A PENTECOSTAL ENCOUNTER WITH EZEKIEL'S VISIONS
THE SPIRIT, POWER, AND AFFECTIVITY

A PENTECOSTAL ENCOUNTER WITH

EZEKIEL'S VISIONS

THE SPIRIT, POWER, AND AFFECTIVITY

LISA R. WARD

CPT

CPT Press
Cleveland, Tennessee

A Pentecostal Encounter with Ezekiel's Visions
The Spirit, Power, and Affectivity

Published by CPT Press
900 Walker ST NE
Cleveland, TN 37311
USA
email: cptpress@pentecostaltheology.org
website: www.cptpress.com

Library of Congress Control Number: 2021942512

ISBN: 9781953358295

CONTENTS

Chapter 7

Overtures Toward a Pentecostal Theology of Spirit-Inspired Visions

Chapter 8

Contributions, Reflections, and Tasks for Further Study

ACKNOWLEDGEMENTS

I would like to acknowledge first and foremost my family and close friends. My grandmother, Mary (I called her Meme), was my champion. She saw something in me that motivated her to encourage and to support me continually throughout the many years required to pursue this project. She went to be with the Lord before I completed this study, but I know she is watching over me and proud that I finished the work the Lord entrusted into my hands. My mother, Judy and brother, Dwight were also very supportive along this journey. They did not complain as I would often cancel family plans in lieu of research and writing commitments. They believed in me and said as much on a regular basis. I am also profoundly grateful to my father, Philip, who is one of the most generous persons I know. There are several close friends of whom I have been blessed to be a part of their lives. Among those who persistently championed my endeavors are Dr William McDonald, Jennifer Marshall, Pam and Samir Idriss, Ahavah Chesed, Lisa Millen, Valerie Landfair, and Carla Jones. Without their prayers and support, I would not have endured the journey. Thank you so much for your love and support.

The calling as a teacher of God's word has continually motivated my life. I taught in various Bible schools internationally that were associated with my local church. I committed to ministry in my local church and several short-term missions' opportunities. After completing my graduate studies at ORU, I questioned as to whether I should return to the mission field or continue with my academic endeavors. The Lord led and inspired me to pursue this project. It has been a journey filled with failure and success, disappointment and joy, and pain and healing. The joys and healings have far surpassed the pain and disappointments. Mostly, because of God's goodness and faithfulness. The Lord's faithfulness and provision came in the form of support from Dr Amos Yong, who introduced me to Dr John Christopher Thomas. God's grace overflowed in abundance as I was accepted into a Pentecostal community of scholars who were more than academic specialists. Drs Thomas and Lee Roy Martin became my entrusted academic advisors, mentors, and role models whom I desire to emulate. Their lives typify true Christ followers and ministers of the gospel. They obeyed and participated with God to create a Spirit-inspired community at the Centre for Pentecostal Theology in Cleveland, TN. I am extremely thankful for the opportunity to sit at the table among many inspiring and talented PhD students over the last four years. The fellowship has been invaluable as we became a body of believers who not only pursued the academic callings upon our own lives, but also invested in each other's lives. I am particularly thankful for the friendships and insights of Becky Basdeo-Hill, Daniel Isgrigg, Rick Wadholm, David Johnson, Steffen Schumacher, and Randall Ackland.

ABBREVIATIONS

Early Pentecostal Periodicals

AF	*The Apostolic Faith*
BC	*Bridal Call*
COGE	*The Church of God Evangel*
PE	*The Pentecostal Evangel*
TBM	*The Bridegroom's Messenger*
TP	*The Pentecost*
WE	*Weekly Evangel*

Other

BDB	Francis Brown *et al., The New Brown, Driver, Briggs, Gesenius Hebrew and English Lexicon (trans. Edward Robinson; Peabody, MA: Hendrickson, 1979).*
CBQ	*Catholic Biblical Quarterly*
CPT	Centre for Pentecostal Theology
DPCM	Burgess, S.M., *et al.* (eds.), *Dictionary of Pentecostal and Charismatic Movements* (Grand Rapids. Zondervan, 1988).
HALOT	Ludwig Koehler & Walter Baumgartner, *The Hebrew and Aramaic Lexicon of the Old Testament (2 vols.; Boston: Brill, 2011).*
Int	*Interpretation*
IVP	Inter-Varsity Press
JBL	*Journal of Biblical Literature*
JEBS	*Journal of European Baptist Studies*
JEPTA	*Journal of European Pentecostal Theology Association*
JETS	*Journal of the Evangelical Theological Society*
JPT	*Journal of Pentecostal Theology*
JPTSup	Journal of Pentecostal Theology Supplement Series
JOTT	*Journal of Translation and Textlinguistics*
JRE	*Journal of Religious Ethics*
JRH	*Journal of Religious History*
JSOT	*Journal for the Study of the Old Testament*

JTS	*Journal of Theological Studies*
NIDPCM	Burgess, S.M., and E.M. van der Maas (eds.), *The New International Dictionary of Pentecostal and Charismatic Movements* (Grand Rapids. Zondervan, 2003).
NIDOTTE	W.A. VanGemeren (ed.), *The New International Dictionary of Old Testament Theology and Exegesis* (5 vols.; Carlisle: Paternoster; Grand Rapids: Zondervan, 1996).
Pneuma	*Pneuma: The Journal of the Society for Pentecostal Studies*
SBL	*Society of Biblical Literature*
TDOT	G.J. Botterweck, H. Ringgren, and H.J. Fabry (eds.), *Theological Dictionary of the Old Testament* (15 vols.; Grand Rapids: Eerdmans, 1974-2006).
TLOT	E. Jenni and C. Westermann (eds.), *Theological Lexicon of the Old Testament* (3 vols.; trans. M. Biddle; Peabody: Hendrickson, 1997).
TJ	*Trinity Journal*
WBC	Word Biblical Commentary
VT	*Vetus Testamentum*

1

INTRODUCTION

I. The Purpose and Task of the Investigation

The purpose of this study is to examine and articulate the literary and theological relationships primarily between the activities of the divine רוח ('Spirit'), the יד־יהוה ('hand of YHWH'), and the affective language (e.g. משמים 'stunned or overwhelmed', and באפי 'my anger') in the four significant visions in the book of Ezekiel (Ezek. 1–3; 8–11; 37.1-14; 40–43). Three of these four visions are accentuated by the theme, the כבוד־יהוה ('the glory of YHWH'). Ezekiel's visions provide the structural framework that underscores the theological themes of the Spirit, the glory of YHWH, the hand of YHWH, and the leitmotif of the affections, which will provide the basis for constructing overtures towards a holistic theology of Spirit inspired visions.[1] Uniquely, in all four of Ezekiel's visions, the term רוח and

---

[1] The Spirit of God in the OT is an interesting topic to evaluate for several reasons: (1) The origin of the concept is difficult to trace, (2) ancient Israelite monotheism does not explicitly discuss God in abstract theoretical terms, but rather in relational terminology throughout history, and (3) the concepts of the immanence and transcendence of YHWH are discussed in anthropomorphic terms in the OT, rather than abstract language, which is familiar to modern thought. Various scholars have written about the concept of God's Spirit in relationship to creation; the semantic meanings and classifications of the רוח and the activities of God's Spirit. Johannes H. Scheepers, *Die Gees van God en die Gees van die mens in die Oud Testamentische Studien* (Kampen: J.H. Kok, 1960). Daniel Lys, *Rûach: le souffle dans l'Ancien Testament. enquête anthropologique à travers l'histoire théologique d'Israël* (Paris: Presses Universitaires de France, 1962). Lloyd Neve, *The Spirit of God in the Old Testament* (Cleveland, TN: CPT Press, 2011). Neve uses the historico-grammatical approach to trace the development of the origin of the term רוח. Leon Wood, *The Holy Spirit in the Old Testament* (CEPS; Grand Rapids: Zondervan, 1976), provides a popular approach to the subject matter with the NT in mind. Robert Koch, *The Holy Spirit in the Old Testament* (Bern: Peter Lang, 1991). Koch directs his study to the concept of messiah and the eschatological role of the Spirit. Wilf Hildebrandt, *An Old*

variations of the phrase, יד־יהוה are emphasized in the narratives and are linked to the affective descriptions of Ezekiel's prophetic encounters with YHWH. This study will not only highlight the prominence placed upon the affective language used in the vision narratives, but it will also underscore the affective influences upon the implied reader or hearer.[2]

A Pentecostal reader not only focuses upon orthodoxy and orthopraxy but also orthopathy.[3] Steven Land rightly proposes that the addition of the role of the affections provides a more holistic approach to reading the biblical text.[4] A Pentecostal hermeneutic is employed to highlight a narrative theological reading of Ezekiel's visions, which includes 'an affective approach'.[5] The conclusions will be put into conversation with Pentecostal spirituality to offer a proposal for a theology of Spirit inspired visions and an appreciation for the affective dimensions that showcase in Ezekiel's visions.

Testament Theology of the Spirit of God (Peabody, MA: Hendrickson, 1995). Hildebrandt offers a canonical approach in English and categorizes passages into four conceptual frameworks. Christopher J.H. Wright, *Knowing the Holy Spirit Through the Old Testament* (Downers Grove, IL: IVP Academic, 2006). Wright categorizes the work of the Spirit throughout the OT.

[2] The term 'hearers' is used rather than 'readers' because Ezekiel is a prophetic message that is heard and later read. Lee Roy Martin, *The Unheard Voice of God: A Pentecostal Hearing of the Book of Judges* (JPTSup 32; Blandford Forum: Deo Publishing, 2008) aptly argues that 'hearing is the most frequent method of encounter with the word of God' since, in part, the command 'to hear' occurs 201 times and all forms of the verb occur 1,159 times in the HB. Martin emphasizes that for the Hebrew culture the term 'hear' is more than listening, but also includes the act of obedience (cf. Exod. 7.16, Deut. 30.17-18, 2 Kgs 14; 17.13-14, Ezek. 12.2 and Neh. 9.17), p. 68.

[3] The broad use of the term 'Pentecostal' is utilized throughout this study and is intended to include the Charismatic stream of the broader movement.

[4] Steven J. Land, *Pentecostal Spirituality: A Passion for the Kingdom* (JPTSup 1; Sheffield: Sheffield Academic Press, 1993), pp. 13-14. See also, Robert O. Baker, 'Pentecostal Bible Reading: Toward a Model of Reading for the Formation of the Affections', in Lee Roy Martin (ed.), *Pentecostal Hermeneutics: A Reader* (Leiden: Brill, 2013), pp. 95-108, and Lee Roy Martin, 'Psalm 63 and Pentecostal Spirituality: An Exercise in Affective Hermeneutics', in Lee Roy Martin (ed.), *Pentecostal Hermeneutics: A Reader* (Leiden: Brill, 2013), pp. 263-84. One of the first scholars who examined the role of the affections in the Hebrew prophets was Abraham J. Heschel, *The Prophets* (2 vols.; New York: Harper & Row, 1962). Heschel's groundbreaking work not only examines the affections of the prophetic consciousness, but also the 'pathos of God'.

[5] For an example of this approach see Martin, 'Psalm 63 and Pentecostal Spirituality', pp. 263-84.

II. Structure and Flow of the Argument

Following the introduction, Chapter 2 will offer a survey of the modern scholarly literature related to the activities of YHWH's רוח in the book of Ezekiel.[6] Currently, there is a lacuna in Pentecostal Ezekiel scholarship which highlights the pneumatological emphasis observed in the book.[7] Therefore, this chapter will also survey the broader scope of Pentecostal scholarship to include the role of the Spirit in the OT.[8]

---

[6] To date, there are only two published monographs highlighting the pneumatological considerations in the book of Ezekiel. James Robson, *Word and Spirit in Ezekiel* (LHBOT 447; New York: T&T Clark, 2006). Dale Launderville, *Spirit and Reason: The Embodied Character of Ezekiel's Symbolic Thinking* (Waco: Baylor University Press, 2007). There are two commentaries that give some attention to the activities of YHWH's רוח: (1) Walther Zimmerli, *Ezekiel 2: A Commentary on the Book of Prophet Ezekiel Chapters 25–48* (trans. J.D. Martin; Philadelphia: Fortress, 1983), pp. 567-68, and (2) Daniel Block's two-volume commentary, *The Book of Ezekiel, Chapters 1—24* (Grand Rapids: Eerdmans, 1997) and *The Book of Ezekiel, Chapters 25–48* (Grand Rapids: Eerdmans, 1998). There are only a handful of articles that examine the presence of the various ways in which the term רוח is employed. For example, Arvid Kapelrud, 'The Spirit and the Word in the Prophets', *ASTI* 11 (1977-78), pp. 40-47; John Woodhouse, 'The Spirit in the Book of Ezekiel', in B.G. Webb (ed.), *Spirit of the Living God Part One* (Sydney: Lancer, 1991), pp. 1-22; Daniel I. Block, 'Empowered by the Spirit of God: The Holy Spirit in the Historiographic Writings of the Old Testament', *SBTJ* 1 (1997), pp. 20-28; Block, 'The Prophet of the Spirit: The Use of *RWH* in the Book of Ezekiel', *JETS* 32 (1989), pp. 27-49; Harold Hosch, 'רוח in the Book of Ezekiel: A Textlinguistic Analysis', *JOTT* 14 (2002), pp. 77-125; Pamela Kinlaw, 'From Death to Life: The Expanding *Ruah* in Ezekiel', *PRSt* 30 (2003), pp. 161-72; and Jacqueline Grey, 'Acts of the Spirit: Ezekiel 37 in the Light of Contemporary Speech-Act Theory', *JBRP* 1 (2009), pp. 69-81.

[7] There are five recent monographs presented by Pentecostal scholars who write about the Spirit of God in the OT literature: Larry McQueen, *Joel and the Spirit: The Cry of a Prophetic Hermeneutic* (Cleveland, TN: CPT Press, 1995), Wilf Hildebrandt, *An Old Testament Theology of the Spirit of God* (Peabody, MA: Hendrickson, 1995), Wonsuk Ma, *Until the Spirit Comes: The Spirit of God in the Book of Isaiah* (JSOTSup 271; Sheffield Academic Press, 1999), Rickie D. Moore, *The Spirit of the Old Testament* (JPTSup 35; Blandford Forum: Deo Publishing, 2011), and Rick Waldholm Jr., *A Theology of the Spirit in the Former Prophets: A Pentecostal Perspective* (Cleveland, TN: CPT Press, 2018).

[8] Rick D. Moore, 'Canon and Charisma in the Book of Deuteronomy', *JPT* 1 (1992), pp. 75-92; and 'Deuteronomy and the Fire of God: A Critical Charismatic Interpretation', *JPT* 7 (1995), pp. 11-33; John Christopher Thomas, 'Women, Pentecostals, and the Bible: An Experiment in Pentecostal Hermeneutics', *JPT* 5 (1994), pp. 41-56; Lee Roy Martin, 'Power to Save!? The Role of the Spirit of the Lord in the Book of Judges', *JPT* 16 (2008), pp. 21-50; and *The Unheard Voice of God*; John Christopher Thomas, 'Reading the Bible from Within our Traditions: A Pentecostal Hermeneutic as Test Case', in Joel Green and Max Turner (eds.),

Chapter 3 will construct a Pentecostal reading strategy based upon contemporary Pentecostal scholarship.[9] A Pentecostal reading strategy is informed and shaped by the Scripture, the Spirit, and the community.[10] In this view, it is the Pentecostal fivefold gospel and the community, which are the catalysts for the transformation that occurs in the reader and intersects with the discussion of the roles of experience and the affections in the task of hermeneutics. According to J.C. Thomas, 'the transformation that accompanies this narrative experiential journey results in changed affections and/or dispositions, as well as for an appreciation for the way in which experience functions as a dynamic part of the interpretative process'.[11] A reading strategy that is informed pneumatically in participation with the believing community (past and present) will inherently respect the pneumatic ethos of Scripture.

A narrative theological analysis is utilized as a method owing to its compatibility with the narrative orientation of Pentecostal thought.[12] A Pentecostal hearing of the biblical texts highlights the text in its final form and derives its primary meaning from the narrative.[13] From

---

Between Two Horizons. Spanning New Testament Studies and Systematic Theology (Grand Rapids: Eerdmans, 2000). Thomas proposes a Pentecostal hermeneutic of Scripture, Word, and community derived from the components that are depicted in the method of the Jerusalem council in Acts 15. He highlights that the Holy Spirit is present to discern testimony, and to guide the believing community to determine which Scriptures are most relevant to their contemporary situation.

[9] Thomas, 'Reading the Bible from Within our Traditions' and *The Spirit of the New Testament* (Leiden: Deo, 2005); Clark Pinnock, *Scripture Principle, Reclaiming the Full Authority of the Bible* (Grand Rapids: Baker, 2006); Kenneth J. Archer, *A Pentecostal Hermeneutic: Spirit, Scripture, and Community* (Cleveland, TN: CPT Press, 2009); Martin (ed.), *Pentecostal Hermeneutics*.

[10] Roger Stronstad, 'Pentecostal Experience and Hermeneutics', *Paraclete* 26.1 (1992), pp. 14-30.

[11] Thomas, 'What the Spirit is Saying to the Church – The Testimony of a Pentecostal in New Testament Studies', in Kevin Spawn and Archie Wright (eds.), *Spirit and Scripture* (London: T & T Clark, 2012), pp. 115-29.

[12] John Goldingay, 'Biblical Story and the Way it Shapes Our Story', *JEPTA* 17 (1997), pp. 5-15. For Goldingay meaning is found in the dynamics of the biblical story and our own stories. He states, 'In general, the biblical story is designed to enable us to discover who we are. We do that by telling our own story, but by telling it in the context of the Bible story. We find ourselves by setting ourselves in that other story ... In fact, we all tell our individual stories in the light of a world-view, a grand narrative.'

[13] Martin's *The Unheard Voice of God* is a groundbreaking work on the book of Judges, which highlights the Pentecostal orientation of 'hearing' the biblical story. I choose to use the term 'hearers' in addition to the term 'readers' because Ezekiel is a prophetic message that needs to be heard not only read. In *The Unheard Voice*

this perspective, a literary and theological analysis of the text will focus on the stories that the narrator tells to understand how they help
the reader or hearer derive meaning in the text with special attention
given to repetition of literary markers, the structure, genre, and main
characters, while drawing theological conclusions.

Chapter 4 will discern and discuss the testimonies of early Pentecostals concerning the book of Ezekiel specifically utilizing the Pentecostal periodicals surveying the Wesleyan-Holiness publications:
The Apostolic Faith, *The Bridegroom's Messenger*, *The Evening Light/Church
of God Evangel*, followed by the Finished Work publications: *The Pentecost*, *Latter Rain Evangel*, *The Pentecostal Evangel*, and *The Bridal Call*.
This survey will be limited to the early years of the Pentecostal movement (1906-1923) because it is considered the theological heart of
the movement.[14] *Rezeptionsgeschichte* (reception history) is a model
utilized by several Pentecostal scholars, such as Kimberly Alexander,[15] Chris Green,[16] Larry McQueen,[17] Melissa Archer,[18] David
Johnson,[19] and Rick Wadholm.[20] The early Pentecostal interpretations of the pneumatological texts of Ezekiel provide an understanding of how early Pentecostal spirituality was informed by their reading of Ezekiel (*Wirkungsgeschichte*).[21] The discernment of early

---

of God, Martin successfully substantiates that 'hearing is the most frequent method
of encounter with the word of God'. He observes that the command 'to hear'
occurs 201 times in the OT and all forms of the verb occur 1,159 times. He cites
Deut. 5.1, Josh. 3.9, 1 Kgs 22.19, Jer. 2.4, 2 Kgs 20.16 and Isa. 55.3 as evidence of
a person(s) who is/are commanded 'to hear' God or his word. Martin also argues
that the biblical term 'hearing' involves more than merely listening because to hear
the word of God is to obey the word of God (cf. Exod. 7.16, Deut. 30.17-18, 2
Kgs 14,11, 2 Kgs 17.13-14, Ezek. 12.2, and Neh. 9.17), p. 68.

[14] W.J. Hollenweger, 'Pentecostals and the Charismatic Movement', in Cheslyn
Jones, Geoffrey Wainwright, and SJ Edward Yarnold (eds.), *The Study of Spirituality*
(New York, NY: Oxford University Press, 1986), pp. 549-53.

[15] Kimberly Ervin Alexander, *Pentecostal Healing: Models in Theology and Practice*
(JPTSup 29; Blandford Forum: Deo Publishing, 2006).

[16] Melissa L. Archer, 'The Worship Scenes in the Apocalypse, Effective History,
and Early Pentecostal Periodical Literature', *JPT* 21.1 (2012), pp. 87-112.

[17] Chris E. Green, *Foretasting the Kingdom: Toward a Pentecostal Theology of the Lord's
Supper* (Cleveland TN: CPT Press, 2012).

[18] Melissa Archer, *I Was in the Spirit on the Lord's Day: A Pentecostal Engagement with
Worship in the Apocalypse* (Cleveland, TN: CPT Press, 2015).

[19] David Johnson, *Pneumatic Discernment in the Apocalypse: An Intertextual and Pentecostal Exploration* (Cleveland, TN: CPT, 2018).

[20] Waldholm, *A Theology of the Spirit in the Former Prophets*.

[21] Ulrich Luz, *Matthew in History: Interpretation, Influence, and Effects* (Minneapolis:
Fortress Press, 1994).

Pentecostal testimonies regarding the book of Ezekiel is also conducive to the integration of the hermeneutical paradigm of the Spirit, the Word, and the community, which has recently been championed by the contemporary Pentecostal academic guild.[22]

Chapter 5 will provide the reader with an overview of the book of Ezekiel to identify the genre, characters, structure, and themes. The purpose is to familiarize the reader with the basic content of Ezekiel's major vision reports and its function within the narrative as a whole. The identification of Ezekiel's overarching theme of visions will provide the structural framework to describe the four central literary units of the entire book, which are under examination for this study.

Chapter 6 will offer a narrative theological hearing of Ezekiel's four major vision narratives (Ezek. 1–3; 8–11; 37.1-14; 40–48).[23] It will give special attention to the genre identified, themes, and the literary markers observed in the text in order to discern the structure of the book of Ezekiel. This chapter will highlight a major theme of the role of the Spirit in the four major visions of Ezekiel as it connects with the leitmotif of the affections. This investigation combines a Pentecostal reading strategy with literary and theological analyses to interpret and fully engage with Ezekiel's visions. The methodological emphasis is placed upon how the text affected or was experienced by the implied hearers. Similar reading methodologies are demonstrated in the work of Walter Brueggemann[24] and Pentecostal scholars like Rickie D. Moore[25] and Lee Roy Martin, who offers a

---

[22] Archer, *A Pentecostal Hermeneutic for the Twenty-First Century*, pp. 156-66, emphasizes the contributions of the Pentecostal community to the interpretative process.

[23] A narrative-theological approach focuses on the story being told rather than the reconstruction of historical events, therefore the sources behind the book of Ezekiel are at best only theoretical. The presuppositions I follow for this study are: (1) the implied author of the book of Ezekiel self identifies the prophet, Ezekiel, (2) the exilic community in Babylon is the narrative's implied audience, (3) the narratives provide a series of date notices prior to several of the visions and oracles (1.1, 2-3; 3.16; 8.1; 20.1; 24.1), which suggests that all the messages were received and delivered within a span of six or seven years in the narrative world, and (4) the story identifies the prophet as Ezekiel, as the main character who was called to prophesy to those carried off to the land of Babylon.

[24] Walter Brueggemann, *A Commentary on Jeremiah: Exile and Homecoming* (Grand Rapids: Eerdmans, 1998).

[25] Moore, Rickie. D., 'Canon and Charisma in the Book of Deuteronomy', *JPT* 1 (1992), pp. 75-92; 'Deuteronomy and the Fire of God: A Critical Charismatic

hearing of the biblical text.[26] It will also present theological reflections upon the text with intention toward constructing a holistic theology of Spirit inspired visions in the book of Ezekiel.

Chapter 7 will summarize and synthesize the results of this exploration. It will attempt to provide overtures toward a holistic theology that is conducive to the construction of a Pentecostal theology of Spirit inspired visions and the implications for the role of the affections. These conclusions will be founded upon a narrative theological reading of Ezekiel's four major visionary accounts that will provide the basis for overtures toward an OT pneumatology.[27]

Chapter 8 will outline the contributions gleaned from this project. It will also reflect on directions for future study. Hopefully the questions raised in this investigation will be answered and provide new perceptions or elicit new enquiries in Ezekiel studies.

Interpretation', *JPT* 7 (1995), pp. 11-33; 'The Prophetic Calling: An Old Testament Profile and Its Relevance Today', in *The Spirit of the Old Testament* (JPTSup 35: Deo Publishing, 2011), pp. 35-64.

[26] Martin, *The Unheard Voice of God.*

[27] The conclusions will make overtures towards Ezekiel's contribution to the broader discussion of OT pneumatology.

2

A Survey of Modern Literature Regarding the Spirit of YHWH and the Hand of YHWH

I. Introduction

Most Ezekiel interpreters recognize that the increased occurrences of the term רוח in the book of Ezekiel are a distinct literary feature. However, despite this distinction, there are still limited comprehensive treatments of its pneumatological emphasis. Additionally, Ezekiel's visionary narratives are not only highlighted with the term רוח ('spirit' or 'wind' or 'breath'), but also the phrase, יד־יהוה, and affective terms such as משמים ('stunned or overwhelmed'), באפי ('in my anger'), בחמה ('in wrath') that describe either the prophet's or YHWH's disposition (Ezekiel 1–3; 8–11; 37.1-14; 40–48). The purpose of this exploration is to examine and articulate the literary and theological relationships between the activities of the divine רוח, the יד־יהוה, and the affective language presented in Ezekiel's visions. Therefore, this chapter will provide a chronological survey of contemporary Ezekiel scholarship grouped by their respective decades, in order to discuss the major contributions to Ezekiel studies on these aforementioned themes. Some of these scholars cited below treat the term in tandem with the Hebrew idiom the יד־יהוה, and some do not. Currently, there is only one distinct scholarly treatment of the role of the affections in the prophetic literature, Abraham Heschel, while most treatments only mention this feature in commentaries. To date there are three commentaries, two monographs, and a handful of articles that give particular attention to the diverse activities of the term רוח in the book of Ezekiel. Several works below emphasize the activities of the רוּחַ ('Spirit') in the OT but will be reviewed because they include the book of Ezekiel. There are also four works below that provide significant contributions to the prophetic corpus that highlight the role of the divine רוּחַ ('Spirit'), the יד־יהוה, and/or the affective language has upon prophetic activities and/or the prophetic consciousness, which includes the prophet Ezekiel. This review will not survey commentaries unless they have extended discussions about the pneumatological themes depicted in Ezekiel's visions.

II. Review of Literature

A. Johannes H. Scheepers, Daniel Lys, Abraham J. Heschel, and Johannes Lindblom

Johannes H. Scheepers

In 1960, J.H. Scheepers utilized a grammatical analysis of each occurrence of the term רוּחַ to classify and determine its various meanings in the OT. He asserts that there is not a definitive chronological development of the term רוּחַ owing to the question of the chronology of the texts. However, he does conclude that it probably meant 'wind' before 'breath'.[1] Scheepers divides his chapters conceptually with the term רוּחַ: (1) as wind, (2) as a human being (and an animal), (3) other derivations of the root r-w-h, (4) as an extra-natural spirit, and (5) the phrase, the רוּחַ of YHWH.[2] He argues that in Ezekiel there are examples of each of the main categories listed above. For example, Scheepers describes and defines the term רוּחַ as 'a wind as part of creation, invisible, incorporeal, moves, blows, seldom used in direct relation with life, and is used figuratively but never as the conveyer of life'.[3] He asserts that the term רוּחַ in Ezek. 37.9 represents the idea of a wind in the sense of 'blowing to and from all the corners of the earth'.[4]

Scheepers argues that when רוּחַ is referring to a human being, then the fundamental idea is 'breath' because it is related to the idea

---

[1] Scheepers, *Die Gees van God en die Gees van die mens,* p. 308.
[2] Scheepers, *Die Gees van God en die Gees van die mens,* pp. 304-22. Scheepers provides a summary of each of the chapters.
[3] Scheepers, *Die Gees van God en die Gees van die mens,* pp. 304-305.
[4] Scheepers, *Die Gees van God en die Gees van die mens,* p. 305.

of *'nesjama or nefesj* as the principle of life', which includes 'capacities, thinking, and the seat of different emotions'.[5] In relation to Ezek. 2.2, רוח as breath is describing the animation of the prophet's spirit, which he maintains means, 'aroused to action'.[6] Scheepers concludes in this sense, the רוח ('breath') is a power because it is brought to life and 'parallels with *nesjama*'.[7]

Scheepers also classifies רוח as 'an extra-natural' spirit, which he asserts does not belong to 'the ordinary, natural life, but cannot always be distinguished from the spirit of man, because the latter is also that which is more closely connected with God than the flesh or the earthly body'.[8] He variably renders the term רוח in this sense: (1) spirit, (2) wind, and (3) power or faculty of the term רוח. For example, Scheepers interprets the term רוח in Ezek. 1.12, 20 as a power working in the nation as a whole and more specifically as the 'the vital power of the *merkaba*' on which YHWH is depicted as riding on his throne.[9] Scheepers also renders the term רוח as the divine Spirit, which 'conveys life and power given to Ezekiel' (Ezek. 2.2 and 3.24); רוח as the divine power which carries Ezekiel, while he is in a visionary state from place to place' (Ezek. 3.12, 14; 8.3; 11.1, 24a; 43.5); and as the symbol of the spirit of YHWH, which will 'bring life to the nation in exile in which they will be gathered from all quarters' (Ezek. 37.9, 14). In all of these diverse meanings, he concludes:

> In these texts of Ezekiel, רוח has an indefinite character (sometimes used without an article or any other determination) because Ezekiel's experiences have an indefinite (cf. the hand in 8.3) or a symbolic character. But the term רוח is closely related to YHWH (cf. the relation with himself in 1.12, 20; with his word in 2.2; with his hand in 8.3, and with his spirit in 37.9).[10]

In Chapter 5, Scheepers classifies 95 instances of the genitive construction of YHWH/Elohim in the OT. He either renders the term רוח as 'wind' when it is in reference to a 'work of the spirit' or the

---

5 Scheepers, *Die Gees van God en die Gees van die mens,* p. 306.
6 Scheepers, *Die Gees van God en die Gees van die mens,* p. 306.
7 Scheepers, *Die Gees van God en die Gees van die mens,* p. 307.
8 Scheepers, *Die Gees van God en die Gees van die mens,* p. 309.
9 Scheepers, *Die Gees van God en die Gees van die mens,* pp. 309-11.
10 Scheepers, *Die Gees van God en die Gees van die mens,* p. 310.

'breath of God' when hyperbole or figurative language is used.[11] Scheepers concludes that typically the phrase, the רוח of YHWH is dependent upon the objects upon which the spirit works. He argues that in Ezek. 11.5; 37.1, the רוח of YHWH is 'like the hand of YHWH (cf. 2 Kgs 3.15 and Ezek. 8.1) and is a dynamic power'.[12] Under this classification, Scheepers identifies the work of the רוח of YHWH as directly connected with (1) the whole nation (Ezek. 37.14), or (2) the individual members of the nation (Ezek. 36.26; 39.29), or (3) in a universal context, such as the heavenly beings (Ezek. 1.12, 20).[13] Scheepers emphasizes 'the רוח of YHWH as the mediator of divine words' even if it is not explicitly stated.[14] He proposes that 'the transcendental spirit is first of all a dynamic power or explosive activity in which the same activities are ascribed to the יד־יהוה and to his רוח ('spirit') (Ezek. 1.3; 8.1 with 11.5 'hand' and 'spirit' in Ezek. 8.3 and 2.2)'.[15] From this perspective, Scheepers argues that 'there is no reason to think the prophets who do not mention the spirit reject the spirit in connection with their prophetic activity, because first they heard and then they spoke the word of YHWH'.[16] Scheepers concludes that specifically, the term רוח in the book of Ezekiel, and the יד־יהוה ('hand of YHWH') is depicted more because of the spiritual state in which the prophet received the revelation, which emphasized its importance.[17]

Daniel Lys

Daniel Lys' *Ruach', le souffle dans l'Ancien Testament* combines an anthropological, theological, and semantics study of the term רוח. He categorizes the term רוח into three possible classifications and concludes that all three are present in the book of Ezekiel: (1) a meteorological wind (1.4), (2) the human ('spirit') (3.14b), and (3) the divine רוח (3.12, 14a, 24; 8.3. 11.1, 5).[18] Lys asserts that there is continuity between the human רוח ('spirit'), which he argues is the center of decisions, and the Spirit of God, which he describes the רוח as

---

[11] Scheepers, *Die Gees van God en die Gees van die mens,* pp. 311-22.
[12] Scheepers, *Die Gees van God en die Gees van die mens,* p. 312.
[13] Scheepers, *Die Gees van God en die Gees van die mens,* pp. 314-16.
[14] Scheepers, *Die Gees van God en die Gees van die mens,* p. 318.
[15] Scheepers, *Die Gees van God en die Gees van die mens,* pp. 316-17.
[16] Scheepers, *Die Gees van God en die Gees van die mens,* pp. 316-17.
[17] Scheepers, *Die Gees van God en die Gees van die mens,* pp. 316-17.
[18] Lys, *Rûach,* pp. 70; 350-55.

'inspiring aspiration, creating, destroying, and invigorating'.[19] The central idea of Lys' book is that the term רוח as 'wind' was 'almost immediately demythicized by Israel, from the oldest texts, and it is the instrument of God in history, and as a result becomes quite versatile, enlivening, or destructive, phenomenon of nature or divine instrument, or a sign of a direction'.[20] Lys concludes that the term רוח as 'wind' in Ezekiel does not represent the divine Spirit, but does express God's actions.[21]

Abraham J. Heschel

One of the first scholars to examine the role of the affections in the prophetic corpus was Abraham J. Heschel. Heschel's magnum opus, *The Prophets*, a two-volume monograph that examined the prophetic consciousness in relation to what he calls the 'pathos of God'.[22] In contrast to the theological tenet of the incorporeality of God, Heschel proposes that God demonstrated his involvement with ancient Israel through 'divine pathos' that was expressed through 'living care'.[23] He asserts that 'God looks at the world and is affected by what happens in it and man is the object of God's care and judgment'.[24] Heschel argues that the Hebrew prophet is affected by God's pathos through an encounter with God:

> The analysis of prophetic utterance shows that the fundamental experience of the Hebrew prophet is a fellowship with the feelings of God, sympathy with the divine pathos, a communion with the divine consciousness, which comes about through the prophet's reflection of, or participation in, the divine pathos.[25]

Heschel further explains that the typical prophetic state of mind is one of being taken up into the heart of the divine pathos. His view of 'sympathy' is related to the prophet's answer to inspiration. From this perspective, prophetic sympathy is a response to 'transcendent sensibility' as attraction to the divine Being.[26] Heschel understood the

---

[19] Lys, *Rûach*, p. 17.

[20] Lys, *Rûach*, p. 73.

[21] Lys, *Rûach*, p. 75.

[22] Abraham Heschel, *The Prophets* (2 vols.; New York: Harper & Row, 1962), II, pp. 1-11.

[23] Heschel, *The Prophets*, II, pp. 99-103.

[24] Heschel, *The Prophets*, II, p. 263.

[25] Heschel, *The Prophets*, II, p. 263.

[26] Heschel, *The Prophets*, I, p. 21, and II, pp. 87-103.

Hebrew prophets as unique in that they had the ability to participate in divine-human communication via 'sympathy' rather than the cross-cultural concept of 'spirit possession', which led some scholars to view the Hebrew prophets as 'ecstatics'.[27] In Heschel's view, the Hebrew prophet could be regarded as unique from other cultures, and psychologically stable to receive messages from God in such a way as to communicate these messages.[28] For Heschel, prophecy was a phenomenon of sympathy, which drew sharp distinctions between the prophetic mind and that of the mystics, mantics, and apocalyptic seers.[29] He viewed the mantics as 'ecstatics', which he defined not unlike others of his time, as a 'psychological state or condition' or as 'one, who is frenzied, out of control, merging with a god, and extinction of self'.[30] From this perspective, Heschel refuted the idea that

---

[27] Heschel, *The Prophets*, II, pp. 170-89.

[28] Scholarly examinations of ecstasy as part of the prophetic experience of the ancient Israelite prophets are widely diverse among biblical scholars. Since Gustav Hölscher's groundbreaking treatment of prophetic ecstasy from the early 20th century, scholarly treatments of the ecstatic nature of prophecy has generally followed three lines of development. Some have disregarded the nature of ecstasy as part of the writing and earlier non-writing prophets as ecstatics. In this view, there are two positions that are considered: (1) acceptance of the non-writing prophets as ecstatics, but later writing prophets are not ecstatics, and (2) acceptance that the writing prophets had a mild form of ecstasy. A second development, although not generally followed, is that the 'true prophets' are not ecstatics, while the 'false prophets' were ecstatic. The third development followed Hermann Gunkel's position, that the prophets received oracles while in a moment of ecstatic inspiration but produced their oracles after their state of ecstasy. In this view, Gunkel sought to understand the ecstatic experiences of the Hebrew prophets by examining their external actions and behaviors.

[29] Heschel, *The Prophets*, I, pp. 20-21; and II, pp. 170-89. For an alternate view, see three works by Benjamin Uffenheimer, 'Prophecy and Sympathy', *Immanuel* 16 (Sum. 1983), pp. 7-24; 'Prophecy, Ecstasy, and Sympathy', in *Congress Volume* (Leiden: Brill, 1988), pp. 257-69; and *Prophecy in Ancient Israel* (trans. David Louvish; Jerusalem: Magnes Press, 1999). He responded directly to Heschel's perspectives and examined the Hellenistic and classical ways in which ecstasy was used and compared these to uses in the NT literature. He observes some NT uses of ecstasy were defined as 'in amazement, or to be amazed', while examples in the classical texts generally use the term as it was defined phenomenologically. Uffenheimer argues that the Greco-Roman influences upon the definition of ecstasy influenced the way biblical scholars use the term', p. 259. He asserts, 'To follow in the footsteps of Plato was to erroneously mistake the term for its etymology, for its phenomenology, or its semantic field', p. 267.

[30] Heschel, *The Prophets*, II, pp. 104-46, 171. For this viewpoint of ecstasy, see Johannes Lindblom, *Prophecy in Ancient Israel* (Philadelphia: Muhlenberg Press, 1962). For a contemporary and comprehensive treatment of ecstasy, see John Levison, 'Allure of Prophetic Ecstasy', in *Filled with the Spirit* (Grand Rapids: Eerdmans,

Ezekiel or the pre-classical prophets were ecstatic despite the intense emotional language or strange symbolic acts that were depicted in the narratives.

Heschel defines the term רוח according to its semantic domains as ('air in motion', 'breath', 'wind', 'vain things', 'spirit', or 'mind'). He argues the רוח reflects the 'pathos', 'passion', or 'emotion, as a state of the soul'.[31] For Heschel, Ezekiel's bitterness and rage (3.14) and his 'week of silence' (3.22-24) is viewed in light of his perspective of 'sympathy', and reflects God's own feelings toward Israel.[32] He saw the emotive words of the prophet, Ezekiel, as 'stern, sour, stinging, but behind his austerity is love and compassion for mankind'.[33]

Johannes Lindblom

Johannes Lindblom's *Prophecy in Ancient Israel* utilizes a cross-cultural approach to examine OT prophecy.[34] He surveys prophecy in light of phenomenology that is recorded in various ancient and modern literatures. Lindblom describes the many characteristic features of the prophetic type in the world of religion: (1) 'the consciousness of having received a special call, (2) the constraint exercised by spiritual powers, (3) the ecstatic phenomena, (4) the ability to hear divine secrets, and (5) the duty of pronouncing oracular messages from the spiritual world'.[35]

Lindblom devotes the majority of his monograph to a discussion of the prophetic activities or phenomena of the ancient Israelite prophets in terms of divine inspiration, symbolic acts, ecstatic visions, and auditions.[36] He concludes that there is a widespread human

---

2010), pp. 154-77; and Levison, *Of Two Minds: Ecstasy and Inspired Interpretation in the New Testament World* (N. Richland Hills, TX: BIBAL Press, 1999). Levison aptly surveys the breadth of impact that Greek and Roman culture with their definitions of inspired ecstasy had on early Jewish authors.

[31] Heschel, *The Prophets*, II, pp. 2-3; 95-97.

[32] Heschel, *The Prophets*, II, pp. 28-47; 96, 224.

[33] Heschel, *The Prophets*, I, pp. 16-19, and II, p. 12.

[34] Lindblom, *Prophecy in Ancient Israel*, pp. 1-46.

[35] Lindblom, *Prophecy in Ancient Israel*, pp. 4-23.

[36] Lindblom, *Prophecy in Ancient Israel*, pp. 47-216. Lindblom categorizes visions according to various reports of the prophet's experience and a psychological assessment of prophetic personality. For other methodological approaches to OT prophetic visions, see M.R. Stead, 'Prophetic Visions' in Mark Boda and J. Gordon McConville (eds.), *The Dictionary of Old Testament Prophets* (Downers Grove: IVP Press, 2012), pp. 818-24. Burke Long, 'Reports of Visions Among the Prophets', *JBL* 95 (1976), pp. 353-65. Long argues, contra to Zimmerli, that Ezekiel's

phenomenon based on personal predisposition in certain individuals and concludes that [Ezekiel] as a 'prophetic type' is viewed in religious and psychological terms as 'a person who, because he is conscious of having been specially chosen and called, feels forced to perform actions and proclaim ideas which, in a mental state of intense inspiration or real ecstasy, have been indicated to him in a form of divine revelations'.[37] Lindblom defines ecstasy as 'an abnormal state of consciousness in which one is so intensely absorbed by one single idea or one single feeling, or by a group of ideas or feelings, that the normal stream of psychical life is more or less arrested'.[38] He argues that there are different facets to ecstasy from 'religious ecstasy, degrees of ecstasy, possession and personal inspiration, psychical and phenomenological forms of ecstasy'.[39] For Lindblom, the 'majority of prophetic visions are ecstatic visions' that are either 'pictorial visions' (eg. Ezek. 1.1-28; 37.1-14) or 'dramatic visions' (eg. Ezek. 2.9) and should be studied in the light of modern psychology of religion'.[40]

Yet, Lindblom distinguishes Ezekiel from all other OT prophets because he states that Ezekiel's descriptions of tasting the scroll (Ezek. 3.1), and the 'awareness of the hand, which on different occasions grasped him, was a muscular hallucination' are 'neurotic and hysterical traits'.[41] Lindblom distinguishes hallucinations from ecstatic visions and auditions by defining hallucinations, 'as a visual, auditory, or other sensory perception which does not correspond to any objective reality in the external world, but (and here it differs from

---

prophetic call narrative is related to the common features identified in ancient Near Eastern and Israelite theophany vision or dream reports (eg. 1 Kgs 3.5-15). Susan Niditch, *The Symbolic Visions in Biblical Traditions* (HSM, Chico, CA: Scholars Press, 1983), argues that as sociological and historical realities change, so the literary form flexibly evolves, thereby remaining a relevant vehicle for prophetic expression. She traces the development through an examination of the language of the visions (from an economical-rhetorical style to narrative prose); their symbols (from everyday objects to complex, otherworldly happenings); and their pattern or structure of content (from a simple question and answer dialogue to dramatic narrative scenes).

[37] Lindblom, *Prophecy in Ancient Israel*, pp. 118-22.
[38] Lindblom, *Prophecy in Ancient Israel*, pp. 4-6.
[39] Lindblom, *Prophecy in Ancient Israel*, pp. 4-23.
[40] Lindblom, *Prophecy in Ancient Israel*, pp. 123-25.
[41] Lindblom, *Prophecy in Ancient Israel*, pp. 123, 190. Lindblom concludes that 'it was not uncommon with ecstatic inspiration for the visionary to experience sensual perceptions such as taste, smell, etc'.

vision and audition) is thought to be apprehended by the bodily senses and has all the characteristic features of a real perception, although it does not correspond to any external reality'.[42] Lindblom discusses the term רוח in the OT to argue:

> [when referencing the divine], רוח in the OT narratives is never regarded as being independent of YHWH, but is YHWH's spirit, a more or less substantial *dynamis*, a force emanating from YWHW; the spirit is always sent by YHWH and runs YHWH's errands. For this reason, it is wrong to suggest that רוח was regarded as a spirit analogous to the spirits of the shamans or the jinn of the pre-Islamic Arabs; nor is there any question of possession in the proper sense of the word, as in the narratives of the demons in the gospels.[43]

Lindblom states that the Israelite prophets understood YHWH's רוח and YHWH's יד are 'substantially identical in their effect', in which they are both expressions of divine power of inspiration and effective in ecstatic experience. He identifies the expressions: the spirit of YWHW and the hand of YHWH as literary markers indicating divine inspiration through ecstatic events.[44] Lindblom draws another distinction in the book of Ezekiel. He argues that although the spirit plays a prominent role in his visionary experience, 'Ezekiel prefers the idea of "the hand" to that of "the spirit" when describing the revelatory state'.[45] He proposes that 'when the hand of YHWH is pressed hard upon Ezekiel, i.e., intense ecstasy, he was filled with an inner glow'.[46]

B. Lloyd Neve, Leon Wood, Stanley Horton, Arvid Kapelrud, Walther Zimmerli, and Robert Wilson

Lloyd Neve

Published in 1972, Lloyd Neve's monograph, *The Spirit of God in the Old Testament*, uses a historico-grammatical approach to trace the development of the origin of the term רוח.[47] He concludes that the

---

[42] Lindblom, *Prophecy in Ancient Israel*, pp. 122-23.
[43] Lindblom, *Prophecy in Ancient Israel*, pp. 57-58.
[44] Lindblom, *Prophecy in Ancient Israel*, pp. 57,
[45] Lindblom, *Prophecy in Ancient Israel*, pp. 176-77.
[46] Lindblom, *Prophecy in Ancient Israel*, pp. 179.
[47] Neve, *The Spirit of God in the Old Testament*.

concept of the divine רוח has evolved over time from its earliest conception as a divine wind to the late formulations depicted in Chronicles.[48] Neve states, 'YHWH's רוח as used in the OT, most often refers to his power, the divine energy, or to his wrath. An uncommon usage is depicted in Isa. 30.1 when it designates YHWH's mind, expressed most commonly in Hebrew by the term לב.'[49] He points out that during the exilic period there was a marked increase in the occurrences of the literary uses of the term רוח with new meanings attributed: (1) spirit as the giver of life, the agent of creation, (2) spirit as the presence of YHWH, and (3) spirit in the human recipient (inner life).[50] Neve highlights that for the first time in the book of Ezekiel the uncommon reference to the 'spirit' as the presence of YHWH ('fullness of his being') is used (Ezek. 39.29; cf. one other text Ps. 139.7).

Neve identifies two usages of רוח in Ezekiel that are carried over from earlier texts: (1) YHWH's guiding will (Ezek. 1.12, 20, 21, and 10.17), and (2) YHWH's energizing and directing power (Ezek. 2.1-2; 3.12, 14, 24; 8.3; 11.1, 5, 24; 37.1; and 43.5). Yet, the רוח as YHWH's רוח as a guiding will, progresses from a communal aspect of Israel as a nation to a predicted future when it will be with the individual (Ezek. 36.27).[51] Neve also compares the 'spirit' in 1 Kgs 18.12 and 2 Kgs 2.16 with the theophany in Ezek. 1.4 to assert that YHWH's spirit controls the prophet's actions.[52] He also suggests that the יד־יהוה in Ezekiel may represent an ecstatic condition and when it is used with the רוח then it is referring to YHWH's רוח and not 'wind'.[53]

Leon Wood

Leon Wood's *The Holy Spirit in the Old Testament* provides a popular approach to the subject matter with the NT in mind.[54] His treatment presupposes a NT lens to the concept of the Spirit of God in the OT and his focus is more contemporary, rather than a critical exegetical examination of the term and its various uses. From this

---

[48] Neve, *The Spirit of God in the Old Testament*, pp. 116-18.
[49] Neve, *The Spirit of God in the Old Testament*, pp. 50-51.
[50] Neve, *The Spirit of God in the Old Testament*, pp. 55-60.
[51] Neve, *The Spirit of God in the Old Testament*, pp. 84-94.
[52] Neve, *The Spirit of God in the Old Testament*, p. 41.
[53] Neve, *The Spirit of God in the Old Testament*, p. 40.
[54] Wood, *The Holy Spirit in the Old Testament*.

perspective, he emphasizes the theological implications of the רוח as YHWH's רוח breathing new life in Ezekiel's vision of the dry bones (Ezekiel 37), and the indwelling רוח 'spirit' in Ezek. 2.2 as a precursor to the indwelling Spirit depicted in the book of Acts.[55]

Stanley Horton

Stanley Horton's *What the Bible Says About the Holy Spirit* provides a biblical theological approach of the OT and the NT to discern a progressive revelation of God through the work of his Spirit. He concludes, 'the entire OT looks on prophecy as the chief activity of the Spirit among his people'.[56] He specifically addresses the experiences of the Spirit in the book of Ezekiel by associating the רוח ('spirit') with 'the hand of the Lord' (Ezek. 1.3; 3.14, 22, 24; 8.1; 11.1). Contrary to most contemporary scholarship, Horton attributes each occurrence of the term רוח as the 'Spirit' and not to the 'breath or the wind of God'.[57] He posits that the Spirit is symbolically representing a power, however he argues that it is the power from God through the Spirit that enters Ezekiel and transports him in visions.

Horton treats the visions more tentatively by translating the term *vision* as 'appearance' at times (Ezek. 10.1; 41.21) and not the more common 'prophetic vision'.[58] Although, he admits the problems associated with this view, he argues that in these instances the visions are appearances or manifestations of God. He observes that the remainder of the references to רוח in Ezekiel is related to Israel's future restoration of receiving a new heart and a new spirit (Ezek. 11.19, 20; 18.31, 32; 36.26, 27; 37.14; 39.29).

Arvid Kapelrud

In 'The Spirit and the Word in the Prophets' Arvid Kapelrud writes a polemic against the notion that the 'prophets of doom' deliberately omitted the use of the term רוח ('spirit') in order to emphasize that

---

[55] Wood, *The Holy Spirit in the Old Testament*, pp. 90-112. Wood discusses the debates surrounding the issue of biblical ecstasy in the prophetic literature and concludes that the Hebrew prophets were not ecstatics.

[56] Stanley Horton, *What the Bible Says About the Holy Spirit* (Springfield, MO: Gospel Publishing, 1976), p. 55.

[57] Horton, *What the Bible Says About the Holy Spirit*, p. 67.

[58] Horton, *What the Bible Says About the Holy Spirit*, pp. 68-9.

the 'word' was from YHWH and not inspired by the spirit.[59] Kapelrud identifies the so-called later prophets as the 'prophets of doom' because he views these prophets according to the messages that they preached, and draws distinctions between the earlier prophets that are generally classified as the 'ecstatic prophets' due to the emphasis placed upon the relationship between the spirit of God/YHWH and phenomenon.[60] He offers a brief analysis of the prophets and their relationship to the 'word and the spirit' concluding that the idea of the 'spirit of God inspiring the words of the prophets' was possibly an established idea, therefore it was not necessary to mention it.[61] Kapelrud recognizes that only Ezekiel and Micah are two of the later prophets who emphasize the spirit of YHWH as the divine רוח, who seized and filled them, and inspired them to speak the word of YHWH.[62]

Walther Zimmerli

Walther Zimmerli's detailed two-volume commentary on Ezekiel is one of the most influential works in Ezekiel scholarship from the last fifty years. He made extensive use of tradition-historical, form-critical, and redaction-critical methodologies to posit that much of the material in Ezekiel went back to the prophet himself.[63] Yet, Zimmerli, in his voluminous work, only dedicates a few pages to the term רוח, which is a key motif in all four of the major visionary accounts. He

---

[59] Arvid Kapelrud, 'The Spirit and the Word in the Prophets', *ASTI* 11 (1977-78), pp. 40-47.

[60] Kapelrud, 'The Spirit and the Word in the Prophets', pp. 40-41.

[61] Kapelrud, 'The Spirit and the Word in the Prophets', p. 46.

[62] Kapelrud, 'The Spirit and the Word in the Prophets', p. 46, treats each occurrence of the term רוח as it is used in Isaiah, to conclude that most of the time it is rendered as a 'wind'. See also, Ma, *Until the Spirit Comes*, pp. 33-70. Ma also supports this perspective as he attests that for the first time, the indefinite form of רוח ('spirit') is used in the exilic era to refer to the 'incomparable attribute of Israel's God (Isa. 31.3) that links YHWH's power with the term רוח ('spirit')'.

[63] Walther Zimmerli, *Ezekiel 1: A Commentary on the Book of Prophet Ezekiel Chapters 1–24* (trans Ronald E. Clements; Philadelphia: Fortress, 1979), p. 20, traces the development of Ezekiel's thought within his theory of a school of disciples. This is a significant contribution that emphasizes the prophet was either involved in the writing process of the events or told the events to his disciples, who later wrote the accounts. Some mainstream debates continue to center around Zimmerli's significant contributions regarding the speech forms and traditions in the book of Ezekiel. For example, see Ronald Hals, *Ezekiel* (FOTL XIX; Grand Rapids: Eerdmans, 1989). Hals presents a form-critical analysis of the book of Ezekiel in its entirety.

argues that the main interpretative challenge in identifying YHWH's
רוח relates to the indistinct ways that the writer(s) uses the term רוח.
For example, the use of רוח without its construct form רוח־יהוה or
רוח־אלהים ('the spirit of YHWH' or 'the spirit of God') is ambiguous and has vexed many interpreters. Zimmerli renders the term רוח
as 'wind' and identifies four categories present in the book of Ezekiel: (1) 'air in motion', (2) 'breath of life', (3) 'prophetic experience
of a call', and (4) 'the world of the divine'.[64]

Zimmerli attests that when the term רוח rendered as ('wind') yet
deals directly with the prophet (Ezek. 2.2; 3.12; 24), then it is interpreted in its theological sense demonstrating an activity of YHWH.[65]
However, Zimmerli is cautious to attribute the simple use of רוח
without the article to YHWH's רוח ('Spirit'). He states, 'It appears to
be an almost independent, effective power'.[66] Zimmerli's category of
a 'prophetic experience of a call' is just as vague. For example, he
observes the term רוח (Ezek. 2.2; 3.12, 24; 8.3; 11.1, 24a; 43.5) is a
mixture of a natural understanding of רוח ('wind') combined with
effects brought about by YHWH.[67]

Zimmerli describes Ezekiel's prophetic experiences as 'an autodrama' indicative of a 'dramatic reality' as it depicts Ezekiel not only
seeing and hearing but also acting within the visions.[68] He argues that
the combination of YHWH's רוח and YHWH's יד reflect a development of 'ecstatic experiences from pre-classical prophecy' (Ezek.
3.12, 14a; 8.1-3).[69] Zimmerli also claims that Ezekiel's transportations
are 'an ecstatic transportation' described in the visions, which are a
working of the spirit and the 'hand of the Lord [that] lifts Ezekiel
out of ordinary time and space into the very presence of God'.[70]

---

[64] Zimmerli, *Ezekiel 2*, pp. 566-68.
[65] Zimmerli, *Ezekiel 2*, p. 567.
[66] Zimmerli, *Ezekiel 2*, p. 566.
[67] Zimmerli, *Ezekiel 2*, p. 567.
[68] Zimmerli, *Ezekiel 1*, pp. 18-19.
[69] Zimmerli, *Ezekiel 1*, p. 234. Zimmerli compares the heavenly being in 1.27
with the 'man' in 8.2 and concluded that since YHWH encounters Ezekiel in the
form of the כבוד, then the 'man' in 8.2 must refer to a heavenly messenger. Zimmerli argues that these Ezekiel texts are a precursor to the apocalyptic tradition that
underscores a heavenly mediator (Zech. 5.9) lifting the prophet between heaven
and earth.
[70] Zimmerli, *Ezekiel 1*, pp. 27, 42, 117.

Robert Wilson

In the 1970's, Robert Wilson wrote a handful of articles using ancient and modern cross-cultural comparison studies to argue that the phrase, the יד־יהוה belongs to the same set of prophetic terminology as the message-reception formula used to communicate the means of divine communication.[71] In this view, the phrase יד־יהוה is often times associated with inspiration through possession of the deity.[72] Wilson also attests that it reflects the presence of intermediation that results in an ecstatic manifestation that at times can depict a trance-like behavior.[73] Yet, he distinguishes spirit possession from a trance. Wilson states, 'Strictly speaking a trance is a psycho-physiological state marked by dissociation and can have a number of different causes besides spirit possession'.[74] He concludes that the repetitive use of the יד־יהוה and the emphasis upon the רוח in Ezekiel represent prophetic inspiration and spirit possession.

C. Moshe Greenberg and Daniel Block

Moshe Greenberg

Moshe Greenberg utilizes a holistic approach in his two-volume commentary on the book of Ezekiel. Greenberg follows Heschel in describing how the phrase, the יד־יהוה is not only used to convey that God's hand is 'a manifestation of his power' but also is 'the urgency, pressure, and compulsion by which he [Ezekiel] is stunned and

---

[71] Robert Wilson, 'Prophecy and Ecstasy: A Reexamination', *JBL* 98 (1979), pp. 321-37 in Robert C. Culley and Thomas W. Overholt (eds.), *Anthropological Perspectives on Old Testament Prophecy* (Semeia 21; Missoula: Scholars, 1982), pp. 404-22. Wilson, *Prophecy and Society in Ancient Israel* (Philadelphia: Fortress, 1980), pp. 260-63, argues that the Judean prophet was characteristically a visionary.

[72] Wilson, *Prophecy and Society*, pp. 260-66.

[73] Wilson, 'Prophecy and Ecstasy', p. 332.

[74] Wilson, *Prophecy and Society*, p. 34. See also, John J. Roberts, 'The Hand of Yahweh', *VT* 21 (1971), pp. 244-51. Roberts seeks to locate the origin of the expression יד־יהוה ('the hand of YHWH') by comparing it to its usage in ancient Near Eastern and Israelite literature. He traces the semantic development of the expression and notes that the phrase at times is related to supernatural manifestations of disaster and at other instances to prophetic experiences. He identifies the prophetic development of the expression יד־יהוה with similarities to physical or psychophysical symptoms and concludes that the development of the prophetic use of the idiom the יד־יהוה may not be related to illness but only subsumes the idea because the prophetic phenomenon resembles sickness.

overwhelmed'.[75] Yet, Greenberg disagrees with Heschel arguing that the phrase in Ezekiel's visions is used to convey that the 'prophet is in a trance brought on by consciousness of being addressed by God'.[76] He draws a distinction between how the phrase is used in the Elijah narratives. For Greenberg, the יד־יהוה in 1 Kgs 18.46 is used to manifest an outward strength and in the visions of Ezekiel it represents a manifestation of a trance in connection with 'some sensory (Ezekiel 2–3) or physical effect (Ezek. 3.22) other than mere audition', and 'detaches him from his surroundings and transports him in the spirit to faraway places' (Ezek. 8.1: 37.1; 40.1), or 'rivets his attention to a psycho-physical change that is to occur in him' (Ezek. 33.22).[77] Greenberg argues that Ezekiel is distinct from other literary prophets because he is 'susceptible to seizure' employing the phrase, the יד־יהוה to describe the 'onset of prophecy'.[78]

Greenberg attempts to define and draw distinctions between biblical ecstasy and pagan ecstasy.[79] He asserts that the biblical visionary must be in possession of himself in order to receive the divine word. He states, 'the ecstasy of biblical prophecy consists in a Godward concentration of consciousness that obliterates circumstances, in contrast to the ecstasy of pagan prophets, in which consciousness itself was obliterated'.[80] From this perspective, Greenberg associates the רוח ('spirit') in Ezek. 2.2 with a 'vigor even courage infused into the prophet by the address of God'[81] and distinguishes it from the רוח ('wind') as 'a mode of locomotion' in Ezek. 3.12-14a; 8.3; 11.1, 24; 43.5 as 'visionary experiences', and ('wind') in Ezek. 3.14b-15, which he concludes represents a 'real experience'.[82]

[75] Moshe Greenberg, *Ezekiel, 1–20: A New Translation with Introduction and Commentary* (AB 22; New Haven, Yale, 1983), p. 41.
[76] Greenberg, *Ezekiel, 1–20*, p. 42.
[77] Greenberg, *Ezekiel, 1–20*, p. 42.
[78] Greenberg, *Ezekiel, 1–20*, p. 42, points out that the phrase, יד־יהוה is used in Isa. 8.11 and Jer. 15.17, but argues that unlike in the Ezekiel texts, it is not used to describe the onset of prophecy.
[79] Greenberg, *Ezekiel, 1–20*, p. 62. See Yezekiel Kaufmann, *Religion of Israel: From Its Beginnings to the Babylonian Exile* (Moshe Greenberg, trans.; London: Allen & Unwin, 1961), pp. 93-111.
[80] Greenberg, *Ezekiel, 1–20*, p. 62.
[81] Greenberg, *Ezekiel, 1–20*, p. 62.
[82] Greenberg, *Ezekiel, 1–20*, p. 70.

Daniel I. Block

Daniel Block published two articles highlighting the Spirit of God in the OT and the book of Ezekiel: (1) 'Empowered by the Spirit of God: The Holy Spirit in the Historiographic Writings of the Old Testament' and, (2) 'The Prophet of the Spirit: The Use of *RWH* in the Book of Ezekiel'.[83] In these articles, he attributes the basic meaning of רוח as 'wind' with a bifurcation of the term. For Block, one fork leads to the meaning of 'side' or 'direction', while the other fork develops five subcategories in Ezekiel: (1) as agent of conveyance, (2) agent of animation, (3) agent of prophetic inspiration as 'mind', (4) as the seal of covenant relationship, and (5) sign of divine ownership.[84]

Block also published a two-volume commentary on Ezekiel studies, which gives special attention to the activities of the term רוח ('wind' or 'breath') as it relates to YHWH and provides a thorough examination of the semantic range of the noun in the prophetic corpus to draw conclusions about the various ways the prophets employ the term רוח in relation to God.[85] He concludes that Ezekiel is the most spiritual prophet of the OT because the term רוח occurs 52 times, more than any other prophet, and the expression is distributed widely throughout the book. Block's conclusions highlight the theological sense of the word רוח, although he oftentimes renders the term as either 'wind' or 'breath'.[86] Block also asserts that רוח as the activity of the divine רוח 'spirit' is closely associated with God himself. He cites, not unlike many others, Aubrey Johnson, 'The spirit throughout the OT is the extension of God's personality'.[87] In this view, the idea of the literature portraying God's personality is compatible with the extensive anthropomorphisms and anthropopath-

---

[83] Block, 'Empowered by the Spirit of God: The Holy Spirit in the Historiographic Writings of the Old Testament', *SBTJ* 1 (1997), pp. 20-28, and 'The Prophet of the Spirit: The Use of *RWH* in the Book of Ezekiel', *JETS* 32 (1989), pp. 27-49.

[84] Block, 'The View from the Top: The Holy Spirit in the Prophets', in David Firth and Paul Wegner (eds.), *Presence, Power, and Promise* (Downers Grove, IL: IVP, 2012), pp. 175-207.

[85] Block, 'The View from the Top', p. 178.

[86] Block, 'The View from the Top', p. 178.

[87] Aubrey Johnson, *The One and the Many in the Israelite Conception of God* (Cardiff: University of Wales, 1961), pp. 6-8, 20, 36-38. Robson, *Word and Spirit in Ezekiel*, p. 77. Ma, *Until the Spirit Comes*, p. 11.

isms that were used in Israelite literature. This type of metaphorical language describes God's attributes of power and emotions. Block's important contributions provide a clearer understanding of the diverse activities of the term רוח ('wind' or 'breath') as an agent of YHWH. He states, 'His (Ezekiel's) prophetic experiences derive from encounters with God that have affected his entire being' and account for his bizarre symbolic acts, yet he denies any presence of ecstasy exists in the narratives.[88]

D. John Rea, Robert Koch, John Woodhouse, Manfred Dreytza, and Wilf Hildebrandt

John Rea

John Rea, a charismatic OT scholar, wrote *The Holy Spirit in the Bible*[89] utilizing grammatical, contextual, and theological perspectives. He identifies two 'renewing functions' for the role of the רוח ('Spirit') in the book of Ezekiel: (1) God's promise of his indwelling Spirit (Ezek. 36.27; 37.14), and (2) the outpoured Spirit as a covenant sign (Ezek. 39.29).[90] Rea argues that Jesus used the term 'water' from Ezek. 36.25 and the 'new spirit' of v. 26 to describe the 'new birth' to Nicodemus in Jn 3.5.[91] He highlights that although, 'Ezekiel did not employ the term new covenant, these concepts of inner cleansing and regeneration with God's promise to impart YHWH's Spirit to indwell believers was a new feature not previously provided in his [YHWH's] covenants with Abraham, Moses, and David'.[92]

Rea concludes that 'the work of spiritual renewal in God's people Israel had begun with his cleansing process of judgment by the Babylonians in Ezekiel's own day' and was a future promise from God through an 'outpoured רוח ('Spirit')' (Ezek. 39.29).[93] He proposes that 'although the outpouring of God's Spirit prophesied by Ezekiel did not occur in his time, it was nevertheless a completed action in God's mind'.[94] He argues that this interpretation is supported through Joel's prediction of the outpouring of the Spirit (Joel 2.28-

---

[88] Block, 'The Prophet of the Spirit', pp. 11, 33.
[89] John Rea, *The Holy Spirit in the Bible: All the Major Passages about the Spirit* (Lake Mary, FL: Creation House, 1990).
[90] Rea, *The Holy Spirit in the Bible*, pp. 101-107.
[91] Rea, *The Holy Spirit in the Bible*, p. 103.
[92] Rea, *The Holy Spirit in the Bible*, pp. 102-103.
[93] Rea, *The Holy Spirit in the Bible*, p. 105.
[94] Rea, *The Holy Spirit in the Bible*, p. 105.

32). Rea draws distinctions between the רוח ('Spirit') in Ezekiel 36–37 as an act for Israel's 'reception of new life' and the רוח ('Spirit') in Ezek. 39.29 as 'an ongoing witness to Israel as well as to the nations that he is their God'.[95] From this perspective, Rea concludes that the 'outpoured Spirit' is the 'seal of the everlasting covenant of peace' (Ezek. 37.26) and is 'a divine mark of ownership' that would ratify the covenant relationship'.[96] In Ezek. 47.1-12, Rea connects the term רוח as 'an outpoured Spirit' to the idea of God's Spirit as a 'life-giving river', which flows from his sanctuary in Jerusalem and the water in the Dead Sea valley (cf. Joel 3.18) to the symbolic idea of 'cleansing, sanctification, renewal, and healing' (2 Chr. 4. 2-10; Titus 3.5; Eph. 5.26). He utilizes other Scriptural references of the רוח and water to emphasize the relationship between God's Spirit and water (Ps. 46.4; Zech. 13.1; 14.8; Jn 7.37; Rev. 22.2).[97]

Robert Koch

In Robert Koch's *Der Geist Gottes im Alten Testament*, he utilizes a historical critical approach to focus his study on the concept of the messiah and the eschatological role of the Spirit.[98] Thus, he gives more space and time to the examination of texts dealing with the messianic figure. Koch traces the development of the term רוח as a natural 'wind' to 'breath of life' to religious categories.[99] He views that רוח is an active agent of the 'supernatural and super-historical God' and 'the personal potency of the acting God'.[100] Koch asserts that the action of 'the spirit of YHWH' upon people is likened to the רוח as the 'wind' or 'life-breath the life giving one' close to YHWH, yet he argues that the 'spirit of YHWH' is not an independent reality but a personification.[101] From this perspective, Koch perceives the רוח in the book of Ezekiel is representative of the actions or personifications of YHWH. Koch concludes that when the term רוח is combined with the דבר ('word'), then it is primarily indicative of God's revelation in the OT.[102]

---

[95] Rea, *The Holy Spirit in the Bible*, p. 106.
[96] Rea, *The Holy Spirit in the Bible*, pp. 106-107.
[97] Rea, *The Holy Spirit in the Bible*, p. 107.
[98] Koch, *Der Geist Gottes im Alten Testament*.
[99] Koch, *Der Geist Gottes im Alten Testament*, p. 31.
[100] Koch, *Der Geist Gottes im Alten Testament*, p. 32.
[101] Koch, *Der Geist Gottes im Alten Testament*, p. 34.
[102] Koch, *Der Geist Gottes im Alten Testament*, p. 13.

John Woodhouse

John Woodhouse's 'The Spirit in the Book of Ezekiel' examines each occurrence of the term רוח to argue that specifically it is emphasized in the first three chapters and the last four chapters of the book of Ezekiel. He renders the term as 'wind' in Ezek. 1.4, 12 and 20a and 'breath' when רוח enters the prophet in Ezek. 2.2. Woodhouse argues that in the context of a storm wind the רוח is the movement associated with a natural wind.[103] For Woodhouse, רוח is not interpreted as the divine ('spirit'). He also renders רוח as 'breath' of the living beings representing 'air in motion' or the breath of the living beings is the motion that is moving the wheels (20b, 21).[104] In Ezekiel's call narrative, Woodhouse interprets רוח as 'breath' likened to Ezekiel's vision of the dead bones (ch. 37).[105]

Manfred Dreytza

In Manfred Dreytza's revised doctoral dissertation from Basel, he utilizes a diachronic semantic approach with a view of salvation history and a history of religion.[106] Through his lexical investigation, Dreytza identifies meteorological and theological meanings for the term רוח in the OT. With regards to Ezekiel, he observes what he calls, 'the divine coercion formula' ותהי עלי שם יד־הוה ('The hand of YHWH was upon me there'), which is a prominent literary feature and interprets it as a 'special experience of God's power upon the prophet, which he observes is similar to the actions of God's רוח ('spirit') upon certain judges of Israel'.[107] In Dreytza's article on the רוח, he emphasizes the force of YHWH's יד to illustrate YHWH's exposition of 'seizing the prophet [Ezekiel]' for entry into his prophetic service.[108] He attests that the Hebrew idiom, YHWH's יד is not only present in

[103] Woodhouse, 'The Spirit in the Book of Ezekiel', pp. 1-22.
[104] Woodhouse, 'The Spirit in the Book of Ezekiel', p. 6.
[105] Woodhouse, 'The Spirit in the Book of Ezekiel', p. 7.
[106] Manfred Dreytza, *Der theolgische Gebrauch von RUAH im Alten Testament: Eine wort-und satzsemantische Studie* (Basal: Brunnen, 1992).
[107] Dreytza, 'רוח', *NIDOTTE*, II, p. 404. Block, *The Book of Ezekiel*, p. 35. Variations of this formula occur seven times in the book of Ezekiel. The variation in the verb 'was upon' is 'to be, exist or become upon; to put on or clothe; to prosper, succeed upon'.
[108] Dreytza, 'רוח', *NIDOTTE*, II, p. 404.

Ezekiel's 'irresistible call ... but also during his lifetime as the Lord seizes him on special occasions'.[109]

Wilf Hildebrandt

Wilf Hildebrandt's *An Old Testament Theology of the Spirit of God* offers a canonical and theological approach to highlight the ways in which the term רוח is used in OT passages.[110] He discusses the Spirit's role in relation to four different categories in the OT, namely, (1) creation, (2) God's people, (3) leadership, and (4) prophecy.[111] He broadly examines the semantic range of the possible meanings of the term רוח, which can be translated as 'spirit', 'wind', or 'breath' in addition to other meanings. Hildebrandt compares the role of the Spirit in prophecy in Israel to that of its larger context of the ancient Near East and concludes that the Canaanite prophetic practices are seen in the OT with the prophets of Baal and Asherah (1 Kings 18).[112]

Hildebrandt observes through his statistical analysis that there are 60 references to God's Spirit in the HB that are not in the construct form[113] to conclude that when the term רוח is identified in its theological sense in Ezekiel, it is the 'active, creative, and vital presence of God'.[114] From this perspective, he argues that the external activity of the רוח was the way in which 'Israel understood their experiences of deliverance, salvation, guidance, and the presence of God'.[115] Hildebrandt argues that in the Former and the Latter prophets, the רוח is closely connected to prophecy. He attributes the term רוח as it is emphasized in Ezekiel, as an empowerment for the task that lay ahead of the prophet. Specifically, he argues that the term רוח is: (1) the motivational guiding force behind the creatures (Ezek. 1.12, 21, 20-21; 10.17), and (2) transports and raises Ezekiel, which is associated to the phenomenon related to inspiration of the prophet (Ezek. 2.2; 3.12, 14, 24; 8.3; 11.1, 5, 24; 43.5).[116] Hildebrandt also draws connections between the יד־יהוה and the term רוח as an indication of prophetic empowerment, and concludes that the term רוח is related

---

109 Dreytza, 'רוח', *NIDOTTE*, II, p. 405.
110 Hildebrandt, *An Old Testament Theology of the Spirit of God*.
111 Hildebrandt, *An Old Testament Theology of the Spirit of* God, pp. 18-27.
112 Hildebrandt, *An Old Testament Theology of the Spirit of* God, pp. 26-27.
113 Hildebrandt, *An Old Testament Theology of the Spirit of* God, pp. 187-90.
114 Hildebrandt, *An Old Testament Theology of the Spirit of God*, p. 18.
115 Hildebrandt, *An Old Testament Theology of the Spirit of God*, p. 18.
116 Hildebrandt, *An Old Testament Theology of the Spirit of God*, pp. 26-27.

to 'prophetic inspiration, whether visionary or auditory, and is a result of the divine רוח'.[117]

E. Harold Hosch, Pamela Kinlaw, James Robson, Christopher J.H. Wright, Dale Launderville, Paul Joyce, Jacqueline Grey, and John Pilch

Harold Hosch

In Harold Hosch's 'רוח in the Book of Ezekiel', he utilizes discourse analysis, surface structure grammatical analysis, case frame analysis, and semantic domain analysis for each usage of the term in order to expand the sense of the meaning.[118] He identifies eight different semantic domains for the term רוח: (1) movement of air, (2) vigor of life, (3) attitudes and emotions, (4) psychological faculties or thought, (5) punishment, (6) reward, (7) spatial orientation, and (8) supernatural beings.[119] Hosch concludes that only the domain that reflects the term רוח as 'supernatural beings' is the divine רוח ('spirit'), and it occurs more than any other semantic domain in the book of Ezekiel. Overall, his category of 'supernatural beings' includes God, Holy Spirit, angels, devil, and demons.[120] He also points out that the 'motion equated with the activity of the divine ('spirit') was important for Ezekiel, and it may define his understanding of the ('spirit') in a special way as reflected in the prophet's encounter with the רוח'.[121]

Hosch, not unlike others, recognizes the emphasis placed upon the mobility motif depicted in its literary context of the chariot-throne vision and subsequent call narrative (Ezek. 1.4-28; 2.2; 3.12, 14a, 24).[122] However, he raises an interesting perspective regarding

---

[117] Hildebrandt, *An Old Testament Theology of the Spirit of God*, pp. 27; 189-90.

[118] Harold Hosch, 'רוח in the Book of Ezekiel', pp. 77-125.

[119] Hosch, 'in the Book of Ezekiel', pp. 77-125.

[120] Demonic spirits are not widely spoken of in OT passages. A few examples are demonstrated when the Spirit of the Lord left Saul, and a spirit from the Lord was sent to Saul to torment him (1 Sam. 16.14-16; 23; 18.10; 19.9), and in Judg. 9.23, God sends an evil spirit between Abimelech and the people of Shechem.

[121] Hosch, 'רוח in the Book of Ezekiel', p. 115.

[122] Hosch, 'רוח in the Book of Ezekiel', p. 87. For other scholars who emphasize the mobility motif, see John Kutsko, *Between Heaven and Earth: Divine Presence and Absence in the Book of Ezekiel* (Winona Lake, IN: Eisenbrauns, 2000), p. 99. See also Joyce, *Ezekiel*, pp. 65-75. Block, *The Book of Ezekiel*, p. 106. Block argues that Divine presence is the one of the major themes in the inaugural visionary accounts, as well as the entire book of Ezekiel that links the mobility motif of departure of the deity from his temple and his eventual return.

the mobility motif as it relates to the occurrence of רוח ('spirit') in Ezekiel 1–3. He states that the activity of the divine רוח 'spirit' in these encounters had 'an irresistible and empowering effect upon the prophet'.[123]

Pamela Kinlaw

In 2003, Pamela Kinlaw's 'From Death to Life: The Expanding רוח in Ezekiel' approaches the text from a literary perspective of an ideal reader to argue that the רוח takes on an 'expanding role' as its meaning evolves or 'expands' throughout the book of Ezekiel.[124] She proposes that this literary strategy provides the reader with an understanding of how the Ezekiel narratives 'guide the perceptions of the implied reader in perceiving God's interaction with the prophet and the readers themselves'.[125] Kinlaw builds upon Block's analysis of the רוח through her methodology that is based upon the work of E.K. Brown. She explains how Brown's use of rhythm, repetition, and an expanding symbol as a literary device, can be used especially when the author 'struggles to communicate an emotion about something that lies behind his story, his people, and his setting or something less definite than any of these'.[126]

Kinlaw focuses upon the term רוח as a dominant symbol and aims to integrate the term as she examines each occurrence in its context. Kinlaw concludes that the expansion of the symbol 'pulls the audience into the drama, depicting the abandonment and destruction to the point of unbearable pain, because only after the fullness of pain can the reader fully experience the life brought by God's presence, by God's רוח, a presence as tangible as the wind on the face and the breath in the body'.[127]

James Robson

In James Robson's revised PhD thesis, *Word and Spirit in Ezekiel*, he employs rhetorical analysis to examine the idea of prophetic inspiration in relation to the דבר־יהוה ('word of YHWH') and YHWH's רוח

---

[123] Hosch, 'רוח in the Book of Ezekiel', p. 117.

[124] Pamela Kinlaw, 'From Death to Life: The Expanding רוח in Ezekiel', *PRSt* 30 (2003), pp. 161-72.

[125] Kinlaw, 'From Death to Life', p. 161.

[126] Kinlaw, 'From Death to Life', p. 163. Kinlaw cites, E.K. Brown, *Rhythm in the Novel* (Lincoln: University of Nebraska Press, 1950), p. 113.

[127] Kinlaw, 'From Death to Life', p. 172.

in the book of Ezekiel. Robson's approach is also theological and synchronic with internal unity and intentionality of the book in mind. He argues that the relationship between 'word' and 'spirit' should be understood in the context of the primary function of God's Spirit, that is, not for prophetic inspiration or authentication of Ezekiel's vocation, but for the transformation of the lives of the hearers of the book.[128] Robson provides an outline of the generally accepted views and disagreements over the meanings of the term רוח in Ezekiel according to their meteorological, anthropological, and theological domains.[129]

Although Ezekiel's visions are not Robson's primary objective, he does address the visions at various points. He argues that Ezekiel 'does not recover the inspiration of pre-classical prophets because, on the one hand, pre-classical prophets are not as inspired as is sometimes said, and, on the other, because classical prophets are more inspired than is sometimes allowed'.[130] Using speech act theory, he classifies two types of inspiration: (1) 'word-communicating' inspiration and (2) 'potentiating' inspiration.[131] For Robson, word-communi-

---

[128] James Robson, *Word and Spirit in Ezekiel* (LHBOT 447; New York: T & T Clark, 2006), builds upon the methodological approach of Thomas Renz, *Rhetorical Function of the Book of Ezekiel* (Boston: Brill, 1999), pp. 1-26. Renz explores the function of the book of Ezekiel as part of the communicative situation in which it originated. He claims that the book in its final form was shaped for the second generation of hearers.

[129] Robson, *Word and Spirit in Ezekiel*, pp. 72-83.

[130] Robson, *Word and Spirit in Ezekiel*, pp. 105-70, offers a full discussion about prophetic inspiration in the pre-exilic and exilic prophets. He argues that the pre-exilic prophets rejected the divine רוח as their source of inspiration due to the occurrences of objections about false prophets or excesses of the ecstatic prophets. The theological view observes that these prophets were focused more upon the 'word of YHWH' and thus, they did not reflect upon the idea of a mediating spirit. Robson argues that the paucity of the mention of the spirit related to prophetic inspiration in certain periods of Israelite history has caused some scholars to question the significance that the role of the spirit has played. For example, the prophets do not directly claim prophetic inspiration by the spirit in the period after 700 BCE until the first exile in 597 BCE. An exception may be represented by Mic. 3.8, 'But as for me, I am filled with power, with the Spirit of the Lord'. For a comprehensive treatment of this debate, see Robson, *Word and Spirit in Ezekiel*, pp. 146-70. Robson categorizes the four perspectives of interpretation on this paucity: (1) antithetical, (2) historical, (3) rhetorical, and (4) theological. For an opposing view of the concept of inspiration in pre-exilic prophets, see Sigmund Mowinckel, 'The Spirit and the Word in the Pre-exilic Reforming Prophets', *JBL* 59.3 (1940), pp. 199-227. Mowinckel argues that the pre-exilic prophets did not see a place for a mediating spirit and they also repudiated such a role.

[131] Robson, *Word and Spirit in Ezekiel*, pp. 11, 99-167.

cating inspiration is observed when the רוח inspires YHWH's word to the prophet (prophetic event) and from or through the prophet to his audience (rhetorical event) (e.g. 2 Sam. 23.2; 1 Kgs 22; Isa. 30.1-2).[132]

Robson defines potentiating inspiration as occurring when the term רוח is involved in the power to evoke a revelatory state of mind.[133] From this perspective, he concludes that YHWH addresses Ezekiel both by visions and by word. Although he does not explicitly link inspiration with YHWH's יד he does point out that the major vision reports in Ezekiel are introduced by the יד-יהוה.[134]

Christopher J.H. Wright

Christopher Wright's 2006 monograph, *Knowing the Holy Spirit Through the Old Testament*, examines the work of the Spirit through a thematic approach. He observes five categories: (1) The Creating Spirit, (2) The Empowering Spirit, (3) The Prophetic Spirit, (4) The Anointing Spirit, and (5) The Coming Spirit.[135] Wright interprets the 'Spirit in the book of Ezekiel as the Spirit of God' who 'literally lifted him up and carried him around the place', either in physical reality or in visions, and 'once even by the hair of his head' (Ezek. 2.2; 3.12, 14, 24; 8.3; 11.24; 37.1).[136] Wright limits his discussion regarding the book of Ezekiel to give more time and space to the vision in Ezekiel 36–37, which he attributes to a 'coming Spirit' of renewal and restoration.[137]

Dale Launderville

In 2007, Dale Launderville's monograph *Spirit and Reason: The Embodied Character of Ezekiel's Symbolic Thinking* combines interdisciplinary and cross-cultural methodological approaches to provide its readers with fresh perspectives in Ezekiel studies. Launderville utilizes his expertise in the classical Greco-Roman literature as a hermeneutical lens to compare and contrast the Pre-Socratic Greek and Mesopotamian traditions with various theological issues within Ezekiel's modes

---

[132] Robson, *Word and Spirit in Ezekiel*, p. 105. Robson uses speech act theory developed by John Searle, *Speech Acts: An Essay in the Philosophy of Language* (Cambridge: Cambridge University Press, 1969).

[133] Robson, *Word and Spirit in Ezekiel*, pp. 106, 120.

[134] Robson, *Word and Spirit in Ezekiel*, pp. 95-101.

[135] Christopher J.H. Wright, *Knowing the Holy Spirit through the Old Testament* (Downers Grove, IL: IVP, 2006).

[136] Wright, *Knowing the Holy Spirit through the Old Testament*, p. 126.

[137] Wright, *Knowing the Holy Spirit through the Old Testament*, pp. 126-36.

of communication, visions, and rhetoric.[138] He uses an analogical approach to shed light upon the symbolic language that is employed in the final form of the Ezekiel texts.

Launderville argues that in the Babylonian exile with all of its traumatic events, the Israelites are challenged to think of YHWH's sovereign rule over history through Ezekiel's visions, rhetoric, symbolic acts, and not by their circumstances. Specifically, he asks how Ezekiel utilizes symbolic thinking as a way in which to communicate his messages. Launderville highlights the key phrase in Ezekiel's theology, 'a new heart and a new spirit', to demonstrate how Ezekiel's theological and symbolic message encourages the Israelites to become living symbols of the spirit of YHWH representing his sovereignty in the world.[139] For Launderville, this activity of becoming a symbol is initiated in Ezekiel's inaugural vision and continues throughout the rest of the book. He observes that the divine Spirit is the connection between humans and the cosmos and concludes that it is this participation between the divine Spirit, humanity, and the cosmos in which the restored exiles will gain a perception of their reality in a new world order from YHWH's perspective.[140]

Paul Joyce

Paul Joyce is a leading contemporary scholar in Ezekiel studies.[141] Joyce states in his 2007 commentary on Ezekiel,

> There is no intention in this volume (commentary) to address every critical issue. My purpose is to make a distinctive contribution to the interpretation and understanding of the book of Ezekiel, particularly in terms of its theology, grounded in both historical research and literary sensitivity.[142]

Although Joyce does not mention pneumatology as one of his theological themes that he develops in the commentary,[143] in an earlier monograph, he does observe five categories for the term רוח in the HB, and identifies all five types in the book of Ezekiel. They are:

---

138 Dale Launderville, *Spirit and Reason: The Embodied Character of Ezekiel's Symbolic Thinking* (Waco: Baylor University Press, 2007), pp. 1-10.
139 Launderville, *Spirit and Reason*, pp. 1-2.
140 Launderville, *Spirit and Reason*, pp. 20-32.
141 Paul Joyce, *Ezekiel, A Commentary* (New York: T & T Clark, 2007).
142 Joyce, *Ezekiel*, p. vi.
143 Joyce, *Ezekiel*, pp. 17-32.

'wind', 'God-given breath of life', 'dynamic power of YHWH', 'the medium of understanding in humans', and 'the moral will'.[144] He posits that when the use of the term רוח is pointing to the 'will', it is in such a way as to describe the moral sense of the word לב ('heart, mind').[145] In Joyce's commentary on Ezekiel, he uses this point to argue that the reference to a new heart and spirit (11.19; 36.26-7; 37.14) is the gift or the result of the outpouring of YHWH that provides the capacity of corporate Israel to obey YHWH's commands. He defines the term רוח as the 'animation by the divine' (2.2; 8.3; 11.5; 37.1) even though רוח is mentioned without the article.[146] He also concludes that these references are alluding to pre-classical prophecy and are 'clearly representing inspiration language'.[147] He argues that the two phrases, 'the word of the Lord came to Ezekiel' and 'the hand of the Lord was on him there' are two recurrent and important formulas for the divine inspiration of the prophet, the latter being especially distinctive of Ezekiel (cf. Ezek. 1.14, 22; 8.1; 33.22; 37.1; 40.1).[148] Joyce agrees with Zimmerli that the prophet Ezekiel stands in a long tradition of ancient Near Eastern prophecy.[149] He argues that Ezekiel's week of silence and the affective term משמים ('stunned or overwhelmed') used to describe the event should be read in light of pre-classical prophecy (Ezek. 3.12-15).[150] From this perspective, Ezekiel's strange behavior is interpreted through the lens of the pre-classical prophets, thus not to be associated with mental illness.

Steven Tuell

In 2009, Steven Tuell's *NIBC* on the book of Ezekiel primarily demonstrates a 'believing criticism' that integrates a full range of historical criticisms to examine the theological theme of divine presence.[151] Tuell concludes that the visions in Ezek. 1.1; 8.3, and 40.2 form a connected plot line that ties the book together in light of this theme of divine presence and absence.[152] Although, Tuell does not

---

[144] Joyce, *Divine Initiative and Human Response in Ezekiel* (JSOTSup 51; Sheffield: JSOT Press, 1989), pp. 109-11.

[145] Joyce, *Divine Initiative*, pp. 109-11.

[146] Joyce, *Ezekiel*, p. 76.

[147] Joyce, *Ezekiel*, p. 76.

[148] Joyce, *Ezekiel*, p. 67.

[149] Joyce, *Ezekiel*, p. 80.

[150] Joyce, *Ezekiel*, p. 80. See also Carley, *Ezekiel Among the Prophets*, pp. 69-81.

[151] Steven Tuell, *Ezekiel* (NIBC; Peabody, MA: Hendrickson, 2009), pp. 1-6.

[152] Tuell, *Ezekiel*, p. 276.

mention pneumatology as a theme in the book of Ezekiel, he does appear to agree with Zimmerli's premise that there is the presence of pre-classical inspiration illustrated by the work of the רוח. He states, it is the same רוח that lifts Ezekiel up (2.2; 3.14) and commands Ezekiel to speak the word of the Lord (2.4; 3.11).[153] Tuell also observes that the combination of YHWH's יד and YHWH's רוח in Ezek. 3.12-15 suggests the presence of ecstasy.[154] He interprets Ezek. 3.12, 14a as the 'prophet's mystical transportation from God's direct interaction'.[155] Tuell states that the phrase the יד־יהוה ('hand of YHWH') reflects the concept of ecstatic prophecy in Ezekiel and is an important formula for the divine inspiration of the prophet (1.3; 3.14, 22; 8.1; 40.1).[156] Tuell follows Joseph Blenkinsopp in that Ezek. 3.14 paints a portrait of a prophet that is in 'a state of ecstatic exaltation' and 'also feels the let-down of his return to mundane reality'.[157]

Jacqueline Grey

In 2009, Jacqueline Grey examined the acts of the רוח in Ezekiel 37.[158] She applies speech-act theory to the narrative of Ezek. 37.1-14 and builds upon the work of John Austin who argues that speech-act theory contributes to biblical studies. Grey agrees with Austin in that words or speech are more than referential or informative but are also performative and indicative of a reality.[159] Grey's examination of discourse is not concerned with authorial intent, but rather with the meaning of the discourse itself and what the speaker did during the discourse. From this perspective, the speech acts of YHWH support the legitimate authoritative role of the words of the prophet and through proclamation change is affected. Regarding the role of the רוח, Grey concludes that Ezekiel's רוח as ('breath') 'produces the

---

153 Tuell, *Ezekiel*, p. 12.
154 Tuell, *Ezekiel*, pp. 10; 19-21; 58-59.
155 Tuell, *Ezekiel*, pp. 10; 19-21; 58-59.
156 Zimmerli, *Ezekiel 1*, pp. 48, 117. Joyce, *Ezekiel*, pp. 67, 251.
157 Tuell, *Ezekiel*, p. 21. Joseph Blenkinsopp, *Ezekiel* (Int 23; Louisville: Westminster, 1990), p. 28.
158 Jacqueline Grey, 'Acts of the Spirit: Ezekiel 37 in the Light of Contemporary Speech-Act Theory', *JBRP* 1 (2009), pp. 69-81.
159 John L. Austin, *How to Do Things with Words* (Cambridge, MA: Harvard University Press, 1962). Walter Houston, 'What did the Prophets think they were doing? Speech acts and prophetic discourse in the Old Testament', *BibInt* 1.2 (1993), pp. 167-88. Matthias Wenk, 'The Creative Power of the Prophetic Dialogue', *Pneuma* 26.1 (2004), pp. 118-29.

reality, which is actuated by the רוח ("Spirit") and inhabits the breath of the prophet's declaration, which works to achieve and fulfill the declaration'.[160]

John Pilch

John Pilch's 2011 monograph, *Flights of the Soul*, dedicates an entire chapter to the call of Ezekiel (Ezekiel 1–3). He uses a 'Kitbashed model', which combines anthropological and other social scientific literature to interpret the dream and vision reports in the biblical narratives.[161] He defines a 'Kitbashed model' as selectively using parts of other's models and constructing a new model. One of Pilch's conclusions is that these biblical reports of visions take place in 'an alternate state of consciousness' (ASC's), in which the visionary is not 'possessed by the spirit or does not hallucinate; but rather is able to communicate for the purpose of solving a problem or convey new information'.[162] He reports 'Ezekiel's commission scene reports the intelligible soundtrack of Ezekiel's ASC experience'.[163] Pilch explains that in many ASC experiences reported in the Bible and elsewhere, the visionary is at first frightened by the experience and usually requires comfort. Yet, he argues that in the narratives about Ezekiel, the prophet is not afraid. Ezekiel's reaction to the vision is a gesture of homage as he reports that he fell on his face.[164] Pilch states:

> The activity of the Spirit (2.1-2) is in light of Ezekiel's usages of the pre-classical ecstatic prophets, Elijah and Elisha, in whom the Spirit was very active. For Ezekiel, the spirit is an energy originating in the divine sphere which manifests itself as a force that propels (Ezek. 1.12, 20-21), lifts up (Ezek. 2.2; 3.12, 14, 24), transports (Ezek. 8.1; 11.1, 24; 37.1), and energizes and renews both individuals and community (Ezek. 11.19; 18.31; 36.26-27; 37.14; 39.29).[165]

Pilch concludes that what is lacking in form analysis is that the visionary reports of these 'prophets took place in ASC's and that

---

[160] Grey, 'Acts of the Spirit', p. 79.
[161] John Pilch, *Flights of the Soul: Visions, Heavenly Journeys, and Peak Experiences in the Biblical World* (Grand Rapids: Eerdmans, 2011), pp. ix-xiii.
[162] Pilch, *Flights of the Soul*, p. 10.
[163] Pilch, *Flights of the Soul*, p. 216.
[164] Pilch, *Flights of the Soul*, p. 217.
[165] Pilch, *Flights of the Soul*, p. 217.

genre always derives from the social system since genres are not part of the language or the linguistic system'.[166] From this perspective, Pilch argues that 'it is quite plausible that the visionaries did behave in just the way that the literary pattern reports', in which Ezekiel's call vision fits the pattern of ASC described by contemporary cognitive neuroscience and cultural anthropology.[167]

III. Conclusions

From the above survey of contemporary Ezekiel scholarship, it is apparent that while the book of Ezekiel is replete with the term רוח (52 references) with a breadth of semantic meanings represented, there are only a few comprehensive treatments in contemporary Ezekiel scholarship that write about the diverse and numerous pneumatological considerations. There is also a lacuna in Pentecostal scholarship in Ezekiel studies, and to date, there are only two published monographs from the wider biblical guild that highlight the role of the רוח in the book of Ezekiel. The most common methodological approach observed from the above scholarly works in which scholars give particular attention to the diverse activities of the term רוח in the OT, is through categorization and a critical analysis of each occurrence of the term רוח.[168] Particularly, in the book of Ezekiel, the scholars above usually render the term רוח as either ('spirit' or 'wind' or 'breath') and categorize these terms either in a (1) meteorological, (2) anthropological, and/or (3) theological sense. The latter sense is further categorized or examined by the various roles or activities of the divine רוח.

However, the theological sense of the term רוח in Ezekiel has led to a diversity of interpretations and generated numerous debates regarding the function or role of the רוח ('spirit') in prophecy. One central argument culminates because the common usage for the

---

166 Pilch, *Flights of the Soul,* p. 222.
167 Pilch, *Flights of the Soul,* p. 222.
168 Zimmerli, *Ezekiel 2*, pp. 566-68. Block, 'Prophet of the Spirit', pp. 27-49; Hosch, 'רוח in the Book of Ezekiel', pp. 77-125; Woodhouse, 'The Spirit in the Book of Ezekiel', pp. 1-22. See also, Robson, *Word and Spirit,* pp. 80-95. Robson provides an outline of the general accepted meanings and disagreements over the meanings of the term רוח in the book of Ezekiel according to their meteorological, anthropological, and theological domains.

divine רוח in the OT involves its representation of the metaphysical or divine power, specifically expressed in its genitive construction as רוח-אלהים ('the spirit of God') or רוח־יהוה ('the spirit of YHWH'),[169] and these phrases occur less frequently in latter prophets and only twice in the book of Ezekiel (Ezek.11.5; 37.1). Additionally, one of the distinctions in the book of Ezekiel is that frequently the term רוח is used without modifiers, which has caused many scholars reviewed above to leave the meaning of the term ambiguous. While there is no general consensus as to the exact nature of the divine רוח in Ezekiel's visionary accounts, many scholars cited above conclude primarily through the context that at times the simple use of רוח without the article can be related to an activity given by YHWH, yet some conclude that it may not refer to YHWH's רוח ('spirit'). For example, some of these activities range from divine animation, inspiration, and conveyance to natural winds moving the prophet or courage given by God.

Furthermore, some scholars reviewed above conclude that the meaning of the term רוח cannot be fully expressed by using word, clause, or verse as the parameters for determining its meaning and argue that the categories must remain fluid. For example, the insights of Zimmerli, Block, and Robson's represent examples of how their respective categorizations are not exclusive to one another. In other words, the function of the role of the term רוח can represent more than one category when read in its wider literary context. Thus, they argue that categorization of ideas is useful for providing a template, but the danger of categorizations is that it can also draw sharp delineations that can impede the proper interpretation of the text.

The current debates not only center on grammatical issues, but also with the prophetic function of the divine רוח as it relates to inspiration, whether visionary or auditory. On a general level, there is a

---

[169] Zimmerli, *Ezekiel 1*, pp. 18-19. Zimmerli emphasizes that the concept of 'the spirit of God' or 'the spirit of YHWH' is unique in Israel because its formulation is only depicted in ancient Israelite literature. See also, John Walton, 'The Ancient Near Eastern Background of the Spirit of the Lord in the Old Testament' in David G. Firth and Paul D. Wegner (eds.), *Power, Presence, and Promise: The Role of the Spirit in the Old Testament* (Downers Grove; IL: IVP, 2011), p. 38. M.V. Van Pelt, W.C. Kaiser, and D. Block, 'רוח', *NIDOTTE*, III, pp. 1073-78. From this perspective, the phrases, 'the spirit of God' or 'the spirit of YHWH' consistently portray a prophetic empowerment given by YHWH's spirit that was familiar to the leaders and prophets in the exilic era.

fundamental understanding of OT literature that the divine רוח inspires prophecy. However, the issue of prophetic inspiration in the
OT is widely debated and more so in the book of Ezekiel.[170] This
argument rests upon the paucity of the mention of the term רוח in
the classical prophets. Robson and Kapelrud attest that the classical
prophets did not disclaim the term רוח as their source of inspiration,
but were more concerned with the word of YHWH, and possibly the
role of the divine spirit was understood. For some scholars, the book
of Ezekiel recovers the role of the term רוח in prophetic activities
from the pre-classical prophets to discuss its usage phenomenologically.[171] For example, the activities of the transporting רוח in 1 Kgs
18.12 and 2 Kgs 2.16 are similar to the רוח that lifts Ezekiel (Ezek.
3.12, 14a). The contributions of these scholars are useful; however,
the lack of clarity or consensus provides space for the continued exploration for the function and uses of the רוח in the book of Ezekiel.

The second motif reviewed above is the יד־יהוה that occurs frequently in Ezekiel's vision narratives. In the prophetic tradition, the
יד־יהוה is an anthropomorphic clause often used metaphorically to
describe an element of God's power ascending upon a prophet,
judge, or ruler. Uniquely, in the book of Ezekiel, the idiom is linked
with Ezekiel's revelatory visions of the glory of YHWH, which includes the word of YHWH, his visionary transportations by the רוח
and various uses of affective language. The Hebrew idiom or its variation ותהי עלי שם יד־הוה ('The hand of YHWH was upon me
there') is present in all four major visions of the glory of YHWH in
the book of Ezekiel (1.3; 3.14; 22; 8.1; 37.1; 40.1).

Contemporary Ezekiel scholarship reveals that there are numerous methodological approaches employed to explore the relationships between the activities of YHWH's רוח and YHWH's יד. Many
scholars draw conclusions regarding the prophetic activities (phenomenon) of the prophet, while others attempt to discuss the prophetic consciousness of the literary disposition of the prophet Ezekiel. There are three views identified: (1) Ezekiel is an ecstatic prophet
and should be read in light of pre-classical prophecy, (2) Ezekiel is

---

[170] George M. Flattery, *A Biblical Theology of the Holy Spirit: Old Testament* (Springfield: Global University, 2009), pp. 93-111.

[171] Zimmerli, *Ezekiel 1*, pp. 42-43. See also, Keith Carley, *Ezekiel Among the
Prophets: A Study of Ezekiel's Place in Prophetic Tradition* (SBT 2nd Series 31; Naperville,
IL: SCM Press, 1974), pp. 30, 71-73.

not an ecstatic prophet, or (3) Ezekiel is pathological. Generally, the scholars who regard Ezekiel as an ecstatic prophet do so on the grounds of the similarities between the phenomenological language and the combined literary motifs of the יד־יהוה and the רוח that is depicted in the literature of the pre-classical prophets and the book of Ezekiel. For example, Neve considers that the יד־יהוה in Ezekiel may represent an ecstatic condition and when it is used with the רוח then the writer(s) is referring to YHWH's רוח ('spirit') and not 'wind'.[172] Likewise, he argues that when the writer(s) uses any affective terms associated with YHWH or other anthropomorphic language, then the term רוח is referring to YHWH's 'spirit' and not 'wind'. Scheepers draws the connection between Ezekiel and the pre-classical prophets, yet he does not make statements about the nature of ecstasy. Additionally, in the book of Ezekiel there is also the emphasis placed upon the affective language that provides additional support for some scholars who view Ezekiel as an ecstatic prophet. Particularly, the call narrative portrays the prophet as having an intense emotion חמה ('heat' 'wrath') in his רוח ('spirit') (3.14b), and he is ultimately left שמם ('stunned or overwhelmed') for seven days (3.15). Tuell agrees with Blenkinsopp, who interprets Ezekiel's emotional portrait in this pericope to conclude that the prophet in 'a state of ecstatic exaltation' feels the letdown of his return to ordinary reality.[173]

Lindblom, Zimmerli, Joyce, and Dreytza also observe that the combined literary motifs of YHWH's רוח and YHWH's יד point to the notion of ecstasy, which they discern help to portray the prophet's affective responses to the visionary encounter.[174] Joyce argues that Ezekiel's week of silence and the affective term שמם ('stunned or overwhelmed') used to describe the event should be read in light of pre-classical prophecy (Ezek. 3.12-15).[175] From this perspective, they associate Ezekiel's strange behavior as similar to the pre-classical prophets, thus not to be associated with mental illness. Mostly, it is not clear how some of these scholars perceive ecstasy, because generally scholars do not discuss how they define ecstasy in

---

[172] Neve, *The Spirit of God in the Old Testament*, p. 40.
[173] Tuell, *Ezekiel*, p. 14.
[174] Zimmerli, *Ezekiel 1*, p. 234. Tuell, *Ezekiel*, pp. 10; 19-21; 58-59.
[175] Joyce, *Ezekiel*, p. 80.

the context of prophecy. A few exceptions emerge from the above literature. Greenberg argues that there is a distinction between biblical ecstasy and pagan ecstasy, while Lindblom and Wilson argue that biblical ecstasy is influenced by pagan ecstasy.

There is one particular study proposed by Pilch who argues that Ezekiel's visions take place in 'an alternate state of consciousness' (ASC's), in which he refutes the definition of ecstasy in light of ancient Near eastern spirit possession to argue that Ezekiel is not 'possessed by the spirit and does not hallucinate'.[176] Pilch argues that ASC is an ecstatic event in which the literary portrait of the prophet is fully capable of receiving and giving communication.

Heschel and Block represent the second view although for different reasons. Block argues that Ezekiel is not in a state of ecstasy, but rather through the use of form criticism, he concludes that Ezekiel is a 'resistant and rebellious prophet'.[177] Heschel paints a unique portrait of a Hebrew prophet to argue against the idea of ecstasy that is quite often proposed through cross-cultural comparative studies. There are a couple scholars, like Edwin Broome and David Halperin, who emphasize the affective language employed in the book of Ezekiel and argue that the language portrays the prophet as mentally ill, although this view is not widely followed.[178] All of these studies outlined above contribute in different ways to the controversial questions raised in these discussions.

Historically, there was some consensus established in various circles utilizing form criticism, although not without its challenges. Generally, the form critics of the twentieth century perceived that the state of ecstasy was an irrational and incoherent psychological state or condition.[179] These assumptions were derived from comparative religious analysis and the belief was that ecstasy was a product of

---

[176] Pilch, *Flights of the Soul*, p. 217.
[177] Block, *The Book of Ezekiel*, pp. 11-12.
[178] Edwin Broome, 'Ezekiel's Abnormal Personality', *JBL* 65 (1946), pp. 277-93. David Halperin, *Seeking Ezekiel: Text and Psychology* (University Park: Pennsylvania State University Press, 1993), interprets the whole book of Ezekiel through Freudian psychoanalysis to assert that Ezekiel was portrayed as pathologically sick.
[179] Lindblom, *Prophecy in Ancient Israel*, pp. 3-46. Lindblom developed categories of inspiration and ecstasy. He viewed inspiration as a more general term of mental excitement and ecstasy as intense inspiration in which the person loses full control of their senses. He further contends that ecstatic manifestation was a universal phenomenon available in all cultures across all times that primarily was the result of a personality type.

folk psychology. If these prophets were irrational or frenzied, then how could they articulate or produce a message? Moreover, how could these messages be transformed into a coherent message and be structured in such a way as to be analyzed? Contemporary scholarship includes many anthropological studies of prophecy and ecstasy, while recent scholarship has tended to bypass the question of how the appearance of ecstatic behavior involves the prophetic process, and instead opted to treat it phenomenologically.[180] The objective, visible activity of the prophet was thought possible to be evaluated through ancient comparative religion analysis and contemporary anthropological studies that includes social role theories.[181]

However, there is a lack of scholarly consensus regarding the presence and nature of ecstatic elements in biblical literature, and more specifically in the book of Ezekiel. More importantly there is also ambiguity in adequately defining the term. The words 'trance' and 'ecstasy' at times are used interchangeably, especially when the treatise includes other disciplines such as anthropology. Socio-anthropological studies tend to associate societal roles of prophetic performance with ecstasy as a state of mind that is variably called 'ecstasy, trance or possession' without delineating the distinctions of how these differences might impact the interpretation of the ancient biblical texts.

Contemporary Ezekiel studies provides scholars with numerous opportunities to employ innovative approaches that combine the literary techniques of interpretation, as well as the integration of other disciplines in hopes of gleaning fresh insights into the enigmatic book. Through this review of literature, it is apparent that Ezekiel's major vision narratives are marked with an increase in the occurrences of the term רוח (52), the Hebrew idiom יד־יהוה, and affective language, which is distinct from any other book in the OT. This is somewhat remarkable since Ezekiel is most like the books of Leviticus and Jeremiah in thought and language, yet both have very few

---

[180] Wilson, 'Prophecy and Society in Ancient Israel', and Wilson, 'Prophecy and Ecstasy: A Reexamination', pp. 321-37. In this volume and in a series of articles (Wilson, 1977a, 1977b, 1978-79, 1979) he has provided a rich and wide-ranging discussion of prophecy in Israel viewed from an anthropological-sociological perspective.

[181] For a treatment on the social roles of the Hebrew prophets, see David Peterson, *The Roles of Israel's Prophets* (JSOTSup Series 17; Sheffield: JSOT Press, 1981).

occurrences of the term רוח. Since the phrase 'the hand of YHWH' is considered a distinct feature in Ezekiel and linked with the רוח, then the expectation is that more time and space be given to the discussion.

Because modern critical scholarship has virtually overlooked how the role of the Spirit interplays with the Hebrew idiom, the יד־יהוה and the affective language as it specifically relates to Ezekiel's four major visions, this gap paves the way for a Pentecostal literary-theological hermeneutical approach. A Pentecostal hearing of the text provides an innovative approach because it is informed by the dynamic nature of Scripture, the Spirit, and the community. A Pentecostal reading strategy will provide a hermeneutical lens that will contribute fresh insights to expound further upon the theological and pneumatological implications that are derived from a narrative that describes prophetic visionary encounters. This reading strategy will also incorporate a literary-theological reading as a method owing to its compatibility with the narrative orientation of Pentecostal thought that is holistic because it does not limit the use of various other methodological tools. This literary theological analysis may then provide the hearers (past and present) with an understanding of how the Ezekiel narratives guide the perceptions and the affections of the implied hearers in discerning YHWH's interaction with the prophet. While traditional tools are useful, they are limited in scope to provide an adequate hearing of the visionary texts that inherently includes supernatural events and experience. This proposed Pentecostal reading strategy will require a thorough explanation that will be provided in Chapter 2 of this study.

3

METHODOLOGY: A PENTECOSTAL READING STRATEGY

I. Introduction

At the heart of Pentecostal hermeneutics is the integration of Scripture, the Spirit, and the community to form a Pentecostal hermeneutical paradigm. For the Pentecostal and Charismatic scholars named below, the discipline of biblical hermeneutics seeks to understand how their identity, social location, and theological formation inform their interpretive lens. Other distinct elements also observed are the emergence of 'an affective approach' to reading the biblical texts and understanding Pentecostal spirituality as a vital instructive quality. Land's method integrates Pentecostal spirituality with the formation of the affections that are expressed and evoked by core Pentecostal and Charismatic beliefs and practices.[1] Martin's affective approach involves identifying the affective language in the narrative as well as discussing how this language affects the hearers (past and present). Yet, to date there are no scholarly treatments of the role of the affections in Ezekiel scholarship. The present study incorporates a Pentecostal reading strategy that is informed and shaped by the reading and hearing of Scripture with the Spirit, which integrates discernment from the Pentecostal community. This reading strategy is rooted in the Pentecostal fivefold gospel with an emphasis placed upon the community, which are the catalysts for the transformation that occurs in the reader through the study of Scripture. Due to space

---

[1] Land, *Pentecostal Spirituality*, p. 1.

and time limitations, the present work will only identify the affective language and observe how the language is used in the narratives to affect the characters in the narratives. Perhaps for a future endeavor, a more comprehensive affective approach will be employed to include the transformation that occurs in the present-day hearer.

This chapter will outline the reading strategy that will be employed for the present endeavor. First, my Pentecostal and Charismatic context provides the hermeneutical lens through which I will interpret how the activities of the Spirit in Ezekiel's four major vision narratives are highlighted (Ezek. 1–3; 8–11; 37.1-14; 40–48). Although each person approaches Scripture with his or her own presuppositions, there are some core foundational principles for Pentecostal or Charismatic hermeneuts. These may not be exclusive, neither are they comprehensive, but to name a few: (1) the authority and dynamic nature of Scripture, (2) the leading, guidance, and transformative power of the Spirit, and (3) the accountability of community with an emphasis on witness, mission, and a passion for encounters with God. The Spirit guides the community through knowledge, understanding, and experiences to interpret Scripture in a meaningful way for their particular community, who also serves as the sounding board for the discerning and hearing of Scripture and the accepting or rejecting of various interpretations. Pentecostals and Charismatics not only engage in hearing the biblical texts but also seek to experience the texts as a living word through the ministry of the Spirit. The Pentecostal traditions are diverse, yet there are still common threads that appear throughout this sampling of scholarly works. The concepts of the Scripture, the Spirit, and the community continue to be at the forefront of the Pentecostal dialogue for the task of interpreting Scripture. This study will build upon Thomas and Martin, who propose that a distinct Pentecostal hearing of the biblical text is based upon integrating the Pentecostal community, past and present through discerning the shared experience and role of the Spirit in the task of hermeneutics.[2] Additionally, in defining a Pentecostal approach to the OT the work of scholars Moore (on Deuteronomy)[3],

---

[2] Ervin, 'A Pentecostal Hermeneutical Option', p. 34. Martin, *The Unheard Voice of God*, pp. 30-38.

[3] Moore, Canon and Charisma in the Book of Deuteronomy', pp. 75-92; 'Deuteronomy and the Fire of God: A Critical Charismatic Interpretation', pp. 11-33.

McQueen (on Joel)[4], and Martin (on Judges and Psalms)[5] is essential. Their work not only demonstrates the variety of ways in which a Pentecostal hermeneutic can be constructed but also provides a solid foundation on which to construct a new reading strategy.

The second facet of this reading strategy not only includes the contemporary Pentecostal community as dialogue partners, but it will also retrieve and discern the testimonies of early Pentecostals through the use of reception history. This tool will provide a way to explore how the early Pentecostal interpretations of the visionary and pneumatological texts of Ezekiel provide an understanding of how early Pentecostal spirituality was informed by their reading of Ezekiel (*Wirkungsgeschicte*).[6] This study will explore early Pentecostal periodical literature to discover the extent to which early Pentecostal spirituality was impacted by the pneumatic emphasis in Ezekiel's visions. Generally, the understanding of the early Pentecostal movement was considered eschatological, theophanic, and revivalist and hopefully, their testimonies will also shed light upon the theological implications of Ezekiel's visions.[7] Since early Pentecostal literature is predominantly comprised of testimonies, which continues to influence contemporary Pentecostal communities, a separate chapter is devoted to listening to their witness.

The third element of this reading strategy incorporates a critical engagement of a narrative-theological hearing of the texts. A Pentecostal narrative hearing of Ezekiel's visions is a method owing to its compatibility with its affinity with testimony as a narrative way of life. The integration of these concepts calls for a literary-theological reading of Scripture in the context of the worshipping community, which includes attention to the affective language utilized in the text. Ezekiel's visions are especially appropriate for an affective Pentecostal interpretation due to the nature of its prophetic narrative structure with its poetic language, in which the rhetoric includes

---

[4] Martin, 'Power to Save!?: The Role of the Spirit of the Lord in the Book of Judges', pp. 21-50; *The Unheard Voice of God*; 'Longing for God: Psalm 63 and Pentecostal Spirituality', pp. 54-76.

[5] McQueen, *Joel and the Spirit*.

[6] Ulrich Luz, *Matthew in History: Interpretation, Influence, and Effect* (Minneapolis: Fortress Press, 1994).

[7] D. William Faupel, *The Everlasting Gospel* (JPTSup 10; Sheffield: Sheffield Academic Press, 1996).

metaphors and symbolism.[8] The author(s) of the narratives of every major vision in the book of Ezekiel employs affective language either to describe the overwhelming emotional portrait of the prophet or the pathos of God in the midst of the theme of divine visionary encounters by the רוח.[9] Ezekiel's dramatic encounters with YHWH's רוח combined with the prophet's affective responses have led scholars, like Daniel Block to conclude that 'Ezekiel is a man totally possessed by the Spirit of YHWH', which 'affected his entire being'.[10] The themes of divine encounter, the power and activities of the Spirit, which includes dreams, visions, and passion, resonate profoundly with the Pentecostal ethos. The Pentecostal hearer of Ezekiel's visions recognizes that the affections in the biblical text correspond to their own passions, which ultimately informs the process of interpretation and transforms the hearer by the Spirit. The present integrative study will also take into consideration Land's landmark contributions concerning Pentecostal spirituality, and subsequent works from Thomas, Baker, and Martin, who argue for the integration of the role of the affections because it offers a more holistic approach to the interpretative process. From this perspective, Ezekiel's visions and its pneumatological and affective qualities and dimensions can contribute in the dialogue toward constructing a Pentecostal theology of Spirit-inspired visions.

The final aspect to this study will integrate the conclusions of a Pentecostal narrative theological reading of Ezekiel's visions in order to contribute towards a Pentecostal theology of Spirit-inspired visions for the service of the contemporary Pentecostal and Charismatic communities.

---

[8] For discussions about prophetic speech, see John L. Austin, *How to do things with Words* (Cambridge, MA: Harvard University Press, 1962). Walter Houston, 'What did the Prophets think they were doing? Speech acts and prophetic discourse in the Old Testament', *BibInt* 1.2 (1993), pp. 167-88. Matthias Wenk, 'The Creative Power of the Prophetic Dialogue', *Pneuma* 26.1 (2004), pp. 118-29.

[9] Heschel, *The Prophets*, II, pp. 432-35. Heschel argues that in the HB, stress is laid on the fact that the individual did not perceive of a bifurcation of the mind, heart, thought, or emotions.

[10] Block, *The Book of Ezekiel, Chapters 1–24*, pp. 11-39.

II. The Origins of Pentecostalism in North America

Pentecostalism emerged out of the Holiness movement of the 20th century with revivals that energized a worldwide phenomenon. Historians generally trace the beginning of the Pentecostal movement in North America to the revivals associated with two significant people and events in the early 1900's: Charles F. Parham's Bethel Bible School in Topeka, KS, (1901), and William J. Seymour, a black holiness preacher from the 'Azusa Street Mission' in Los Angeles, CA (1906-1909).[11] There is a general (but not universal) consensus among historians that the defining belief of Pentecostalism, namely 'that in apostolic times, the speaking in tongues was considered to be the initial physical evidence of a person's having received the baptism in the Holy Spirit' was first established by Charles Parham at his Bethel Bible School at the end of 1900 in Topeka, Kansas.[12] This key

---

[11] While the focus of this thesis is on North American Classical Pentecostalism, it is important to note that there were several international Pentecostal revivals, contributing to the globalization of Pentecostalism, such as the Welsh, Indian, and Korean revivals. For the origins and developments on these international revivals see, Alan Anderson, *An Introduction to Pentecostalism* (Cambridge: University Press, 2004), pp. 35-38. It is also noted that Pentecostalism continues to be a fast-growing movement with the majority of its adherents found in Asia, Africa, and Latin America. For the origins and development of North American Pentecostalism, see Vinson Synan, *The Holiness-Pentecostal Movement in the United States* (Grand Rapids: Eerdmans, 1971), later published as *The Holiness-Pentecostal Tradition: Charismatic Movements in the Twentieth Century* (Grand Rapids: Eerdmans, 1997); Donald Dayton, *Theological Roots of Pentecostalism* (Peabody: Hendrickson Publishers, 1987); Walter Hollenweger, *The Pentecostals* (Peabody, MA: Hendrickson, 1988); Harvey Cox, *Fire From Heaven: The Rise of Pentecostal Spirituality and the Reshaping of Religion in the Twenty-First Century* (Reading: Addison-Wesley, 1995), and Faupel, *The Everlasting* Gospel, 1996.

[12] For the accounts of the Bethel Bible school revival, see Sarah Parham, *The Life of Charles F. Parham, Founder of the Apostolic Faith Movement* (Baxter Springs, KS: Apostolic Faith Church, 1930), p. 54. Parham, *The Life of Charles F. Parham*, p. 54. A part of Parham's story records:

> The Pentecostal blessing fell, that the indisputable proof on each occasion was, that they spake with other tongues. About 75 people beside the school, which consisted of 40 students, had gathered for the watch night service. A mighty spiritual power filled the entire school. At 10:30 p.m. sister Agnes N. Ozman asked that hands might be laid upon her to receive the Holy Spirit as she hoped to go to foreign fields. At first, I refused, not having the experience myself I laid my hands upon her head and prayed. I had scarcely repeated three-dozen sentences when a glory fell upon her, a halo seemed to surround her head and face, and she began speaking in the Chinese language, and was unable to speak English for three days.

event in the history of Pentecostalism was marked by the experience of Parham's students who spoke in tongues and later perceived it as the evidence of Spirit baptism. Their theological tenets of tongue speech, which they interpreted as the baptism in the Holy Spirit, still remains an essential doctrine to classical Pentecostalism.[13]

The revival that arose in the small band of believers led by Seymour yielded different results as he preached racial reconciliation and the restoration of biblical spiritual gifts. The Azusa Street Revival soon became a local sensation that attracted thousands of curious seekers and pilgrims from all around the world. The spiritual intensity of the revival continued for over three years, making Azusa Street one of the most significant Pentecostal centers in the early 20th century. Speaking in tongues through Spirit baptism was not the only spiritual experience witnessed at the revival at the Azusa Street Mission. These women and men experienced a socio-religious phenomenon of their day. The Azusa revival represented multi-racial worship with expressions of overwhelming love and unity for one another, people singing in the Spirit, dreams and visions, and many testimonies of healings, salvations, and deliverances were recorded in the mission's periodical, *The Apostolic Faith* (*AF*).[14] The first issue of *AF* was published in September of 1906 with subsequent monthly publications from 1906–1908. The editor and writers reported the revival events of the Azusa Mission, sermons from Seymour, and the testimonies from missionaries from all over the world.[15] *The Apostolic Faith* is a testament of the influence that the Azusa revival had upon the globalization of Pentecostalism.

The Azusa Street Mission sent out many missionaries, both women and men, to preach a fivefold gospel: Jesus as savior, sanctifier, healer, Spirit baptizer, and soon coming King.[16] The women and men who shared leadership roles primarily regarded that Spirit baptism was given for the sake of evangelism. Believing that they were living in the end times, they discerned that the Spirit's outpourings of the spiritual gifts were to empower the church for missions. However, early Pentecostals were not attempting to produce a systematic

---

[13] Synan, *The Holiness-Pentecostal Tradition*, p. 89.

[14] *The Apostolic Faith* 1.1 (Sept. 1906), p. 2; 1.2 (Oct. 1906), p. 3; 1.3 (Nov. 1906) p. 4; 1.4 (Dec. 1906), pp. 1-2.

[15] Alexander, *Pentecostal Healing*, p. 75.

[16] Archer, *A Pentecostal Hermeneutic for the Twenty-First Century*, pp. 31-32.

theology. They were concerned with living a 'sanctified' life as an empowered witness of Jesus Christ within their community and beyond. In the words of the movement's founder, Seymour states, 'We are not fighting men or churches, but seeking to displace dead forms and creeds and wild fanaticism with living, practical Christianity'.[17] Later, this Pentecostal movement was defined as a 'paramodern revivalistic, restorational movement, held together by its common doctrinal commitment to the Full Gospel message'.[18]

Unfortunately, critics attacked the congregation in part because of its racial unity. Additionally, theological and racial issues quickly spawned from the Azusa revival and began to divide the movement. The interracial religious phenomenon soon faded.[19] Theological questions regarding sanctification, the gift of speaking in tongues, and the nature of the Godhead brought tensions within the movement.[20] While women enjoyed ministerial freedom in early Pentecostalism, this freedom has declined in various ways in contemporary Pentecostal and Charismatic denominations.[21] Despite these challenges, the early Pentecostal movement produced widespread renewal movements in the U.S. and internationally. For example, some Catholics, Episcopalians, and mainline Christian denominations experienced the baptism of the Spirit with spiritual gifts as speaking in tongues, healings, and prophecy, later known as the Catholic and Charismatic renewal movements. The editors and contributors of *The New International Dictionary of Pentecostal and Charismatic Movements* report of these rapidly growing renewal movements across the globe. They describe how these renewal movements developed into:

> various other forms of worship patterns, cultural attitudes, ecclesiastical structures, and methods of evangelism ... that comprise independent, indigenous, post-denominational denominations, and groups that cannot be classified as either Pentecostal or Charismatic, but share a common emphasis on the Holy Spirit, spiritual

---

[17] *AF* 2.1 (Jan. 1907), p. 2.

[18] Archer, *A Pentecostal Hermeneutic for the Twenty-First Century*, pp. 34.

[19] Synan, *The Holiness–Pentecostal Movement in the United States*, pp. 153, 168-84; Cox, *Fire From Heaven*, pp. 62-63.

[20] Stanley Burgess and E.M. van der Maas (eds.), *NIDPCM*, pp. xviii-xix.

[21] Burgess and Maas (eds.), *NIDPCM*, pp. xviii-xix.

gifts, pentecostal-like experiences, signs and wonders, and power encounters.[22]

According to the editors of *NIDCPM*, the early Pentecostal revivals and their spirituality greatly influenced Christendom at large and prompted many branches of Christendom to review their theological perspectives on the work of the Holy Spirit.[23] In a recent survey, it is suggested that together the Pentecostal and Charismatic Christianity exceed approximately 600 million adherents worldwide.[24] David Barrett describes the movement more specifically,

> These members are found in 740 Pentecostal denominations, 6,530 non-Pentecostal mainline denominations with large organized internal charismatic movements, and 18,810 independent neo-charismatic denominations and networks. Charismatics are now found across the entire spectrum of Christianity. They are found within all 150 traditional non-Pentecostal ecclesiastical confessions, families, and traditions.[25]

III. The Emergence and Rise of Pentecostal/ Charismatic Hermeneutics

Pentecostalism and the subsequent Charismatic movements have become a major worldwide religious phenomenon since the twentieth century.[26] In addition to their theological and spiritual influences, in the last generation, Pentecostal scholars have increasingly engaged in the ecclesial dialogue for the task of hermeneutics. These Pentecostal and Charismatic interpreters are quite diverse in their approaches to biblical hermeneutics. Some of the hermeneutical questions posed are related to identifying what is unique about a Pentecostal or Charismatic reading of Scripture and how does a Pentecostal perspective affect one's interpretation of Scripture? For example, these groups are interested in how might the Holy Spirit mediate meaning from

---

[22] Burgess and Maas (eds.), *NIDCPM,* pp. xx-xxi.
[23] Burgess and Maas (eds.), *NIDCPM,* pp. xx-xxi.
[24] Anderson, *An Introduction to Pentecostalism,* p. 3.
[25] Vinson Synan, *The Century of the Holy Spirit: 100 Years of Pentecostal and Charismatic Renewal* (Nashville, TN: Thomas Nelson, 2001), p. 383.
[26] For the classifications, definitions, and descriptions of the current global Pentecostal and Charismatic movements, see Burgess and Maas (eds.), *NIDCPM,* (2003).

the text; how does the implications for the affections influence biblical interpretation; how do the experiences of the *charismata* of the Spirit related to supernatural occurrences shape the hermeneutical lens of the biblical scholar? In the last few decades, there are numerous Pentecostal scholars who are constructing hermeneutical models that reflect their ethos and biblical convictions in order to interpret the texts in a holistic perspective.[27] The growing impact of the paradigm shift between modernity and postmodernity to literary analysis, which emphasizes the narrative and stories in the biblical text, has inspired Pentecostal scholars to forge new inroads into the discussion of contemporary biblical hermeneutics. While several Pentecostal scholars[28] began probing the challenge of beginning the discussion of what constitutes Pentecostal hermeneutics,[29] there were several scholars who developed the discipline. The following survey of

---

[27] Green, *Toward a Pentecostal Theology of the Lord's Supper*, p. 183.

[28] The late Pentecostal scholar, Howard Ervin wrote the first article to propose a Pentecostal hermeneutic. Howard Ervin, 'A Pentecostal Hermeneutical Option', in Paul Elbert, (ed.), *Essays on Apostolic Themes: Studies in honor of Howard M. Ervin* (Peabody, MA: Hendrickson Publishers, 1985), pp. 23-35. Ervin argued for a 'pneumatic epistemology' that is grounded in biblical faith with a phenomenology that meets the criteria of empirically verifiable sensory experience and does not violate the coherence of rational categories. He posited that this approach would yield a viable hermeneutic that deals responsibly with the apostolic witness of Scripture in terms of an apostolic experience, and in continuity with the Church's apostolic traditions. See also the late charismatic theologian Clark Pinnock, *The Scripture Principle* (San Francisco: Harper & Row, Publishers, 1984), who made significant contributions towards the discussion of the role of the Holy Spirit and biblical interpretation. Pinnock argues that the Holy Spirit is the major crux for mediating the understanding of Scripture, transforming the reader and for making the text an ontological reality, as the 'living word'. He explains that when the reader embraces Scripture through the illumination of the Holy Spirit, then he/she is not only informed but also transformed. Pinnock also articulates that the original inspiration of Scripture of the canonical formation extends to the contemporary understanding of Scripture.

[29] See Gerald Sheppard, 'Word and Spirit: Scripture in the Pentecostal Tradition Part Two', *Agora* 2.1 (1978), pp. 14-19; Mark McLean, 'Toward a Pentecostal Hermeneutic', *Pneuma* 6.2 (1980), pp. 35-56; Russell Spittler, 'Scripture and the Theological Enterprise: View from a Big Canoe' in R.K. Johnston (ed.), *The Use of the Bible in Theology: Evangelical Options* (Atlanta: John Knox, 1985), pp. 56-77; and John McKay, 'When the Veil is Taken Away: The Impact of Prophetic Experience on Biblical Interpretation', *JPT* 5 (1984), pp. 17-40. For a comprehensive review of these Pentecostal scholars who began the dialogue of Pentecostal hermeneutics and the characteristics of the discipline see J.C. Thomas, 'Pentecostal Interpretation', in Steven McKenzie (ed.), *The Oxford Encyclopedia of Biblical Interpretation* (Oxford: Oxford University Press, 2013), II, pp. 89-97.

Pentecostal scholarship will highlight some of the major works that began and developed the discipline of Pentecostal hermeneutics.

One of the first significant contributions toward the development of a Pentecostal hermeneutic was from a distinguished OT scholar, Rick D. Moore. He began to argue in the late 1980's that Pentecostals must find their way to defend the biblical texts from deconstruction-ism of the historical-critical methodology of hermeneutics in lieu of a Pentecostal hermeneutic.[30] He urged Pentecostal scholars to begin the arduous work to conceptualize a clear Pentecostal approach to reading the biblical texts. Moore also offers an outline of what he proposes are elements towards a distinct Pentecostal approach: (1) 'the role of the Holy Spirit', (2) 'the role of experience', (3) 'the Pentecostal understanding of the prophet-hood for all believers', and (4) 'the inseparable connection between knowledge of the truth as proposition and truth that is integrated into one's calling as a "witness" of Christ'.[31]

This clarion call generated two subsequent studies by Moore in the book of Deuteronomy. In 1992, 'Canon and Charisma in the Book of Deuteronomy', Moore argues that the book of Deuteronomy demonstrates two revelatory channels, that of canon and charisma in Israel's progressive revelatory experience.[32] In this view, Moore contends that the 'written word and the charismatic word are joined to form a revelatory synergism that leads to a theophanic encounter'.[33] He contends that a critical charismatic interpretation requires the interpreter to hear the voice of the Spirit 'outside' oneself.[34] He states, 'a voice from the text is much better than our own',[35] which is a common theme among Pentecostal and Charismatic traditions.

In 1995, Moore articulates a 'critical charismatic interpretation' through a literary-theological reading of the book of Deuteronomy. Moore's article, 'Deuteronomy and the Fire of God: A Critical Charismatic Interpretation' is a prime illustration of how he integrates a critical assessment of the book of Deuteronomy with his Pentecostal

[30] Moore, 'Canon and Charisma in the Book of Deuteronomy', pp. 75-92.
[31] Moore, 'A Pentecostal Approach to Scripture', *Seminary Viewpoint* 8.1 (Nov. 1987), pp. 4-5.
[32] Moore, 'Canon and Charisma in the Book of Deuteronomy', pp. 75-92.
[33] Moore, 'Canon and Charisma in the Book of Deuteronomy', p. 78.
[34] Moore, 'Deuteronomy and the Fire of God', pp. 11-33.
[35] Moore, 'Canon and Charisma in the Book of Deuteronomy', p. 76.

traditions' beliefs and literary analysis. He uses a comparative analysis to highlight the similarities of the theological expression of the Hebrew canon's narrative stories and the Pentecostal traditions' use of testimony.[36] Moore does not claim a new hermeneutical formula; however, he proposes his perspective provides a fresh approach to the book of Deuteronomy through a Pentecostal orientation combined with a literary-theological approach.

Moore's hermeneutical approach, which reflects a kind of dialogical experience, intersects with the challenges related to the role of experience and presuppositions that the interpreter brings to the text. At times, critics reduce this type of approach to a modern reader response theory. The philosophical argument culminates in the dichotomy between rationalism and subjectivism. From a modernistic perspective, the rational tools of reason and logic are the valid means of criteria to approach the interpretive process, and subjectivism leads to faulty interpretations. However, Pentecostals not only have a high regard for the truth of Scripture but also a belief that the supernatural events depicted in the narratives of Scripture provide the basis for the possibility that these types of encounters with God are not just concepts to believe as theological truths, but are also realities for the contemporary believer.

Increasingly, Pentecostal scholars also highlight the importance of integrating the role of the community in this dialogical experience to form a trialectical hermeneutic, in which the Spirit forms the Pentecostal community, and the community interprets Scripture under the direction of the Spirit. Similar to the biblical view of the Bereans, the Pentecostal community searches the Scripture and reasons with one another in the interpretive process. The communal activity of reading Scripture promotes ecclesial dialogue and fresh insights for meaningful application, as well as prevents dogmatism. The hearing and discerning of testimonies of others in the community, whether past or present, is also significant to the hermeneutical task for Pentecostals.

John Christopher Thomas, a prominent Pentecostal NT scholar and theologian, offers numerous contributions to Pentecostal hermeneutics. He was the first scholar to develop the Spirit, Word, and community paradigm, which is still at the forefront of the discussion of Pentecostal hermeneutics today. Additionally, he made contribu-

---

[36] Moore, 'Deuteronomy and the Fire of God', pp. 11-33.

tions to the dialogue on the role of affections in the transformation of the hearer in reading Scripture, and also championed the narrative theological approach to Scripture as a means to write overtures towards the construction of Pentecostal theology. In one of his earliest works, in 1994, he constructed a Pentecostal hermeneutic through a close narrative reading of Acts 15. He examines the Jerusalem Council's deliberations regarding whether or not new Gentile believers should first convert to Judaism to become accepted as Christian believers.[37] Thomas observes the active participation of the Jerusalem community with the Spirit in order to interpret Scripture and resolve their debate. He states, 'the Holy Spirit is present to discern testimony, guide the believing community, and discuss which Scriptures are most relevant to their contemporary situation'.[38] Thomas concludes that there is the presence of an implicit hermeneutical paradigm which is modeled in the Acts 15 narrative: (1) the role of the community, (2) the role and experience of the Spirit, and (3) the place of Scripture.[39] From this perspective, Thomas proposes that a Pentecostal hermeneutic that integrates the Scripture, the Spirit, and the community is noteworthy because it is similar to the components that are portrayed in the method of the Jerusalem council in Acts 15.[40] Thomas is one of the leading proponents in the discussion that regards the community as a pivotal factor for the task of hermeneutics. He argues that the role of community acts as the 'discerning body' in the task of interpreting Scripture.[41]

Thomas also advanced the discussion of Pentecostal hermeneutics through his emphasis upon the role of the affections. He asserts that 'the Pentecostal fivefold gospel and the community are the catalysts for the transformation that occurs in the reader' and intersects with the discussion of the role of experience in the task of hermeneutics.[42] He highlights five affections that broadly correspond to the fivefold gospel: Salvation/Gratitude, Sanctification/Compassion, Spirit Baptism/Courage, Healing/Joy, Return of Jesus/Hope.[43]

---

[37] Thomas, 'Women, Pentecostals and the Bible: An Experiment in Pentecostal Hermeneutics' *JPT* 5 (1994), pp. 41-56.

[38] Thomas, 'Reading the Bible from Within our Traditions', pp. 118-19.

[39] Thomas, 'Women, Pentecostals and the Bible', pp. 41-56.

[40] Thomas, 'Reading the Bible from Within our Traditions', pp. 118-19.

[41] Thomas, 'Reading the Bible from Within our Traditions', pp. 118–19.

[42] Thomas, 'Women, Pentecostals, and the Bible', pp. 41-56.

[43] Thomas, 'What the Spirit is Saying to the Church', pp. 115-29.

Thomas continued to contribute to Pentecostal scholarship with a book of essays titled, *The Spirit in the New Testament*.[44] He compiled several of his previously published articles and a couple of new pieces that reflected not only major contributions to the academic guild, but also as he states, 'this collection represents markers along the way of my own academic, theological, and spiritual journeys'.[45] Thomas provides an overview of the characteristics of Pentecostal theology in the 21st century and the current trends in the landscape of Pentecostal scholarship. His articles in this book include several narrative theological treatments of the Gospels highlighting a diversity of topics and a comparative study of the fourth Gospel and rabbinic Judaism.

Thomas' most recent work, co-authored with Frank Macchia, is a 624-page commentary on the book of Revelation in *The Two Horizons New Testament Commentary Series*.[46] This series gives special attention to the theological interests of the text with a focus on a narrative engagement of each paragraph in the book of Revelation.

The works of Larry McQueen and Mark Stibbe also emphasize the role of the 'prophetic community'. McQueen's *Joel and the Spirit*, is the first Pentecostal treatment of an entire biblical book. He utilizes a Pentecostal reading strategy to incorporate reception history and a narrative theological analysis to explore the role of the prophetic community in the book of Joel. McQueen argues that through discerning the voices of the early Pentecostal community of believers and their appropriation of the themes in Joel are instructive for interpreting the book of Joel. In this view, he observes that the 'hearer(s)' of the text plays a vital role in the interpretative process in the context of community.[47] Through this Pentecostal reading strategy, a constructive proposal of a Pentecostal eschatology is set forth.[48]

Stibbe provides a clear description of the distinctions between the dynamics of integrating the original meaning of the text (grammatico-historical criticism) and meaning derived for the here and

---

[44] Thomas, *The Spirit in the New Testament*, pp. 233-47.

[45] Thomas, *The Spirit in the New Testament*.

[46] John Christopher Thomas and Frank Macchia, *Revelation: Two Horizons New Testament Commentary Series* (Grand Rapids: Eerdmans, 2016).

[47] McQueen, *Joel and the Spirit*, pp. 111-12.

[48] McQueen, *Joel and the Spirit*, pp. 110-15.

now (Stibbe refers to this as the *prophetic significance*).[49] Another useful term that Stibbe uses is 'discernment'. He outlines a three-stage Anglican Church (AC) charismatic hermeneutical approach. He begins with the discernment of the believer and follows with a second stage that reflects the process of sharing testimonies and then searching Scripture for 'shared experience'.[50] The third stage involves the integration of AC tradition (liturgy). Although, the AC tradition is described in terms of liturgy, Pentecostals and Charismatics have their own unique forms of tradition.

In 2005, Kenneth Archer added to the conversation through a comprehensive treatment, *A Pentecostal Hermeneutical Strategy for the Twenty-First Century*. He sought to articulate a distinct Pentecostal hermeneutical strategy informed by a Pentecostal identity. Archer argues that early Pentecostal hermeneutical strategies could be 'retrieved and critically re-appropriated to construct a contemporary Pentecostal hermeneutic'.[51] He builds upon Thomas' earlier proposal to argue that there are three common themes in the early Pentecostal hermeneutic: (1) Scripture, (2) Spirit, and (3) community.[52] According to Archer, historically, the North American Pentecostal's hermeneutic used what he calls 'The Bible Reading Method', and proposes their identity and story could be understood through 'Central Narrative Convictions'.[53] These central narrative convictions emphasized verbal inspiration, inerrancy and end-time events that were influenced by Keswickianism, pre-millennialism, and dispensationalism that found their basis in the Baconian Common Sense method.[54] Archer combines semiotics, narrative analysis, and reader-response theory with an appreciation for the ways in which the early Pentecostal

---

[49] Mark Stibbe, 'This is That: Some Thoughts Concerning Charismatic Hermeneutics', *Anvil* 14.3 (1998), pp. 181-93.

[50] Stibbe, 'This is That: Some Thoughts Concerning Charismatic Hermeneutics', pp. 181-93.

[51] Archer, *A Pentecostal Hermeneutical Strategy for the Twenty-First Century*, pp. 1-5.

[52] Archer, *A Pentecostal Hermeneutical Strategy for the Twenty-First Century*, pp. 156-85. For a theological treatise utilizing the Spirit, Word, and community paradigm, see Amos Yong, *Spirit-Word-Community: Theological Hermeneutic in Trinitarian Perspective* (Eugene: Wipf & Stock, 2002). Yong, a Pentecostal theologian also attempts to explicate the dynamic relationship between the Spirit, the Word, and the community in the task of constructing theology.

[53] Archer, *A Pentecostal Hermeneutical Strategy for the Twenty-First Century*, pp. 12-22; 94-124.

[54] Archer, *A Pentecostal Hermeneutical Strategy for the Twenty-First Century*, pp. 35-63.

community interpreted Scripture to construct a distinct Pentecostal approach to reading the biblical text.

The following contribution given to the landscape of Pentecostal hermeneutics is by Robby Waddell, a NT scholar and theologian. Waddell's *The Spirit of the Book of Revelation* is the first monograph that provides a comprehensive treatment of the pneumatology of the Apocalypse.[55] Through his literature review he points out that contemporary NT scholarship has given little attention to the role of the Spirit in the book of Revelation.[56] Waddell allocates two chapters to explain and discuss the developments in 'intertextuality' as a methodology, and second, to construct his argument to support how the 'location of a Pentecostal interpreter' is employed as a hermeneutical lens.[57] He employs intertextuality and a narrative theological reading to highlight and construct a pneumatology from the book of Revelation. Waddell provides a full discourse on the development of what he calls a 'profile of a Pentecostal reader of the Apocalypse'.[58] His construction toward a Pentecostal theological hermeneutic is informed by this proposed Pentecostal profile, which consists of four elements: (1) the word Apocalypse serves as the 'event of revelation' and the Pentecostal ethos of 'revelation as a prerequisite for a valid interpretation of Revelation' with the expectation of encounter; (2) the status of Scripture in Rev. 1.3 serves to reveal the emphasis upon the written and aural dimensions, and the prophetic interpretation from the local community; (3) the Pentecostal ethos of communal participation with the Spirit leads to interpretation of the 'word'; and (4) a Pentecostal theological approach to reading Scripture includes a theology of encounter, which is informed by the fear of God in worship.[59] Waddell argues that 'a Pentecostal reading is both synchronic, focusing on the final form of the text, and theological, allowing the ethos and experience of the tradition to inform the interpretation theologically'.[60] He writes, 'A Pentecostal theological hermeneutic has

[55] Robby Waddell, *The Spirit of the Book of Revelation* (JPTSup 30: Blandford Forum, UK: Deo Publishing, 2006).

[56] Waddell, *The Spirit of the Book of Revelation*, pp. 7-38.

[57] Waddell, *The Spirit of the Book of Revelation*, pp. 3-4; 97-118.

[58] Waddell, *The Spirit of the Book of Revelation*, pp. 97-131.

[59] Waddell, *The Spirit of the Book of Revelation*, pp. 122-29.

[60] Waddell, *The Spirit of the Book of Revelation*, p. 101.

less to do with Greek philosophy than with theophany, a divine encounter, a revelation, and an experience with the living God'.[61]

In an innovative contribution (2008) by Lee Roy Martin, *The Unheard Voice of God: A Pentecostal Hearing of the Book of Judges*, he provides a method owing to Pentecostal ethos, which encourages the reader to 'hear' the voice of the text, through recognizing the world in the text.[62] He analyzes the three main speeches in the book of Judges through a rhetorical-theological reading. In this view, rather than examining the book for historiographical concerns, he argues that it should be 'heard' as a prophetic voice. This Pentecostal hearing of the book represents a 'Spirit empowered re-appropriation of the text through the same apostolic experience of the Spirit at Pentecost'.[63] Martin presents a proposal that grounds the meaning in its historical context through his literary-theological reading of the text combined with a Pentecostal reading strategy. Martin's groundbreaking work on the book of Judges highlights the Pentecostal orientation of 'hearing' the biblical story. Additionally, he satisfies his further aim to serve the church and academia through his work. In 2013, Martin continued to advance the discussion of Pentecostal hermeneutics through his development of an affective hermeneutical approach to read Psalms 63 and 107.[64] For Martin, 'an affective approach calls for the hearer to attend to the affective tones that are present in the text and to allow the affections of the hearer to be shaped by the text'.[65] The results of these articles and the contributions of other Pentecostal scholars who interpreted other Psalms and wrote about similar topics of worship recently led Martin to compile and edit *Toward a Pentecostal Theology of Worship*.[66]

---

[61] Waddell, *The Spirit of the Book of Revelation*, p. 111.

[62] Martin, *The Unheard Voice of God*; 'Power to Save!? The Role of the Spirit of the Lord in the Book of Judges', *JPT* 16 (2008), pp. 21-50. Martin argues that 'hearing is the most frequent method of encounter with the word of God' and the command 'to hear' occurs 201 times while forms of the verb occur 1,159 times in the HB.

[63] Martin, *The Unheard Voice of God*, pp. 30-38.

[64] Martin, 'Longing for God: Psalm 63 and Pentecostal Spirituality', pp. 263-84. The article was first written by Martin, 'Longing for God: Psalm 63 and Pentecostal Spirituality', *JPT* 22 (2013), pp. 54-76.

[65] Martin, 'Longing for God', p. 264.

[66] L.R. Martin (ed.), *Toward a Pentecostal Theology of Worship* (Cleveland, TN: CPT Press, 2nd edn, 2020).

In 2012, Chris Green articulated six theological presuppositions that he appreciates for the construction of a Pentecostal theology.[67] He follows Walter Hollenweger, who first argued that the spirituality of early Pentecostalism represents the 'heart and not the infancy of the movement'.[68] Green exhorts, not unlike others, that a Pentecostal hermeneutic should include the witness of these early Pentecostals as a helpful method called *Wirkungsgeschichte* ('history of effects').[69] He incorporates Terry Cross' premise that the Pentecostal experience provides a unique lens in which to construct theological methods.[70] In the spirit of ecumenism, Green adds that a robust Pentecostal hermeneutic should dialogue with the 'church catholic, so that the finished product is not only distinctly Pentecostal but also recognizably *Christian*'.[71] For Green, the Pentecostal tradition's core beliefs in the formation of theology are also biblical, canonical, and sensitive to the narrative.

Melissa Archer's article on the worship scenes in the Apocalypse presented in 2012 provides the foundation for her further contribution to NT studies through her PhD thesis, *'I Was in the Spirit on the Lord's Day'*, which was published in 2015.[72] She advances Pentecostal hermeneutics through her literary-theological interpretation of the worship scenes in the book of Revelation by combining reception history to provide overtures toward the construction of a Pentecostal theology of worship. David Johnson follows Archer with a literary-theological interpretation of the theme of discernment in the Apocalypse and adds to the discussion with an intertextual reading.[73] Both

---

[67] For a discussion on all six points review Green, *Toward a Pentecostal Theology of the Lord's Supper*, pp. 1-3.

[68] W.J. Hollenweger, 'Pentecostals and the Charismatic Movement', in Cheslyn Jones, Geoffrey Wainwright, and S.J. Edward Yarnold (eds.), *The Study of Spirituality* (New York, NY: Oxford University Press, 1986), pp. 549-53.

[69] Hollenweger, *The Pentecostals* (Peabody, MA: Hendrickson, 1988), p. 551.

[70] Terry Cross, 'The Divine-Human Encounter: Towards a Pentecostal Theology of Experience', *Pneuma* 31.1 (2009), pp. 3-34. See also, Roger Stronstad, 'Pentecostal Experience and Hermeneutics', *Paraclete* 26.1 (1992), pp. 14-30.

[71] Green, *Toward a Pentecostal Theology of the Lord's Supper*, p. 2 (emphasis original).

[72] Melissa L. Archer, 'The Worship Scenes in the Apocalypse, Effective History, and Early Pentecostal Periodical Literature', *JPT* 21.1 (2012), pp. 87-112; *I Was in the Spirit on the Lord's Day: A Pentecostal Engagement with Worship in the Apocalypse* (Cleveland, TN: CPT Press, 2015).

[73] Johnson, *Pneumatic Discernment in the Apocalypse: An Intertextual and Pentecostal Exploration.*

Archer and Johnson incorporate insights from the voices of early Pentecostals through reception history.

The contributions surveyed above provide a sampling of the major contours in the landscape of Pentecostal hermeneutics as the discipline emerged and as it continues to develop.

Although Pentecostal and Charismatic scholars represent a diversified group, there appears to be common characteristics identified, which are shared among the people of the movement.

IV. Reception History

This study will also feature a Pentecostal and Charismatic context, in part, by means of *Wirkungsgeschichte,* history of effects or otherwise called, reception history. *Wirkungsgeschichte* is a contemporary methodology[74] utilized by various scholars for the purpose of interpreting Scripture. Ulrich Luz employed this approach in his commentary on the Gospel according to Matthew.[75] Luz's methodological approach and hermeneutical convictions are defined through his exegetical approach as a modified historical-critical method. He criticizes classical historical-critical exegesis because it tends to isolate the biblical texts in their own time, rendering the contemporary meaning irrelevant. Luz takes into account the text's history of interpretation, as well as the text's history of influence to provide its relevance and understanding of the texts in its contemporary context.[76] He is convinced that this approach to gain an understanding of the influences or effects of biblical hermeneutics throughout history has significantly influenced the Church and society.[77] Similarly, Hans Jauss argues that reception history adds an important historical component to the biblical text through the integration of the past interpretation of the texts.[78] He asserts contemporary hearers cannot come to the text without being impacted by their previous tradition's interpretations.

---

[74] See Mark Elliott, 'Effective-History and the Hermeneutics of Ulrich Luz', *JSNT* 33.2 (2010), pp. 161-73. He provides an overview of how Ulrich Luz' work stimulated the rising interest in the use of effective history in the biblical text as a means to interpret the text.

[75] Luz, *Matthew in History.*

[76] Luz, *Matthew in History*, p. 63.

[77] Luz, Matthew in History, p. 64.

[78] Hans Robert Jauss, *Toward an Aesthetic of Reception* (T. Bahti [trans.]; Minneapolis, MN: University of Minnesota Press, 1982).

Various Pentecostal scholars, such as Kimberly Alexander, Chris Green, and Melissa Archer agree with Thomas, who suggests that by listening to and discerning the voices of previous Pentecostals as they sought to interpret the biblical texts 'provides the basis for a more robust theology that can be constructed for the benefit of Pentecostal hermeneutics and the Church at large'.[79] From this perspective, an examination of early Pentecostal interpretations of Ezekiel's visions and its pneumatological and affective dimensions in the book of Ezekiel will provide an understanding of how early Pentecostal spirituality was informed by their reading of Ezekiel's visions (*Wirkungsgeschicte*).[80] The discernment of early Pentecostal testimonies regarding Ezekiel is also conducive to the integration of the hermeneutical paradigm of the Spirit, the Word, and the community.[81]

Thomas describes the Pentecostal believer as experiencing a 'narrative way of life' and draws parallels between the narrative aspects of Scripture and a Pentecostal way of life.[82] In keeping with a Pentecostal orientation is the use of a narrative-theological analysis of the biblical texts. Offering a close reading of the text in its final form is employed for the purpose of deriving its theological meaning from the story in the world within the text.

V. Narrative-Theological Analysis

The rise of the use of narrative criticism in biblical studies is, in part, a response to the limitations of form and redaction criticism.[83] Narrative criticism focuses on the stories a writer tells to understand how they help the reader derive meaning. According to Walter Fisher, narratives are fundamental to communication and provide structure for human experience and influence people to share common

---

[79] Kimberly Ervin Alexander, *Pentecostal Healing: Models in Theology and Practice* (JPTSup 29; Blandford Forum: Deo Publishing, 2006); Archer, 'The Worship Scenes in the Apocalypse', pp. 87-112; Green, *Foretasting the Kingdom*; and Thomas, 'What the Spirit is Saying to the Church', pp. 115-29.

[80] Luz, *Matthew in History*, p. 85.

[81] Archer, *A Pentecostal Hermeneutic for the Twenty-First Century*, pp. 156-66. Archer emphasizes the contributions of the Pentecostal community to the interpretative process.

[82] Thomas, 'Reading the Bible from Within our Traditions', pp. 118-19.

[83] For a comprehensive discussion on the rise of narrative criticism and literary analysis, see Kevin Vanhoozer, *Is there a Meaning in this Text? The Bible, the Reader, and the Morality of Literary Knowledge* (Grand Rapids: Zondervan, 1996).

explanations and understandings. Fisher defines narratives as 'symbolic actions-words and/or deeds that have sequence and meaning for those who live, create, or interpret them'.[84] The study of narrative criticism, therefore, includes form (fiction or non-fiction, prose or poetry), genre (myth, history, legend, etc.), structure (including plot, theme, irony, foreshadowing, etc.), characterization, and communicator's perspective. Characteristics of a narrative were defined as early as Aristotle in his *Poetics* under plot. He called plot the 'first principle' or the 'soul of a tragedy' and is the arrangement of incidents that imitate the action with a beginning, middle, and end.[85] Plot includes introduction of characters, rising action and introduction of complication, development of complication, climax, and final resolution. Narrative studies recognize that there is meaning found in the text as a whole. Generally, narrative critics define a narrative as any piece of literature, whether it is religious or secular, that tells a story. However, there is a diversity of ways that narrative critics define and implement narrative analysis. For example, David Gunn defines narrative criticism as, 'Interpreting the existing text (in its final form) in terms primarily of its own story world, seen as replete with meaning, rather than understanding the text by attempting to reconstruct its sources and editorial history, its original setting and audience, and its author's or editor's intention in writing'.[86]

Generally, Pentecostal scholars are concerned with the narrative of Scripture in its final form of the biblical text. This is not to say that all Pentecostal scholars utilize narrative approaches to the biblical text. However, some OT scholars, as well as the interpreters reviewed above, maintain that the primary meaning is found in the stories embedded in the narrative. For example, John Goldingay asserts that one of the major features of how the dynamics of the biblical story is retold in various contexts provides the chief meaning of the text. This perspective highlights the point of view from the characters in the narrative. Every author or narrator has a message to communicate to the reader, which produces an effect upon the reader.

---

[84] Walter Fisher, *Human Communication as Narration: Toward a Philosophy of Reason, Value, and Action* (Columbia: University of South Carolina Press, 1987), p. 21.

[85] Fisher, *Human Communication as Narration*, p. 23.

[86] David M. Gunn, 'Narrative Criticism', in Steven L. McKenzie and Stephen R. Haynes (eds.), *To Each Its Own Meaning: An Introduction to Biblical Criticisms and Their Approaches* (Louisville, KY: Westminster, John Knox Press, 1993).

Goldingay posits that the dialogue between story and context in Scripture has the capacity to bring out new significance in varying events.[87] He also highlights that the relevance of retelling of these stories is how readers identify with their own story. He states, 'In general, the biblical story is designed to enable us to discover who we are. We do that by telling our own story but by telling it in the context of the Bible story. We find ourselves by setting ourselves in that other story. In fact, we all tell our individual stories in the light of a world-view, a grand narrative'.[88] Therefore, according to Goldingay, it is not enough to know about the conventions of the narrative but to 'live' and 'perceive oneself' in what Paul Ricoeur calls 'the world of the text'.[89]

Likewise, Brueggemann denies the possibility of obtaining absolute meaning based upon data collected from 'behind the text'.[90] He suggests that the central truth-claims of Israel in the OT are not a declaration of 'historical facts', but are testimonies offered by witnesses.[91] For Brueggemann, biblical truth is located not in the historical events that may or may not lie behind the offered testimony but in the testimony itself. He asserts that the interpreter has access only to the testimony itself for the purpose of making theological constructions from the OT Scriptures and applying them to contemporary contexts and situations.

An OT hermeneut in search of the theological implications of the texts will often grapple with the tensions of integrating theological and hermeneutical convictions. A narrative theology that treats Scripture as story invites the reader into a story-world and that, from within the worldview of that story-world, makes claims upon the reader's perception of reality. In Brueggemann's commentary, *Jeremiah*, he follows Leo Perdue who validates the imaginative alternative methodologies in light of 'positivistic, historicist, objective claims' as a means of exploring the final form of the text in its canonical formation.[92] Brueggemann argues that the book of Jeremiah does not

---

[87] Goldingay, 'Biblical Story and the Way it Shapes Our Story', pp. 5-15.

[88] Goldingay, 'Biblical Story and the Way it Shapes Our Story', pp. 5-15.

[89] Goldingay, 'Biblical Story and the Way it Shapes Our Story', p. 15.

[90] Brueggemann, *Theology of the Old Testament Testimony, Dispute, Advocacy* (Minneapolis: Fortress Press, 1997), p. 68.

[91] Brueggemann, *Theology of the Old Testament Testimony*, p. 118.

[92] Leo G. Perdue, *The Collapse of History. Reconstructing Old Testament Theology* (Overtures to Biblical Theology; Minneapolis: Fortress Press, 1994). See also,

belong to 'the scholarly guild' but to the church.[93] Yet, he skillfully integrates the book's historical context and its theological significance maintaining the tension between these methodological approaches providing a major contribution to Jeremiah studies for the academic guild and the church.[94]

A literary-theological reading of Ezekiel's visions is employed in this study as a method owing to its compatibility with the narrative orientation of Pentecostal thought. This writer will follow the proposals set forth by Martin, a Pentecostal 'hearing of the biblical texts' that highlights the text in its final form, and Brueggemann, Goldingay, and many Pentecostal scholars who support that meaning is derived from the testimony 'within' the narrative.[95] Martin accentuates the idea of 'hearing' the text as it is a primary biblical concept in the HB and it also resonates with the Pentecostal orientation towards a culture of orality. Generally, the book of Ezekiel is perceived as one of the most cohesive books in the HB comprised of poetry and prose with voluminous speeches, symbolic acts, and vision reports. Yet, it was written for the purpose of its audience(s) to hear and obey the prophetic exhortations and warnings given in its numerous speeches embedded in and around the vision reports. In this way, the book invites Pentecostal and Charismatic hermeneuts to engage in the plethora of opportunities of hearing its testimonies.

VI. An Affective Approach

The use of affective language is a powerful tool used in literary works. Affective language provides the reader with the emotional disposition of the characters in the story. Affective language also provokes emotions in the hearers or readers (past and present) as they respond to the language. A fourth characteristic of Pentecostal hermeneutics in this survey observes that there is a distinct Pentecostal approach that

---

Brueggemann, *A Commentary on Jeremiah* and Vanhoozer, *Is there a Meaning in this Text?* Vanhoozer states that since Jesus is 'the Word incarnate', then words are God's means of endorsing a truthful way of life and values and adds that an OT hermeneut needs to allow the text to speak meaningfully and in a new context.

[93] Brueggemann, *A Commentary on Jeremiah*, p. xiii.

[94] Brueggemann, *A Commentary on Jeremiah*, p. 419. He states that the book of Jeremiah does not make sense apart from its history and politics of the ancient Near East.

[95] Martin, *The Unheard Voice of God*, p. 13.

appreciates the affective language in the text and discerns its theological contributions.[96] There are three Pentecostal scholars who provide
insight regarding how the role of affective language provides a hermeneutical lens in hearing the biblical text.

As a Pentecostal theologian, Land's primary purpose was to present a treatise to interpret and 're-vision' the Pentecostal tradition,[97]
yet he also makes noteworthy insights about how Pentecostal theological beliefs and spiritual practices that contribute to the interpretative process are integrated in the affections.[98] In Land's third chapter of *Pentecostal Spirituality: A Passion for the Kingdom*, he proposes new
categories of how to perceive and discuss the affections, over and
against the dated dichotomy of the terms 'reason' and 'feelings'.[99] As
mentioned previously, Land argues that religious affections (gratitude, compassion, and courage) are the 'integrating core of Pentecostal spirituality'.[100] He describes Pentecostal spirituality as 'a passion for the kingdom',[101] which necessitates that the affections have
a role to play in the act of biblical interpretation. He proposes that
attention given to the role of the affections provides a more holistic
approach to reading the biblical text.[102]

Robert Baker's 'Pentecostal Bible Reading: Toward a Model of
Reading for the Formation of the Affections' followed Land's work
to propose a synthesis of orthodoxy, orthopraxy, and orthopathy
through a construction of an affective approach to the biblical text.[103]
Baker argues, 'to seek to understand the ideational/rational content
of a text without also seeking to experience and reflect upon its emotive effect is to skew the text's message'.[104] Baker is also informed by
semiotics and utilizes a literary analysis to offer an affective reading

---

[96] Thomas, 'What the Spirit is Saying to the Church', p. 121. See also, Moore,
'And Also Much Cattle': Prophetic Passions and the End of Jonah', *JPT* 11 (1997),
pp. 35-48, and Heschel, *The Prophets*, II, p. 123.

[97] Land, *Pentecostal Spirituality*, pp. 122-81.

[98] Land, *Pentecostal Spirituality*, pp. 122-81.

[99] Land, *Pentecostal Spirituality*, p. 122.

[100] Land, *Pentecostal Spirituality*, pp. 2, 75, 97, 120. See also, Cartledge, 'Affective
Theological Praxis', pp. 34-52.

[101] Land, *Pentecostal Spirituality*, pp. 2, 97, 120. Cartledge, 'Affective Theological
Praxis', pp. 34-52.

[102] Land, *Pentecostal Spirituality*, pp. 13-14.

[103] Baker, 'Pentecostal Bible Reading', pp. 95-108.

[104] Baker, 'Pentecostal Bible Reading', p. 96.

of Jesus' death in John.[105] He contends that the book of John was 'structured in order to inculcate the Christian affections of love and fear in the actual reader'.[106] Baker concludes that to 'understand the message of the biblical texts, one must submit to the Spirit who breathed the Scriptures and indwells the reading process. A reading strategy that coheres with and is informed by Pentecostal spirituality is a treasure that Pentecostal scholars can offer the church and its scribes.'[107]

Martin argues that biblical scholarship has neglected the affective dimension of biblical poetry largely due to the mysterious nature of the role of the affections. Yet, he points out that the literary function of poetry is to 'evoke the passions and to form the affections'.[108] He also incorporates Brueggemann's functional approach, which allows for scholarly considerations of the affective qualities of the poetic literature and 'argues that a holistic interpretation of Scripture must include attention to the affective tones of the text and to the affective concerns of the interpreter'.[109] Specifically, in Martin's work in the Psalms, he argues that 'the process of affective interpretation requires at least four cooperative moves on the part of the hearer': (1) 'the hearer of the psalm must identify and acknowledge the affective dimensions in the text', (2) 'the hearer of the psalm must acknowledge his or her own passions that are brought to the interpretive process', (3) 'the hearer of the psalm must be open to the emotive impact of the text', and (4) 'the hearer must allow himself or herself to be transformed by the affective experiencing of the psalm'.[110]

The insights of Land, Baker, and Martin argue generally that an affective approach to Scripture is three-fold: (1) Pentecostal spirituality is informed theologically through the affective biblical language, (2) the hearer(s) must attune to the affective dimensions of Scripture, and (3) the hearer(s) is encouraged to seek to engage the affective language as a dynamic and living word that transforms the hearer(s) by the Spirit. A Pentecostal spirituality includes the dimensions of the affections in the task of biblical hermeneutics. The affections are

---

[105] Baker, 'Pentecostal Bible Reading', pp. 104-108.
[106] Baker, 'Pentecostal Bible Reading', p 104.
[107] Baker, 'Pentecostal Bible Reading', p 108.
[108] Martin, 'Longing for God', p. 57.
[109] Martin, 'Longing for God', pp. 59-60.
[110] Martin, 'Longing for God', pp. 58-60.

not only transformed in the reader by an encounter with the biblical text and the Spirit, but also an affective approach can provide theological implications for Pentecostal spirituality. Agreeing with Land that a Pentecostal or Charismatic reader not only focuses upon orthodoxy and orthopraxy, but also orthopathy, which provides the space and motivation to examine not only the affective language in the biblical texts, but also shows how the texts impact the hearers (past and/or present). He rightly proposes that 'the addition of the role of the affections provides a more holistic approach to reading the biblical text'.[111] However, due to time and space limitations, this study will only examine the affective language as it appears in Ezekiel's four major vision narratives as it relates to either the prophet's or YHWH's disposition in such a way as it enhances the overall story of the narratives, and its characters.

The conclusions derived from hearing the testimony of Ezekiel's vision reports will provide the basis for overtures towards an OT pneumatology, specifically as it relates to Spirit-inspired visions. The theological reflections based upon the narrative analysis of the texts will support a dialogue for the construction of a holistic theology of Spirit-inspired visions in Ezekiel. A holistic theology is advantageous to the construction of a Pentecostal theology of Spirit-inspired visions and the associations that are derived from the affective language used in the narratives.

VII. Conclusions

This outline highlights the major contributions in Pentecostal hermeneutics which provides the basis for the construction of a Pentecostal reading strategy designed to integrate a narrative theological approach in which to hear the four-major vision reports in Ezekiel. Some of the key characteristics identified through this survey of Pentecostal hermeneutics includes that generally, Pentecostals and Charismatics view Scripture as the dynamic 'living word', which is authoritative for the interpretation for Christian experience, doctrine, and practice. It is viewed as dynamic and living because it is read theologically through which the believer can experience/encounter the living

---

[111] Land, *Pentecostal Spirituality*, pp. 13-14. See also, Baker, 'Pentecostal Bible Reading', pp. 95-108, and Martin, 'Psalm 63 and Pentecostal Spirituality', pp. 263-84. Heschel, *The Prophets*, II, pp. 85-109.

God, and also be transformed, healed, and even participate in the biblical narrative by the Spirit. The primary goal in reading or hearing the Bible is not an intellectual pursuit void of an expectation of how the Spirit will encounter and transform the believer through hearing the Scripture. Typically, Pentecostals do not seek the Scripture for propositional truths, but rather it *is the theological truth* and is read and heard theologically as the divinely inspired Scripture, which can be applied to their contemporary situation. Generally, Pentecostals read Scripture for the plain meaning of the text, yet they are open to multiple meanings by the Spirit as the primary interpreter of Scripture.

Pentecostal hermeneutics is not predisposed with the classic debate of illumination vs. original inspiration. Pentecostals adhere to the doctrine of the Spirit's role in original inspiration and illumination, yet they forge new ground in the discussion of how the Spirit participates in the interpretative process. First, it is apparent through the preceding works that the interpreters who describe experiences and encounters with the Spirit, view the role of the Spirit as a legitimate presupposition or hermeneutical lens for the discipline of Pentecostal hermeneutics. In other words, the Pentecostal hermeneut is informed by his/her shared experience by the Spirit with the Pentecostal communities, past and present, and testimonies described in Scripture. One of the distinguishing marks of Pentecostals and Charismatics is that the Spirit is not only present for the illumination of the biblical texts, but also present to transform the interpreter as he/she reads, hears, and understands Scripture.

Second, the role of experience is highlighted in Pentecostal hermeneutics due to the ethos and worldview of Pentecostals and Charismatics. The transforming process of the interpreter by the Spirit is an essential element of a Pentecostal ethos because the shared experiences of the *charismata* of the Spirit such as, Spirit baptism witnessed by the worshipping community, is a primary element of the full Gospel message. The participation with the community is how the interpreter develops a pneumatic epistemology. For example, Jesus as Spirit baptizer with the signs of tongues, prophecy, healing, deliverance, and miracles are experienced through the worshipping community. It is in this context of experiential faith that the interpreter comes to hear and understand this full Gospel message, which results in the Spirit's transformation of the interpreter, and by and large, Pentecostals discern that the transformation by the Spirit occurs in the interpreter's passions, affections or dispositions. From this perspective, a Pentecostal worldview includes an expectancy for a supernatural encounter or for the Spirit to participate in the interpretative process.

Third, Pentecostal and Charismatic hermeneuts understand that it is impossible for any interpreter to approach the task of hermeneutics without the influence from their context, pre-understandings, and presuppositions, which are directly generated from their socio-religious location in the believing community. The believing community for the hermeneut consists of three major influences: (1) voices from the roots of the movement, the early Pentecostals, (2) the local community of faith, and (3) the academic guild.

Uniquely, Pentecostal hermeneuts are sensitive to hear from the Pentecostal community past and present because it is in the context of 'community' that the spiritual formation is established and affords the interpreter the possibility of 'hearing' the biblical texts through their Pentecostal ethos. Primarily these early Pentecostal voices are heard through the use of testimonies, stories, and sermons as they sought to interpret Scripture. These early Pentecostal voices serve to inform and enrich the interpretive process for those who are called to contribute to the discipline of Pentecostal hermeneutics. Fortunately, there is an increasing number of Pentecostal and Charismatic scholars within the academy, which is a development that affords a new generation of scholars with the opportunity to dialogue and critique their academic works and to participate in a communal activity that is bonded through the Spirit of Christ for the task of interpreting Scripture. The Pentecostal interpreter is informed by his/her shared experience of the Spirit with the worshipping communities, past and present. This communal experience with the Spirit is the seedbed for the transformation of the affections of the interpreter.

Thus, a Pentecostal reading strategy is constructed with the outlined above considerations as a methodological approach to hear the visions in the book of Ezekiel. As a member of a new generation of Pentecostals and Charismatics, this writer chooses to embrace critical scholarship combined with a methodology that is informed by our tradition's faith and spirituality. This approach includes, yet is not limited to, a pneumatic epistemology that inherently respects the pneumatic ethos of Scripture, and the community's passionate desire to be transformed through an encounter with God in the interpretative process of the biblical text.

A Pentecostal theology is not simply an attempt to interpret spirituality in the biblical narratives, but it also seeks to construct a biblical theology that explains the spiritual events in Scripture, which can be applicable for the church at large. According to Land, spirituality is not separate from theology, but is the essence of theology in theory and practice; therefore, it shapes a Pentecostal epistemology.[112] Since there are numerous pneumatological considerations in the biblical texts, the primary focus of this study will narrow the pneumatological discussion to the theme of Spirit-inspired visions and its affective dimensions in the text.

Visions for Pentecostals and Charismatics are considered an eschatological promise as part of the outpouring of the Spirit before the second coming of Christ (Joel 2.28-32). These groups also regard visions as part of the apostolic witness as a result of the outpouring of the Spirit on the day of Pentecost (Acts 2). According to Peter Hocken, visions and dreams were considered part of the experiential aspect of early Pentecostal worship and served 'as a kind of icon for the individual and the community'.[113]

Yet, there is a lacuna in contemporary Pentecostal scholarship dealing with the vision narratives and their pneumatological and affective literary features described in Scripture. As discussed in the previous chapter, there are three monographs by Pentecostal scholars who give special attention to the Spirit in the OT, yet none of whom discuss the implications for Spirit-inspired visions. As a result, this study will incorporate their works and hopefully forge new ground in Ezekiel studies.

The conclusions from this investigation will discuss the theological implications that will be examined primarily between the activities of the divine רוח ('Spirit'), the יד־יהוה ('hand of YHWH'), and the affective language in the four significant visions in the book of Ezekiel (Ezek. 1–3; 8–11; 37.1-14; 40–43). It will also provide the structural framework that underscores the theological themes of the Spirit, the glory of YHWH, the hand of YHWH, and the leitmotif of the affections, which will provide the basis for constructing

---

[112] Land, *Pentecostal Spirituality*, pp. 32-56.

[113] Peter Hocken, *The Challenges of the Pentecostal, Charismatic, and Messianic Jewish Movements: The Tensions of the Spirit* (Farnham: Ashgate Pub. Ltd, 2009), p. 9.

overtures towards a holistic theology of Spirit-inspired visions. A holistic theology is also conducive to the construction of a Pentecostal theology of Spirit-inspired visions and religious affections. Agreeing with Martin, who argues 'a holistic interpretation of Scripture (especially the poetic literature) must include attention to the affective dimension of the text and to the affective concerns of the interpreter'.[114] Yet, the Ezekiel texts, which are primarily prophetic literature with poetic nuances, will limit the affective approach to attend primarily to the affective language in the narratives. As part of the construction of a theology of Spirit-inspired visions, this writer will suggest ways in which Ezekiel's visions can contribute to the affective formation of the contemporary Pentecostal and Charismatic communities. This study will employ a Pentecostal reading strategy informed by these aforementioned views combined with literary tools that are theologically motivated to engage in a close narrative reading of the four major visions in Ezekiel (1–3; 8–11; 37.1-14; 40–48).

---

[114] Martin, 'Longing for God', p. 54.

4

RECEPTION HISTORY: EZEKIEL'S VISIONS AND THE SPIRIT IN EARLY PENTECOSTAL LITERATURE

I. Introduction

In this chapter I will explore the early Pentecostal periodical literature to discern the extent to which early Pentecostals and their spirituality were influenced by their interpretations of the Ezekiel's four major vision narratives, which includes its pneumatological emphasis (Ezekiel 1–3; 8–11; 37.1-14; 40–48). Additionally, the following reception history (*Wirkungsgeschichte*) of the early Pentecostal periodical literature offers insight into the many ways in which these biblical texts may have shaped Pentecostal pneumatology in the U.S. This task will be accomplished through special attention given to the sermons and testimonies of the men and women from the North American Pentecostal movement as they engaged with Ezekiel's visions. Agreeing with Hollenweger's premise that approximately the first ten years represents the 'heart' and early formation of the movement's spirituality, this survey will combine his insights with Luz's application of *Wirkungsgeschichte*, which traces the effects that a particular piece of literature has had on certain readers, as a proposal methodology for reading.[1] A number of Pentecostal scholars have followed Hollenweger's

---

[1] Hollenweger, 'Pentecostals and the Charismatic Movement', pp. 549-53. Land's *Pentecostal Spirituality* follows Hollenweger's assertion that the first ten years represents the 'theological heart' of the Pentecostal movement, rather than the 'infancy', p. 47.

premise in conjunction with Luz's work as a way in which to hear the early Pentecostal literature for its contribution to contemporary Pentecostal theologies.[2] I chose to extend the survey to the first seventeen years of the North American Pentecostal movement (1906–1923) because a more comprehensive view is needed to engage with an early Pentecostal periodical that is key for its contribution to their interpretations of Ezekiel's vision reports and its pneumatological considerations observed in the text. It is not the intent to re-appropriate or construct a methodology from these early Pentecostal periodicals. The purpose is to allow the Pentecostal voices from the past to contribute to the conversation with contemporary Pentecostal and/Charismatic scholarship in hopes for a way forward in producing a constructive holistic theology of the role of the Spirit in the book of Ezekiel. Specifically, this chapter will examine the Pentecostal periodicals surveying the Wesleyan-Holiness publications: *The Apostolic Faith*, *The Bridegroom's Messenger*, *The Evening Light/Church of God Evangel*, followed by the Finished Work publications: *The Pentecost*, *Latter Rain Evangel*, *The Pentecostal Evangel*, and *The Bridal Call*.[3]

---

[2] Thomas and Alexander, '"And the Signs Are Following": Mark 16.9-20 – A Journey into Pentecostal Hermeneutics', *JPT* 11.2 (2003), pp. 147-70; and Thomas, 'Healing in the Atonement: A Johannine Perspective,' in *The Spirit in the New Testament* (Blandford Forum: Deo, 2005), pp. 175-89. Alexander, *Pentecostal Healing*; Green, *Toward a Pentecostal Theology of the Lord's Supper*, pp. 74-181; H.O. Bryant, *Spirit Christology in the Christian Tradition: From the Patristic Period to the Rise of Pentecostalism in the Twentieth Century* (Cleveland, TN: CPT Press, 2014), pp. 464-508; Archer, '*I Was in the Spirit on the Lord's Day*', pp. 68-118; and Johnson, *Pneumatic Discernment in the Apocalypse*.

[3] In 1910, William Howard Durham preached a sermon entitled 'the Finished Work of Calvary' at a Midwestern Pentecostal convention. His finished work teaching 'sought to nullify the understanding of sanctification as wholly realized in the believer by a crisis experience subsequent to and distinct from conversion'. This teaching began the controversy that divided the Pentecostal movement into a three-stage and two-stage Pentecostalism. Three-stage Pentecostalism held the Wesleyan view that there are three distinct experiences of grace: (1) conversion, (2) sanctification, and (3) baptism in the Holy Spirit. Two-stage Pentecostalism, which was the non-Wesleyan view proposed by Durham, held that sanctification was a lifelong process that began at conversion, thus this view only professed two stages (1) conversion and (2) Spirit baptism. Durham wrote in his magazine, *The Pentecostal Testimony*:

> I ... deny that God does not deal with the nature of sin at conversion. I deny that a man who is converted or born again is outwardly washed and cleansed but that his heart is left unclean with enmity against God in it ... This would not be Salvation. Salvation ... means a change of nature ... It means that all the

The early Pentecostal literature consists primarily of testimonies, hymns, and sermons from multi-cultural and multi-racial laypersons, ministerial leaders, and missionaries from both genders who were discerning and testifying to their Pentecostal experience. Generally, these testimonies provide the basis for contemporary Pentecostals to discern and investigate the early formation of Pentecostal spirituality. For Hollenweger, there are several distinct characteristics of early Pentecostalism: (1) 'orality of liturgy', (2) 'narrative theology', and (3) 'inclusion of dreams and visions into public and personal worship'.[4] The latter has specific bearing for discerning early Pentecostal spirituality as it relates to the visionary texts in Ezekiel. The purpose of examining these primary sources is to assess not only the doctrinal teaching of these editors and writers, but also to discern any similarities or distinctions between their beliefs and practices, which may have been shaped by the descriptions of the Spirit's activities in Ezekiel's visions.

The following chronological review of the periodicals will also be arranged according to similar themes identified in the book of Ezekiel.

II. Wesleyan-Holiness Publications

The Apostolic Faith

Many historians have dated the North American Pentecostal movement to the summer of 1906 in the city of Los Angeles at the Azusa Street Mission led by William Seymour.[5] Seymour was an African-American holiness preacher, who had been invited to speak, but had been locked out of the Holiness Church on Santa Fe Street because he insisted on preaching the doctrine of the baptism with the Holy Spirit with the initial evidence of speaking in tongues. Seymour was then invited to stay in the home of Mr. and Mrs. Edward Lee, who were members of the church, and after which, he began to preach in

---

old man or old nature, which was sinful and depraved and which was the very thing in us that was condemned, is crucified with Christ.

[4] Hollenweger quoted in Land, *Pentecostal Spirituality*, p. 52.

[5] See James R. Goff, *Fields White unto Harvest: Charles F. Parham and the Missionary Origins of Pentecostalism* (Fayetteville: University of Arkansas Press, 1988), p. 11, who claims that Charles Parham from Topeka, KS should be recognized as the founder of the Pentecostal movement.

their living room at the Asberry home on Bonnie Brae Street. Subsequently, Seymour himself experienced the baptism of the Holy Spirit and then the crowds grew so large that they had to relocate to an abandoned AME church at 312 Azusa Street. From this point, according to historian Vinson Synan, a 'monumental revival began'.[6] The revival continued for three and a half years at what became known as the Apostolic Faith Mission.

The Apostolic Faith (AF) was a free monthly periodical produced out of the Azusa Street Revival.[7] It is an indispensable resource to garner understanding of the people and events that helped to shape the contours of the global Pentecostal movement. The first issue was published in September of 1906 and there were subsequent monthly publications from 1906–1908. The editor and writers report about the revival events of the Azusa Mission, sermons from William Seymour, and the testimonies from missionaries from all over the world, as the emerging Pentecostal movement became a worldwide phenomenon.[8] These testimonies include the stories of manifestations of the Holy Spirit as described in supernatural vision experiences, healings, miracles, tongues, and exuberant worship. *The Apostolic Faith* is a testament of the influence that the Azusa revival had upon subsequent globalization of Pentecostalism.

In the second issue, the opening article is titled, 'The Pentecostal Baptism Restored: The Promised Latter Rain Now Being Poured Out on a Humble People'.[9] One of the ways in which the early Pentecostal community saw itself was as 'the bride of Christ' preparing for the great Marriage Supper of the Lamb and living with the expectation of the soon-coming return of Jesus Christ.[10] More specifically, the promise of the latter rain exemplifies how these early

---

[6] Synan, *The Holiness Pentecostal Tradition*, p. 97.

[7] Alexander, *Pentecostal Healing*, p. 75. The *Apostolic Faith* was first published in September of 1906 and there were subsequent monthly publications from 1906–1908. The editor and writers reported the revival events of the Azusa Mission, sermons from William Seymour, and the testimonies from missionaries from all over the world. Although, there are no direct references to the book of Ezekiel, there are many testimonies of visions of the heavens that appear to relate indirectly to Ezekiel's 'open heaven' visionary reports. See *AF* 1.3 (November, 1906), *AF* 1.6 (February-March, 1907), pp. 1, 2, 8; *AF* 1.7 (April, 1907), p. 1; p. 4; *AF* 2.13 (May, 1908), p. 1.

[8] Alexander, *Pentecostal Healing*, p. 75.

[9] *AF* 1.2 (October, 1906), p. 1; *AF* 1.12 (January, 1908), p. 2.

[10] *AF* 1.3 (November, 1906), p. 2.

Pentecostals believed that according to Joel 2.28 they were part of the latter outpouring of the Spirit, which would usher in the soon-coming King. As a result of this outpouring, believers would see dreams and visions.[11] In a teaching about visions in this publication, the writer discusses the biblical reports of visions as a way to defend the numerous testimonies of visions in the early Pentecostal movement. He writes, 'We know that some look with disfavor upon falling under the power, and many regards with suspicion visions and revelations. But, how can any who really believes in the Bible doubt the genuineness of that which fully bears the marks of being of God, and which is also in fulfillment of the prophecies and promises of his word?'[12]

The Apostolic Faith records numerous testimonies of 'visions of God' and descriptions of the Spirit's manifestations that occurred during their visionary experiences that relates to the language used to describe Ezekiel's visionary reports.[13] The opening statement of three of Ezekiel's four major vision narratives describes the prophet receiving 'visions of God' and connects these visions with various descriptions of the Spirit (Ezek. 1.1; 8.3; 40.2). In the *AF*, there are testimonies of those who fall under the power of God during their descriptions of throne room visions. For example, a testimony from India exclaims, 'And the Spirit of God came upon me, after which I saw the vision of the Almighty, falling into a trance but having my eyes open. I was left alone, and saw this great vision, and there remained no strength in me; and I became dumb.'[14] Individuals testify to being 'slain under the power of God' and 'falling prostrate under the power of God', and 'falling like dead men'.[15] These kinds of experiences were at times associated with involuntary movements lasting minutes or hours. For example, W.H. Durham testifies about such an experience when he visited the Azusa Mission:

> But on Friday evening, March 1, His mighty power came over me, until I jerked and quaked under it for about three hours. It was

---

[11] *AF* 1.3 (November, 1906), p. 2.

[12] *AF* 1.8 (May, 1907), p. 3.

[13] *AF* 1.6 (February-March, 1907), pp. 1, 2, 8; *AF* 1.7 (April, 1907), p. 1; p. 4; *AF* 2.13 (May, 1908), p. 1. One testimony recites, 'Great blessings have come upon the lowly and humble. Many have seen visions of Jesus and of the heavenly fire.'

[14] *AF* 1.8 (May, 1907), p. 3.

[15] *AF* 1.6 (February-March, 1907), p. 1; *AF* 1.7 (April, 1907), p. 1.

strange and wonderful and yet glorious. He worked my whole body, one section at a time, first my arms, then my limbs, then my body, then my head, then my face, then my chin, and finally at 1 a.m. Saturday, March 2, after being under the power for three hours, He finished the work on my vocal organs and spoke through me in unknown tongues.[16]

The close association between the Spirit's manifestation of controlling the person's body as the power of God was over them is remarkably similar to the idea of the power by 'the hand of YHWH' coming over Ezekiel (1.4; 3.12-15; 8.3; 40.1). The language in the book of Ezekiel describes the prophet 'falling prostrate' after witnessing 'visions of God' all the while the power of the 'hand of YHWH' was upon him and after the Spirit entered him (1.4; 2.2; 3.15, 22, 26). The prophet also is struck silent at the end of the inaugural vision narrative of the glory of God (Ezek. 1.28).

Some early Pentecostals of *The Apostolic Faith* believed that they could experience being 'carried away' by the Spirit as they saw visions of Jesus, heavenly beings, or the New Jerusalem. For example, a testimony states, 'Many have received visions of Jesus and report he is coming soon. In Minneapolis, others report to see visions while they were under the power and were caught up to Heaven and saw the New Jerusalem.'[17] The idea of being 'carried away' or 'lifted up by the Spirit' is a unique literary feature used in Ezekiel's vision reports and these early Pentecostals most likely would have been influenced by these kinds of Spirit texts in Ezekiel (Ezek. 3.12, 14; 8.3; 11.1, 24; 43.5).

Another connection with the vision reports in Ezekiel is the visions of angelic beings that are mentioned in the *AF*. Seymour describes how 'Los Angeles is being visited from a rushing mighty wind from heaven' and the presence of angelic beings from heaven are heard, 'No choir – but bands of angelic beings have been heard by some in the Spirit and there is a heavenly singing that is inspired by the Holy Spirit'.[18] Brother G.W. Evans testifies about how he fell under the power of God and was in a trance for approximately ten minutes. After he arose, he describes that at first, he saw the faces of

---

[16] *AF* 1.6 (February-March, 1907), p. 4.
[17] *AF* 1.11 (October to January, 1908), p. 2.
[18] *AF* 1.3 (November, 1906), p. 1.

angelic beings that filled the room and then he saw Jesus who came and stood in the room.[19] These kinds of testimonies express the idea that Pentecostal meetings included what came to be called 'The Heavenly Anthem'.[20] For example, one writer exclaims, 'No choir, but bands of angels have been heard by some in the Spirit and there is a heavenly singing that is inspired by the Holy Ghost'.[21] It is possible that these speakers were thinking of the angelic beings observed in the throne room vision reports of Ezekiel, Isaiah, and Revelation (Ezekiel 2–3; Isaiah 6; Revelation 4). The connection between heavenly angels singing as a choir is closely connected with the Spirit as it is the Spirit who baptizes and gives the utterance of either a heavenly language or song.

The *AF* also publishes songs in their periodical, which conveys their commitment to their belief in the fivefold gospel.

> Jesus is coming. Jesus is coming for me!
> Jesus is coming. I'll see his glory.
> The clouds are his chariots.
> The angels are his guard.
> Jesus is coming! How plain is his word.[22]

This particular chorus repeats several times and describes their belief in Jesus, as the soon coming King. What is significant for this study is the way in which the song utilizes Scripture to describe Jesus as riding on the clouds as his chariot is surrounded by angels (angelic beings) and connected to seeing a vision of his glory. Whether this song directly reflects Ezekiel's inaugural vision of the glory of God is unclear, but it is interesting that the language in both accounts mentioned above describe a chariot-throne vision with angelic beings (Ezek. 1.4-28).

Summary

The *Apostolic Faith* testifies how these early Pentecostals directly relate their visionary experiences to the Spirit's manifestations. Their testimonies of visions include being 'slain or falling prostrate in the Spirit' and 'carried by the Spirit', all while hearing and seeing throne-room

---

[19] *AF* 1.3 (November, 1906), p. 4.
[20] *AF* 1.3 (November, 1906), pp. 1, 3.
[21] *AF* 1.3 (November, 1906), p. 3. See also, *AF* 1.5 (January, 1907), p. 1.
[22] *AF* 1.4 (December, 1906), p. 4.

visions of Jesus or angelic beings. The theme of worship and the heavenly choir is rich throughout this periodical as they are given a gift by the Spirit to hear the heavenly choir or participate in song with the heavenly choir. Their testimonies of visions that include the Spirit's activities use similar language observed in some of the Ezekiel texts, which emphasis the Spirit's role and manifestations. As described above, some of the early Pentecostals also testify of 'being under the power of the Spirit', a phenomenon often called 'being slain in the Spirit' in most contemporary Pentecostal and Charismatic churches.[23] From this perspective, there are several instances where a case could be made that perhaps some of these early Pentecostals were influenced by the myriad of descriptions of the Spirit's activities in Ezekiel's vision narratives.

The Bridegroom's Messenger

The Bridegroom's Messenger is a periodical that emerged in Atlanta, Georgia in 1907 edited first by Gaston B. Cashwell and soon thereafter by Elizabeth Sexton.[24] I will examine these publications from 1907–1923. *The Bridegroom's Messenger* contains testimonies, scriptures, hymns, and prayers that were collected from a variety of people from various continents. A major purpose for the periodical was to hear testimonies from their community of believers. One of the central themes observed in these testimonies was the emphasis upon the manifestations of the Holy Spirit through supernatural visions, healings, miracles, tongues, and exuberant worship. Similar to the *AF*, they believed according to Joel 2.28 that visions and dreams were a result of the 'latter rain' outpouring of the Spirit. These early Pentecostal communities interpreted scripture in light of a 'promise-fulfillment' ideology, and particularly among the various Holiness groups, this 'latter rain' concept was common and purposed due to their beliefs surrounding the idea of the soon coming King.[25] As such, the promise of the outpouring of the Spirit was a fulfillment, which resulted in the manifestations of the Spirit through Spirit Baptism,

---

[23] *AF* 1.2 (October, 1906), pp. 1, 2; *AF* 1.3 (November, 1906), pp. 1, 4; *AF* 1.6 (February-March, 1907), p. 7; *AF* 1.8 (May, 1907), p. 2.

[24] Alexander, *Pentecostal Healing*, p. 75.

[25] Archer, *A Pentecostal Hermeneutic for the Twenty-First Century*. Archer argues that the 'early Pentecostals held to a distinct narrative of which the Latter Rain motif played a significant role in the construction of the Pentecostal story', p. 101. *TBM* 15.239 (August, 1922), p. 1.

dreams and visions, and other supernatural experiences. Many testimonials in *TBM* described below, report how their vivid vision reports are a direct result to their beliefs related to the baptism of the Spirit.

The sermons and testimonies observed in the early Pentecostal literature discern that the baptism of the Holy Spirit was not only for speaking in tongues,[26] but also for seeing visions and dreams, hearing heavenly choirs in the midst of visions, intercessory prayer, and spiritual and moral cleansing in the believer.[27] Specifically, *The Bridegroom's Messenger* contains several direct references to Ezekiel in which some sermons or testimonies reflect how they interpret Ezekiel's visions or describe how their own visions relate to Ezekiel. Among these sermons identified, it is interesting that they use language which directly associates the Spirit's role to their visions. Additionally, some testimonials reference discrete passages in the book of Ezekiel to convey how the writers were influenced by the theme of prayer. For example, a letter by brother McIntosh records a Chinese believer who cites Ezek. 22.30, 'I looked for someone among them who would build up the wall and stand before me in the gap on behalf of the land so I would not have to destroy it, but I found no one'.[28] Brother McIntosh interprets this passage as a clarion call for believers to receive a spirit of intercession for their fellow believers who are struggling in foreign lands. He writes, 'So we can only kneel in the gap and pray for their lives to be spared. Oh! We are praying for God to speak to them with our tongues. We are waiting on Him.'[29] He continues,

---

[26] *TBM* 1.11 (April, 1908), p. 2. Mrs. Anna Kelly writes, 'I heard of the Holy Ghost being poured out in Los Angeles, CA. They were speaking in tongues and I realized that they had an experience above me. It was their speaking in tongues that convinced me. I saw I did not have the Bible evidence of the baptism, although I had been taught to think so.' Archer proposes that the early Pentecostals used a 'Bible Reading Method' or used scripture to interpret scripture to provide their doctrinal understanding of baptism in the Spirit. See Archer, *A Pentecostal Hermeneutic for the Twenty-First Century*, p. 77. He argues that William Seymour, the editor of *Apostolic Faith*, illustrates the Bible Reading Method of baptism of the Spirit and tongues in one of his articles.

[27] *TBM* 1.11 (April, 1908), p. 2. Ione Waldron reports, 'I praise God that when He sent His Spirit to me and convicted me of sin'.

[28] *TBM* 1.11 (April, 1908), p. 1; For the theme of prayer see also *TBM* 9.187 (October, 1916), p. 3.

[29] *TBM* 1.11 (April, 1908), p. 1.

The work here is that God has given to this precious band a spirit of intercessory prayer; they have real soul travail; they have caught the mind of the Spirit and are abreast of God's thought for the human family. The Spirit is drawing the baptized ones everywhere to a deeper, more definitive and intelligent prayer than ever before.[30]

Brother McIntosh also references Ezek. 2.4-6, 'The people to whom I am sending you are obstinate and stubborn. Say to them, this is what the Sovereign Lord says, whether they listen or fail to listen, for they are a rebellious people, and they will know that a prophet has been among them.'[31] He draws correlations between the way that the writers describe Ezekiel's audience in his call narrative as a rebellious and hard people to the present-day Chinese believers. Brother McIntosh bemoans that despite some of the Chinese believers being filled with the Holy Spirit, their preaching did not always prove fruitful because he thought they too were a hard and rebellious people. He writes, 'Filled with the Holy Spirit, they retained settled conviction that they were in divine order and expected that God would seal their work in China. But when they tried to pour out the message of love to the darkened minds around them, they found themselves unable to make them understand'.[32] Like the message that the prophet Ezekiel was to deliver to his people, so too, Brother McIntosh's message did not seem to penetrate 'the darkened minds'.

One of the more prominent themes identified in *TBM* as it relates to Ezekiel, is how these early Pentecostals interpreted scripture in light of a 'promise-fulfillment' ideology and how they connect this idea to the phrase, 'the hand of the Lord'.

The Latter Rain Motif and the Hand of the Lord

As early Pentecostals were a people expecting the promise of the outpouring of the Spirit for empowerment and the end time harvest, they often associated the power of God with the phrase, 'the hand of the Lord'.[33] This phrase is used 26 times in the book of Ezekiel, which is more than any other book in the OT. Specifically, the Hebrew idiom is emphasized in all four of Ezekiel's major visionary

---

[30] *TBM* 1.11 (April, 1908), p. 1
[31] *TBM* 1.11 (April, 1908), p. 1.
[32] *TBM* 1.11 (April, 1908), p. 2.
[33] *TBM* 1.18 (July, 1908), p. 5; *TBM* 1.18 (July, 1908), p. 3.

accounts (Ezekiel 1–3; 8–11; 37.1-14; 40–43). The phrase, 'the hand of the Lord' is a distinct literary tool used in the narrative reports of Ezekiel to describe how the prophet: (1) hears the word of the Lord and, at times, angelic beings, (2) falls prostrate after seeing a vision of the glory of the Lord, (3) is lifted and transported to a heavenly throne vision, and (4) sees a mysterious man with, at times, angelic beings. Frequently, this phrase is used in tandem with the Spirit of the Lord in the context of Ezekiel's vision reports (Ezek. 3.12-14, 22-24; 8.1-3; 37.1; 40.1-3). It is conceivable that this recurring Hebrew idiom in the book of Ezekiel influenced some of these early Pentecostal believers. Susan A. Duncan testifies to the connections between the manifestations of the Spirit by the power of God's hand as it came upon Pentecostal believers.

She writes,

> While a meeting was going on in the church, a few had gathered in Elim's home for further waiting, and it was there the power fell. During the day about seven were prostrated under the hand of God, speaking in tongues, singing, and prophesying. Truly the 'Latter Rain' had come, and God was doing a new thing in the earth. Later, many others were baptized in the Spirit and prostrated under the power of God.[34]

It is clear that Duncan regards that these manifestations of Spirit baptism (tongues and prophecy) *and* singing came as a result of being 'prostrated under the hand of God'. The idea of 'falling prostrate' or 'being slain under the power of God' is well documented in the early periodicals of Pentecostals.[35] Often these believers describe that while prostrated under the power of God by the 'hand of God', they would also hear angelic beings. For example, a testimonial records, 'We had read about the heavenly choir that the Spirit is forming, but we never imagined its power and sweetness until we actually heard its notes, sounding out like a grand oratorio of angelic voices … like the waves of the sea for power'.[36] Two of the four major visions in Ezekiel describe how the prophet hears angelic beings, 'Then the Spirit lifted me up, and I heard behind me a loud rumbling sound, "May

---

[34] *TBM* 1.18 (July, 1908), p. 5.
[35] *TBM* 1.9 (March 1, 1908), p. 3; *TBM* 1.16 (June, 15, 1908), p. 3; *TBM* 2.45 (September 1, 1909), p. 4.
[36] *TBM* 1.18 (July, 1908), p. 5.

the glory of the Lord be praised in his dwelling place!" It was the sound of the wings of the living creatures brushing against each other and the sound of the wheels beside them, a loud rumbling sound' (Ezek. 3.12-13; 10.1).

Interestingly, those who fell under the power of God's hand experienced visions of Jesus, the throne of heaven, angelic beings, all while having the ability to communicate how they were feeling during the vision. A testimony from Mattie Ledbetter recounts her visions of Jesus on a throne of glory,

> I had visions of Jesus on a throne of glory, and the Holy Ghost used all my powers to praise and adore Him for some time. I did not talk very much in tongues, but on Thursday the Holy Spirit manifested Himself in a much more wonderful way. I had two visions of Jesus, and was filled with rapturous love and it seemed that if God did not stay His hand, I would die of pure love and joy, and desire to praise and adore Him, as it was revealed to me He deserved I beheld Him on the throne of His glory.[37]

Mattie Ledbetter describes how it is the Spirit who inspired her to praise Jesus during her vision of the Lord upon the throne of glory. The connection between the Spirit and visionary experiences of Jesus and his throne of glory recur several times in *The Bridegroom's Messenger*.[38] At times it is not clear whether these testimonies were influenced by the throne room vision reports in Ezekiel 1 or Revelation 4. Because the language is very similar, it is possible that they were influenced by both accounts.

Ledbetter states,

> In a vision I saw Him far above my head beneath a dome of rainbow light and glory. As I sang and wafted my hand, He descended, coming down to me, which was the longing desire in my soul. All

---

[37] *TBM* 1.18 (July, 1908), p. 3.

[38] See Archer, '*I Was in the Spirit on the Lord's Day*', pp. 68-118. Archer's chapter on 'Effective History' documents comprehensively on the connections between worship, praise, and singing testimonies with that of visions described in the early Pentecostal literature. For example, see *TBM* 5.120 (November 1, 1912), p. 3.

day and all night I was thrilled with waves of joy and glory in every fiber of my being. [39]

Her testimony of a vision of the throne of glory is likened to that of Ezekiel's vision of the throne of YHWH's glory. Both visions describe how the throne was a dome above them that was filled with light and a rainbow of colors. Significant for this study is that both visions also describe the overwhelming feelings that were experienced by the visionary and their ability to report their emotional disposition during such an encounter.

Some of these early Pentecostal testimonies of the glory of God specifically describe that it is the 'hand of God' that carried them in visions, which for these early Pentecostals and ancient Israelites, represented the power of God. Three of Ezekiel's visionary narratives describe how the Spirit transports the prophet while 'the hand of YHWH is upon him' (Ezek. 3.12-15; 8.3; 40.1). Generally, these early Pentecostals viewed that the 'hand of God' symbolized the power of God that was responsible for 'transporting' them in a vision and leading them to see and hear in the vision. Mattie Dennis describes her visionary experience,

> Then I was carried, or led upward through a heavenly atmosphere with the light remaining over my head. Then I saw the walls of the great city of God. Oh, the beautiful colors can never be told! And it dazzled like the sun. I now saw many bands of angels flying over and about the city. Then the 'hand' led me through a shining gate, and all the host of heaven was praising God with voices with all the music of heaven, and I saw it was the Lord Jesus. [40]

This testimony is remarkably similar to the language used to describe Ezekiel's first two major vision reports (Ezekiel 1–3; 8–10). Ezekiel's vision reports and the testimony above illustrate how the visionary transportation by the Spirit from earth to heaven includes visual and auditory elements. The testimony and Ezekiel's narrative convey the visionary as seeing vivid colors, light imagery, angelic beings, as well as hearing praises to God. Both accounts describe a vision of Jesus or 'mysterious man' on a colorful throne of glory, or a

---

[39] *TBM* 1.18 (July, 1908), p. 3. The mention of 'false prophets' in the context of the 'last days' is also prevalent throughout this periodical, 'False prophets will continue to prophesy lies, and many will be deceived'.

[40] *TBM* 5.105 (March 1, 1912), p. 3.

brightly lit heaven with angelic beings, while hearing a heavenly choir at the same time. Both connect these visual and auditory experiences with 'the hand of God'. Dennis appears to have been influenced with Ezekiel's visionary transportation reports to the heavenly realms (Ezek. 2.24; 3.12-15). She states, 'the hand then let go of me and I saw it was the Lord Jesus, and he said to me that you are home but not to stay'.[41] The Ezekiel text reads,

> Then the Spirit lifted me up, and I heard behind me a loud rumbling sound as the glory of the Lord rose from the place where it was standing. It was the sound of the wings of the living creatures brushing against each other and the sound of the wheels beside them, a loud rumbling sound. The Spirit then lifted me up and took me away, and I went in bitterness and in the anger of my spirit, with the strong hand of the Lord on me (Ezek. 3.12-14).

Dennis' testimony reports how she was allowed to be in the presence of Jesus in the heavens by the hand or power of the Spirit but was not allowed to stay. The Ezekiel text also reports how the prophet was transported to see the glory of the Lord by the Spirit, but not allowed to stay.

The next two sections report how these early Pentecostals interpreted Ezekiel's inaugural vision and the last temple vision in Ezekiel 47.

Ezekiel and the Four Living Beings

Ezekiel's inaugural vision report of the four living beings is often times symbolically interpreted in the early Pentecostal literature. In a response to an article about 'the rapture', E.H. Blake writes a sermon about the four faces of the living beings in Ezekiel 1,

> The four faces are expressive of perfect character: the lion is that of boldness and strength; the ox, that of endurance, patience, and humble service; the eagle, that of an elevated life, one above the things of this world, affection on things above, of spiritual insight and truth; they are said of having eyes that see every way, seeing the deep things of God; the man of intelligence. We notice that in Ezekiel 1 and Revelation 6 that the living creatures are the expression of the living expressions of the throne, or in other words

[41] *TBM* 5.105 (March 1, 1912), p. 3.

the Spirit of God in the throne are worked out through them, so they have sat down in Christ in his throne, being perfect overcomers.[42]

Blake interprets the living creatures who have over their heads the color of crystal (Ezek. 1.22) as representing 'the highest order of saints' or the 'Bride', who demonstrates perfection, unity, and perfect obedience in service.[43] He suggests that the feet of the four living beings, which are described as 'burnished brass' in Ezek. 1.7, is a close likeness to the feet of Jesus described as 'bronze glowing in a furnace' in Rev. 1.15.[44] Blake also perceives that the twenty-four elders in Revelation 4 are 'attendants' of the next rank who will be 'raptured' after the highest order, the 'Bride'. For Blake, Ezekiel's inaugural vision of the four living beings is the same living beings in John's revelation, and both represent the 'Bride of Christ' sitting on his throne, empowered to overcome through the Spirit.

Ezekiel's Throne Vision in Ezekiel 47, The Latter Rain Motif, and Spirit Baptism

Sexton, the editor of *The Bridegroom's Messenger*, writes a sermon about Ezekiel's temple vision (Ezekiel 47), which is the last and fourth major vision in Ezekiel that utilizes water imagery. The temple vision highlights a river overflowing from under the threshold and pouring out from the throne.[45] Sexton's sermon, 'River of Water of Life' emphasizes the symbols of water, oil, and wind to interpret Ezekiel 47.[46] She states, 'The pure river of the water of life, which we behold in the New Jerusalem let down from God out of heaven is the prophetic fulfillment in Ezekiel 47'.[47] She proposes that the water of life is the restored Edenic beauty and perfection, with the added glory of redemption privileges and possessions'.[48] She interprets the entire

---

[42] *TBM* 6.121 (November 15, 1911), p. 4.
[43] *TBM* 6.121 (November 15, 1911), p. 4. Blake states that the next rank of whom is caught up after the living creatures and the elders are found in Rev. 7.9, after the tribulation and the sixth seal.
[44] *TBM* 6.121 (November 15, 1911), p. 4.
[45] *TBM* 2.42 (July, 1909), p. 1; *TBM* 7.158 (July, 1914), p. 3. *TBM* 15. 235 (January, 1922), p. 4.
[46] *TBM* 3.48 (October, 1909), p. 1.
[47] *TBM* 3.48 (October, 1909), p. 1.
[48] *TBM* 3.48 (October, 1909), p. 1.

chapter of Ezekiel 47 in light of how she perceives the working of the Spirit in the 'sanctified life of Pentecostal baptism'.[49] She writes,

> This [Ezekiel's] vision marvelously applies to the Spirit's working. Where the Holy Spirit goes, it carries life and healing as this stream of living water. Our first going through the waters is with the waters to our ankles. It suggests the walking in newness of life, born of the Spirit and walking by faith. The second bringing through the waters, takes us deeper, but in the same water. The waters are to the knees.[50]

It is apparent that for Sexton the water that overflows the temple in Ezekiel 47 symbolically represents the Spirit whom she associates with 'the rivers of living water that flows from the throne of God' and comes to bring life, healing, cleansing, and holiness.[51] Sexton argues that Ezekiel's temple vision illustrates how the 'water cleanses from physical filth and the Spirit cleanses from sin and the pollutions of sin'.[52] She also determines that Ezekiel's temple vision is a promise of the Pentecostal outpouring of the working of the Spirit.[53]

Sexton describes,

> The same Spirit that comes to quicken in the new birth takes us deeper in God and uses us in the ministry of prayer as priests unto our God sanctified and set apart for his service. Again, the going through the waters, the waters are up to the loins. This suggests strength and power. We see its application to the Holy Spirit's mighty work upon the sanctified life in Pentecostal baptism. The next measurement finds a great river that cannot be passed over.[54]

As previously mentioned, one of the ways in which early Pentecostals saw themselves was through the lens of the Latter Rain motif. The Latter Rain motif is further developed in Sexton's interpretation of Ezekiel 47 as she discerns that the promise of the Pentecostal outpouring is a prophetic fulfillment in her interpretation of the Spirit's outpouring symbolized by the water flowing through Ezekiel's final temple vision.

---

[49] *TBM* 3.48 (October, 1909), p. 1.
[50] *TBM* 3.48 (October, 1909), p. 1.
[51] *TBM* 3.48 (October, 1909), p. 1.
[52] *TBM* 3.48 (October, 1909), p. 1.
[53] *TBM* 3.48 (October, 1909), p. 1.
[54] *TBM* 3.48 (October, 1909), p. 1.

Sexton associates the Spirit's outpouring of the Pentecostal Spirit baptism with love. In keeping with a Wesleyan Holiness view of Spirit baptism, Sexton perceives that the outpouring of the Spirit is given to a heart that is pure allowing it to love God fully.[55] She writes,

> Waters to swim in. The saints now stand on the brink of a grand ocean of love, too broad to pass over, too deep to fathom. You may wade in the borders of it, and plunge into its healing currents; you may view the river of life on either side of it, but the fullness of the glory is not yet.[56]

Hannah A. James also writes that the temple vision with the emphasis upon the water imagery in Ezekiel 47 is like the baptism of the Holy Spirit and love. She states, 'Ezekiel's wondrous vision of the ever-deepening river should be like the baptism. Oh! That we all should plunge into the mighty torrents of God's love and be swept along upon its waters ... to be without measure.'[57] The reliance upon Ezekiel's temple vision can hardly be missed as the editor draws upon the water imagery and clearly associates it with the Latter Rain motif and Spirit baptism.

Summary

The Bridegroom's Messenger provides several testimonies that are salient for the present study. The sermons reveal that the early Pentecostals often interpreted the Ezekiel texts symbolically. The testimonies reveal that the early Pentecostal spirituality was influenced by Ezekiel's visions primarily because they believed they were part of the 'Latter Rain' movement in which the Spirit's outpouring (Spirit baptism) was given for the reception of dreams and visions, cleansing, and holiness, which all represented manifestations by the Spirit. These visions describe how they discerned that their eyes were opened by the Spirit of God to receive visions of Jesus on the throne of heaven, angelic beings, and the glory of God. They associated the power of the Spirit

---

[55] Archer, *A Pentecostal Hermeneutic for the Twenty-First Century*, pp. 14-15. Archer traces the Holiness movements and their influences upon early Pentecostalism. He distinguishes a Keswickian Spirit baptism, which according to Archer is a second experiential work for empowerment for service, with that of a Wesleyan Holiness Spirit baptism, which views that Spirit baptism totally eradicates Adamic sin and comes to the purified heart to love God fully.

[56] *TBM* 3.48 (October, 1909), p. 1.

[57] *TBM* 7.58 (July 1, 1914), p. 3.

with the 'hand of God' in receiving visions. Additionally, they under-stood that a vision constituted several elements; (1) seeing in the spir-itual world, (2) hearing heavenly choirs or angelic beings, and the word of the Lord, (3) reports of participation in the vision through all one's senses, (4) the ability to describe overwhelming feelings that often-initiated worship by falling prostrate, and (5) the ability to recall the events experienced in the vision. Their testimonies describe vivid and bright colors seen in heaven, hearing heavenly choirs, and feel-ings of joy as they were under the power of God by 'the hand of God'. These stories also reflect how these believers respond to their visions either with verbal praise, repentance, or decisions to answer a call to follow Christ. But also, these testimonies record their physical bodily responses of prostration and shaking in response to 'the hand of God upon them' in these visions that were given by the Spirit. In these ways, similar to the prophet Ezekiel, they saw themselves re-ceiving visions by the Spirit of God and participating in their visions through all of their senses.

The Evening Light/Church of God Evangel

The General Overseer of the Church of God, A.J. Tomlinson, served as editor of *The Evening Light and Church of God Evangel* from 1910 to 1922 in Cleveland, TN. The headquarters of this Pentecostal denom-ination continues to be located in Cleveland, TN.[58] It is evident that the book of Ezekiel influenced this periodical because there are sev-eral direct reflections of Ezekiel texts in the pages of this publication. In the very first edition, Tomlinson quotes passages from Ezekiel 34 to highlight its shepherd imagery. He emphasizes that the Lord, as the shepherd, will continue to look for his sheep and draw them out of a 'dark and cloudy day' (Ezek. 34.12-13). Tomlinson proceeds to paint a picture of how he perceives that the 'dark and cloudy' day has passed and now the church is in the 'evening of the gospel age' be-fore the coming tribulation. He correlates the dark days of Ezekiel, the prophet in exile, and the dawn of the light of the glory of God with the storm and fire imagery in Ezekiel's inaugural vision (Ezek.

---

[58] See Alexander, *Pentecostal Healing*, pp. 68-69. The *Evening Light and Church of God Evangel* began in March 1910. Its name shortened to *Church of God Evangel* in March 1911.

1.4-28) to the Spirit's outpouring in the new present age of the church.[59] He continues,

> They (sheep) are coming as the light is now shining ... The full blaze of light beamed forth from the Pentecostal chamber, and shined forth with radiant glory in the early morning of the gospel day and its beams have pierced through the dark ages and created a warmth to many almost discouraged lives at intervals ever since the pouring out of the Spirit on that memorable day. I am the Alpha and the Omega, the first and the last, said Jesus; and as the light burst forth with such glory and power in the first or early morning.[60]

Tomlinson associates Ezekiel's exile with the dark ages and his inaugural vision that occurs in Ezekiel 1 with the age in which the Spirit's outpouring will usher in the gospel age.[61] He also concludes that Jesus is the light and radiant glory who has come to gather the sheep that were scattered. He states that Ezekiel's inaugural vision of the four living beings is likened to the 'church that was planted in the early morning and burst out on the sea of humanity like a thunderbolt from the clear sky'.[62]

Like Blake in *TBM*, Tomlinson's sermon in the second issue of *COGE* symbolically interprets Ezekiel's four living beings as 'the Bride of Christ'.[63] He urges his readers to get ready for the 'Day of the Lord' as he draws a correlation between the four living beings in the book of Ezekiel and the 'Bride of Christ'.[64] Tomlinson testifies that 'Jesus is getting a crowd ready who are going to be exactly of one mind and of one accord. His prayer in the seventeenth chapter of John compels an answer. No guessing at this. Like Ezekiel's living creatures, they are all joined together, and all going in the same direction at the same time' (Ezek. 1.9).[65]

---

[59] *COGE* 1.1 (March, 1910), p. 1. Similar to *TBM*, the sheep and shepherd imagery in Ezekiel is referenced again in *The Evening Light and Church of God Evangel* as brother MacArthur is inspired by Ezekiel 34 as a call to intercede for the church and its leaders or shepherds. See *COGE* 1.12 (October, 1910), p. 7.

[60] *COGE* 1.1 (March, 1910), p. 1.

[61] *COGE* 1.1 (March, 1910), p. 1.

[62] *COGE* 1.1 (March, 1910), p. 1.

[63] *COGE* 1.12 (October, 1910), p. 7.

[64] *COGE* 1.12 (October, 1910), p. 7.

[65] *COGE* 1.2 (March, 1910), p. 2.

Ezekiel and the Manifestations of the Spirit

Sometimes the idea of 'falling prostrate' or 'being slain under the power of God' among the early Pentecostals was associated with kinetic movements that lasted either minutes or hours.[66] In a homily entitled, 'The Operations of the Holy Spirit', Z.R. Thomas addresses critics of the manifestations of the Spirit in the Pentecostal people (falling prostrate, dancing, trembling, and shaking). He traces several instances in the Scriptures, which he cites as examples of these kinds of manifestations of the Spirit. Thomas writes,

> Dear friends God's power doesn't stop at shaking people, but shakes even this old earth. When they had prayed the place was shaken where they had assembled (Acts 4.31). Dear reader, I don't wonder at people jumping, leaping, dancing, trembling, shaking or falling under the mighty power of God. While a great many people say it is indecent for people to fall about as some of the Pentecostal people do, but now we want to see what the Bible says about that. The prophet Ezekiel fell to his face when he encountered a vision of the glory of the Lord (Ezek. 1.18).[67]

Thomas continues to emphasize the Spirit's activities in the prophet Ezekiel,

> The spirit lifted me up and brought me unto the east gate of the Lord's house, which looks eastward (Ezek. 11.1, 24). Afterward the Spirit took me up and brought me in a vision by the Spirit of God into Chaldea and he put forth the form of a hand and took me by the lock of my head; and the Spirit lifted me up between the earth and the heaven, and brought me in the visions of God to Jerusalem (Ezek. 8.3). Then the Spirit took me up and I heard behind me a voice of a great rushing (Ezek. 3.12-15). So, the Spirit lifted me and took me away and I went away in bitterness in the heat of my spirit, and the hand of the Lord was strong upon me, and I fell on my face, then the Spirit entered me and I fell on my face.[68]

Thomas explains, 'Dear reader whether you like it or not it lines up with the Bible just the same'. He cites several passages of

---

[66] *AF* 1.6 (February-March, 1907), p. 5; *AF* 1.7 (April, 1907), p. 1.
[67] *COGE* 15.26 (June 13, 1914), p. 8.
[68] *COGE* 15.26 (June 13, 1914), p. 5.

Scripture to argue that trembling is a manifestation of the Spirit. For example, Thomas cites the book of Ezekiel,

> Son of man, eat thy bread with quaking and drink thy water with trembling and with carefulness (Ezek. 12.18). They shall clothe themselves with trembling, they shall wait upon the ground and shall tremble at every moment and be astonished at thee (Ezek. 26.16), and when he had spoken this word, I stood trembling.[69]

Tomlinson, the editor of *COGE*, also adds to the conversation in a response to an article in the 'Florida Baptist Witness' called 'The Fallacy of the Modern Holiness Propaganda'.[70] He addresses the critiques towards the Pentecostal tradition relating to the manifestations of the Spirit and specifically, 'falling under the power of God'.[71] Tomlinson uses the biblical narratives of Ezek. 1.28 and 3.23, which describe Ezekiel falling prostrate by the Spirit, to defend current day testimonies of similar reports. Clearly, these early Pentecostals perceived that the Spirit's manifestations they read in the Scriptures substantiated their own experiences.

Physical manifestations of the Spirit were only part of how these early Pentecostals viewed the outpouring of the Spirit. There are several testimonies that emphasize the themes of cleansing and holiness through the water imagery and the Spirit depicted in the book of Ezekiel. Sam C. Perry writes an article in which he urges his readers to read Ezek. 36.25-27, 'I will sprinkle clean water on you, and you will be clean; I will cleanse you from all your impurities and from all your idols. I will give you a new heart and put a new spirit in you; I will remove from you your heart of stone and give you a heart of flesh. And I will put my Spirit in you and move you to follow my decrees and be careful to keep my laws.' Perry interprets the 'new heart' and a 'new spirit' in Ezek. 36. 26-27 as a promise from God. He argues that it is only a 'new heart' and a 'new spirit' that assures one can live a holy life that is pleasing to him.[72]

---

[69] *COGE* 15.26 (June 13, 1914), p. 5.
[70] *COGE* 6.29 (September 25, 1916), p. 1.
[71] *COGE* 6.29 (September 25, 1916), pp. 1, 8.
[72] *COGE* 6.49 (December 4, 1915), p. 1.

Summary

The Evening Light and Church of God Evangel gives further testimony to the influence that the book of Ezekiel had upon early Pentecostal spirituality and their doctrine of Spirit baptism. Their testimonies confirm that the descriptions of the Spirit portrayed in Ezekiel's visions were used to support their beliefs and practices regarding the manifestations of the Spirit that included falling prostrate under the power of God, shaking or other bodily responses, and cleansing and purification. This periodical emphasizes the testimonies and sermons of believers who read Ezekiel as a seer who was encountered by 'the glory of YHWH'; overpowered by YHWH's hand; engaged by the diverse activities of Spirit, which ultimately provided them with biblical support for how they could conceive of having the same kinds of experiences. Similar to *TBM*, the *COGE* records how the four living beings in Ezekiel's inaugural vision are interpreted symbolically as the 'Bride of Christ' and are correlated to the four living beings in Revelation.

III. Finished Work Publications

The Pentecost
In 1908, J. Roswell Flower published *The Pentecost* in Indianapolis, IN. Later, A.S. Copley became the editor and changed the name to *Grace and Glory*. *The Pentecost* highlights sermons, teachings, and reports from their community of believers. *The Pentecost* contains a few articles directly dealing with Ezekiel's inaugural vision (Ezekiel 1).[73]

The editor, A.S. Copley writes about the four gospels using Ezekiel's inaugural vision (Ezekiel 1). In an attempt to support the different views of the life of Jesus Christ presented by the gospel writers, he appeals to a symbolic interpretation of Ezekiel's vision of the four living beings. He states, 'In Ezekiel, is given a possible symbolic teaching for those four gospels. The lion symbolizes Jesus anointed as King; the ox as servant; the face of a man represents a human; and the face of an angel as divine.'[74] Similar to some contemporary interpretations of Ezekiel's inaugural vision of the four creatures, this teaching demonstrates how some early Pentecostals also used a NT

---

[73] *TP* 1.3 (November, 1908), p. 1.
[74] *TP* 1.3 (November, 1908), p. 1.

lens to interpret the imagery in Ezekiel's inaugural vision (Ezek. 1.4-28).

The Spirit and the 'Heavens Were Opened'

As this study has shown, the visions of the early Pentecostals are filled with testimonies of vivid descriptions of the supernatural realm that is typified by bright lights, amber colored fire, and either the glory of God, angelic beings, or the Spirit. However, the phrase 'the heavens were opened' is not as common as it only occurs twice in the entire Bible, once in Genesis, and once in Ezekiel's opening vision (Gen. 7.11; Ezek. 1.1). The Ezekiel text reads, 'the heavens were opened and I saw visions of God'. This statement precedes an elaborate description of a 'whirlwind, and immense cloud with flashing lighting and surrounded by brilliant light. The center of the fire looked like glowing metal, and in the fire, was what looked like four living creatures. In appearance, their form was human' (Ezek. 1. 4-5). Therefore, for an early Pentecostal to make mention of this uncommon phrase is quite remarkable. Martha J. Lewis from Canada cites Ezekiel 1 as a way to describe how 'the heavens were opened' in her experience with the baptism of the Spirit at a church altar call. She tells of her 'stubborn will' and how through prayer she became broken and willing to confess her sins. She reports that she continued to pray at home for the next three days for the baptism of the Spirit and then suddenly was awakened out of her sleep by the 'sound of a roar of fire'.[75] Ms. Lewis describes her vision of the Spirit of God using the storm and fire motifs that were used in Ezekiel's opening vision,

> I saw fire all about me and fire above me. I saw nothing of earth. The fire above me was in strips or widths. Cloven tongues of fire were in the background. Truly the heavens were opened onto me and I saw the Spirit of God, like a dove descending and lighting upon me at my throat. The dove was all fire and had a circle of light about Him.[76]

Ms. Lewis continues to tell her story of how this light came upon her body and caused her to tremor in the bed. She testifies that she was rendered powerless to move hand or foot. Ms. Lewis states,

---

[75] *TP* 1.3 (November, 1908), p. 7.
[76] *TP* 1.3 (November, 1908), p. 7.

The fire I saw above me came also on my body and burned through my flesh like ashes going through a sieve. I was speechless. I was filled with the Holy Ghost in all my being, worshipping God, for the first time, in spirit and in truth. I praised God as the Spirit gave utterance in an unknown tongue. This new tongue seemed to be akin to my new state of my body, soul, and spirit.[77]

Ms. Lewis relates the fire and light metaphors to the Spirit. As she reports that the heavens were opened, she reports she saw the Spirit descending upon her. She connects Ezekiel's vision of the heavens renting to her own experience, yet she interprets it as an experience of the baptism of the Spirit.

The Latter Rain Evangel (TLRE)

Pastor William Piper of Stone Church in Chicago led the publication of *The Latter Rain Evangel* between the years of 1908 and 1911.[78] *The Latter Rain Evangel* contains numerous sermons from Stone Church regarding manifestations of the Spirit that occurred in their church services, and sermons from leaders around the world. *The Latter Rain Evangel* gives testimony to the influence Ezekiel's visions had upon the early Pentecostals, as there are several direct references to Ezekiel that can be observed in its pages. For example, Miss Minnie F. Abrams tells the story of someone who was baptized in the Spirit and became struck dumb in speech likened to the prophet Ezekiel.[79] She recounts how some who were baptized in the Spirit had a habit of speaking what they pleased,

And their tongues had been saying bad things, but they had become dumb, and they could not say anything in their own tongue. Some had remained dumb for as long as three weeks, not able to speak a word in a language, and thus God taught them the use of the tongue. He taught them what it was to be shut up unto Himself. He taught them the idleness of the tongue; He taught them what separation unto God for this tongue means. It was a wonderful lesson to His children. There is no Teacher like unto Him. I remember when the first person was struck dumb, we didn't

---

[77] *TP* 1.3 (November, 1908), p. 7.

[78] *TLRE* 1.1 (July, 1908), p. 1. See Archer, *A Pentecostal Hermeneutic in the Twenty-First Century*, pp. 103-105 for a full treatment of the life of and contributions of D. Wesley Myland (1858-1943).

[79] *TLRE* 1.12 (September, 1909), p. 8.

understand it and we said, 'Lord, teach us, show us something in the Word about it', and the Lord showed us how when Ezekiel was dumb, and we found something in the Word to explain all these works of the blessed Holy Ghost.[80]

Miss Abrams uses the Ezekiel text to interpret her testimonies of 'dumbness'. She compares their 'dumbness' with how the narrative portrays Ezekiel as so overwhelmed by his visionary encounter with God that he sat silent for seven days (Ezek. 3.15).

D. Wesley Myland also associates Ezekiel's vision with Spirit baptism. He presents a series of homilies on the 'Latter Rain' and the Pentecostal outpouring. His first lecture is titled, 'A Setting Forth of the Seven-Fold Condition'. Myland associates the meaning of the number seven with the glory. He explains how Ezekiel's vision of the glory is related to his 'latter rain' experience of Spirit baptism. Myland lists several scriptural accounts of people who received visions of the glory of God,

> Moreover, the light of the moon shall be as the light of the sun, which shone like the light of the sun and it shall be a seven-fold (perfection) as the light of seven days, 'in one day. It was like that the night God baptized me. It was like that when the Lord Jesus Christ revealed Himself to Saul in mid-day on the way to Damascus. Why it is the old Shekinah glory! I have been tracing it through the Bible recently; it is away beyond the light of the sun at mid-day. It is that glory that stood at the gates of Eden, that appeared to Moses in the burning bush; it is that glory that was in the pillar of cloud and at the door of the tabernacle; it is that which flashed before Isaiah; and gave Ezekiel his vision, and that swept the gloomy isle of Patmos into the sea of glory, with Jesus in the midst of it.[81]

Myland concludes that his experience of the baptism of the Spirit is likened to Ezekiel's visions of the glory of God (Ezekiel 1–3; 8–10).

---

[80] *TLRE* 1.12 (September, 1909), p. 8.
[81] *TLRE* 1.10 (July, 1909), p. 17.

Ezekiel's Vision of the Four Living Creatures and Pentecost

While one might now expect symbolic interpretations of Ezekiel's vision of the four living creatures from the early Pentecostal periodicals, there are also sermons that associate Ezekiel's inaugural vision with Pentecost. In a homily titled, 'Ezekiel's Pentecostal Vision', Charles F. Hettiaratchy perceives that Ezekiel's inaugural vision of the four living creatures in Ezekiel 1 is a vision of Pentecost.[82] He explains, 'I just pass on to you some thoughts the Lord gave me one day as I was on my knees studying the scriptures. I was waiting for a message to deliver at a Bible reading, and the Lord gave me these thoughts.'[83] Hettiaratchy writes,

> These four living creatures were under the throne of God. Upon the throne, there was a Man, that Man is our Elder Brother. He is on the throne. These four living creatures were under the throne. We read of them again in the fourth chapter of the book of Revelation; there we read they were in the midst of the throne and round about the throne. The sixth verse says, 'And before the throne there was a sea of glass like unto crystal; and in the midst of the throne, and round about the throne, were four living creatures.' There is not a word in scripture that is not given for a purpose.[84]

Hettiaratchy compares the throne from John's revelation (Rev. 3.21) to that of Ezekiel's throne. He points out that Ezekiel saw the living creatures under the throne while John saw them on the throne. He concludes that the living creatures are believers, 'We find these overcomers sat on the throne, and we find these four living creatures were on the throne; so to me the logical conclusion is that the four living creatures would be those who are the Bride of Christ, and it seems to me Ezekiel had a vision of Pentecost'.[85] He proposes that

---

[82] *TLRE* 3.2 (November, 1910), p. 1.
[83] *TLRE* 3.2 (November, 1910), p. 1.
[84] *TLRE* 3.2 (November, 1910), p. 1.
[85] *TLRE* 3.2 (November, 1910), p. 1. The early Pentecostals believed they were the Bride of Christ and lived their lives in expectation of the soon return of Christ the King. Hettiaratchy emphasizes,

We have first to be ruled then we become rulers. First, we suffer with Him, then we reign with Him. First, we are ruled and then He chooses us as rulers. In Revelation 3.21 we read, 'To him that overcomes will I grant to sit with Me in My throne, even as I also overcame, and am set down with My Father on His

Ezekiel's fiery description of the vision of the chariot-throne may represent a 'vision of Pentecost or the fire of God'.[86] Hettiaratchy compares the day of Pentecost in Acts 2 with the description of a rushing mighty wind and the cloven tongues of fire that rested upon each one of them as they were all filled with the Holy Ghost with that of Ezekiel's vision of the four living creatures in Ezekiel 1. He concludes that the 'wind' represents the 'baptism of the Holy Spirit' and the 'color of amber' as 'fire' represents the four living beings as the 'fire-baptized sons of God'.[87]

Hettiaratchy also explains how the cherubim in Ezekiel 1 and 10 are in the presence of God because the Holy Spirit purifies them. He writes that the two cherubim, who stood at each end of the mercy seat, and the Shekinah glory that dwelt between these two, were made of solid 'genuine' gold.[88] For Hettiaratchy, the mercy seat is related to Jesus Christ, and he concludes that since the cherubim were made of the same piece of gold, so the Bride (cf. Revelation 4) must partake of the very nature of the Bridegroom, of the nature of the slain Lamb.[89] He explains,

> We also read that the cherubim are made of beaten gold. These are all types and there is teaching in them; we must be of beaten gold. We must have that love that is without dissimulation, the love of God shed abroad in our hearts, not merely the outer coating, the gold plating, but through and through gold. The Holy Ghost is purifying the gold now. Who shall stand when He appears; He is like a refiner's fire? He shall sit as a refiner and purifier of silver and purify the sons of Levi. The Holy Ghost is to purify us until we become like beaten gold, to be shaped and fashioned unto his image, so that when the Bridegroom comes the Bride may be prepared to meet Him.[90]

---

throne.' The overcomers shall sit on the throne, and we are looking forward to the day when the Lord Jesus Christ will come in the glory of the Father and His holy angels, and on His vesture and on His thigh a name written, KING OF KINGS AND LORD OF LORDS. He is coming as King of kings, and somebody will reign with Him in His kingdom.

[86] *TLRE* 3.2 (November, 1910), p. 1.
[87] *TLRE* 3.2 (November, 1910), p. 2.
[88] *TLRE* 3.2 (November, 1910), p. 2.
[89] *TLRE* 3.2 (November, 1910), p. 2.
[90] *TLRE* 3.2 (November, 1910), p. 3.

Hettiaratchy argues that there are seven characteristics that are emphasized in Ezekiel's vision of the four living creatures (Ezek. 1.4-27). The first feature is related to 'walking upright' before the Lord, and he interprets the 'living creatures' as human beings and not angelic beings since they had the appearance of the likeness of a man.[91] He highlights that the straight feet 'signify that there is no crooked walk with them'.[92] Hettiaratchy states that the second characteristic emphasizes 'toughness' because the sole of their feet was like the sole of a calf's foot.[93] He concludes that the calf's foot is made hard so that he [the believer] may walk in the rough places of the earth without being hurt.[94] Hettiaratchy connects John's vision of the glorified Jesus with feet that were like the color of burnished brass, with the prophecy of Isaiah, 'How beautiful upon the mountains are the feet of them that brings good tidings'.[95] He uses these connections to conclude that the feet that 'sparkled like the color of burnished brass' in Ezekiel 1 must represent feet that are shod with the preparation of the Gospel of peace and witnesses for God.[96]

Hettiaratchy contends that the third characteristic is portrayed in Ezek. 1.8, 'And they had the hands of a man under their wings on their four sides'.[97] He interprets that the hands of a man mean, 'they used their hands, but those hands are covered with wings. Wings signify a heavenly nature, and whatever they did with their hands they were covered with a heavenly nature and they did all to the glory of God.'[98] For Hettiaratchy, the fourth characteristic deals with how the living beings' wings were joined one to another as a 'sign of real unity among the saints of God'.[99] He connects the storm motif and the Spirit to interpret that fire represents God's testing, which he posits is for the purpose to unify the believers. Again, Hettiaratchy makes correlations between the day of Pentecost and Ezekiel 1. He describes the unity of the disciples who were of one accord and one

---

[91] *TLRE* 3.2 (November, 1910), p. 3.
[92] *TLRE* 3.2 (November, 1910), p. 4.
[93] *TLRE* 3.2 (November, 1910), p. 4
[94] *TLRE* 3.2 (November, 1910), p. 4
[95] *TLRE* 3.2 (November, 1910), p. 4.
[96] *TLRE* 3.2 (November, 1910), p. 4.
[97] *TLRE* 3.2 (November, 1910), p. 4.
[98] *TLRE* 3.2 (November, 1910), p. 4.
[99] *TLRE* 3.2 (November, 1910), p. 5.

mind when they were all filled with the Holy Ghost with the storm motif and the unity in Ezekiel 1.[100]

Hettiaratchy interprets the four faces in Ezek. 1.8b-10 symbolically: (1) the face likened to that of a 'man' represents 'humanity', (2) the face likened to that of a 'lion' represents the king of all beasts and is made bold and fearless by the Holy Spirit, (3) the face that is likened to an 'ox' represents the 'beast of burden that carries heavy loads, more over are they patient and forbearing', and (4) the face likened to that of the 'eagle' represents 'one that is never weary of life as we fly upward'.[101] His fifth feature highlights the characteristic of 'humility' because the four living creatures' wings, which covered their bodies, meant that they were not seen and represents a sign of humility (Ezek. 1. 11-12).[102] He proposes that 'the burning coals of fire' depicted in Ezek. 1.13 symbolizes the seventh characteristic, a passion or the baptism of the Spirit.[103] He states that this fire 'sets our hearts aglow with the love of God because he who dwells in love, dwells in God, for God is love'.[104] For Hettiaratchy, 'baptism in the Spirit means baptism into God, and the baptism of the Spirit means baptism of love, for God is love'.[105] He also interprets the storm and fire motifs symbolically to epitomize the 'unseen power of God that when it comes to touch the people they are set aflame'.[106] From this perspective, he connects the baptism of the Spirit with the symbol of fire and the idea of love.

Hettiaratchy perceives that the 'wheel within a wheel' in Ezek. 1.15-21 symbolizes the final characteristic of submission. He states, 'The wheel within a wheel signifies that the small wheel is your will, and the big wheel is God's will. The work of the Holy Ghost is to blend our wills with the will of God, and as the big wheel turns, the small wheel will turn along with it, and the four living creatures were in the wheels, moving right along in the center of God's will.'[107] He concludes that the likeness of a man above the firmament in Ezek. 1.22, is 'the Man that is our Elder Brother on the throne, in the place

[100] *TLRE* 3.2 (November, 1910), p. 5.
[101] *TLRE* 3.2 (November, 1910), p. 5.
[102] *TLRE* 3.2 (November, 1910), p. 5.
[103] *TLRE* 3.2 (November, 1910), p. 5.
[104] *TLRE* 3.2 (November, 1910), p. 5.
[105] *TLRE* 3.2 (November, 1910), p. 6.
[106] *TLRE* 3.2 (November, 1910), p. 6.
[107] *TLRE* 3.2 (November, 1910), p. 6.

of majesty and place of glory at the right hand of God. He ever lives to make intercession for us.'[108] He also highlights that the clarity of the throne means that there are 'no clouds of doubts and fears, and unbelief and discouragement; all these things come from the devil, and when the devil comes, we must resist him. And when the prophet saw this vision, he fell upon his face.'[109] For Hettiaratchy, Ezekiel 1 represents seven characteristics that are a result of the baptism of the Spirit likened to the day of Pentecost.

The Hand of the Lord in Ezekiel

The phrase, 'the hand of the Lord' is often times referenced in this periodical and continues to provide evidence of how the early Pentecostals associated the visions in the book of Ezekiel with their own experiences or manifestations of the Spirit of God. Myland writes several articles regarding the numerous times that he was miraculously healed, then delivered 'by death', and called to preach. Myland asserts that his deliverance comes from his belief that 'For we which live are always delivered unto death and that the life also of Jesus might be made manifest in our mortal flesh' (2 Cor. 4.10-14).[110] In one of his entries, he emphasizes the phrase 'the hand of the Lord' in Ezekiel 37 as it relates to his last or 'seventh' deliverance. He pens,

> That was my first Pentecostal message. I tell you it was not I that spoke. It was God's 'the hand of the Lord was strong upon me' like Ezekiel. When the Spirit of the Lord gets you, then the hand of the Lord is upon you. Your spirit may shrink, but the hand of the Lord is upon you. He carried me away. First, He carried me up, then He carried me out into service to other people, and that is why I am here tonight.[111]

From this passage, Myland perceives that 'the hand of the Lord' is synonymous with the Spirit of the Lord who 'carried' him, likened to the way in which Ezekiel's visions use the Hebrew idiom in direct relation to the Spirit (Ezek. 3.12-14, 22-24; 8.1-3; 37.1; 40.1-3). He continues to write that this experience is the last of his deliverances or a 'death by fire that results in Pentecostal baptism'.[112] Significant

---

[108] *TLRE* 3.2 (November, 1910), p. 7.
[109] *TLRE* 3.2 (November, 1910), p. 7.
[110] *TLRE* 2.3 (December, 1909), p. 5.
[111] *TLRE* 2.3 (December, 1909), p. 6.
[112] *TLRE* 2.3 (December, 1909), p. 6.

for this study, the early Pentecostals closely associate the hand of God with various manifestations of the Spirit, including baptism.

Cossum begins his treatment of the phrase, 'the hand of the Lord' by interpreting the Zionist movement through the lens of Ezekiel's prophecies.[113] He chooses another Ezekiel passage to add support, 'Can your heart endure, or can your hands be strong, in the days that I shall deal with thee? I, the Lord, have spoken it, and will do it. And I will scatter thee among the heathen and disperse thee in the countries, and I will consume thy filthiness out of thee' (Ezek. 22.14-18). Cossum states, 'God has been scattering his people for the purpose of taking the dross out of them in that way'.[114] He emphasizes Ezek. 22.21-22, 'I will scatter you among all the nations, and then I will call you in my fiery wrath, in your unbelief and with my judgment still upon you. I will call you up to Jerusalem and then I will pour my wrath upon you'. Cossum concludes,

> Two of these scriptures point to the time of complete and final restoration with no more scattering, and the other two speak, I believe, of the gathering of Israel in unbelief just before The Great Tribulation. Judah was carried away to Babylon because of the sin of idolatry. They have been cured of their idolatry, because they have never since lapsed into idolatry, and therefore, they must have repented, and God because of their repentance, returned them from their captivity after seventy years. Israel was again scattered in the year 70 A.D., this time because of their rejection of the Messiah, the great sin of Calvary. They have never repented of the sin of rejecting Jesus, and therefore are still scattered. Seventy years as compared with eighteen centuries! Here is food for thought![115]

Ezekiel's Visions and the Latter Rain Motif

In one of Cossum's last sermons, he draws connections to passages in Ezekiel with modern day applications. He interprets the prophecy of judgment and promise in Ezek. 34.20-31 as a latter-rain promise that the Lord will rescue his scattered and persecuted people to give them hope that they will return to their land.[116] For Cossum, one of

---

113 *TLRE* 2.7 (April, 1910), p. 4.
114 *TLRE* 2.10 (May, 1910), p. 5.
115 *TLRE* 2.10 (May, 1910), p. 5.
116 *TLRE* 2.1 (October, 1910), p. 17.

the 'marvels of prophecy is that the Bible is supernatural' and lends itself to a modern-day interpretation.[117] For example, he asserts that the Jews who were scattered to Romania and Russia were persecuted, but God will restore them to their land. Cossum states, 'we are supposed to be a type in a microcosm, a little world now for that which a whole world will be in the millennium'.[118] He asserts that the latter-rain connection is depicted in Ezek. 34.25-26, 'I will make a covenant of peace ... I will send down showers in season and there will be showers of blessing'.[119]

Vision and Prophecy of Ezekiel's Dry Bones (Ezek. 37.1-14)

W.H. Cossum utilizes several passages from the book of Ezekiel to interpret the prophecies in Ezekiel 34, 36, and 37 in light of contemporary Jews who were scattered to many nations. The first sermon is titled 'Mountain Peaks of Prophecy and Sacred History of the Indestructible Jew'.[120] Cossum interprets the passage, Ezek. 36.6–26, as a prophecy that was fulfilled in its time, but also lends itself to support that God will continue to fulfill his promises to the scattered 'indestructible' Jews throughout the centuries.[121]

In Ezekiel 37, there are two prophecies: (1) The dry bones, and (2) The two sticks. In this passage, the Lord tells Ezekiel that the bones were very dry, and he should put flesh upon them, and that Ezekiel should prophesy unto the רוח ('wind') that it might breathe upon them so that they 'might live'. Cossum observes the 'breath' as a type of the Holy Spirit and that this prophecy represents a time when the dead, dry, and scattered Israel will be filled with the Holy Spirit.[122] He asks a rhetorical question,

> Are the Jews in their own land? They are going back but they have not been in their own land, except a very small fragment of them. But notice how clear the interpretation of the prophecy. The Lord distinctly says here it is the *whole* house of Israel, and the coming of the wind is the coming of the Holy Spirit, which God will pour

---

[117] *TLRE* 2.1 (October, 1910), p. 17.
[118] *TLRE* 2.1 (October, 1910), p. 18.
[119] *TLRE* 2.1 (October, 1910), p. 18.
[120] *TLRE* 2.7 (April, 1910), p. 1.
[121] *TLRE* 2.7 (April, 1910), p. 3.
[122] *TLRE* 2.7 (April, 1910), p. 3.

upon them when He restores them to the land. He has spoken and it will be done.[123]

Cossum states that the Jewish people have never been united since their first separation, but they will be united according to Ezekiel's prophecy as they are called back to their land (Ezek. 37.15-28). He combines the Ezekiel text with Hosea and Amos 9 to conclude that the same promise is in all three texts; the Jews will not be scattered anymore.[124] Cossum states that he disagrees with many commentators who say that the prophecies were satisfied after the Jews returned from Babylon. But Cossum contends this view is impossible for the Jews had a worse scattering and scourging under Titus in 70 CE than they ever had before.[125]

Cossum describes that just like the ancient Jews returned to Jerusalem from Babylon, the terms 'hard heartedness' in Ezekiel 36 is associated with the modern Jews that are coming back to their own land in 'unbelief' before the tribulation time and before the coming of Christ.[126] He uses the aforementioned Ezekiel texts and Zephaniah to support his argument that the 'Jews are in the providence of God, being turned, as Ezekiel puts it, into God's fire-pot, or as Zephaniah gives it, they are getting ahead of God and going up in unbelief before the day of the Lord'.[127] Cossum describes the modern Jews as spiritually strong. He states, 'they are not strong in the ordinary acceptance of that term, but they have a strong spiritual nature. They have spiritual capacity, and when the time comes, they will be touched and quickened, and purified by the blood of Jesus Christ. They will be filled with the outpoured Spirit of God, and they will be a tremendous power.'[128] For Cossum Ezekiel 36–37 is interpreted through the 'latter rain' motif because he views that these chapters describe how the ancient Jews and the modern Jews are in need of God's outpouring of the Spirit to renew, sanctify, and give them a new heart to accept God.[129]

---

[123] *TLRE* 2.7 (April, 1910), p. 4.
[124] *TLRE* 2.7 (April, 1910), p. 4.
[125] *TLRE* 2.7 (April, 1910), p. 4.
[126] *TLRE* 2.10 (May, 1910), p. 5.
[127] *TLRE* 2.10 (May, 1910), p. 5.
[128] *TLRE* 2.10 (May, 1910), p. 7.
[129] *TLRE* 2.11 (August, 1910), pp. 1-2.

Summary

The Latter Rain Evangel gives further testimony to the influence that the book of Ezekiel had upon early Pentecostal spirituality. These writers generally interpreted Ezekiel's visions through their present-day experiences. They viewed the Pentecostal doctrine of Spirit baptism, which included visions and other manifestations by the Spirit, as part of their perception of the latter rain motif. Specifically, this periodical highlights voices that read Ezekiel through a NT lens. For example, they used: (1) symbolism to interpret Ezekiel's four living beings to conclude that the creatures represent the 'Bride of Christ', (2) correlates the throne vision in John's revelation with Ezekiel's throne vision, and (3) read Ezekiel's inaugural vision in light of the day of Pentecost found in Acts.

Pentecostal Evangel

The fifth finished work periodical went through several names. It was first published in 1913 as the *Christian Evangel (CE)*.[130] Founders J. Roswell and Alice Flower created the *Christian Evangel* to report on revivals and missions' activities from around the globe. It was also called the *Weekly Evangel (WE)* from 1915 to 1919, coinciding with the General Council locating its headquarters in St. Louis, Missouri.[131] The name *Christian Evangel* returned when the headquarters moved to Springfield, Missouri, its current location.[132] The last name it settled upon was the *Pentecostal Evangel (PE)*.[133] *PE* was chosen because of the 'initial evidence controversy' and the desire to 'speak out with conviction for the distinctiveness of the Pentecostal position'. Bell was the managing editor of both periodicals for a brief period of

---

[130] The *Christian Evangel* was published at Plainfield, IN from Jul 19, 1913 to Jul 4, 1914, at Findlay, OH from Jul 11, 1914 to Jan 30, 1915, and at St. Louis, MO from Feb 13, 1915 to Mar 6, 1915.

[131] The *Weekly Evangel* was published at St. Louis from Mar 13, 1915 to May 18, 1918. This name change was at the request of the Post Office which had another publication with a similar name being published from St. Louis, Joseph R. Flower, 'The *Evangel's* Roots', *PE* 4132 (Jul 18, 1993), pp. 7, 22 (p. 22).

[132] The *Christian Evangel* was published at Springfield, MO from Jun 1, 1918 to Oct 4, 1919, and on Jul 1, 1918 it became bi-weekly for the duration of this study's window. 'Due to paper shortage and high production cost brought on by World War I, the Weekly Evangel went bi-weekly' and returned to weekly in March 1923, Joseph R. Flower, 'The *Evangel's* Roots', *PE* 4132 (Jul 18, 1993), pp. 7, 22 (p. 22).

[133] The *Pentecostal Evangel* was published at Springfield, MO from Oct 18, 1919 to Jun 9, 2002.

time.[134] It appears that these writers were also conditioned by their eschatological beliefs.[135] For example, as one writer wrote, 'The most important of all messages, and one which the Holy Ghost emphasizes above everything else is this: "Jesus is coming soon"'.[136] The second coming of Jesus was not just another important doctrine to be believed, it was an imminent reality they thought would come to pass in their lifetime. The signs were everywhere that the return of Jesus was near. One article observes, 'Jesus is coming. The skies are darkening. The clouds are lowering. The lightings are flashing. The thunders are rolling. The signs are multiplying that proclaim the birth throes of the new creation are at hand.'[137] Many also testified to astronomical phenomenon they labeled as 'signs in the heavens'.[138]

There were many testimonies of revival, which included the baptism in the Spirit. Some of these testified that they received visions, not unlike Ezekiel. A two and half month revival meeting held by Reverend S.D. Kinne and his wife exclaimed that 'thirty-four people were saved and baptized. It looked like Ezekiel's vision and the resurrection of the dry bones that came together.'[139]

As previously discussed, early Pentecostals were influenced by the promise in Joel that God will pour out the Spirit, which was accompanied by a promise that God would give 'visions' and 'dreams'. Many of whom testified to having received visions of the coming of Christ.[140]

For example, during a 1917 Maria Woodworth-Etter meeting, an attendee noted there were 'strong messages given in the Spirit in

---

[134] This was 'during the interval from July 1914 to March 1915 when the national headquarters was located in Findlay, Ohio', Joseph R. Flower, 'The *Evangel's* Roots', *PE* 4132 (Jul 18, 1993), pp. 7, 22 (p. 22).

[135] *WE* 85 (Apr 10, 1915), p. 1; 'Signs of the Approaching End', *WE* 206 (Sep 8, 1917), p. 8; James McAlister, 'Startling Signs of the End', *PE* 248/249 Second Coming Supplement (Sep 10, 1920), pp. 1-3; 'Signs of the Times', *PE* 526 (Dec 15, 1923), p. 8.

[136] D.H. McDowell, 'The Purpose of the Coming of the Lord', *PE* 595 (May 2, 1925), p. 2.

[137] 'How Long', *WE* 236/237 (Apr 20, 1918), p. 8.

[138] *WE* 10.1 (Jan 20, 1914) p. 1; *PE* 203 (Aug 18, 1917), p. 13; *PE* 201(Aug 4 1917), p. 11; *PE* 204 (Aug 25, 1917), p. 11; *PE* 799 (May 25, 1929), p. 11; *PE* 1346 (Feb 24, 1940), p. 3.

[139] *WE* 133 (April 01, 1916), p. 15.

[140] *PE* 526 (Dec 15, 1923), p. 3; *PE* 189 (May 12, 1917), p. 4; *PE* 207 (Sept 15, 1917), p. 15; *PE* (Nov 11, 1922), p. 14. Such testimonies disappear after the mid 1920s.

other languages, with clear interpretation relative to the imminent appearing of our Lord, and the urgent need of the bride to make herself ready'.[141] There were also testimonies of visions in which the Spirit revealed the details of the coming events that often reinforced commonly accepted interpretations of prophetic texts.[142]

Alice Evelyn Luce offers numerous articles that were taken from her book *Pictures of Pentecost: In the Old Testament* in *WE* and advertised in the *PE*. Four articles are written about Ezekiel: (1) 'The Ever-Deepening River: Ezekiel's vision of the waters to swim in', (2) 'Spirit-filled Messenger: Ezekiel's Pentecostal Visions', (3) 'Men that are a Sign: Ezekiel's Pentecostal Experiences', and (4) 'Life from the Dead: Dry bones turned into a living army as described by Ezekiel'.[143] Luce calls the prophet Ezekiel, 'the prophet of the Holy Ghost' and exhorts her readers to consider that the entire book be read as an example of 'a life abandoned to the Spirit of God'.[144] In the first article, Luce attributes the water to be as a symbol of the Holy Spirit as appeared on the Day of Pentecost. She attributes the vision in Ezekiel 47 as 'a picture of the Holy Spirit bringing life and fertility wherever its waters came', which was a foreshadow of the day of Pentecost when the promise of the baptism of the Holy Spirit would be given first to the disciples.[145] Luce describes the 'ever-deepening waters' in Ezekiel 47 as stages of the life of service one is called to after the baptism of the Spirit. She states, 'the beginning of our life of service for Jesus, is only the starting point of an ever-deepening experience of His power. This speaks to us of what will always be the first result of the Spirit's power in us, namely a consistent walk'.[146] Luce continues to compare the next level of water is 'the Spirit's

---

[141] 'Mighty Warnings of the Imminence of the Lord's coming at the Woodworth-Etter Meetings in Los Angeles California', *WE* 168 (Apr 21, 1917), p. 14.

[142] 'Prophetic Vision of the Lord's Second Coming, the Great Tribulation and the End of the World', *PE* 338/339 (May 1, 1920), pp. 1-3; J.N. Gortner, '666', *CE* 284/285 (Apr 19, 1919), pp. 1-2; *CE* 288/289 (May 17, 1919), p. 3; 'Remarkable Visions of Things to Come', *PE* 526 (Dec 15, 1923), p. 3. It is interesting to note that in each of these visions, the events described did not deviate from the common premillennial and dispensational script.

[143] *WE* 171 (Jan 6, 1917), pp. 4-5; *WE* 207 (Sept 15, 1917), pp. 6-7, *WE* 210 (Oct 13,1917), pp. 8-9, *WE* 211 (Oct 20, 1917), p. 6, and *PE* 340/341 (May 15, 1920), p. 15.

[144] *WE* 171 (Jan 6, 1917), p. 4.

[145] *WE* 171 (Jan 6, 1917), p. 4.

[146] *WE* 171 (Jan 6, 1917), p. 4.

control of our prayer life'.[147] As the waters rise to the loins, Luce associates the term 'loins' with strength and states, 'clearly the next result of the Spirit's power in our lives is strength of character manifested, also a detachment from earthly things, and a readiness of mind to serve the Lord and run on His errands'.[148] Luce goes on to exhort her readers that 'how often we have grown cold in our service and our ministry has seemed to dry up, just because we have not let the Lord lead us on into those waters to swim in'.[149] She describes that the waters in Ezekiel 47 that were too high to pass over is the ultimate 'glorious fullness of this pentecostal experience upon which we have entered! Here we see for the first time in this vision a picture of utter abandonment to the Spirit of God.'[150]

In Luce's second article, she asserts that the whirlwind and the fire are symbols of the Holy Spirit and that 'the cherubim spoke in pictures to the saints of OT days what is so clearly revealed in the New Testament'.[151] She describes these cherubim 'as a prophecy of salvation and restitution at the closed portals of Eden. They were shown as a pattern of perfect service to Ezekiel, and reappearing as the four Living Creatures of Revelation in the very midst of the throne with Jesus.'[152] Luce continues to describe how she views these cherubim as servants 'carrying the knowledge of the Lord to others, going as His representatives to extend His kingdom and increase the number of those who will own Him as their King'.[153] Luce encourages her readers to view 'the four faces of the cherubim in light of the Four-fold Gospel' and that 'these Spirit-filled messengers possess godly characteristics'.[154]

Luce's third article cites several references to the ways in which Ezekiel, the prophet was called as a sign. She argues that the book of Ezekiel emphasizes the call to believers to live a life of abandonment to the Spirit of God because it shows how 'the obedient, surrendered prophet is told that he is to be God's sign to the disobedient,

---

[147] *WE* 171 (Jan 6, 1917), p. 4.
[148] *WE* 171 (Jan 6, 1917), p. 5.
[149] *WE* 171 (Jan 6, 1917), p. 5.
[150] *WE* 171 (Jan 6, 1917), p. 5.
[151] *WE* 207 (Sept 15, 1917), p. 6.
[152] *WE* 207 (Sept 15, 1917), p. 6.
[153] *WE* 207 (Sept 15, 1917), pp. 6-7.
[154] *WE* 207 (Sept 15, 1917), pp. 6-7.

unbelieving people'.[155] Luce attributes the Latter Rain outpouring of the Spirit as the power of the Spirit coming upon believers and causing them to lie prostrate. However, she testifies to 'many times those under the power, unconscious of the things of time and sense, have been seen to weep, mourn, and groan over those who were rejecting Christ, as they have seen visions of hell and judgment to come, and have been made to realize the exceeding sinfulness of sin'.[156] Luce does not go so far to say that Ezekiel interceded for the Israelites while laying prostrate under the power of God, but she believes that he was humbled before the Lord and shown his sin and the sin of the people.[157]

Luce's final article on Ezekiel is about the working of the Spirit of God in Ezekiel's vision of valley of dry bones (Ezek. 37.1-14). She claims that the Spirit breathed life into the dry, dead bones and 'were transformed into a host of living warriors by the entrance of the breath of God!'[158] She distinguishes between the infusion of 'the Spirit of God brings power of the Spirit, but it is the breath of God that comes to impart new life'.[159] Luce laments how the church needs 'an infusion of the Spirit of God to bring life and power', but also that the church needs 'prophets, men of strong faith, humble enough to get His message, and bold enough to proclaim it without fear or favor'.[160] She believes that it takes 'the mighty infilling of the Spirit of God to preach to dry bones and without becoming dried up oneself' and Ezekiel gives the example of 'success when he tells us that it is the hand of the Lord that comes upon him and the Spirit of the Lord is the one who carried him out'.[161]

The Bridal Call

Cecil Robeck, Jr. observes that Aimee Semple McPherson was the most prominent woman from the early Pentecostal movement. She was the founder of the International Church of the Foursquare Gospel (ICFG), which was theologically based upon her sermons from

---

155 *WE* 210 (Oct 13,1917), p. 8.
156 *WE* 210 (Oct 13,1917), pp. 8-9.
157 *WE* 210 (Oct 13,1917), pp. 8-9.
158 *WE* 211 (Oct 20, 1917), p. 6.
159 *WE* 211 (Oct 20, 1917), p. 6.
160 *WE* 211 (Oct 20, 1917), p. 6.
161 *WE* 211 (Oct 20, 1917), p. 6.

Ezekiel's inaugural vision (Ezek. 1.4-10).[162] McPherson began her monthly magazine, *The Bridal Call* (*TBC*) and was the editor between the relevant dates of June 1917 and December 1920. The journal eventually became the official publication of the ICFG. McPherson wrote many articles based upon her ministry teachings. She writes,

> While in Savannah, Ga., the first editions of the Bridal Call, our monthly magazine, were printed. The Lord had been laying it upon my heart to edit such a paper, and gave me, Himself, the name — THE BRIDAL CALL and the cover design, the Lord appearing in the clouds, and the angels with their trumpets. Over and over the Lord spoke to me, Write the vision and make it plain, that he may run who reads it. Hab. 2.2.[163]

McPherson wrote several autobiographical works in her lifetime.[164] Regarding her initial hesitancy to publish *The Bridal Call*, she pens,

> At first, I hesitated, saying that there are so many Pentecostal papers, and more capable writers who are able to give their entire time and thought to the matter. It would be impossible for me having no office, nor abiding city, holding many meetings, traveling in the Gospel car, mothering the children, and many other things, to write or take the burden of a paper. The Lord replied, 'With me, nothing is impossible'. He showed me His exact plan for the Bridal Call; that its message was not to be one of

---

[162] For a brief biography of Aimee Semple McPherson, see Cecil Robeck Jr., 'McPherson, Aimee Semple', in *NIDPCM,* pp. 856-59. Robeck highlights her contributions to the Pentecostal tradition, as she was a prolific writer, musician, communicator, and the founder of the ICFG. First, she and her first husband, Robert Semple were ordained by William H. Durham on January 2, 1909. In 1919 Aimee received ordination with the Assemblies of God (AG) as an evangelist and held these credentials until January 5, 1922, when she returned her fellowship papers to general council chairman. When her ministry continued, she received a membership in the Hancock Memorial Methodist Church, the Methodist Episcopal Church, and the First Baptist Church in San Jose. In 1923 the Angeles Temple was dedicated and in 1923 the International Church of the Foursquare Gospel (ICFG) was born. See also, Edith Blumhofer, *Aimee Semple McPherson: Everybody's Sister* (Grand Rapids: Eerdmans,1993).

[163] Aimee Semple McPherson, *This is That: Personal Experiences of Aimee Semple McPherson, Evangelist* (ed. Douglas Harrolf; HJ Publishing, 1919), pp. 135-36.

[164] See Robeck, 'McPherson', in *NIDCPCM*, p. 857. Robeck lists several of McPherson's autobiographical works: *This Is That* (1919, 1921, 1923); *The Story of My Life* (1951); *Divine Healing Sermons*; *Fire from on High* (1969).

controversy, fighting, great wisdom or eloquence, but simply what its name implied, a call to the bride to prepare for her heavenly Bridegroom. So, whatever reports, testimonies or other matter may be in the paper, we endeavor to have one article making plain the way of salvation, one on the baptism of the Holy Ghost, and one on the coming of the Lord and the preparation to meet Him. So plainly the Lord spoke, giving me articles to write, in such bursts of revelation that the tears streamed down my face, while my fingers flew over the typewriter keys.[165]

Later, in 1921 McPherson published *The Bridal Call* from Angelus Temple at Echo Park an interdenominational church that she built and purchased herself.[166] She writes, 'The Lord is now opening for us *The Bridal Call Publishing House*, centrally located at 125 South Spring Street, Los Angeles, Cal., and has commissioned a brother here to print it, so that now we will be able to send the paper promptly on a given date'.[167]

Inspired from her sermon on Ezek. 1.4-10, McPherson founded the ICFG. She preached Jesus as Savior, Baptizer in the Holy Spirit, Healer, and Coming King from her interpretation of Ezekiel's inaugural vision of the glory of God. In her first editorial of *The Bridal Call*, McPherson records a teaching from her interpretation of Ezek. 1.4-10. McPherson explains that the background to Ezekiel's inaugural vision represents the theme of judgment in the OT.[168] She argues that there is present in Ezekiel's vision the idea of the indignation of an angry God that will fall upon the Israelite nation of idolaters because they had transgressed his Law.[169] However, McPherson also perceives that Ezekiel's inaugural vision of the glory of God represents God's grace. She observes that there is a distinction with the 'north wind' that is surrounded in light or the 'whirlwind' that comes from the north (Ezek. 1.4) from any other preceding wind in the OT, because it has an unfolding light within it.[170] McPherson points out that this wind did not have a mystery of black darkness, but rather

---

[165] *TBC* (May, 1920), p. 1.
[166] *NIDCPCM*, p. 857. Angeles Temple held daily services for conversion, healing, the baptism of the Holy Spirit, and the deepening of the spiritual life.
[167] McPherson, *This is That*, p. 137.
[168] *TBC* (May, 1920), p. 1.
[169] *TBC* (May, 1920), p. 1.
[170] *TBC* (May, 1920), p. 1.

was full of light, brightness in it as it is the color of amber. She exclaims, 'What a vision! What a revelation came to Ezekiel through the fiery cloud that day! And what a picture, vision, revelation of a cloud of Grace, and of a fiery power of the glory of the four-fold, four square Gospel which it contains, comes to us through the vision of Ezekiel today!'[171]

McPherson continues,

> And out of the midst of the cloud there comes the four-square Gospel of our Lord and Savior, Jesus Christ, as the four living creatures of the appearance of a Man. The Gospel which is borne to us is indeed a four-square Gospel facing the world four square, revealing four different faces or phases of the Gospel, all of which bear faithful likeness to man, Jesus Christ.[172]

She concludes that the first face, which Ezekiel caught a glimpse of was the face of the man who is Jesus Christ the only Savior, gazing upon the four-square Gospel. She describes 'the face of the man' as: (1) 'The Victorious Conqueror' who returns from the wilderness, (2) 'The Good Shepherd' who feeds his flock, and (3) 'The Intercessor' who prays alone on the mountainside.[173]

McPherson discerns that the second face Ezekiel saw was the lion, which is the symbol of Jesus Christ, who is the baptizer with the Holy Spirit. She states, 'also we see in the living word the lion of the tribe of Judah, the all glorious baptizer with the Holy Ghost and fire'.[174] McPherson writes that the third face, which Ezekiel saw, was the face of an ox that represents Jesus Christ, the Great Physician.[175] She explains that the ox is the 'burden bearer, the patient, plodding, unfaltering, and sacrificial burden bearer'.[176] The fourth face is that of the eagle, and represents Jesus the soon coming King. McPherson describes, 'the eagle with its piercing gaze that looks into the high and lofty heavens with its searching gaze that sights and notes the smallest objects in the earth beneath, is the eagle that soars in the clouds'.[177] Similar to some of her predecessors, McPherson symbolically

---

[171] *TBC* (May, 1920), p. 1.
[172] *TBC* (1920, 05), p. 1. *TBC* 8.3 (August, 1923), p. 6.
[173] *TBC* (1920, 05), p. 1. *TBC* 8.3 (August, 1923), p. 6.
[174] *TBC* (1920, 05), p. 1. *TBC* 8.3 (August, 1923), p. 6.
[175] *TBC* (1920, 05), p. 1. *TBC* 8.3 (August, 1923), p. 6.
[176] *TBC* (1920, 05), p. 1. *TBC* 8.3 (August, 1923), p. 6.
[177] *TBC* 8.3 (August, 1923), p. 6.

interprets Ezekiel's vision of the four living beings. She does not interpret the faces as the 'Bride of Christ', but rather she perceives that the four faces are representations of Christ in light of her theological views of Jesus and the Spirit of God.

The Spirit and 'The Hand of the Lord was Upon Me'

McPherson does not directly cite the phrase, 'the hand of the Lord was upon me' as seen frequently in the book of Ezekiel. However, she appears to connect the ideas of 'knowing' the Lord and receiving visions with the hand of the Lord. She states,

> What a wonderful thing it is for an individual to know that the hand of the Lord is upon him! Away down in Florida, when we were preaching to the dear colored people, they used to love to sing this verse: 'Chil'en, Ah knows de Lawd, Chil'en, Ah knows de Lawd, Ah knows de Lawd, Dun got His han' on me, and O, this afternoon I am so conscious of the hand of the Lord resting upon me. Praise His Name!'[178]

McPherson emphasizes the connections between the 'hand of the Lord' and the Spirit in Ezekiel's visions. She cites, 'the hand of the Lord was upon me and carried me out in the Spirit of the Lord' (Ezek. 1.28; 10.4). She highlights,

> This was by no means the first time the hand of the Lord had been upon Ezekiel. Had he not been caught up unto mountain-tops of Revelation? Had he not seen the four living creatures, the cherubim and the Ark? Had he not beheld the glory of the Lord? The mighty moving of his power seen in Ezek. 1.28 and 10.4. Doubtless, when the hand of the Lord came down upon him and carried him out in the Spirit, Ezekiel longed to be lifted again to some ethereal height of glory. The Lord was moving him out and what wonders was the Lord about to show him now?[179]

McPherson identifies and questions how the prophet Ezekiel might feel as he describes his encounter with the glory of the Lord. She states, 'Have you ever wondered what Ezekiel's feelings must have been when he opened his eyes and discovered that the Lord let him down in the midst of the valley (Ezekiel 37). Being set suddenly

---

[178] *TBC* 8.3 (August, 1923), p. 6.
[179] *TBC* 8.3 (August, 1923), p. 6.

down in a valley after a hilltop experience is enough, but that was not the worst of it, this was a valley WHICH WAS FULL OF BONES.'[180] From this perspective, she observes the affective qualities in the book of Ezekiel in order to draw conclusions about the prophet Ezekiel. McPherson continues to approach the Ezekiel text affectively as she states,

> I think that perhaps some of us know in a little measure how to appreciate and understand what the feelings of Ezekiel were. We, too, have felt the hand of the Lord upon us. We too have, at many times, beheld His glory and dwelt in the midst of life and power. We too have had the Spirit of the Lord set us down in a certain assembly, home, neighborhood, or city wherein we have opened our eyes to discover with a start, that we have been deposited right in the midst of a valley which is literally full of bones.[181]

Summary

It is remarkable that McPherson, as one of the most prominent early Pentecostals, chose to establish the ICFG based upon her theological interpretations of Ezekiel's inaugural vision of the glory of God (Ezek. 1.4-10). She preached Jesus as Savior, Baptizer in the Holy Spirit, Healer, and Coming King directly from a symbolic reading of Ezekiel's vision of the four living beings. Additionally, it is interesting that McPherson ponders how Ezekiel may have felt from the visionary encounter with God. She is the first of the early Pentecostals, noted in this study, who highlights the affective tones in Ezekiel's visions.

IV. Conclusions

The early Pentecostal readings of the Spirit in the visions of Ezekiel offer several points for overall reflection, which may serve to contribute to our contemporary context. The testimonies and sermons from the early Pentecostal groups and their respective periodicals that they represent between the years of 1906 to 1923 reveal that the book of Ezekiel did have direct bearing upon early Pentecostal spirituality, beliefs, and practice. In these early Pentecostal writings, we find

---

[180] *TBC* 8.3 (August, 1923), p. 7.
[181] *TBC* 8.3 (August, 1923), p. 7.

testimonies of their own visions that are directly related to the book of Ezekiel, which both shape and are shaped by the author's experience of what they refer to as their personal Pentecost. Their testimonies were written in such a way as to demonstrate that the vision texts proved to serve as a confirmation for their own visionary experiences. Primarily it was discovered that visions for the early Pentecostals were considered as part of an eschatological promise of the outpouring of the Spirit before the second coming of Christ (Joel 2.28-32). The early Pentecostal literature is filled with testimonies and reports of visions that they regarded as part the 'latter rain' outpouring. These groups perceived that visions as part of the apostolic witness were a result of the outpouring of the Spirit on the day of Pentecost (Acts 2). As such, visions and dreams were not only considered as part of the experiential aspect of early Pentecostal worship and spirituality but were also expected by these communities.[182] From this perspective, at times Ezekiel's visions were interpreted eschatologically, and frequently directly associated with the work of the Spirit. As such, visions were pneumatologically grounded in their spirituality. Additionally, the early Pentecostals saw themselves living in the last days, awaiting the soon coming King and often times interpreted Ezekiel's vision narratives in light of present-day events.

Visions as an eschatological promise as part of the outpouring of the Spirit before the second coming of Christ also encouraged the development of Pentecostal spirituality and teaching regarding their views of Spirit baptism. These early Pentecostals viewed the biblical text as reliable and that it mirrored their own experiences through the testimonies recorded in scripture. They perceived that their visionary experiences and other manifestations of the Spirit were a result of their Spirit baptism, and for some, they also perceived that Ezekiel's inaugural vision was a prophecy of the Pentecostal baptism of the Spirit that was to come. Their beliefs affected their spirituality because they would report how their visionary experiences would lead them to worship God. Specifically, they would describe how they would fall prostrate in worship to God, much like the prophet Ezekiel fell prostrate in his inaugural vision of the glory of YHWH (Ezek. 1.4-28).

---

[182] Hocken, *The Challenges of the Pentecostal, Charismatic, and Messianic Jewish Movements*, p. 9.

Their beliefs and practices regarding Spirit baptism became central to the lives of the men and women during the Azusa Street revival. Generally, the baptism of the Spirit meant that they experienced empowerment to witness, deliverance, and nearness to Christ.[183] Through this survey, it is apparent that early Pentecostals associated the baptism of the Spirit with visions. There are numerous testimonies that draw upon Ezekiel's frequently cited Hebrew idiom of the 'hand of the Lord' and the Spirit as support for their own visionary experiences. Both, the Wesleyan-Pentecostals and the Finished Work Pentecostals include testimonies of how 'the hand of the Lord' was an intense spiritual experience that included (1) visionary transportations by the Spirit, (2) hearing angelic voices, (3) seeing Jesus, his glory, heavenly beings, thrones, and (4) descriptions of overwhelming feelings in the midst of the vision experiences.

Alexander argues that there are significant distinctions in the pneumatology of Wesleyan-Pentecostals and the Finished Work Pentecostals. These two distinct streams among the early Pentecostal literature emerged out of a theological controversy.[184] Alexander explains that for 'Wesleyan-Pentecostals, the Spirit is given and responded to and the believer is transformed' and for Finished-Work Pentecostals, the 'implications are that the Spirit actualizes the work already accomplished by Christ'.[185] This distinction provides the basis for numerous trajectories in the beliefs of the activities of the Spirit's role in the life of the believer. She argues that the relevant issues at hand are the ideas of immanence and transcendence of the Spirit.[186] The Finished Work theology emerging from these early Pentecostals that can be discerned through their testimonies is of a pneumatology that the Spirit's activities are brought in his fullness *now* to the believer.

Alexander explains that for Wesleyan Pentecostals, such as those in the Pentecostal Holiness Church, Spirit baptism is identified as a third experience which follows upon an experience of heart purity,

---

[183] Alexander, *Pentecostal Healing*, p. 78.

[184] Alexander, *Pentecostal Healing*, pp. 77-78. Alexander describes how this schism emerged when Charles Durham resigned his pastorate in Chicago and took his message to the Azusa Street Mission in 1911 to try to convince Wesleyan-Holiness Pentecostals under Seymour's leadership to abandon the second work theology.

[185] Alexander, *Pentecostal Healing*, p. 233.

[186] Alexander, *Pentecostal Healing*, p. 233.

or entire sanctification. This may explain a distinction noted between the testimonies of the visionary experiences described by both streams. The Wesleyan-Pentecostal groups seem to include more testimonies of the affective dimensions of their visionary experiences, though it was McPherson who went so far as to identify the affective language used in Ezekiel's visions as a way to read Ezekiel's vision reports. The Wesleyan-Pentecostals also associated Ezekiel's visions with cleansing and sanctification as some emphasized the symbol of water representing not only the Spirit, but also the cleansing of the believer. For this group, Alexander reports that the Baptism in the Holy Spirit is identified as that which is 'continually abiding and flowing out of you as rivers of living water'.[187] However the theological distinctions were developed, it is evident through this survey that both groups associate 'the hand of the Lord' with manifestations of the Spirit. Both groups also use the Ezekiel text to support the physical manifestations of the Spirit that occurred during their visionary experiences.

Some of the early Pentecostals also interpreted the OT with a NT lens and saw the scriptures Christologically. Thus, the symbolic interpretation of the four living beings was interpreted as the four characterizations of Jesus Christ narrated in the four gospels. It is astonishing that McPherson founded an entire denomination (ICFG) from her theological interpretation of Ezekiel's inaugural vision of the glory of God.

Generally speaking, the contemporary Pentecostal and Charismatic communities can relate to the ways in which these early Pentecostal voices perceived Ezekiel's visions. The idea of encounter with the living God through the Spirit and Scripture was not only expected, but also central to their lives and mission. They understood that an encounter with the Spirit through baptism would not only result in seeing visions and dreams, but also cause them to worship God, and empower them for their mission in the last days as they awaited the second coming of Christ. The early Pentecostals demonstrate a rich spirituality articulated through the pages of these periodicals. They are unabashedly artful in the ways in which they testify of their Pentecostal experience. They describe how their latter rain outpouring of the Spirit has baptized, sanctified, and given them

---

[187] Alexander, *Pentecostal Healing*, p. 234.

tongues, prophecy, and visions and dreams. What has emerged is a fuller understanding of the continuity/discontinuity of Spirit-inspired visions and various other interrelated pneumatological themes these early Pentecostals discerned from the visions in the book of Ezekiel.

5

Overview of Ezekiel's Visions: Genre, Characters, Structure, and Themes

I. Introduction

This chapter provides the study of Ezekiel's visions with an overview of the genre, characters, structure, and themes identified in the vision reports. The purpose of this section is to familiarize the reader with the basic content of Ezekiel's major vision reports and their function within the narrative as a whole. Additionally, it is proposed here that the book is structured according to its genre of prophetic visions. This study utilizes a narrative–theological approach to Ezekiel's visions to identify their genre, main characters, themes, and literary connections. Moreover, I argue that the visions provide the structure for the book.[1] The book has its own distinctive literary style from other prophetic books because of its extended vision narratives marked by its pneumatological emphasis, colorful imagery and poetic flair, mixed with its numerous oracles, autobiographical style, and

---

[1] A narrative theological analysis is utilized as a method owing to its compatibility with the narrative orientation of Pentecostal thought. See Goldingay, 'Biblical Story and the Way it Shapes Our Story', pp. 5-15. For Goldingay meaning is found in the dynamics of the biblical story and our own stories. A Pentecostal hearing of the biblical texts highlights the text in its final form and derives its primary meaning from the narrative. From this perspective, a literary and exegetical analysis of the text will focus on the stories that the narrator tells to understand how they help the reader or hearer derive meaning in the text with special attention given to repetition of literary markers, the structure, genre, and main characters, while drawing theological conclusions.

affective language.[2] Ezekiel's visions underscore the theological themes of the Spirit, the glory of YHWH, the hand of YHWH, and the leitmotif of the affections. It is proposed here that Ezekiel's genre of visions provides the overall structural framework to the book (Ezek. 1–7; 8–36; 37–39; 40–48) and is underscored by Ezekiel's four central vision reports (Ezek. 1–3; 8–11; 37.1–14; 40–48) that are strategically placed in the book. Uniquely, in all four of Ezekiel's visions, the term רוח and variations of the phrase, the יד־יהוה are emphasized in the narratives and are linked to the affective descriptions of Ezekiel's prophetic encounters with YHWH. For example, the shared literary feature of the affective language is used to describe either the emotional disposition of the prophet (1.28; 3.14-15; 43.3), the house of Israel (37.11), or YHWH (8.3-6, 17-18; 43.7-8; 44.4). Thus, the affective language contributes to identifying the structure of the book as well as enhancing the quality of the hearing and imagining of the imagery in the narratives. The following brief overview of Ezekiel's visions provides initial support that the four key vision narratives mark a literary structure that through shared literary features highlights a pneumatological emphasis. The identification of Ezekiel's overarching theme of visions will provide the structural framework to describe the four larger literary units of the entire book, and the four smaller literary units, which are under examination for this study.

---

[2] For a variety of treatments on vision reports, see Lindblom, *Prophecy in Ancient Israel*. Lindblom categorizes visions according to various reports of the prophet's experience and a psychological assessment of prophetic personality. See also, Long, 'Reports of Visions Among the Prophets', pp. 353-65. Long argues, contra to Zimmerli that Ezekiel's prophetic call narrative is related to the common features identified in ancient Near Eastern and Israelite theophany vision or dream reports, in which theophany was a legitimating device (e.g. 1 Kgs 3.5-15). Niditch, *The Symbolic Visions in Biblical Tradition*, argues that as sociological and historical realities change, so the literary form flexibly evolves, thereby remaining a relevant vehicle for prophetic expression. She traces the development through an examination of the language of the visions (from an economical-rhetorical style to narrative prose); their symbols (from everyday objects to complex, otherworldly happenings); and the pattern or structure of content (from a simple question and answer dialogue to dramatic narrative scenes). From a sociological perspective, see Wilson, *Prophecy and Society in Ancient Israel*, pp. 260-63. Wilson argues that the Judean prophet was characteristically a visionary. Stead, 'Prophetic Visions', pp. 818-24.

II. Genre

The book is a composite of visions (chs. 1–3; 8–11; 37.1-14; 40–48), prophetic oracles (eg. chs. 6–7; 12–14; 25–36), sign or symbolic acts (4.1–5.4; 12.1-20; 24.15-18, 24,27; 37.15-28), extended metaphors (chs. 15; 16; 21; 23), laments (ch. 19), and proto-apocalyptic prophecies (chs. 38–39).[3] Narratively, there are numerous ways ancient Israelite seers or visionaries report their encounters or experiences and receive messages from YHWH.[4] Some of these central ways are conveyed through dream or vision reports.[5] Visions occur frequently in both the Old and New Testaments as instruments of supernatural revelation, and at times, in theophanic texts. Although there are distinctions between visions and theophanies, there are similarities as well. Visions and theophanies are both terms that can be associated with biblical reports of divine-human encounters and generally in the HB, theophanies describe the ways in which YHWH discloses, reveals, or allows himself to be seen.[6] Both terms imply a communicative event through non-verbal symbolic imagery, which may include verbal discourse, and imply the presence of divine self-manifestation.[7]

Literarily, vision texts are usually replete with symbolic imagery, metaphors, and anthropomorphic terms that are used to describe the events in these narratives. They function as audiovisual modes of communications between the heavenly realm, which include supernatural beings, and an earthly recipient. The terms used to designate

---

[3] R. Moore and B. Peterson, *Voice, Word, and Spirit: A Pentecostal Old Testament Survey* (Nashville, TN: Abingdon, 2017), pp. 206-15.

[4] Visionary experiences are also found in earlier written prophecy (Amos 7.1-8; 8.1-11; 37.1-14; Isaiah 6; Jer. 4.23-26; 24.1-10). In the history of interpretation there have been a number of approaches employed in attempts to define the genre of prophetic visions: (1) Psychological approaches that attempt to analyze the experience of the prophet, (2) Categorizing visions into various types based upon structure, content, and intention, (3) Historical analysis that attempts to trace the development of the traditions, dates, and events, and (4) Form-critical analysis.

[5] The semantic overlap between dreams and visions is present in various biblical accounts. For example, not all dreams are prophetic visions (e.g. Gen. 20.3), and a prophetic vision may also be demonstrated in a dream (e.g. Daniel 7; Zech. 4.1).

[6] Jeffrey Niehaus, 'Theology of Theophany', in *NIDOTTE*, III, pp. 1247-50. The connection between the traditional theophanies and Ezekiel 1 can be seen in the biblical narratives (Deut. 33:2) and in the storm theophanies (Hab. 3.4-6).

[7] For the discussion of ראה ('see') see Jackie A. Naudé, in *NIDOTTE*, III, pp. 1007-15. For a discussion of חזון ('vision') in relation to theophany see also, Naudé, in *NIDOTTE*, II, pp. 56-61.

visions in both Testaments include verbs of 'seeing' and 'perceiving'. Although this list is not exhaustive, two key HB terms commonly associated with visions are ראה ('see, have visions, look at, appear, or make oneself visible'), and its variable form, מראה ('sight, appearance, or supernatural vision').[8] The semantic range of meanings of the verb include: 'to discern', 'to discover', 'to encounter', 'to know', 'to perceive', and 'to understand'.[9] The theological use of ראה in the HB indicates the wide range of descriptions that are used to convey these reports of divine-human encounters. One of the distinguishing literary features included in the book of Ezekiel is the emphasis placed upon the numerous prophetic vision reports. The term ראה occurs approximately 73 times in the book.[10]

The vision reports are literarily connected to each other, which underscores the importance of the visions as the book's primary literary setting. Prophetic speeches are also prominent in the book as they are embedded in the vision narratives and serve to develop the plot from beginning to end. The emphasis placed upon these key terms to identify the book's genre is also supported by its main characters illustrated in the vision narratives.

III. The Main Characters Portrayed in Ezekiel's Vision Reports

While there are a plethora of characters mentioned in the book of Ezekiel, there are three prominent figures: Ezekiel, YHWH or the glory of YHWH, and the divine Spirit.[11] All that is known about the character of Ezekiel is from the literary portrait in the book.[12] The

---

[8] Naude, ראה ('see, have visions') in *NIDOTTE* 3, pp. 1007-15.

[9] See *BDB*, p. 919; *HALOT*, II, pp. 1156-61.

[10] Abraham Even-Shoshan, *A New Concordance of the Old Testament: Using the Hebrew and Aramaic Text* (Jerusalem: Kiryat-Sefer, 2nd edn, 1989), pp. 1041-45.

[11] Although the 'living creatures' later identified by Ezekiel as the 'cherubim' play a significant role in Ezekiel's inaugural vision (1.4-28) and are mentioned in the second vision of the glory of YHWH (ch. 10), they do not play a significant role in the other two major visions that are treated in this investigation. Therefore, these characters will be highlighted as appropriate in the narrative, but are not listed in the four main characters featured for the purposes of this narrative theological hearing.

[12] Many scholars attempted to explain the nature of his behavior in terms of mental illness and even diagnosed him as a schizophrenic. Since the 1950's these theories and interpretations have been dismissed and abandoned. However, in

title comes from the name of the prophet, which is the same in the LXX and the Hebrew text traditions. Ezekiel's name means, 'God makes hard or strengthens'. Ezekiel is identified early on as a visionary and recipient of YHWH's message to his immediate audience or hearers, the exiles. The literary portrait of Ezekiel is closely identified through the combination of the descriptions of his visions and hearing the word of YHWH, which is indicative for identifying Hebrew prophets or seers in their communities.[13]

The occurrences of the divine Spirit in Ezekiel are illustrated through a variety of activities or roles.[14] There are fifty-two references to the term רוח in the book with a breadth of semantic meanings represented. For example, the activities of the divine רוח in Ezekiel are observed, but not limited to (1) indwelling and empowering the prophet or the people of Israel (2.2; 37.14), (2) transporting the seer (3.12, 14a; 24; 8.3; 11.24; 37.1, 14; 43.5), and (3) inspiring the seer (2.2; 11.24). Other uses of the term רוח also occur in references made to either the רוח ('spirit') of the living creatures (1.4; 10.17) or Ezekiel's disposition (3.14b).[15]

1993, David Halperin revived these theories and expanded them. Halperin, *Seeking Ezekiel: Text and Psychology*, interprets the whole book of Ezekiel through Freudian psychoanalysis to assert that Ezekiel was portrayed as pathologically sick. See also, Broome, 'Ezekiel's Abnormal Personality', pp. 277-93. For a more nuanced view, see David Jobling, 'Towards an Adequate Psychological Approach to the Book of Ezekiel', a paper presented at the Annual Meeting of SBL, Orlando, Nov. 23, 1998. For similar methodological approaches, see Daniel L. Smith-Christopher, 'Ezekiel in Abu Ghraib: Reading Ezekiel 16.37-39 in the Context of Imperial Conquest', in *Ezekiel's Hierarchical World: Wrestling with a Tiered Reality* (SBL Symposium Series 31, 2004), pp. 141-58, and Nancy Bowen, *Ezekiel* (AOTC; Nashville: Abingdon, 2010), p. 1. Smith-Christopher and Bowen utilize a post-colonial and psychological analysis in its historical-socio-cultural context. Smith-Christopher presents a socio-psychological reading of Ezekiel 16 and argues that the events and experiences of the Exile combined with the imagery presented by the writer(s) of Ezekiel is evidence of a post-traumatic distress disorder.

[13] The first and most common Hebrew term for prophet is נביא from a root meaning 'to bubble forth, as from a fountain', hence 'to utter' (Ps. 19.2). In the time of Samuel another word ראה ('seer') began to be used (1 Sam. 9.9).

[14] Aubrey Johnson, *The One and the Many in the Israelite Conception of God* (Cardiff: University of Wales, 1961), pp. 6-8, 20, 36-38, argues that YHWH's Spirit is an extension of YHWH's personality

[15] Scheepers, *Die Gees van God en die Gees van die mens*, p. 308, argues that when רוח is referring to a human being, then the fundamental idea is 'breath' because it is related to the idea of '*nesjama or nefesj* as the principle of life', which includes 'psychical life and capacities and thinking', and the 'seat of different emotions'.

In three of the four visions, the theme of the 'glory of YHWH' is emphasized. The word כבוד appears about two hundred times in the HB. With reference to theophanies, the כבוד־יהוה appears to be associated with God's self-manifestation.[16] Ezekiel's visions describe the כבוד־יהוה frequently in anthropomorphic terms (1.27-28; 3.22-23; 8.3; 9.3; 11.22-23; 43.3). The glory of YHWH is at times described as a mysterious figure surrounded with fire and light, speaking, standing, hovering, and moving from place to place. In keeping with the central genre identified, it is not surprising that three of the main characters are of supernatural origin.

IV. Structure of Ezekiel's Vision Narratives

The book of Ezekiel is the third of the Latter Prophets in the Tanakh and one of the major prophetic books in the HB, following Isaiah and Jeremiah. According to the book itself, it spans the years from 593–571 BCE. Ezekiel's genre of prophetic visions is highlighted not only in the opening statements, but also is featured throughout the book, which sets the stage for the hearer to understand that the central message of the book is primarily communicated in picture form through symbolic images. The book is arguably one of the most literarily cohesive texts in the HB, and while it is common for most scholarly treatments to structure the book historically or thematically, it is proposed here that the book should be structured by its primary genre of prophetic visions.[17] As the book begins and ends with extended vision narratives, which are filled with vivid and sometimes bizarre imagery, symbolic actions, speeches, and allegorical word pictures, it is reasonable that due to the book's primary genre, it simply does not lend itself to an austere historical reconstruction.[18]

---

[16] Kutsko, *Between Heaven and Earth*, p. 80, posits that the 'glory' was a 'significant element in Priestly theology' (cf. Exod. 16.7, 10; 24.16-17; 29.43; 40.34-35; Lev. 9.6, 23).

[17] The chronological ordering is grounded upon the dated oracles in the book (1.1-2; 3.16; 8.1; 20.1; 24.1; 26.1; 29.1, 17; 30.20; 32.1; 40.1). The thematic structure has also been variously arranged (1) judgment on the house of Israel (1–24); (2) judgment on the nations (25–32); and (3) restoration of the house of Israel (33–39); and the (4) the new temple (40–48).

[18] See the major vision reports that introduce the structural framework of the book of Ezekiel (1–3, 8–11, 37.1-14, 40–48).

Initial support for this premise is observed in the superscription, which sets the stage for the book, וָאֶרְאֶה מַרְאוֹת אֱלֹהִים ('I saw visions of God' Ezek. 1.1). The initial literary setting introduces to the hearers (past and present) from the onset that the prophet claims he saw visions.[19] The dating formula that is specific to the day is linked to the recurring title 'visions of God' and marks the beginning of each vision of the כְּבוֹד־יהוה presented in the book (1.1; 8.3; 40.2).[20] Moreover, 'the word of YHWH' (v. 3) that comes to Ezekiel identifies the visions of God (v. 1) as the 'word of YHWH'.[21] The first vision is an elaborate description of the glory of YHWH, which highlights the literary marker, the glory of YHWH and its pneumatological emphasis of the term רוּחַ. The opening vision paints the picture of Ezekiel's inauguration to prophetic service, which immediately precedes his commissioning (1–3). Ezekiel's extensive inaugural vision is linked with the call narrative and can further be divided into three parts: (1) the superscription (1.1-3), (2) Ezekiel's inaugural vision (1.4-28), and (3) Ezekiel's call narrative (2–3.27).[22] The conclusion of the narrative

---

[19] Block, *The Book of Ezekiel*, p. 85, argues that in Ezekiel the term אֱלֹהִים functions as an appellative 'divinity' rather than the proper noun and therefore it does not refer to God himself.

[20] Within the discussion of unity, authorship, and redaction many scholars observed that since the book of Ezekiel was written in a distinctive orderly format with its specific date formulas and first-person narrative, which led scholars to consider even up to the 20th century that the book of Ezekiel was for the most part a homogenous whole, likely written by the prophet himself. The beginning of the twentieth century ushered in the first significant opposition to the unity of the book, to the association of authorship primarily with Ezekiel, and to the exilic dating of the book. For a discussion of the distinct feature of the autobiographical format of the book that supported a thesis of unity and to view the words of Ezekiel as authentic, see Paul Joyce, *Ezekiel: A Commentary* (LHBOTS 482; New York: T&T Clark International, 2009), pp. 16-66.

[21] Taylor, *Ezekiel: An Introduction and Commentary*, p. 53.

[22] The idea of the call or commissioning of God is deeply rooted in biblical thought and depicted in the narratives where God summons and inaugurates the person into a prophetic ministry (cf. Isa. 6.1-13; Jer. 1.4-19; Ezek. 1.1-3.27). Many modern critics agree that the vision is a single literary unit with some evidence of later additions by the prophet's disciples or the prophet himself and concludes with YHWH's personal instructions for the prophet at 3.15 or 3.27. See Block, *The Book of Ezekiel 1–24*, pp. 78, 150-60. He observes the coherence and unity of the inaugural vision with the call narrative as a literary unit. Block argues that 3.22-27 is the initiation of Ezekiel to his new vocation. The commissioning can also be structured in smaller literary units, see Block, *The Book of Ezekiel 1–24*, pp. 111-31. He observes that the commissioning of Ezekiel is comprised of three subunits: (1) 2.3-7 represents the first commissioning speech by YHWH, (2) 2.8–3.3 represents the vision of the scroll, and (3) 3.4-11 represents the second commissioning

ends with v. 27 because the chronological information at 3.16 appears to note a second type of visionary encounter, but also a continuation of the preceding visionary encounter.[23] The Hebrew idiom, יד־יהוה ותהי עלי שם ('The hand of YHWH was upon me there' 3.22) and the term רוח appear again to connect this paragraph to the preceding texts by echoing the same motifs. Thus, it seems likely that the inaugural visionary call narrative concludes with the end of the instructions that comes at 3.27 and before the first sign acts (4.1).[24] This smaller literary structure highlights the coherence of Ezekiel's visionary call narrative and supports the claim that the prominent literary themes are interrelated. The bizarre and lavish language in this initial vision is provocative. The affective language serves to accentuate the overwhelming effects upon the main character, Ezekiel. The seer is described as angry מר בחמת רוחי ('bitterness; in the heat of my spirit') as he is left משמים ('stunned or overwhelmed') for seven days (3.14-15) after his encounter with the glory of YHWH.

The second major vision narrative thematically describes the departure of the glory of YHWH from the Temple (8–11). The narrator highlights the connections between 'the hand of YHWH' and the Spirit with Ezekiel as he claims to see detestable idolatrous acts that are performed by the priests in the sacred Jerusalem Temple. This section ends with a charge to Ezekiel as a prophetic watchman, which precedes prophetic proclamations of YHWH's promise of restoration.

---

speech. For an opposing view, see Norman Habel, 'The Form and Significance of the Call Narratives', *ZAW* 11 (1965), pp. 297-323.

[23] Margaret Odell, *Ezekiel* (Macon, GA: Smyth & Helwys, 2005), pp. 13-17; 53-5, argues that the symbolic acts (3.22-5.5) are part of the prophet's preparation to be a prophet and are not a record of his public ministry. She posits that there are no literary breaks between the sections, no textual evidence to support that these acts were performed, and that the prophet does not begin speaking YHWH's decrees until after the symbolic acts are completed. She further contends that due to the verbal parallels, the events describe two encounters: one by the river Chebar (1.1–3.21) and the second by the plain of the Chebar (3.22–5.17). However, with the use of the future tense in the vv. 22-27, the narrative appears to be a continuation of what YHWH intends to do that is distinct from the present tense of YHWH's commands of the symbolic acts in 3.27–5.17.

[24] For a more detailed structural outline see Block, *The Book of Ezekiel 1–24*, p. 78. The structural components of his outline are as follows: (1) the superscription (1.1-3), (2) the inaugural vision (1.4-28a), (3) the commissioning of Ezekiel (1.28b-3.11), (4) the preparation of Ezekiel (3.12-15), (5) YHWH's induction speech (3.16-21), and (6) the initiation of Ezekiel (3.22-27).

Ezekiel's third major vision commences with God's commandment to Ezekiel to prophesy to the 'valley of the dry bones', which symbolizes the existing death and destruction that will be brought to life (37.1–14). Although, this vision is much shorter than the other vision reports, it is still considered significant because it marks the turning point in the entire book. It is considered in the current examination for three primary reasons: (1) it highlights the visual presentation of the transition from the themes of judgment and death to hope and life, (2) it presents the continuity of the pneumatological emphasis observed, which is represented by the role of the Spirit's activities, and (3) the presence of the recurrent literary markers the יד־יהוה and the רוח that appear to be interrelated.

The fourth major vision comprises several chapters that detail how God will restore the land, the Temple, and the priesthood through his glory returning to the Temple. The message of God's promise of hope and life entrusted to Ezekiel provides the overarching story in the last two vision cycles. All four of these vision narratives introduce oracles marked by דבר־יהוה ('the word of YHWH') and at times, include reports of symbolic acts.[25]

While there are a variety of options about the structure for the book, the opening words of the four major sections may well provide the overarching literary structure to describe the story of the entire book: (1) Vision of the glory of YHWH with warnings against Jerusalem (1–7); (2) Vision of the departure of the glory of YHWH with judgment oracles against Israel's leaders and the nations (8–36); (3) Vision of the Valley of Dry Bones and oracles against Gog (37–39); and (4) The new Temple Vision and the glory of YHWH with instructions regarding the Temple/Priests/Land (40–48). Ezekiel's four central vision reports (1–3; 8–11; 37.1–14; 40–48) are outlined as follows:

I. The Opening Vision of the glory of YHWH and Call Narrative (1–3)

II. The Vision of the Departure of the Lord's glory (8–11)

---

[25] See Block, *The Book of Ezekiel*, p. 23. Block emphasizes the oracles in Ezekiel are used to demarcate the book in four general parts. He also organizes the book around three themes: (1) Judgment on Israel (chs. 1–24); (2) Judgment on the nations (chs. 25–32); and (3) Future blessings for Israel (chs. 33–48). Its themes include the concepts of the presence of God, purity, Israel as a divine community, and individual responsibility to God.

III. The Vision of the Valley of the Dry Bones (37.1–14)

IV. The Return of the glory of YHWH in the Vision of the New Temple (40–48)

Each of these vision narratives emphasize special literary markers that represent recurring themes associated with the prophet: (1) the hand of YHWH, (2) the divine Spirit, and (3) an array of affective language.[26] These literary markers guide the hearers through the narrative, direct the hearers to new geographical locations, and accentuate the underlying pneumatology present throughout the entire narrative. Thus, the theological themes derived from the connections between the activities of the Spirit, the hand of YHWH, the glory of YHWH, and the affective language presented in the narratives will provide the basis for constructing overtures towards a holistic theology of Spirit-inspired visions.

V. Overview of the Themes in Ezekiel's Vision Narratives

A. Superscription (1.1–3)

Superscriptions in the biblical narratives can be useful to set the stage for the subsequent narratives.[27] Specifically, the superscription in the book of Ezekiel isolates the priestly-prophet's ministry in narrative time, place, and mode of prophetic inspiration.[28] The superscription

---

[26] Three out of the four visions share two other literary features: (1) an anthropomorphic description of the glory of YHWH as a figure like that of a man (1.26-28; chs. 8; 40–47), and (2) the living beings, which later are identified as the cherubim (chs. 1 and 10). The Cherubim/cherubs are angelic beings involved in the worship and praises to God. The cherubim are first mentioned in the Bible in Gen. 3.24, 'After He drove the man out, He placed on the east side of the Garden of Eden cherubim and a flaming sword flashing back and forth to guard the way to the tree of life'. Prior to his rebellion, Satan was a cherub (Ezek. 28.13-15). The tabernacle and temple along with their articles contained many representations of cherubim Exod. 25.17-22; 26.1, 31; 36.8; 1 Kgs 6.23-35; 7.29-36; 8.6-7; 1 Chron. 28.18; 2 Chron. 3.7-14; 2 Chron. 3.1-13; 5.7-8; Heb. 9.5.

[27] While the book of Ezekiel is the only prophetic book largely written in the first person, the superscription combines first and third person resulting in scholarly debates regarding the presence of redaction.

[28] Block, *The Book of Ezekiel 1–24*, pp. 15, 77. Block argues that the series of the date notices attached to the oracles and visions (1.1, 2-3; 3.16; 8.1; 20.1; 24.1) provides sufficient evidence to support that all the messages were received and delivered within a span of six or seven years. Block agrees with Zimmerli that Ezekiel was called to prophesy to those carried off to the land of Babylon beginning in 597 BCE.

describes the primary character, Ezekiel, as either 'the son of Buzi, a priest' or 'a priest, son of Buzi', depending upon how the verse is read.[29] The priestly language in the book of Ezekiel is prominent and his priestly heritage provides a lens through which to interpret the words, idioms, and actions in light of the established priestly traditions. The superscription also conveys that Ezekiel was given 'visions of God' while he was near the exiles in Babylon approximately five years after the reign of King Jehoiachin.[30] The mode of inspiration described in these opening verses is striking as it reads, 'the heavens were opened and I saw visions of God' (1.3). The superscription highlights the overarching theme of visions for the entire book.

B. The Inaugural Vision Report (1.4–28) and Call Narrative (2.1–3.27)

The extensive and elaborate opening vision of the glory of YHWH is one of the most distinctive literary features in the book of Ezekiel.[31] The use of metaphors, symbolic imagery, affective language,

---

[29] Marvin Sweeney, 'Dating Prophetic Texts', *Hebrew Studies* 48 (2007), p. 67. Sweeney attests that the chronology of the 30th year is significant for understanding the theological worldview of the book because it marks the active years of a Judean priest who would serve in the Temple from the age of thirty to the age of fifty. See also, Marc Zvi Brettler, *How to Read the Bible* (Philadelphia: Jewish Publication Society, 2005), pp. 185-97. Brettler argues that this superscription sets the prophet apart from any other. He posits that his mention of the 30th year of his own age is in order to mark his entering a priestly ministry to his fellow Hebrew exiles (that being the usual age, Num. 4.23; 30). Thus, he would have been 25 when carried away into exile and could have been inducted into the priesthood. In either instance, the narrative implication is that it is likely that Ezekiel was in training for the priestly office at Jerusalem prior to his captivity. For a Jewish interpretation, see Moshe Eisemann, *Yechezkel, A New Translation With A Commentary Anthologized From Talmudic, Midrashic and Rabbinic Sources* (Artscroll Series; Brooklyn, NY: Mesorah Publications, 2005), p. 88. Eisemann argues that the importance of the date formula, 'in the thirtieth year' refers to the *Merkavah* vision, and that Ezekiel's contemporaries represent the thirty years after finding the Sefer Torah (2 Kings 22). For a discourse on Ezekiel's priestly role see Baruch Schwartz, 'A Priest Out of Place: Reconsidering Ezekiel's Role in the History of the Israelite Priesthood', in Stephen Cook and Corrine Patton (eds.), *Ezekiel's Hierarchical World Wrestling with a Tiered Reality* (Boston: Brill, 2004), pp. 61-67. Schwartz is critical of attempts to see Ezekiel as actively fulfilling any formal priestly function in an exilic environment. He argues that without an altar, 'Ezekiel, the priest was unemployable'.

[30] For the geographical possibilities related to the region of the Chebar River, see Odell, *Ezekiel*, pp. 14-16. Odell argues that there is a resemblance between the book of Ezekiel and Assyrian traditions, and this supports that the prophet was influenced by Neo-Assyrian contact in the region of Nippur.

[31] This chapter's primacy is echoed down throughout the centuries of Christianity, and even more so in Judaism, where it can be considered the taproot of the

and emphasis upon the diverse activities of the רוח portrayed in Ezekiel's inaugural vision is also remarkable. Ezekiel's visionary account
emphasizes three key motifs:

(1) the כבוד־יהוה (1.28b; 3.12b, 23), (2) the יד־יהוה (1.3; 3.14a, 22),
and the (3) רוח (2.2; 3.12a, 14b, 24). The repetitive literary pattern
and motifs suggest the terms and phrases are important and interrelated.[32]

The phrase, 'the hand of YHWH' introduces the vision (1.3) and
is present in all four major visions (1.3; 8.1; 37.1; 40.1).[33] Narratively,
this Hebrew idiom appears to be linked with Ezekiel's revelatory visions of the glory of YHWH, and his visionary transportations by
the Spirit (3.14; 22).[34] It also removes Ezekiel's silence (3.22-27).
Thus, the following questions emerge: (1) What are the connections
between the hand of YHWH and the Spirit in the context of

Merkabah tradition, and also, arguably the apocalyptic tradition. For discussions
regarding Ezekiel as the beginning of the apocalyptic genre, see John J. Collins,
'Introduction: Towards the Morphology of a Genre' in John J. Collins (ed.), *Apocalypse: The Morphology of a Genre* (Semeia 14; Missoula: Scholars, 1979), p. 3. Collins
argues that the word *apocalyptic* has generally been used rather loosely in academic
writing; however, he defines it saying, 'The abstraction apocalyptic hovers vaguely
between literature, sociology, and theology'. See also Paul Hanson, *The Dawn of
Apocalyptic: The Historical and Sociological Roots of Jewish Apocalyptic Eschatology* (Philadelphia: Fortress, 1975), pp. 11-12. Hanson defines apocalyptic eschatology as a
'religious perspective, which focuses on the disclosure (usually esoteric in nature)
to the elect of the cosmic vision of Yahweh's sovereignty'. For a different perspective see Christopher Rowland, *The Open Heaven: A Study of Apocalyptic in Judaism and
Early Christianity* (New York: Crossroads, 1982).
[32] According to Wilson's cross-cultural comparison, the expression 'the hand
of YHWH' belongs to the same set of prophetic terminology as the message-
reception formula used to communicate the means of divine communication. The
prophetic command of YHWH is associated with his power upon the prophet.
Wilson also attests that the ecstatic manifestations are a result of mechanisms of
intermediation that depict trance-like behaviors that are often times associated with
spirit possession. Since the idiom 'the hand of YHWH' is consistently associated
with the activities of the רוח.
[33] Dreytza, יד ('hand, power, side') in *NIDOTTE*, II, p. 403. In the prophetic
tradition, the hand of YHWH is an anthropomorphic clause, which is at times,
used metaphorically to describe an element of God's power ascending upon a
prophet, judge, or ruler. The theological metaphor of God's hand also has its roots
in salvation history as God redeems Israel from slavery in Egypt (Exod. 3.20; 4.17;
6.1; 7.19; 13.3). In other instances, יד can be used to describe God's mighty acts of
judgment over his people (Isa. 19.16; Zech 2.9; Ezek. 20.5) or against Israel's enemies (1 Sam. 5.6, 11).
[34] 1 Kings 18.46; 2 Kgs 3.15; Isa. 8.11; Jer. 15.17; Ezek. 1.3; 3.14, 22; 8.1; 33.22;
37.1; 40.1.

Ezekiel's visionary encounters, (2) how are these terms used in the narratives, and (3) how are these theological themes understood by the hearers?

Ezekiel's call narrative immediately follows the opening vision (2.1). In the HB, call narratives generally serve to authenticate the messenger and his message to his audience given through modes of prophetic inspiration.[35] The seer or prophetic messenger would see a vision and receive revelation that resulted in a perception through the other senses, e.g., understanding or hearing.[36] In Ezekiel's visions, one of the functions of the divine Spirit as inspiration is observed in the narratives through several factors. First, on a general level, the role of the Spirit of God in the inspiration of prophets in the HB is well attested.[37] Prophets depended upon the divine Spirit for their credibility as messengers for their God. Secondly, in the book of Ezekiel, it is the divine Spirit that enters the prophet with YHWH speaking commands to the prophet, which occurs at the same time (Ezek. 2.2; 3.24). Third, two references point to divine inspiration, (1) 'The spirit came into me' (2.2; 3.24), which is a distinguishing pneumatological feature of Ezekiel's visionary call narrative, and (2) 'the spirit of YHWH fell upon me, and he said to me' (11.5). Additionally, in 36.27, the Spirit is linked with the house of Israel's obedience to YHWH's word. In 37.1–14, the Spirit comes at the command of

---

[35] In the HB, the word of YHWH often times follows visions (Gen. 12.1–2; Exod. 3.1–6; Num. 22.31–35; Judg. 6.11–17, 36–40; Isa. 6.1–13; Ezek. 1.1-3.27; Amos 7). From a form-critical approach, the 'call narrative' is used to identify a literary genre that illustrates the commissioning of a prophet or messenger to prophetic ministry usually found in the prophetic tradition (Isa. 6.1–13; Jer. 1.4–19; Ezek. 1–3; Hos. 1.2; Amos 7.14; Jon. 1.2; Zechariah 1). Some of these are considered complete call narratives by form-critical analysis and others are limited and deemed to be call experiences. Yet, there are also a number of texts that describe the motif outside the prophetic books (Exod. 3.1–4.7; Judg. 6.11–17, 36–40), the anointing of Saul (1 Sam. 9.1–10.16), and Micaish ben Imlah's throne-room vision (1 Kgs 22.1–28).

[36] Naudé, ('see'), *NIDOTTE,* III, pp. 1007–15.

[37] James Robson, *Word and Spirit in Ezekiel* (LHBOT 447; New York: T & T Clark, 2006), pp. 99-126; 146-70. Robson outlines the concept of inspiration of the classical prophets and provides a discussion of the רוח as agent of inspiration in Ezekiel directly related to the word of YHWH. However, in the pre-exilic classical prophets there was a decline in the writer(s) uses of the ('spirit') related to prophetic inspiration. See Ma, *Until the Spirit Comes,* pp. 33-70; 109-12, observes that during and after the exile, the frequency of the occurrences of the ('spirit') is notable, which is illustrated in Second Isaiah, the book of Ezekiel, and the Haggai-Zechariah corpus.

YHWH's word, spoken by the prophet. Fourth, the purpose of the HB call narratives is to report the commissioning of a Hebrew prophet to their prophetic service.[38] Thus, the context also links the activity of the divine Spirit with divine prophetic inspiration, hence supporting the function in its theological sense.

More than any other call narrative in the HB, the combination of Ezekiel's elaborate vision and call depicts the power of YHWH in many ways. YHWH's powerful attributes are represented by the glory of YHWH, the hand of YHWH, and the activities of the divine Spirit. These motifs are used as literary tools to describe the forceful ways in which YHWH encounters the prophet, which serves to contribute to the affective literary portrait of the prophet. Imbedded in the visionary call narrative are accounts of YHWH's speeches to Ezekiel, which combined with his inauguration, serve to introduce YHWH's instructions to the seer.

The backdrop of the extreme political and social climate of the Exile provides the setting for how Ezekiel would serve as YHWH's messenger or prophet.[39] The meaning of Ezekiel's name, 'God makes hard or strengthens' adds to the literary portrait of the prophet in this setting. The representation of Ezekiel as a priestly-prophet elucidates the socio-religious context of his opening vision and call narrative as the book highlights priestly language.[40] The narrative

---

[38] Hildebrandt, *An Old Testament Theology of the Spirit of God*, p. 97, argues that specifically for Ezekiel's call, the 'role of the spirit is present in inspiring, motivating, and guiding the prophet'.

[39] Oded Lipschits, *The Fall and Rise of Jerusalem: Judah under Babylonian Rule* (Winona Lake, IN, Eisenbrauns, 2005), pp. 1-35; 72-88. Lipschits postulates a historical reconstruction of this time period in Chapter 1. A turning point in Israelite history of the southern kingdom occurred in 605 BCE when King Nebuchadnezzar defeated the Egyptian army at Carchemish and began to advance military assaults in Judah (Jer. 25.1-14). With the siege and surrender of Jerusalem in 597 BCE and the deportation of the king and the leading citizens, these major events mark the beginning of the 'Exile' (2 Kings 25). Presumably three waves of destruction and subsequent deportations transpired. In 587/586 BCE, the Babylonian forces returned to destroy the city and further depopulate the land (Jer. 52.6). The ministry of the prophet Ezekiel can best be understood against the background of the last days of Judah. As a youth, Ezekiel saw the decline and fall of Assyria, the growing power of Babylon, Egypt's control of Jerusalem in 609 BCE, and the defeat of Egypt and Assyria by Nebuchadnezzar at Carchemish. Ezekiel stood between the old and the new worlds in the narratives of redemptive history. His message spanned the time from 593 to 571 BCE with oracles of judgment and hope.

[40] According to 2 Kgs 24.14-16, Ezekiel may have been carried into exile in Babylon in 597 BCE with many of the nation's elite. 2 Kings records that King

highlights that the entrance of YHWH's glory appearing to the visionary in the foreign land of Babylon was a dramatic statement of YHWH's sovereign rule (1.1-28). YHWH's appearance in Exile also demonstrates that he is still present to keep his covenant with his people in spite of their disobedience.[41] Ezekiel's prophetic call in the midst of the Exile provides the foundation for revealing his ministry as a priestly-prophetic seer and watchman to this exilic community in Babylon.[42]

C. The Vision of YHWH's glory departs from the Jerusalem Temple (8–11)

The account of Ezekiel's first temple vision is the second extended vision report (8–11). The 'hand of the YHWH falls upon Ezekiel' as he sees a man surrounded by light and fire similar to the first extended vision report. Yet, this mysterious figure acquires a new role and becomes a more prominent character in the narrative. He not only seizes Ezekiel by his hair, but later he becomes Ezekiel's tour guide through the temple vision (8.3; 5-18; 9). Again, the language describes forceful activities of the divine Spirit as it (1) levitates Ezekiel between heaven and earth and (2) brings Ezekiel to the glory of YHWH (8.3). Ezekiel is unique among the classical prophets in that

---

Jehoiachin along with members of the royal family, government officials, trained soldiers, smiths, artisans, and the leading elite of the land totaling approximately 10,000 people. Since Ezekiel was either 'a son of a priest, Buzi' or 'a priest', then he would have been considered one of the nation's elite. Block, *The Book of Ezekiel 1–24*, pp. 28-34. Block discusses the historical debates. He proposes that while scholars remain divided on exactly what Ezekiel and his fellow deportees experienced, yet the majority of interpreters conclude that the exiles were allowed to live together and maintain some aspect of their ethnic and social customs. There are other prophetic books that portray prophets as priests (Jeremiah and Zechariah).

[41] Even in the midst of judgment there are numerous citations that support YHWH is faithful to his covenant and has not forgotten his people. The covenant language, 'I will be your God, and you shall be my people' occurs in various places in the HB and is present throughout the book of Ezekiel (11.20; 14.11; 34.24; 30-31; 36.28; 37.23).

[42] Block, *The Book of Ezekiel 1–24*, pp. 5-6. See Block for a discussion on the political practices of forced Israelite immigration by the Babylonians. The issue will not be addressed in this investigation. Block utilizes the documents of the Murashu Archive to confirm that the integration of the exilic community took place near the Chebar canal. Additionally, Psalm 137 locates the *Judean* exiles 'by the rivers of Babylon'. If a return to their land should occur, as promised in the Law (Deut. 30.4), then the only explanation for the deconstruction of Jerusalem/Judah was likewise in the Law, which had prophesied such events (Lev. 26.21–45). Therefore, the exiles in Babylonian likely would have expected their lives to be transformed spiritually as it was prophesied in the new covenant (Jer. 31.31–34; Ezekiel 36).

the story portrays Ezekiel being transported by the Spirit in a vision hundreds of miles away from Babylon to Jerusalem.[43] The entire unit is a single visionary scene in which YHWH reveals to Ezekiel the abominations that are occurring in the Jerusalem Temple (Ezekiel 8), YHWH's response to these abominations (Ezekiel 9), and the departure of the divine glory from the city (Ezekiel 11). The affective language is used throughout the vision narratives either to describe Ezekiel's emotional responses to YHWH's judgment or to YHWH's responses to Israel's abominations.

D. The Vision of the Valley of the Dry Bones (37.1–14)

The third vision report represents a smaller literary unit, yet theologically significant and other than the opening vision is as well known. One of the overarching theological themes in the book's story signifies a promise of internal renewal to the problem of rebellion and sin against YHWH (Ezek. 36.27).[44] God endured their rebellion for years, in which the exilic era necessitated a time for radical intervention. Spiritual transformation would be discernible when Israel exhibited a heart to obey the Law as a covenantal response to the faithfulness of YHWH. The vision of the resurrection of YHWH's people in 37.1–14 is one of the first signs of hope in Ezekiel. Similar to the prophet's translocations by the Spirit in the first major vision, he is also carried off by the Spirit into a valley in this vision and commanded to prophesy to the symbolic imagery of dry bones.

E. The Vision of the glory of YHWH Returning to the Restored Temple (40–48)

The last major vision in the book is Ezekiel's second temple vision and is marked with the dating formula, the Hebrew idiom, 'the hand of YHWH was upon me', the Spirit, and the mysterious man (40-43). Again, the literary features of the hand of YHWH is connected to a transportation by the Spirit of the seer in a vision (43.1-5), and the story explicitly reiterates that this vision is like Ezekiel's opening vision, 'And it was according to the appearance of the vision which I saw, even according to the vision that I saw when I came to destroy

---

[43] See the account regarding Elijah, which is the nearest analogy (1 Kgs 18.12; 2 Kgs 2.1–12, 16–18), and that relating to Elisha (2 Kgs 5.26; 6.17, 32–33).

[44] Odell, *Ezekiel*, pp. 15-17. Odell attests that the political events of this period coincide with the dating of Ezekiel's first vision (cf. Jer. 27; 28.1; 51.59). Ezekiel prophesied during the years 593-571 BCE.

the city: and the visions were like the vision that I saw by the river Chebar, and I fell upon my face' (43.3).

The story unfolds in the narratives as they are further divided thematically into five sections: (1) the vision of the new Temple with the glory of YHWH returning (40–43.11), (2) YHWH's new instructions for the Temple (43.12–44), (3) the divisions of the land and instructions on Holy Days and Festivals (45–46), (4) the new Temple with water flowing from the throne (47.1-12), and (5) the allotted distribution of the healed land to the Twelve tribes (47.13–48.1-35).[45]

In the final Temple vision, Ezekiel is shown the mysterious man again as his tour guide; only this time the man has a line of flax and a measuring rod to measure the dimensions for the building of the new Temple. The next section highlights the glory of YHWH entering the new Temple (43.1–5):

> Then he led me to the gate, the gate facing toward the east; and behold, the glory of the God of Israel was coming from the way of the east. And His voice was like the sound of many waters; and the earth shone with His glory. And *it was* like the appearance of the vision, which I saw, like the vision, which I saw when He came to destroy the city. And the visions *were* like the vision, which I saw by the river Chebar; and I fell on my face. And the glory of the Lord came into the house by the way of the gate facing toward the east. And the Spirit lifted me up and brought me into the inner court; and behold, the glory of the Lord filled the house.

The theme of holiness is emphasized as the glory of YHWH enters the new Temple and the nameless man instructs Ezekiel regarding (1) the altar, (2) the offerings, (3) the sacrifices to be offered by the Levitical priesthood who are the sons of Zadok, and (4) the festivals. This section emphasizes that the teachings of the Torah are to be holy. The third section in Ezekiel's extended temple vision report represents the healing of the land by the water imagery flowing from the throne to bring life to the land and every living creature. Next, YHWH instructs Ezekiel on the divisions of the land to be portioned

---

[45] Greenberg, 'The Design and Themes of Ezekiel's Program of Restoration', *Int* 38 (1948), pp. 189-90, focuses on the law codes as providing the major structure and themes in Ezekiel 40–48. See also, Tuell, *The Law of the Temple in Ezekiel 40–48* (HSM; Atlanta: Scholars Press, 1992), pp 35-49, provides an arrangement for chs. 40–48 giving special emphasis to the legislation or law code at its center. For a chiastic structure, see Renz, *The Rhetorical Function of the Book of Ezekiel*, p. 128.

out to the tribes of Israel as their inheritance. The final section is brief but gives the dimensions of the new city and its name: 'The Lord is There' (48.35).

This final vision report concludes the book with the glory of YHWH returning to his new Temple to dwell among his newly consecrated people, with a healed land. In a literary sense the book of Ezekiel has corresponding visions that form somewhat of an inclusio around the book.

VI. Conclusions

Based upon the identification the book's genre, central themes, and its recurring literary markers, it is proposed here that the book of Ezekiel is organized by its major vision reports (Ezek. 1–3; 8–11; 37.1-14; 40–48). These vision reports introduce the oracular portions and at times, symbolic acts. The preceding overview of Ezekiel's visions provides initial support that the four major vision narratives mark a literary structure for the book of Ezekiel. In this context, there are numerous recurring themes that suggest literary and theological connections. All four of Ezekiel's visions emphasize language that describes the power and sovereignty of God through the use of the Hebrew idiom, the יד־יהוה, and the diverse activities of the divine Spirit. This overview also reveals that the use of affective language used to describe the emotive disposition of the main characters appears to be directly associated to these recurring motifs. It is concluded here that a narrative theological hearing of Ezekiel's four major visions with special attention given to these literary connections observed above, ground Ezekiel's visions pneumatologically and provide a way forward to explore their theological implications.

6

EZEKIEL'S VISIONS: BY THE 'HAND OF YHWH' AND BY THE 'SPIRIT'

I. Introduction

In the previous chapter, I offer an overview of the book of Ezekiel proposing its structure through highlighting its genre, major themes, and main characters in the four key vision narratives. This overview identifies the overarching structure of the book (1–7; 8–36; 37–39; 40–48). For the purposes of this investigation, in this chapter, along with the earlier proposal for a Pentecostal interpretative strategy, I will offer a narrative theological hearing of Ezekiel's four central vision narratives that highlight the overall structure (Ezekiel 1–3; 8–11; 37.1-14; 40–48), which until now, has not received sufficient pneumatological or affective considerations. For ease of the reader, this study will provide short overviews of the sections in Ezekiel's visions not selected here. Specifically, the study will draw particular attention to passages that associate the divine רוח, the יד־יהוה, with the affective terms that accentuate the dynamic themes portrayed in the narratives, such as מר בחמת רוחי ('bitterness; in the heat of my spirit'), משמים ('stunned or overwhelmed'), and באפי ('my anger'). Narratively, the text will be considered in its final form and as a coherent whole with aims to examine the vision narratives and their relationship to its characters and themes with aims towards drawing theological conclusions. This close hearing of the text will highlight other appropriate texts that intersect with the themes of the divine רוח and the יד־יהוה as it relates to Ezekiel's visions.

Although Ezekiel's inaugural vision is closely connected to the call narrative, for the purpose of clarity, the inaugural vision will be heard before proceeding to Ezekiel's call to prophetic service.

II. Ezekiel's Inaugural Call Vision (Ezekiel 1–7)

A. Superscription (1.1-3)
The first three verses, or the superscription, introduces the hearer to the date, location, characters, and most importantly sets the stage for the overarching theme of prophetic visions as the primary genre for the entire book.[1] The first verse reads, 'In the thirtieth year, in the fourth month on the fifth day, while I was among the exiles by the Chebar River, and נפתחו השמים ואראה מראות אלהים ('the heavens were opened and I saw visions of God').[2] The first verse informs the hearers of the calendrical date that Ezekiel's visions occurred and links to the dating in the second verse, 'On the fifth of the month, it was the fifth year of the exile of King Jehoiachin, the word of the Lord came to Ezekiel'.[3] The setting is the land of the Chaldeans by the River Chebar, where Ezekiel is living among the exiles. The opening verses and the subsequent visionary accounts are written in an autobiographical style that presents Ezekiel as the implied author and narrator of his visions.[4] As the implied author and narrator, all of the events in the book are understood and presented from this

---

[1] See Horton, *What the Bible Says About the Holy Spirit*, p. 55, who treats the visions more tentatively by translating the term *vision* as 'appearance' at times (Ezek. 10.1; 41.21) and not the more common 'prophetic vision'. Although, he admits the problems associated with this view, he argues that in these instances the vision is actual appearances or manifestations of God. See also, Kirsten Nielson, 'Ezekiel's Visionary Call as Prologue: From Complexity and Changeability to Order and Stability', *JSOT* 33.1 (2008), p. 100.

[2] See Block, *The Book of Ezekiel 1–24*, pp. 79-89. Block outlines the current debates of the various interpretations of the superscription. Block attests that the use of first and third person is likely an expansion that is a redaction. In this sense, it differs from other superscriptions. The superscription is written in first person and the redaction is in third person that lends to the autobiographical element.

[3] For discussions regarding the precise dating in Ezekiel's visions, see George Ricker Berry, 'The Title of Ezekiel (1.1-3)', *JBL* 52 (1932), pp. 54-57; and Block, *Ezekiel 1-24*, pp. 79-89.

[4] Ezekiel 1.2-3 are the only verses written in third person. It is possible that these verses were added later by an editorial hand. No other prophetic book in the HB opens in an autobiographical style.

perspective.[5] The superscription provides the literary setting in which the telling or hearing of Ezekiel's visions are received and presented to the hearers. The hearers would understand that Ezekiel, as Hebrew prophetic seer, not only is about to receive visions of God, but also hear YHWH's divine word. The close proximity of seeing and hearing in the opening verses leads the hearers to understand the prophetic nature of the events about to unfold. Ezekiel also provides his hearers with clarity as to the setting in which he would describe the visions.

Although, the story does not imply that the exiles saw the visions, it does highlight the communal aspect that Ezekiel was among the exiles when the visions occurred. The exiles as the implied hearers do not appear to have had an active internal participation in the story of Ezekiel's visions because they are not shown to be included in the speech events that occur later between YHWH and Ezekiel. However, it is conceivable that the exiles as the implied hearers are invited into the visionary world through their imagination, as they would be required to imagine what the seer later reported to them in order to perceive or understand what they were hearing.[6] From this perspective, the exilic community would share indirectly in the visions through the use of imagination, as they would 'see what they were hearing'.[7] Moreover, the opening verses closely connects the דבר of YHWH (v. 3) with 'the visions of God' (v. 1).[8] Ezekiel's opening statements convey for his hearers that the event he was about to describe for them was a prophetic event that was seen, yet these visions were also the 'word of YHWH' as they revealed to the prophet messages about YHWH's glory. Their imagination would afford the hearers to hear these visions as YHWH's word given to Ezekiel. In this way, it is the prophetic vision that can be considered the vehicle with

---

[5] Ezekiel's distinct superscription adds to the support for understanding the genre for the entire book. See Zimmerli, *Ezekiel 1*, p. 101 and Hals, *Ezekiel*, p. 363, both of whom see Ezek. 1.3a as the superscription for the entire book.

[6] See Walter Brueggemann, *Hopeful Imagination: Prophetic Voices in Exile* (Philadelphia, PA: Fortress Press, 1986). Brueggemann presents a biblical theological discourse regarding the exilic community.

[7] The hearers could not see what Ezekiel sees. They could only have access to the visions through the descriptions of the images that Ezekiel provided the hearers.

[8] Moore, 'The Prophetic Calling: An Old Testament Profile and Its Relevance for Today', p. 59, describes the ways in which the prophetic literature in the OT directly points to the דבר of YHWH as an event that is seen and heard.

which the divine word comes providing the prophet and his hearers understanding of YHWH's word.[9] Stated differently, the words as symbols in the vision narratives can be received as a divine speech event along with the hearing of YHWH's words given to Ezekiel in the oracular narratives. Therefore, Ezekiel's visions, as the word of YHWH, include visual, aural, and oral elements within the vision experience.

The sentence נפתחו השמים ואראה מראות אלהים not only offers unique perspectives on the reports of Ezekiel's visionary encounters, but also sets the stage for the powerful multi-dimensional drama that is about to unfold. What is interesting is that Ezekiel distinctly uses the terms נפתחו השמים.[10] As in a film at a theatre where the curtains are opened to unveil the drama that is about to begin, so the literary scene of Ezekiel's book uses the phrase, 'the heavens are opened', which signifies the unveiling of the visions of the heavenly world of YHWH.[11] In its visionary context, the seer was granted access to gaze into the heavenly realities as the opening verses read, 'the heavens were opened'.[12] This opening language elicits suspense and an expectation for what lies behind the disclosure of the heavenly realm. From the outset, the genre is provided to the hearers by the phrase, אלהים מראות ('visions of God'). This is not to say that the use of this phrase implies that the hearers would perceive that it is a direct vision of God, because the term אלהים usually is interpreted as an appellative, 'divinity', rather than a proper noun.[13] From this perspective, the

---

[9] Yehezekel Kaufmann, *The Religion of Israel: From Its Beginnings to the Babylonian Exile* (trans. Moshe Greenberg; London: Allen & Unwin, 1961), argues that 'the symbolic vision is not the essence of revelation, but the divine interpretation that follows is how YHWH speaks in riddles' (cf. Num. 12.8), pp. 93-111.

[10] The only other occurrence in the HB of the phrase, 'opening of the heavens' is Gen. 7.11.

[11] Zimmerli, *Ezekiel 2*, p. 567, describes Ezekiel's prophetic experiences as 'an autodrama' indicative of a 'dramatic reality' as it depicts Ezekiel not only seeing and hearing but also acting within the visions.

[12] There are many HB passages that draw connections between YHWH, a whirlwind, storm, and the heavens: (1) 'Elijah went up by a whirlwind into heaven' (2 Kgs 2.11), (2) 'the Lord answered Job out of the whirlwind' (Job 38.1), (3) 'YHWH has his way in the whirlwind and in the storm (Nah. 1.3), (4) 'the Lord will blow the trumpet and go with the whirlwinds' (Zech. 9.14). The language ascribed to the majesty of YHWH occurs in the appearing of YHWH to Moses at Sinai (Exod. 19.16) or on Horeb to Elijah (1 Kgs 19.11–13),

[13] See Greenberg, *Ezekiel 1–20*, p. 41, who offers a full discussion on the names of God in Ezekiel.

hearers would understand that the prophet was given the opportunity to see into the divine heavenly world.[14] The term מראות ('visions'), as opposed to the term חזון ('vision'), conveys that Ezekiel saw many visions rather than just a single vision.[15] The phrase, מראות אלהים ('visions of God') is repeated in subsequent visions and later identified as the כבוד־יהוה (1.28; cf. 8.4; 43.1-3).[16] Yet, at this point, the hearers likely would discern that Ezekiel is and will be seeing many visions of the heavenly world.

Verse 3 of the superscription also adds to the description of the character of Ezekiel, 'The word of YHWH came to Ezekiel, the son of Buzi, the priest, in Babylon by the Chebar River'. It is not certain whether Ezekiel is called a priest or the son of a priest. Regardless, if the narrative describes Ezekiel as the son of a priest or a priest, a priestly heritage contributes to the hearer's understanding of Ezekiel as a priestly-prophetic seer. For example, if he were portrayed as a priest or son of a priest in the Jerusalem Temple, then likewise he would have been exposed to a set of symbols that would have influenced the ways in which he perceived YHWH, the כבוד־יהוה, and the idea of holiness.[17] So too, the hearers would have made associations with Ezekiel's visions to Israelite priestly traditions because the opening verses highlight this priestly aspect of Ezekiel's character as a visionary prophetic seer in Babylon.[18] However, the vision narrative

---

[14] The language is reminiscent of the theophanic event that is used in the Moses narrative (Num. 12.6). In the Moses narrative, the narrator reports that יהוה ומדע יבט ('he beholds the form of YHWH' Num. 12.8).

[15] The more common term, חזון ('vision') is typically used with the collection of oracles and visions in the prophetic literature (Isaiah 1; Obadiah 1; Nahum 1). See Odell, *Ezekiel*, pp. 15-17. Odell argues that the more common term חזון implies a more ambiguous event and message, and the masculine term for 'appearance', implies a direct encounter instead of a vague visionary event (cf. Num. 12. 6-8). Her proposal is compelling from a contextual viewpoint.

[16] Block, *The Book of Ezekiel 1–24*, p. 185.

[17] Norman Snaith, 'The Spirit of God', in *The Distinctives Ideas of the Old Testament* (New York: Schocken, 1964), pp. 143−58.

[18] For example, the priestly language, cultic concerns, sacrifices, temple matters, and the concern for regulations and purity that occur throughout the book confirm for the hearers that Ezekiel was a priestly-prophetic seer (4.13-14; 11; 20.12-13; 40.1–48.35). Ezekiel refuses to cook with human dung and refutes YHWH by stating that he has never defiled himself from his youth (4.12-15). The final vision narratives also underscore the influence of the priestly traditions of the southern establishment as indicated by the prominence of the Jerusalemite theme of the restoration of the Temple (40–48).

does not make mention of Ezekiel serving as a priest in any official capacity.[19] The hearers of Ezekiel's opening visionary statements likely would have understood that an Israelite priestly-prophetic seer would have been opposed to the notion of seeing God in human form, but not to the idea of seeing the כבוד־יהוה as representative of the divine presence.[20] The end of v. 3 introduces the phrase, יהוה־ ותהי עליו שם יד, which provides a unique aspect to the introduction of Ezekiel's opening vision. The variation in the verb 'was upon' is 'to be, exist or become upon; to put on or clothe; to prosper, succeed upon'.[21] At first blush, it would appear that the hearers would understand the term metaphorically as the Hebrew idiom has its roots in their history.[22] From this perspective, the יד־יהוה may represent God's power in the act of deliverance. Contextually, the hearers likely may anticipate that the word of YHWH was coming to Ezekiel either to deliver the exiles or to pronounce judgment upon them.[23] At this point in the story, its meaning is not clear.

In the prophetic tradition, the יד־יהוה is an anthropomorphic clause often used to describe a characteristic of God's power descending upon the prophet.[24] Ezekiel, portrayed early on as a seer

---

[19] Sweeney, 'Ezekiel, Zadokite Priest and Visionary Prophet of the Exile', in *Form and Intertextuality in the Prophetic and Apocalyptic Literature* (Tübingen: Mohr Siebeck, 2005), pp. 125-43. Sweeney contends that Ezekiel's character was a distinctive mark of his personality as demonstrated throughout the book in practical, literary, and theological ways.

[20] Sweeney, *Reading Ezekiel*, p. 27, argues that Ezekiel's throne chariot imagery is based in part upon the imagery of the Ark conveyed to Jerusalem on a wheeled cart during the reign of David (2 Samuel 6; cf. 2 Chr. 28.15), In Ezekiel 1, the chariot throne is traveling across the heavens (Habakkuk 3; Ps. 18.68). The two chariots of YHWH's presence are juxtaposed as they represent the Lord's immanent presence amidst the Israelites and his presence in the heavens (cf. Exod. 33.18).

[21] Dreytza, יד ('hand') in *NIDOTTE*, II, p. 403. The term יד ('hand') can also be used to describe God's mighty acts of judgment over his people (Isa. 19.16; Zech 2.9; Ezek. 20.5) or against Israel's enemies (1 Sam. 5.6, 11). In the Elijah narratives, the יד־יהוה represents an overwhelming effect that God exerts upon the prophets for the purpose of accomplishing a task (cf. 1 Kgs 18.46). In this context, the יד־יהוה in 1 Kgs 18.46 is used to convey an outward strength.

[22] Cf. Exod. 3.20; 4.17; 6.1; 7.19; 13.3 for example of Israel's salvation history.

[23] Block, *Ezekiel 1–24*, p. 108, discusses the possibility of the exiles perceiving the glory of YHWH coming to the exiles in Babylon as judgment for their apostasy.

[24] Dreytza, יד ('hand') in *NIDOTTE*, II, p. 403. Dreytza notes this designation for this idiom occurs more often in the book of Ezekiel than any other prophet (1 Kgs 18.46; 2 Kgs 3.15; Isa. 8.11; Jer. 15.17; Ezek. 1.3; 3.14, 22; 8.1; 33.22; 37.1; 40.1).

who hears YHWH's word, provides the hearers with understanding that the idiom primarily is associated with idea of YHWH's 'power'.[25] From this perspective, the phrase may convey that the power of YHWH's hand was near Ezekiel even in exile as he was far away from their sacred city, Jerusalem, and their temple. The placement of the יד־יהוה in Ezekiel's introduction provides additional information. YHWH's hand was upon the seer during a particular place while experiencing his inaugural visionary event. The question is whether the hearers would perceive or draw connections with YHWH's hand and the reception of Ezekiel's vision. The close proximity of the יד־יהוה with the announcement of what Ezekiel saw (וארא) begs this question.

Since, what follows is an extended and detailed account of a vision and not a story of a particular task performed, then the יד־יהוה appears to be related to the revelatory state of the seer or mode of inspiration instead of a power given for a specific act. The placement of the idiom highlights the context of Ezekiel's reception of visions of supernatural realities and the hearing of the word of YHWH.[26] From this perspective, ותהי עלי שם יד־יהוה points to a special experience of YHWH's power upon the prophet, which is similar to how the divine רוח came upon certain judges of Israel.'[27] The hearers likely would have been familiar with the oral tradition of Israel, which would help connect YHWH's רוח with the ideas of power and inspiration.[28]

B. Ezekiel's Opening Vision (1.4-28)

After setting the stage, Ezekiel's description of his opening vision commences with a long description of bizarre symbolic imagery that

[25] See Block, *The Book of Ezekiel 1*, p. 79, who argues that the Hebrew idiom represents YHWH's power. Zimmerli, *Ezekiel 1*, p. 128.

[26] See Block for a detailed account of the repetitive formulaic expressions used throughout the book of Ezekiel. Block, *The Book of Ezekiel 1*, pp. 31-39, argues that this prophetic formula represents the 'physical dimension of Ezekiel's prophetic role'.

[27] Dreytza, *NIDOTTE*, II, p. 404. Block, *The Book of Ezekiel*, p. 35.

[28] Robson, *Word and Spirit in Ezekiel*, pp. 105-70, offers a full discussion about prophetic inspiration in the pre-exilic and exilic prophets. He argues that the pre-exilic prophets rejected the divine רוח as their source of inspiration due to the occurrences of objections about false prophets or excesses of the ecstatic prophets. The theological view observes that these prophets were focused more upon the 'word of YHWH' and thus, they did not reflect upon the idea of a mediating spirit.

is identified later as YHWH's glory (1.4-28; cf. 8.4). The vision language is emphasized again, 'I looked ('ראה') and behold ('הנה') a windstorm coming out of the north, an immense cloud with flashing lightning that is surrounded by a brilliant light' (1.4). The term הנה ('behold'), as a demonstrative participle, serves to accentuate what Ezekiel saw. The use of the particle הנה ('behold') is the transition between the announcement and the visionary sequence. It has a close semantic relationship with the verb ראה. The term הנה usually appears after verbs of seeing or discovering that makes the narrative graphic and vivid, which plausibly would enable the hearer to enter into the surprise or satisfaction of the speaker or actor concerned.[29] Thus, the use of this particle attests to the hearer's discernment of the visionary and the auditory experience as a surprise event and not an event brought on by divination, as in the prophet seeking divine wisdom from the council of YHWH.[30]

The first reference to the term רוח is notable in the opening description of the vision, 'I looked and behold a windstorm coming out of the north, an immense cloud with flashing lightning and surrounded by brilliant light' (1.4a).[31] The term רוח in this context is

---

[29] For the full treatment of how the particle הנה ('behold') relates to the verb ראה ('see') see Jackie A. Naudé, *NIDOTTE*, III, pp. 1007-15.

[30] The narrative describes King Jehoshaphat asking for the prophet Micaiah ben Imlah to seek divine counsel from the Lord (1 Kings 22). This type of throne theophany is somewhat different in that Micaiah seeks the wisdom of the council of the Lord. Isaiah and Ezekiel are portrayed as prophets who are not seeking counsel, but are surprised by the visionary encounter initiated from YHWH.

[31] As discussed previously in the literature review, there are three most common categories of 'spirit': (1) meteorological, (2) anthropological, and (3) theological. In its meteorological sense, 'spirit' refers to wind or 'air in motion' (Job 4.15; Gen. 3.8; Jer. 4.12). The anthropological concept of 'spirit' retains this sense of 'air in motion' and primarily refers to the physical act of breathing. Furthermore, 'spirit' incorporates a variety of psychological and emotional dispositions (Gen. 6.17; 7.15; Num. 16.22) in its anthropological sense, which exact translation often derives from the immediate context of the word (Gen. 41.8; Dan. 2.3; 7.15; Isa. 54.6). The emotions are understood to come forth out of the spirit and affect both disposition and behavior. The theological meaning is 'Spirit', as in God's Spirit. In this sense, 'spirit' is often qualified as e.g. רוח אלהים (God's Spirit), הרוח (the Spirit) or רוחי (my Spirit) (Gen. 41.38; 2 Sam. 23.2; 1 Kgs 22.24), though it may never really lose its meteorological sense as wind. This results in some instances where ambiguity arises between the two senses, for example, when the meteorological concept mixes with the theological (Ezek. 1.4). It is often integrated into a theological context of meaning, e.g. when the wind is presented as the instrument of healing, again merging the concepts together.

translated as ('wind') because the noun is coupled with 'storm' (1.4).[32] In this instance the meaning does refer directly to the divine Spirit, but rather denotes a ('wind') in a theological sense.[33] In other words, in the context of a vision, the hearer likely would have a sense that the רוח as ('wind') is a supernatural wind closely associated to, or caused by YHWH.[34]

Ezekiel's description of his opening vision utilizes thunder, fire, and storm theophany motifs (vv. 4-5), which signals to the hearers a supernatural sense for the use of רוח as ('wind') and not a natural wind.[35] In other words, 'the windstorm coming out of the north, as an immense cloud with flashing lightning that is surrounded by a brilliant light' is language and imagery that provides the hearer with a sense that YHWH is associated with this windstorm. Furthermore, Ezekiel and the exilic community would have been acquainted with the oral tradition of the Torah and how they were led out of Egypt and guided in the wilderness by 'a pillar of a cloud by day and a fire by night' (Exod. 13.21-22). The fire motif as God's presence, would also have elicited the idea of judgment, thus possibly evoking a sense

---

[32] The term רוח commonly refers to 'wind' in storm theophanies in the HB. The storm and fire motifs are reminiscent of the distinctive elements in the Israelite tradition of the symbolic understanding regarding a vision of the Lord upon a throne chariot was understood as the representative of the Lord's transcendence and immanence among his people. See Sweeney, *Reading Ezekiel*, p. 27. Sweeney argues that Ezekiel's throne chariot imagery is based in part upon the imagery of the Ark conveyed to Jerusalem on a wheeled cart during the reign of David (2 Samuel 6; cf. 2 Chr. 28.15). The two chariots of YHWH's presence are juxtaposed as they represent the Lord's immanent presence amidst the Israelites and his presence in the heavens.

[33] Koehler & Baumgartner, רוח, *HALOT*, II, pp. 1189-99.

[34] Scholarship affirms that there is a wide range of meanings or senses, which correspond to the English word for 'spirit'. So, it can be difficult at times to isolate one word that encapsulates the idea that is associated with an invisible phenomenon. Frequently, when the term occurs in the HB without direct association with animals or a person, it means 'wind'. For example, 'The heavens grew black with clouds and "wind", and there was a great rain' (1 Kgs 18.45). When the term is linked to speech it generally refers to 'breath' as 'air in motion' (Pss. 33.6; 135.16-17). The rendering of רוח as breath can also refer to a life sustaining function (Gen. 6.17; Job 12.10; Isa. 38.16; Ezek. 37.5-14). Regarding mood or disposition behind one's words, it can be said that the term רוח may refer to one's 'spirit' (Exod. 6.9; Num. 5.14; Job 7.11; Ezek. 3.14).

[35] Leslie Allen, 'The Structure and Intention of Ezekiel I', *VT* 43. 2 (1993), pp. 153-60.

of fear in Ezekiel and the hearers.[36] In the vision's theological context, this windstorm would be linked with notions of YHWH's power and mobility as Ezekiel described the windstorm moving.

The theophanic windstorm commences the vision narratives as an action drama. This powerful renting of the heavens introduces the description of the four living beings with intensely bright and colorful language. Ezekiel describes the vision in a multi-dimensional fashion. First, as the prophet gazes upwards toward the north, he describes for the hearers flashing lightening, brilliant light, fire, and glowing metals. One can only imagine how daunting was the idea of seeing a violent storm with dazzling but blinding lights that suddenly appear. Along with the storm motif, uniquely to Ezekiel's inaugural vision, there are explicit references to sparkling gemstone colors, some with metallic qualities, which enhances the affective dimensions of the text as these descriptions quite possibly would elicit excitement along with fear in the visionary and his hearers.[37]

After Ezekiel draws the hearer's attention upward, he then directs the hearer inward to emphasize the elements in the center of the storm imagery (1.4b). First, Ezekiel underscores the אש ('fire') language that appears twice in close connection to the terms, כעין האמל ('like glowing metal' vv. 4, 27). The second mention of the term האמל appears at the end of the vision to form an *inclusio*, underlining its importance. The term האמל is unique to Ezekiel in the HB appearing three times (1.4; 27; 8.2). The LXX renders the term ἤλεκτρον, 'electron', which distinguishes both amber and a gold or silver alloy.[38] The rare term is also combined with the term נגה ('brightness') in both places (vv. 4, 27) and understandably serves to accentuates the idea of a substance that brightly shines or is radiant. The first mention of the term האמל leaves the hearer without discernment of its meaning. However, with the second mention of האמל, Ezekiel sees and discloses quite a bit more detailed information. Ezekiel describes that

---

[36] Cf. Gen. 19.24, 2 Kgs 1.10-14, Isa. 66.15 for the symbolism between fire and divine judgment.

[37] Ross Winkle, 'Iridescence in Ezekiel', *Andrews Seminary Studies* 44.1 (2006), pp. 51-77, points to the explicit references to the rainbow in the OT that occur only in Gen. 9.13,14,16, and Ezek. 1.28. Winkle writes about the rainbow imagery (i.e. iridescence) that is explicit in Ezekiel 1, and argues that it is also underscored elsewhere in Ezekiel.

[38] Cf. Vulg. 'electrum' or 'amber', which is also a gold or silver alloy.

he saw the figure like that of a man (v. 26). This mysterious man from the waist up, כעין חשמל כמראה־אש תיב־לה סביב ('looked like glowing metal, and fire inside and around it' v. 27a), and אש ונגה לו סביב וממראה מתניו ולמטה ראתי כמראה ('from the appearance of his loins downward, I saw it had the appearance like fire and it had brightness all around it' v. 27b). This mysterious figure is specifically related to the rare and significant terms חשמל, אש, and נגה. Thus, Ezekiel is seeing a vision of a figure like that of a man full of fire, shining brightly like that of glowing hot metals.

The portrayal of a 'man' with spectacular imagery of blinding lights and flashing colors is quite bizarre. It is not surprising that Ezekiel presents the mysterious figure ambiguously as he uses simile and repetitive terms, such as, 'like' or דמות ('likeness'). These terms occur 16 times in the inaugural vision alone to describe the visionary events (1.4-28). The vagueness is juxtaposed with bold anthropomorphic analogies that are later used to describe the vision of the glory of YHWH.[39] In the context of his priestly heritage, it is also not unexpected that Ezekiel is timid to admit what he is seeing. While the imagery is elusive and mysterious, there is a sense that Ezekiel is seeing a radiant supernatural being on the throne of sapphire (v. 26).

The notion of seeing a vision with such electric colors could only enhance the mysteriousness and develop the affective dimensions for Ezekiel and the hearers. The fire language elicits the notions of the affective terms of volatility and passion, as fire is associated with the intense colors of red, orange, and silver. Thus, words used in storytelling are not just for the purpose of conveying information, but

---

[39] See Kutsko, *Between Heaven and Earth,* utilizes intertextual analysis to argue that Ezekiel presents the concept of human likeness in the image of God in two ways in chs. 1 and 8. He asserts Ezekiel presents the concept negatively to denounce foreign gods, and positively to describe the human-divine relationship. Kutsko's basis for this argument relies on the premise that Ezekiel knows about primeval history, specifically the creation tradition, in such a way as to emphasize this anthropological concept. Even though the image of God is not technically utilized in the Ezekiel texts, he argues that the anthropomorphic language implies this concept. In this view, Ezekiel intentionally chooses to use the terms 'likeness' and 'appearance' in Ezek. 1.26; 28, with knowledge of the terms 'likeness' and 'image' in Gen. 1.26. It is not clear in this intertextual analysis that the possible allusion to the creation tradition is for the purpose Kutsko proposes. It is not clear in the overarching context that Ezekiel's emphasis is upon humanity created in the image of God. Ezekiel seems to be more concerned with the corruption of humanity (Ezekiel 20), and the need for humanity to be reformed (Ezekiel 37).

affective words are used to elicit the hearer's affections. The idea of a violent storm with lightening and fire occurring in a vision narrative would naturally incite an affective response of fear as the hearers heard and visually imagined the words used to describe the vision. Fear can also include the positive affective dimensions of reverence and awe. The response of fear and awe possibly would have enflamed the Israelite notions of divine power and presence, as fire combined with the associated storm images recollects the literary presentations of the divine presence of YHWH.[40] This text also associates YHWH's appearance with storm language accentuating sounds (vv. 7-14).[41] The hearers likely would sense Ezekiel was seeing or encountering the divine presence of YHWH as they heard the story. As they used their imagination it is reasonable that they too would experience affective responses of fear (both positive and negative), which would be associated with honor combined with passion, power, and worshipful awe. Thus, the intensity of the storm and color images used to describe the vision, which later is recognized by Ezekiel as the glory of YHWH (1.28), only serve to heighten the affective impact upon the hearers.

Second, in his next words, Ezekiel ambiguously introduces the character of the four 'living creatures' (v. 5).[42] Ezekiel continues to describe the vision multi-dimensionally instead of linearly. In the center of the fire, Ezekiel describes the various sides of the four living beings (vv. 4, 5-12, 14, 23-24). Again, the use of 'like' and רמות is emphasized to elicit ambiguity of what Ezekiel claims to see.

---

[40] For example, YHWH's appearance to Israel on Mount Sinai was accompanied by thunder, flashes of lightning, and a dense cloud (Exod. 19.16). There are links with the theophanic text of Psalm 18 as YHWH is depicted in the poetry of antiquity riding on a chariot (v. 11). The use of fire is one of the most enduring images used by the authors of the HB to depict the divine presence. It appears in several literary genres spanning across many periods. The idea of YHWH's self-revelation is found in the burning-bush episode in Exod. 3.1–6 or the frequent 'pillar of fire' motif. The latter, a symbol of YHWH's presence during the exodus wanderings articulated in both (Exod. 13.21–22; 14.24; Num. 14.14) and (Num. 9.15–16) literary strands, not to mention its use in Deut. 1.33, Ps. 78.14 with 'fiery light' and as late as Neh. 9.12, 19.

[41] YHWH's appearance is symbolically characterized as thunder, lightning, dark clouds, brightness, and fire (Ps 18.6-19), and elsewhere anthropomorphized to paint a picture of a Divine warrior coming to do battle against the enemies of Israel (Hab. 3.3-15; Deut. 33.26; Judg. 5.4).

[42] Taylor, *Ezekiel*, p. 55, suggests that the living creatures represent various parts of creation.

Out of it emerged the appearance of the form of four creatures. This was their appearance: they had human form. But each one had four faces, and each had four wings. Their legs were straight and their feet were the hooves of a calf, gleaming like burnished bronze. Under their wings on their four sides were human hands. And each of the four had faces and wings (1.5-8).

He explains how the four living creatures appear to have a human form with four different faces: (1) a man, (2) a lion, (3) an ox, and (4) an eagle. These four-headed creatures, later recognized as cherubim (ch. 10), were given the task of carrying YHWH's divine throne, which serves to emphasize the theme of mobility in the narrative. The recurrent use of the number four is underscored in the description of the creatures and may symbolically represent character traits. The four faces may illustrate: (1) the image of God, (2) courage, (3) strength, and (4) majestic swiftness. The living creatures not only have four faces, but they are also described as having wings that 'spread out upward' with 'one touching the wing of another creature on either side, and two wings covering its body' (v. 11).

The first mention of the term רוח in association with the living creatures occurs here, 'wherever the Spirit would go, they went, without turning as they went' (v. 12). In this context, there is the idea that the divine רוח is controlling or guiding the direction of the living creatures.[43] The beings followed the divine רוח without turning as if they were in total submission to the רוח. The context highlights the idea that the beings did not turn themselves against the guidance of the רוח, thus submitting to the Spirit's guidance. The theme of mobility is underscored again in this scene with the mention of wings and their movements, 'the creatures sped back and forth like lightening' (v. 14).

Ezekiel's frequent use of the literary marker 'I looked' (ראה v.15) cues the hearer that more particulars of the vision are about to be revealed. This multi-dimensional style of telling the story of the vision serves to assist the hearer to behold or imagine what Ezekiel reports to see. Ezekiel describes the mysterious wheels כעין תרשיש ('sparkle like beryl' v. 16) and have intersecting wheels and rims that are filled with eyes all around. Ezekiel's use of color again to describe

---

[43] There is ambiguity as to whether the living being(s) represent the plural form or a collective singular.

the wheels would not go unnoticed. More than likely, the hearers would be amazed at the sparkling quality of the wheels in the vision, which enhances the heavenly scene.[44] The eyes that are positioned all around might be confusing. Would Ezekiel's hearers perceive the eyes symbolically? It is possible that they would discern that the eyes were representative of sight to navigate in a directional sense. It would be reasonable for Ezekiel's hearers to associate these kinds of anthropomorphic terms with natural meanings. They were accustomed to depicting YHWH in anthropomorphic and anthropopathic terms to relate spiritual notions with natural ones. This hearing is conceivable, but the anthropomorphic depiction of wheels possessing eyes all around them is bizarre and the hearers would be forgiven if they were perplexed by the ambiguity.

Consistent with the theme of mobility, Ezekiel connects the living creatures with the term רוח again: (1) 'wherever the spirit would go, they went, without turning as they went' (vv. 12, 20a), and (2) 'and the wheels rose along with them, for the spirit of the beings was in the wheels' (v. 20b, 21).[45] In the context of a chariot-throne vision, the wheels underscore the mobility motif. The living creatures appear to control the wheels as if responsible for driving the chariot-throne. There appears to be a distinction between the רוח that is in the living creatures in vv. 20b and 21 and the רוח used in vv. 12 and 20a that guides or controls the living creatures. In vv. 20b and 21 the living creatures are identified as ones possessing a רוח. It is possible that the hearers would understand the expression of the 'breath of life' as representing how YHWH gives life to creatures.[46] From this perspective, the term רוח is what describes these creatures as 'living' in somewhat a similar fashion as Ezekiel describes his own רוח (3.14). In vv. 12 and 20a, the context supports that the divine רוח is responsible for guiding and directing the living creatures. Ezekiel

---

[44] Winkle, 'Iridescence in Ezekiel', pp. 51-77, highlights the various colors in Ezekiel 1 with the rainbow imagery in the OT.

[45] רוח with the article signifies 'the spirit' (vv. 12, 20a), in contrast to the earlier use of רוח without the article, which signifies the theophanic 'wind' (v. 4).

[46] The views are quite varied. See Woodhouse, 'The Spirit in the Book of Ezekiel', p. 6, who renders the term as 'breath' in 20a and 'breath' when רוח enters the prophet in Ezek. 2.2. He defines רוח as 'breath' of the living beings representing 'air in motion' or the breath of the living beings is the motion that is moving the wheels (20b, 21). Block, 'The View from the Top', p. 191, renders the term רוח 'breath' and defines it as 'agent of animation'.

emphasizes the close connection between the actions of the living creatures and the wheels almost as if they were a part of each other as their movements appear synonymously.

Ezekiel's variable use of the term רוח without the ambiguous use of analogies conveys that he and possibly the hearers understood the different concepts of the רוח. The leitmotifs of guidance or leading, control or submission, and mobility are subsumed in the activities of the divine רוח as it relates to the living beings in these initial references. Ezekiel's depiction of the function of the term רוח along with the variable uses described for the term רוח suggests that Ezekiel possessed an understanding of the concepts for the רוח. Additionally, the lack of his repetitive use of the terms, 'like' or 'likeness' to emphasize ambiguity may indicate that the hearers understood the uses of the רוח as well.

However, the semblance of clarity quickly dissipates as Ezekiel returns to analogies as a means to describe the living creatures. He narrates, 'the appearance of the living creatures was like burning coals of fire or like torches. Fire moved up and down among the creatures; it was bright, and lightning moved out of it. The creatures sped back and forth like flashes of lightning' (vv. 13-14). Notice the dramatic effect of the compounding of fiery images emanating from and moving among the creatures: from אש to הגנ to ברק together with the kinetic verbs of בצרות, לכתמתה, איוצ, and קהבז. The multi-dimensional action-packed drama continues to unfold as Ezekiel draws his hearer's attention still higher to a place above the wheels and the living beings where he reports to see a רקיע ('firmament ') כעין הקרח ('sparkling like crystal' vv. 22, 26).[47]

Ezekiel, for the first time, illuminates to the hearers that he reports to hear sounds during the vision, (1) wings of the living beings touching like the roar of rushing water, and (2) like the voice of the Almighty, like the tumult of an army (v. 24). Although, his language is still couched in analogies, it appears Ezekiel attempts to provide details so as to help the hearers 'see' what they are hearing through their use of imagination. The visionary clearly emphasizes what is seen

---

[47] Cf. Josephus *Ant.* 3.137. Greek text taken from *Jewish Antiquities*, Books 1, vol. 4 of Josephus (trans. H. St. J. Thackeray, LCL; London: Heinemann, 1930), p. 380. In relation to the ark of the tabernacle, Josephus reports that Moses saw the two cherubim sculpted on the throne of God.

and not heard in the overall vision narrative, yet in this scene, Ezekiel also underscores the vision through its auditory elements. He mentions that he heard the sound of the wings of the living creatures and relates it to the 'like the roar of rushing waters', 'like the voice of the Almighty', 'like the tumult of an army', and yet distinguishes this voice from 'a voice that came from above the expanse over their [living creatures] heads' (v. 25a). The sounds of rushing water and the hearing of an advancing army are natural sounds, yet they are in a list with that of the voice of the Almighty. The hearers at this point might assume Ezekiel is familiar with the voice of the Almighty since he reports what he hears is like the voice of the Almighty. The sounds Ezekiel reports to hear appear at first, to be associated with the living creatures and with the voice of the Almighty, but then, as the story continues, clarity pervades. The voice is coming from the 'figure like that of a man' on the throne (vv. 25-28).[48]

The dramatic visionary journey continues as Ezekiel redirects his hearer's attention away from the sounds and towards what he reports to see. Ezekiel introduces the hearers to even a higher place in the heavenly visionary world, 'above the firmament looked like a throne of sapphire stone' (אבן־ספיר) (v. 26). The use of a majestic color to describe the throne serves to emphasize the royal tone of what is to follow in the story.[49] As Ezekiel leads the hearers to visualize higher levels of his vision, the unique term חשמל appears again as Ezekiel introduces one of the main characters in the book, the nameless or mysterious figure like that of a man (vv. 26b-27).

Ezekiel reports that the nameless figure is high above on the throne and describes, 'I ראה that what appeared to be from his waist up; he looked like כעין חשמל, as if full of אש, and that from below he looked like אש and brilliant light surrounded him' (vv. 26b-27).

---

[48] Robert G. Hall, 'Living Creatures in the Midst of the Throne: Another Look at Revelation 4.6', *NTS* 36 (1990), pp. 608-613, suggests that the text assumes that the throne is patterned on the OT tabernacle ark, and concluded that one should take the text just as it reads (i.e., the creatures are both in the midst of the throne and around it), with the living creatures in the midst of the throne as components of it.

[49] Winkle, 'Iridescence in Ezekiel', p. 68, names lapis lazuli as the platform upon which the throne of God rests (Exod. 24.10). Winkle also proposes that it is possible that the text is alluding to the concept of stone bodies, which may be related to the Jewish tradition of angelic beings being engraved on the pedestal of the divine throne. In the Qumran Songs of the Sabbath Sacrifice, one reads of such beings (4Q405 19 5-7a).

The language supports the idea that Ezekiel is not only seeing but discerning what he is seeing. He likens the brilliant light that surrounds 'the figure on the throne' with that of 'a rainbow in the clouds on a rainy day' (1.27-28). The nameless figure appears to be engulfed with electric glowing fire surrounded by a brilliant rainbow of lights. What a sight to behold! The identity of the one on the throne is clouded in mystery. Ezekiel uses metaphorical language accentuated by brilliant colors associated with sparkling gems and a rainbow. Ezekiel's final analogy used in this scene connects the 'the figure on the throne' with 'the likeness of the glory of YHWH' (v. 28b). Although, in keeping with his character portrayed as a priestly-prophetic seer in Babylon, he carefully uses simile so as not to describe the glory of YHWH in tangible terms.[50] Expectedly, the hearers would also be tentative in their understanding because the glory of YHWH is notably associated with its sacred dwelling place.[51] Ezekiel's description of the כבוד־יהוה is remarkable as it portrays God's glory as representing his attributes of holiness, dynamic power, majesty, and splendor.[52] His use of anthropomorphic terms to describe the כבוד־יהוה is similar to what can be called a theophany or the immanent manifestation of God's glory.[53] Ezekiel's hearers may perceive the יהוה־

---

[50] See Odell, *Ezekiel*, pp. 19-26. Odell compares ancient Israelite throne-room and storm theophanies with ancient Near Eastern iconography to note some similarities, yet she adds, 'there are no direct parallels in either the biblical or ancient Near Eastern traditions to Ezekiel's depiction of the four living beings'.

[51] The glory of YHWH is associated with the tabernacle (Exod. 40.34), and then later in the holy Temple (1 Sam. 1.9), and not in a foreign land that would be perceived as a defiled unholy place. See Collins, כבוד ('glory') in *NIDOTTE*, III, pp. 581-87. The term כבוד־יהוה first appears in Exod. 16.7, which emphasizes that the glory is something seen, and it is associated with a cloud. Collins provides an outline of contemporary scholarship, which tends to focus upon the nom. כבוד and the interconnected themes associated with it. Generally, the idea of the glory of YHWH represents God's presence that manifests in the events of ancient Israelite history, but it also conveys a revelation of God's attributes. Eiseman, (*Yechezkel*, p. 64) discusses that the idea of the divine abode was connected with worship in Israel somewhat before the Josianic reform and significantly thereafter.

[52] Naudé, 'חֲזוֹן' ('vision') in *NIDOTTE*, II, pp. 1012-13. Naudé explains, 'typically in a vision, the auditory aspect is dominant over the visual and the visual side of prophetic visions is not God himself'.

[53] Ezekiel's vision of the glory of YHWH can be likened to Moses' encounter (Exod. 33.18), which can be categorized as an anthropomorphic theophanic narrative. For example, Moses asks to see the face of YHWH and is favored by YHWH's glory revealed in terms of YHWH's אחר ('back'), while he is protected by YHWH's

כבוד as an theophanic visionary encounter and would be forgiven if they were uncertain as to whether the כבוד־יהוה was actually appearing to Ezekiel in Babylon.

The final scene features the motifs of clarity, discernment, and understanding. The message conveys that Ezekiel discerns or understands what he is seeing and affectively responds as he falls prostrate in a demonstration of worship in reverential fear and awe, 'When I saw it [glory of YHWH], I fell on my face' (1.28b). The act of worship or falling prostrate depicts Ezekiel's affective response and provides the context for prophetic discernment.[54] This prostration conveys that Ezekiel finally understands what he is seeing. Expectedly, Ezekiel would have given honor to the divine presence by falling prostrate. Yet, Ezekiel as a priestly-prophetic seer in exile, surprised by the presence of the chariot-throne vision of the כבוד־יהוה in a foreign land would also have likely been fearful of the possibility of judgment.[55] Considering the shared context of the exiles and Ezekiel, it naturally elicits the element of surprise and underscores the affective dimensions of the story. The hearers engaging in their imagination would have likely been surprised by the grand entrance of the glory of YHWH in Babylon, fearing judgment, but also simultaneously responding with a sense of awe as YHWH demonstrated his power by announcing sovereign rulership through his presence in Babylon.[56]

In the midst of worship, Ezekiel claims to hear 'the voice of one speaking' (v. 28), which supports the motifs of clarity, discernment, and understanding. Not only does the seer specifically tell the hearers what he is seeing, but he also reports that he hears a voice speaking. At this point in the story, Ezekiel does not identify the voice, but the

---

יד, are ways in which anthropomorphic terms are used to describe what can be considered indescribable concepts.

[54] The affective language in Ezekiel also echoes the story of when the Spirit of God came upon Balaam, who afterwards was given a vision of the Almighty (cf. Num. 24.3-4, 15-16). Ezekiel and Balaam both fell prostrate in an appropriate act of reverence, awe, and submission not only to see but to discern what is being seen: a vision of the glory of YHWH. These stories not only share in the emphasis placed upon the affective responses, but also in the leading role of the רוח.

[55] W. VanGemeren, כבוד ('glory') in *NIDOTTE*, II, pp. 579-82. The כבוד־יהוה is a technical term for the manifest presence YHWH and often appears in judgment.

[56] Sweeney, *Reading Ezekiel*, p. 31.

context points to the figure of the man upon the throne and the identification of the vision of the glory of YHWH.

Summary

Ezekiel's chariot-throne vision of the glory of YHWH that precedes his call narrative is unique in many ways.[57] First, in Ezekiel's vision, YHWH's glory makes a surprising entrance into a foreign land without a sacred dwelling place. The chariot-throne imagery elicits the themes of majestic mobility and sovereign power. The grand entrance of YHWH moving from his abode in the Jerusalem Temple to a foreign land in Babylon illustrates his universal sovereign power over the cosmos. Yet, at this point, it is not certain whether YHWH is coming for the purpose of defending his covenant people or judging them.[58] YHWH's universal power over the cosmos is also illustrated by the use of the number four, as it is symbolically indicative of the four corners of the cosmos. The dimensional aspect is emphasized not only in the way Ezekiel begins to describe the vision, but also in the symbolic language of the use of the number four. The four corners can also convey four spatial dimensions: (1) width, (2) length, (3) height, and (4) depth or the intersections of the other three dimensions.

Second, Ezekiel appeals to the hearers' imagination not only through the genre, but also through his use of analogy. In some sense, Ezekiel invites the hearers to see what he sees as a means to hear YHWH's prophetic word given in symbolic form. He artistically presents what would be called in contemporary terms, a 3-D dramatic film or virtual reality experience. The action drama is intensified with its fire language, constant unpredictable movements, vivid electrifying colors, commanding voices, allusions of majestic imagery, and dynamic forces at work in and around the characters. Naturally, a

---

[57] Expectedly, Isaiah's throne-room vision occurs while in the Temple of Jerusalem and he sees God seated upon the throne. For a different view, see Sweeney, *Reading Ezekiel*, pp. 26-27. Sweeney emphasizes the similarities between the imagery of the Ark of the Covenant with that of Ezekiel's inaugural vision to argue that while Ezekiel's vision is similar to throne-room theophanies, it is distinct due to the chariot motif.

[58] Zimmerli, *Ezekiel 1*, p. 120. The original setting of the motif of YHWH coming from his dwelling place from Sinai (Deut. 32.2) was to come to the aid of his people during battle. This motif expanded to the prophetic announcements of judgments and salvation, which no longer saw YHWH coming from Sinai but that of his dwelling place in Zion (Ps. 50.3).

drama of this magnitude would elicit a myriad of emotional responses with its use of poetic nuances that inherently provoke the
hearer's affections. For example, the fire and storm language used to
describe the glory of YHWH elicits volatility and passion with its
association to intense colors of red, orange, and silver. Thus, this 3-
D film, if you will, is complete with its appeal to an ancient sight and
sound generation, a prophetic generation that responds not only cerebrally but also affectively.

Third, the close proximity and context supports that the Hebrew
idiom יד־יהוה in Ezekiel's superscription conveys an emphasis upon
the revelatory state of the seer.[59] The beginning of the book highlights the context of Ezekiel's reception of visions of supernatural
realities. In fact, the hearing of the word of YHWH to Ezekiel is not
mentioned until after the vision narrative is completely told and imagined by the hearers. Ezekiel's vision drama is marked by the mode
of inspiration as Ezekiel tells the hearers that it was received while
the 'hand of YHWH was upon him there' (v. 3). It is from this perspective that the seer is given the vision by the power of YHWH and
not perceived, at this point, for a specific task.

Fourth, linguistically, Ezekiel juxtaposes the themes of ambiguity
and clarity. His use of analogy emphasizes ambiguity, yet it also provides some clarity for the hearers. While his repetitive use of the
terms 'like' or 'likeness' attempt to describe what seems indescribable; it does convey ambiguity, but it also leads the hearer to use their
prophetic imagination. In this way, Ezekiel's use of natural terms to
describe supernatural realities provides understanding for the hearers.
The language of ambiguity also lends to the quality of the affective
dimensions of the hearers. For example, his repetitive use the words
'like' or 'likeness' conveys to the hearers that he is seeing these specific supernatural realities for the first time and he is perplexed,
amazed, and/or hesitant to describe what he sees. Specifically, the
distinctive term חשמל combined with אש and brilliant light serve to

---

[59] Neve, *The Spirit of God in the Old Testament*, pp. 40-46, proposes that the phrase
יד־יהוה in Ezekiel may represent an ecstatic condition and when it is used with רוח
the writer(s) is referring to YHWH's 'spirit' and not 'wind'. Likewise, he argues that
when the writer(s) uses any affective terms associated with YHWH or other anthropomorphic language, then the term is referring to YHWH's 'Spirit' and not
'wind'.

emphasize the connections between the leitmotifs of color, movement, passion, and power in the visionary experience.

Ezekiel, as illustrated like a 3-D film, is not only presented in the
language of analogy, but also in anthropomorphic terms, and painted
from several dimensions: (1) the כבוד־יהוה is described in hierarchal
and horizontal layers, (2) voices are heard from the living creatures
and the mysterious figure on the throne, (3) various activities of the
רוח interact with the characters, and (4) Ezekiel's affective responses
conclude the vision with the act of discernment and understanding,
which provides clarity to the seer. Ezekiel's multi-dimensional approach to describe his visions serves to stimulate the hearers through
most of the senses, (1) sight, (2) hearing, and (3) the affections. The
hearers may have also experienced a 'whirlwind' of dramatic stimu-
lation as they attempt to imagine the action-packed vision in 3-D.
From this multi-dimensional perspective, the seer is inviting the hearers to imagine what he is seeing so as to entice participation in the
drama that is unfolding. In these ways, the idea of seeing a prophetic
message is indistinguishable from hearing a prophetic message, as
Ezekiel's presentation of the vision requires a multi-dimensional interpretation instead of a linear understanding.

In contrast to the ambiguity illustrated with the use of analogy,
Ezekiel does not use analogy when referring to the diverse activities
of the רוח. In the midst of perplexing ambiguity, Ezekiel underscores
elements of discernment and clarity when he refers to the diverse
activities of the divine רוח that feature the leitmotifs of the themes
of power, submission or dominance, and mobility. Ezekiel highlights
the term רוח in several passages (1.12, 20, 21; 2.2; 3.12, 14, 24) and
the absence of the use of analogy to describe the activities implies
that the hearers would have had a clearer understanding for the diverse uses for the term רוח. Narratively, Ezekiel links the יד־יהוה and
the רוח to emphasize YHWH's power, the reception of his vision,
and clarity and discernment of the vision, which all are associated to
the hearer's perception and understanding of the inaugural vision:
The glory of YHWH.

C. Ezekiel's Call Narrative (2.1–3.27)

Ezekiel 2.1–3.27 is closely connected to the inaugural throne vision
(1.1-28) and is generally considered a whole literary unit. As previously mentioned, the unit will be treated independently for the

purpose of clarity for the reader. After Ezekiel's lengthy account of the majestic and awe-inspiring vision of the glory of YHWH, which provokes the prophet to fall prostate in worship, he claims to hear 'a voice speaking' (1.28). The first scene in this section begins with a title used to address the seer, 'Son of man', which represents a transitional marker, as the hearers soon discover Ezekiel employs frequently throughout his visions to introduce a prophetic speech (2.1-10).[60] This expression would communicate to the hearers that Ezekiel, as a mere mortal is distinguished from YHWH and the living beings of ch. 1, yet he is also special to YHWH as his messenger.

Ezekiel reports that he was commanded to stand up on his feet and instructed that YHWH will soon speak to him (2.1). Though not stated explicitly, it appears that the hearers would understand the רוח to be the mediator of YHWH's divine words.[61] This is the first mention of the רוח in relation to the prophet and it is closely associated with Ezekiel's hearing YHWH's commissioning speech (2.1-10), which adds to the significance of one of the main characters, the רוח. The fact that 'the voice' commands him to stand suggests that Ezekiel was still lying prostrate in worship, fear, and reverence to the magnificent vision of the glory of YHWH.[62] Ezekiel's description in the narrative is not clear as to whether he was too afraid to get up or if he was so engrossed in the awe-inspiring vision of YHWH's chariot throne ushering in YHWH's glory that he could not get up.

---

[60] The 'Son of man' phrase is used in Ezekiel approximately 93 times (cf. 2.1, 3; 3.1; 4.1, 16; 5.1; 6.2; 12.27; 17.2; 21.2; 22.2; 24.2; 33.2; 36.1; 39.1). It is also used elsewhere in the HB, in various apocalyptic works of the intertestamental period, and in the Greek NT. It is used as an address to distinguish between human beings, God, angels, or the eschatological figure to come at the end of history.

[61] Scheepers, *Die Gees van God en die Gees van die mens,* pp. 316-18. The paucity of the mention of the spirit related to prophetic inspiration in certain periods of Israelite history has caused some scholars to question the significance the role of the spirit has played. For example, the prophets do not directly claim prophetic inspiration by the spirit in the period after 700 BCE until the first exile in 597 BCE. An exception may be represented by Mic. 3.8, 'But as for me, I am filled with power, with the Spirit of the Lord'. For a comprehensive treatment of this debate, see Robson, *Word and Spirit in Ezekiel,* pp. 146-70. Robson categorizes the four perspectives of interpretation on this paucity: (1) antithetical, (2) historical, (3) rhetorical, and (4) theological. He argues that 'there is no reason to think the prophets who do not mention the רוח [of YHWH] reject the רוח [of YHWH] in connection with their prophetic activity, because first they heard and then they spoke the word of YHWH'.

[62] Perhaps Ezekiel's hearers would recall that the prophet Moses encountered YHWH 'face to face' (Exod. 33.11).

Certainly, the visionary images of the living creatures and a throne with a figure of a man engulfed in flames encased with light was overwhelming. Whatever the reason, the role of the affections in the act of worship underscores the tone for the entire scene. Likely the hearers would understand that Ezekiel was not able to stand in the divine presence of the glory of YHWH without assistance from the רוח because he claims that בי רוח כאשר דבר אלי ותעמדני על־רגלי ותבא ('The Spirit came into me as he spoke and caused me to stand to my feet' 2.2; 3.24).[63] From this perspective, the Spirit empowers the prophet to stand before the sacred presence of the glory of YHWH.

This transition in the story is key as it introduces the activities of the divine רוח with the prophet. The hearers are presented with the image of the indwelling רוח engaging the seer. This is the first occurrence of the רוח encountering the seer in the vision narrative. It is unique in the sense that the story emphasizes the רוח indwelling the prophet, which results in controlling or empowering the prophet's bodily functions as the רוח raises him to his feet. Ezekiel and the hearers would likely have believed the Hebrew leaders were divinely inspired and endued with divine power because the רוח אלהים בו

---

[63] See Lindblom, *Prophecy in Ancient Israel*, p. 57. Lindblom states that the Israelite prophets understood YHWH's Spirit and YHWH's hand are 'substantially identical in their effect', in which they are both expressions of divine power of inspiration and effective in ecstatic experience. He identifies the expressions: 'Spirit of YHWH' and the 'hand of YHWH' as literary markers indicating divine inspiration through ecstatic events. He argues that the phrase, 'The Spirit came into me' is similar to what can be called the divine inspiration formula, 'the Spirit of YHWH fell upon me'. See also, Kapelrud, 'The Spirit and the Word in the Prophets', p. 46. He recognizes that only Ezekiel and Micah are two of the later prophets who emphasize the spirit of YHWH as the divine רוח, who seized and filled them, and inspired them to speak the word of YHWH.

('Spirit of God was in him') or רוח־יהוה came upon them.[64] Linguistically, the preposition ב can either mean 'in' or 'on'.[65]

In Ezekiel, the רוח language and the description of its activities provides the visionary plot for the developing role of the רוח as one of the book's primary characters. This scene to some degree mirrors the activities of the רוח in the inaugural vision. For example, Ezekiel's use of the article before the term רוח highlights the divine Spirit's activities in both scenes. Like, the living creatures identified as ones possessing a רוח (v. 20b) and the divine רוח (vv. 12, 20a), which functions to guide and direct or possibly controls, mirrors its activities with the seer in 2.2. Second, Ezekiel omits the use of simile when referring to the רוח. Since, Ezekiel's presentation of the רוח language in the inaugural vision is clearer than the ambiguous language used to describe the chariot-throne and the glory of YHWH, it suggests that the hearers would have had a clearer sense of these activities that are occurring in the current scene.

The recurrent transitional marker, 'Son of man' continues to introduce YHWH's speeches throughout the call narrative (2.1-3.27). Embedded in the prophetic speeches are affective terms that accentuate the tenor of the scene. As Ezekiel is given his prophetic mandate to be a messenger to the Israelites, he uses variations of the word מרד ('rebellious') seven times to describe the Israelites in the next

---

[64] In the HB, it was primarily the mediators of God's covenant who experienced the Spirit on an individual basis. In Israelite history, beginning with Joseph and continuing through David the Spirit came upon leaders for the sake of empowering them for a specific task (Gen. 41.38; Num. 11.17, 25; 27.18-19; Deut. 34.9; Judg. 3.10; 6.34; 14.6,19; 15.14; 1 Sam. 10.1, 6, 10; 11.1-11). These passages raise questions as to the operation of the Spirit 'dwelling' inside the OT believer. Block argues that a common misperception is that the Spirit of God only 'comes upon' in the OT but indwells in the NT believer. For a discussion on this issue see Block, *Empowering By the Spirit of God*, p. 45. See also, Richard Sklba, '"Until the Spirit from on High is Poured out on Us" (Isa. 32.15). Reflections on the Role of the Spirit in the Exile', *CBQ* 46 (1984), pp. 1-17. (cf. Isa. 61.1-3; Mic. 3.8; Zech. 4.6). For a cultural anthropological view, see Wilson, 'Prophecy and Ecstasy', pp. 321-37, who associates the indwelling as 'spirit possession' and argues that it can be viewed positively or negatively in a society, according to what spirit they attribute has possessed the individual.

[65] See *HALOT*, ב ('in' or 'on'), pp. 103-105. An example of the Spirit 'filling' is found in the Torah, as the רוח filled the craftsman, Bezalel and Oholiab as they were empowered to do the work on the tabernacle (Exod. 31.1-5; 35. 30-35).

several passages.[66] The recurrent term cues the hearer that the prophet is called to a disobedient, stubborn, and defiant group of people, the Israelites. These affective terms not only serve to describe the affective disposition of the Israelites, but also would probably elicit affective responses of the hearers, as they were the Israelites exiled in Babylon.

For the first time, Ezekiel confirms for the hearers that he is among them (2.5). The introduction of YHWH, the mandate that is commissioned to the prophet, and the vision of the glory of YHWH to Ezekiel, supports that the hearers would understand Ezekiel was a prophet among them and about to receive a message from YHWH.[67] YHWH's description of the Israelites would likely produce fear and prompt an expectation of impending judgment that might be coming to their community as they waited to hear what YHWH would speak to them through Ezekiel. The tension in the story builds, as Ezekiel juxtaposes YHWH's harsh affective descriptions of the Israelites with that of YHWH's somewhat reassuring words to the prophet. Twice YHWH exhorts Ezekiel not to be afraid (v. 6). Ezekiel reports that YHWH commands him not to rebel or be afraid whether the rebellious Israelites listen or fail to listen (vv. 6-8). The task would not be easy. The affective language provides the hearers with the intense nature of YHWH's prophetic commissioning to the prophet. Yet, YHWH's encouragement not to be afraid is also mixed with a warning as YHWH tells the prophet not to rebel like his fellow Israelites.

---

[66] The prophetic mandate from YHWH to one of his messengers is in sharp contrast to a 'false prophet' or one 'YHWH has not sent you' (Jer. 43.2).

[67] Until recently, the common view asserts that the overall function of the prophetic call narratives was to authenticate and legitimate the prophet as the messenger of YHWH. However, the rise in the use of rhetorical analysis as a means to identify communicative intent has generated fresh insight and challenged this view. For example, see Robson, *Word and Spirit in Ezekiel*, pp. 146-70, who argues that Ezekiel's call narrative functions not to authenticate the prophet, but rather to portray him as an example of the obedience that YHWH desires of all his people. He concludes, 'The relationship between YHWH's רוח and YHWH's דבר in the book of Ezekiel is to be understood in terms of the transformation of the book's addressees'. In a similar vein, Renz, *The Rhetorical Function of the Book of Ezekiel*, pp. 1, 229, argues that the book of Ezekiel 'received its final shape to function in a specific way for the second generation of exiles to shape the self-understanding of the exilic community'. He concludes that the rhetorical purpose was accomplished in part through the visual and aural strategies using Ezekiel as 'the medium of the message'. See also, Block, *The Book of Ezekiel*, p. 15. Renz and Block argue that the central rhetorical function of the book is to transform the audience's perception of their relationship with YHWH.

The story does not indicate as to whether Ezekiel was a rebellious prophet or not. Only a warning is given not to be like his rebellious Israelite compatriots.

The repetitive literary marker ואראה links the earlier visionary scenes and cues the reader to pay particular attention to what is about to unfold. Structurally, it serves to demarcate the previous speech from the next vision and oracular scene (2.9-10). YHWH once again emphasizes the visual and oral aspects in the narrative as Ezekiel describes, 'I looked, and I saw a hand stretched out to me. In it was a scroll' (v. 9). The hearers may recall YHWH's hand that came upon Ezekiel (1.3). The scroll that Ezekiel sees has words, קנים והגה והי ('lamentations, mourning, and woe') written on both the front and the back (2.10).[68] All three words are synonymous with wailing and grief giving the hearers reason to become anxious as they may discern that the 'outstretched hand' was possibly YHWH's hand giving Ezekiel impending words of distress as a result of judgment.

Unexpectedly, Ezekiel's initial introduction to the vision of the scroll emphasizes the act of obedience, rather than what the scroll represents. He reports that he is commanded three times to 'eat what is before you' by the outstretched hand and then 'go and speak to the house of Israel' (2.8; twice in 3.1).[69] As Ezekiel complies, he reports that the scroll tastes sweet as honey. Given the previous emphasis upon the affective description of the Israelites as disobedient, it is likely the hearers would understand that YHWH was testing the will or obedience of the prophet. Ezekiel's use of honey to describe the taste of the scroll is in sharp contrast to the revealed words written on the scroll קנים והגה והי ('lamentations, mourning, and woe'). The affective language of extreme distress and sadness underscores the previous motif of impending judgment that was introduced with Ezekiel's commission. The symbolism conveys that Ezekiel found the דבר־יהוה to be pleasant even though it represents judgment.

It also suggests that Ezekiel's hearers would understand that the prophet embodied YHWH's word as he ate the scroll. Ezekiel was commanded to consume the words of YHWH before he was

---

[68] Zimmerli, *Ezekiel* 1, p. 135. Peter Craigie, *Ezekiel* (Philadelphia: The Westminster Press, 1983), p. 17.

[69] Cf. Thomas and Macchia, *Revelation*, p. 196, observe a connection between Rev. 10.8-11 and Ezek. 2.8-3.2. Like Ezekiel, John is commanded to 'take' and 'eat' the book that is in the angel's hand.

commanded to speak the words of YHWH. The contents of the words became a part of Ezekiel. In essence, the symbolic act may point to the idea that if the hearers receive the harsh words of YHWH, then they too would be filled and would also surprisingly experience sweetness of YHWH's words.

After Ezekiel narrates that he willingly obeys YHWH's commands, the recurrent themes of Israel's disobedience and an unwillingness to listen prevails. Ezekiel's obedience likely would demonstrate to the hearers that the Ezekiel's willingness to receive or hear YHWH's words is closely tied to his obedience, unlike the spiritual deafness of his compatriots (v. 7). As Ezekiel is obedient, YHWH decrees that he will make Ezekiel 'as unyielding and hardened' as the Israelites before he finally instructs him to go and speak to his fellow exiles (3.4-11). Yet, before Ezekiel discloses to the hearers what YHWH's message entails, the plot twists and diverts their attention to a unique description of the Spirit's activity. The second occurrence that highlights the רוח in Ezekiel's call narrative interrupts the story, as Ezekiel claims, 'Then the Spirit lifted me up' (3.12a). This unique phrase conveys the idea of an upward transportation by the רוח or what can be referred to as the 'ascension motif'.[70] The ascension motif represents the characteristic of an upward mobility and it occurs elsewhere in the book where the רוח lifts the prophet and transports him in a vision by 'the Spirit of YHWH' (11.24).[71] It demonstrates the activity of the רוח transporting the prophet as the words נשׂא ('lift, carry, or take up') by הרוח are highlighted. Given the context emphasizing that the prophet was caught up in 'divine visions' (1.3; cf. 8.3 and 11.24), the hearers are not likely to understand this to mean a literal carrying away. For the same reasons, neither could הרוח represent a gust of wind, but rather is indeed the Spirit of YHWH.[72]

---

[70] The term 'ascension' is my language used to describe the transporting action of the Spirit. It conveys that the Spirit lifts up the prophet in a divine vision and takes him to another place.

[71] The רוח language of ascension also occurs in the Elijah narrative, 'The Spirit of the Lord carries Elijah' (1 Kgs 18.12) and, 'The Spirit of the Lord caught him up and casts him' (2 Kgs 2.16).

[72] The other occurrences in the book only support the claim that the רוח is the divine רוח since the context of the Temple vision references the same type of transportation by הרוח (8.3; 11.1), and in 11.24 as Ezekiel parallels this form to the construct form, 'Spirit of God'.

After Ezekiel is transported upward to a place that is later revealed, it is the idea of worship that is emphasized again: ורוח נשׂאתני ('Then the Spirit lifted me up') and I heard behind me a great rushing voice, "Blessed is the glory of YHWH in his place!"[73] Ezekiel ambiguously associates the sound of a great rushing voice with sounds of the wings of the living beings as they touch each other (3.13). Within the context of YHWH's chariot throne theophany, the implied connotation is that the living beings are the ones that are speaking the blessing. Given that Ezekiel conveys to the hearers that he has been taken up by the Spirit to the place where the glory of YHWH is located, it is likely that the hearers would understand that the Spirit took Ezekiel in a vision to encounter the glory of YHWH just like he described previously in the inaugural vision. Ezekiel is given a unique opportunity to witness the living creatures worship the glory of YHWH in his visionary experience.

Since Ezekiel is not described as leaving a physical place, it is apparent that Ezekiel is lifted by the רוח in a vision to the throne-room of YHWH where the living creatures praise the Lord in his dwelling. A visionary encounter is confirmed by the description of the prophet as he hears a voice as a great earthquake and the wings of the living beings that touch each other (vv. 12, 13). Thus, for a second time in this visionary call narrative, the יד־יהוה is associated with a vision of the כבוד־יהוה and now is connected with the ascension motif by the Spirit. In the first visionary encounter with the כבוד־יהוה, the prophet falls on his face in reverential fear and awe (1.28b). However, something very unusual is conveyed in this encounter. The scene is interrupted again by the phrase ורוח נשׂאתני ותקחני (3.14).[74] Uniquely, Ezekiel reports that as he is lifted by the רוח and taken away, which the hearers would likely perceive that it was the divine Spirit who was taking the prophet away in a vision from YHWH's dwelling place. The language informs the hearers that it is the divine Spirit that is guiding and controlling the prophet's movements in the vision.

---

[73] This occurrence may be seen as in parallel with Pss. 72.19 and 135.21, yet the doxology towards the כבוד־יהוה remains unmatched. See Block, *The Book of Ezekiel 1–24*, p. 134. In both Psalms, the usage relates the name to the glory. In Isaiah 6, the seraphim also refer to the holiness of the name, Lord.

[74] Zimmerli, *Ezekiel 1*, pp. 117-18. Zimmerli argues that this idiom is distinct in ancient Israelite culture and religion.

The difference in this vision scene is that Ezekiel identifies הרוח that transports him as the same רוח that enters him in 2.2, which provides support that the divine Spirit is responsible for the diverse activities linked to empowerment, inspiration, and transportation depicted in the story. In the previous vision scene of the Spirit's activity with the prophet, Ezekiel reports to hear a voice speaking to him, now the prophet hears praises and sounds of the wings of the living beings (3.12-13). In the inaugural vision, Ezekiel describes the sounds of the living beings and their wings, like the roar of rushing waters, like the voice that resembled the Almighty God (1.24-25). In both vision narratives, the יד־יהוה is upon Ezekiel as he saw and heard the vision of the glory of YHWH (1.3; 3.14).[75] However, the hearers likely would now recall that not only was the יד־יהוה upon the prophet, but the divine רוח entered Ezekiel (2.2), raised him (2.2), and now lifted him up (3.12) to see the glory of YHWH. Immediately following, Ezekiel hears the praises given to the glory of YHWH in his dwelling place (3.12), and the wings of the living beings brushing against each other (3.13), and a loud rumbling sound (3.14). The close proximity between the recurring themes of the Spirit's activity and the hand of YHWH with the prophet and the themes of seeing and hearing heavenly visions convey to the hearers that it is the יד־יהוה and the divine Spirit that enable and inspire the prophet to see and hear.

Ezekiel proceeds to describe for the hearers that he is emotionally affected by the Spirit's transportation. He conveys that while being taken away from YHWH's dwelling place, ואלך מר בצמת רוחי ('I went in bitterness and in the heat of my spirit') with יהוה־ליע חזקה ויד ('The hand of YHWH being strong upon me') (3.14).[76] The

---

[75] Dreytza, יד־יהוה ('hand of YHWH'), *NIDOTTE*, II. p. 404. Dreytza attests that this idiom is not only present in Ezekiel's 'irresistible call, … but also during his lifetime the Lord seizes him on special occasions'. He observes that especially in the book of Ezekiel, what he denotes as the divine coercion formula 'The hand of YHWH was upon me there' means a 'special experience of God's power upon the prophet, which is similar to the actions of God's רוח upon certain judges of Israel'. In the story of Elisha in 2 Kgs 3.15, the terms יד and רוח are used interchangeably.

[76] Greenberg, *Ezekiel, 1–20*, p. 42. He argues that the phrase, the יד־יהוה is not only used to convey that God's hand is 'a manifestation of his power' but also is the urgency, pressure, and compulsion by which he [Ezekiel] is stunned and overwhelmed (cf. Ezek. 3.27).

Hebrew affective term מר with the distinguishing clause בחמת רוחי heightens Ezekiel's emotional disposition.[77] The variation of the Hebrew idiom, the ויד־יהוה ליע חזקה adds to the intensity of the story. The use of the verb חזקה ('strong') elicits a forceful and dynamic quality to the descriptions of the activities of the divine רוח and YHWH's יד. Ezekiel also reports that while he is being transported to and from the divine presence of the כבוד־יהוה in a vision, he is left angry and upset.[78] Would Ezekiel's hearers draw conclusions that the descriptions of the prophet's negative affections were a sign of his resistance to YHWH or possibly that he would rebel against YHWH? Only the unfolding of the story could provide clarity as to how the affective disposition of Ezekiel would influence his response. What is clear, is that the רוח is closely associated with the phrase the יד־יהוה, and it accentuates the themes of power, submission or dominance, and mobility. Understandably the hearers would perceive that YHWH's power and authority were in sharp contrast to Ezekiel's vulnerability and dependence upon YHWH even in the midst of emotional turmoil.

Ezekiel continues to feature the central literary motifs of the יהוה־יד, the כבוד, and הרוח highlighted in the inaugural vision (1.1-28).[79] Therefore, it is possible that Ezekiel's hearers would recall how the יד־יהוה and the Spirit were connected in the inaugural vision and make the same correlations in this scene (3.12-16).[80] Similarly, as the theme of mobility was connected to the Spirit with the chariot throne

---

[77] The Hebrew word מר is used to describe Esau's emotional response when he learned that his brother, Jacob, stole his blessing (Genesis 34). It is also used to illustrated the mood of the Israelites as they were enslaved by the Egyptians (Exod. 1.14).

[78] Neve, *The Spirit of God in the Old Testament*, p. 40, argues the יד־יהוה in Ezekiel may represent an ecstatic condition when affective terms are associated with YHWH's Spirit or other anthropomorphic language. He argues that the combination of YHWH's Spirit and YHWH's יד reflect a development of 'ecstatic experiences from pre-classical prophecy' (Ezek. 3.12, 14a; 8.1-3). See also, Zimmerli, *Ezekiel 1*, pp. 27, 42, 117. Zimmerli also claims that Ezekiel's transportations are 'an ecstatic transportation' described in the visions and are a working of the spirit and the 'hand of the Lord [that] lifts Ezekiel out of ordinary time and space into the very presence of God'.

[79] For a detailed structural analysis, see Block, *The Book of Ezekiel*, p. 133. Block proposes the formal commissioning is followed by three small subunits (3.12-15; 16-21; 22-26) that represent the prophet's preparation.

[80] Dreytza, יד־יהוה ('hand of YHWH'), *NIDOTTE*, II, p. 404.

vision and the living beings, so too the Spirit is described to transport the prophet. The רוח lifts Ezekiel up to the throne and then away from the divine presence all the while under the power or the יהוה־ יד. Here, Ezekiel associates the power of YHWH through the ascension motif depicted in visionary transportations from one place to another as if he is being influenced and controlled by the רוח and the יד־יהוה.[81] Again, the connections between YHWH's power and the divine רוח result in underscoring the leitmotifs of (1) inspiration, in the sense that the Spirit inspires the prophet to hear and perceive, (2) empowerment, in the sense that the Spirit enables the prophet to stand in the presence of YHWH; endowment of power for the prophetic ministry to the rebellious Israelites that lay ahead of the prophet, and (3) mobility, in the sense that the Spirit and the hand of YHWH is transporting the prophet from place to place in the vision.

The affective language heightens the portrayal of Ezekiel's emotional disposition by concluding the pericope with the seer sitting for seven days among the exiles at Tel-abib, משמים ('stunned' or 'overwhelmed' (3.15).[82] Is it possible that the hearers would perceive that Ezekiel is a resisting his call? It is not clear by the passage that the prophet was resisting his prophetic call while he sat stunned. It simply communicates he sat overwhelmed for seven days while the ליע חזקה ויד־יהוה. It may be likely that the hearers understood as the power of YHWH's hand was heavy or weighty upon him, that it was in some way preventing him from moving so quickly. It is also possible that the hearers perceived that Ezekiel was simply emotionally overwhelmed by all the dramatic events that took place in his visions. After all, Ezekiel's descriptions of the sequence of events that took place by the Spirit in the vision narratives are quite remarkable and it is conceivable that the hearers were also משמים ('stunned' or 'overwhelmed') by what they heard, imagined, and felt by the events described. From this literary perspective, it is the power of YHWH's

---

[81] See Long, 'Reports of Visions Among the Prophets', pp. 353-65. Ezekiel's inaugural visionary call report is also closely related to two other major visions in the book, the judgment upon Jerusalem (8.1–11.25), and temple vision for the restoration of Israel (40.1–48.35) in other distinctive ways.

[82] Block, *The Book of Ezekiel 1–24*, pp. 90-97. Bowen, *Ezekiel*, p. 11. Using form criticism, Block and Bowen align the overwhelming mood to the objection to the prophetic call, which are standard components in call narratives.

hand and the Spirit that affects the prophet not only in a physical sense, but an emotional one as well.

Whether one wants to interpret the seven days literally or figuratively, Ezekiel is conveying that an extended period of time is taking place.[83] The affective language and the context supports that the unusual affective responses of the seer is directly associated with his visionary encounter with הרוח and the manifestation of YHWH's power symbolized by the יד־יהוה. However, this emotionally charged encounter does not leave the seer unable to report the event to the hearers.[84] It is conceivable the hearers would make these connections as Ezekiel consistently connects the יד־יהוה with affective language. Ezekiel narrates that the יד־יהוה is used to communicate YHWH's power that is exerted over him, not only at the beginning of the vision encounters (1.3), but also increases in intensity as the prophet reports to sit down overwhelmed for an extended period of time (3.14-15).

The overwhelming events occurring in the preceding visionary scenes are now over and are in sharp contrast to the inactivity reported in the aftermath. The story climaxes with Ezekiel telling the hearers that he is stunned and angry. The hearers are affected along with Ezekiel as they are witnesses to Ezekiel's visions. YHWH calls the prophet to a difficult prophetic task, empowers and infuses him by YHWH's Spirit, and influences him by the power of YHWH's Spirit and hand. The power motif is emphasized by the force of YHWH's יד possibly understood by the hearers to underscore the significance of power that is needed for Ezekiel's call into his

---

[83] See Heschel, *The Prophets*, I, pp. 16-19, and II, pp. 12, 28-47; 96, 224. For Heschel, Ezekiel's bitterness and rage (3.14) and his 'week of silence' (3.22-24) in light of 'sympathy' reflected God's own feelings toward Israel. He saw the emotive words of the prophet, Ezekiel, as 'stern, sour, stinging, but behind his austerity is love and compassion for mankind'.

[84] Greenberg, *Ezekiel, 1–20*, pp. 41-45, argues that the יד־יהוה is used to convey that God's hand is 'a manifestation of his power' but also is 'the urgency, pressure, and compulsion by which he [Ezekiel] is stunned and overwhelmed'. Greenberg also posits that in Ezekiel's visions the יד־יהוה is used to convey that the 'prophet is in a trance brought on by consciousness of being addressed by God'. He draws a distinction between how the phrase is used in the Elijah narratives in 1 Kgs 18.46 to symbolize an outward strength and in the visions of Ezekiel it represents a manifestation of a trance in connection with 'some sensory (Ezekiel 2–3) or physical effect (Ezek. 3.22) other than mere audition'.

prophetic service.[85] Not surprisingly, the intense inaugural vision of the glory of YHWH and subsequent call to prophetic service with the forceful and dynamic visionary encounters with YHWH's Spirit culminate at this juncture with overpowering effects upon the visionary and the hearers.

After the end of this seven-day overwhelming period, Ezekiel reports that YHWH speaks again. The prophet had received his initial commissioning in 2.28b–3.11 to the rebellious Israelites (3.11-15) and he is charged as a watchman in 3.16-21.[86] The anticipated דבר־יהוה to Ezekiel, the son of man, comes to him as a warning to the Israelites to repent of their evil ways and sin (3.16-21). The voice of YHWH likely would be experienced by the exilic community as direct communication from YHWH mediated to them through the prophet. The importance of the warning of impending judgment to the Israelites is augmented by YHWH's declaration of holding Ezekiel accountable if he does not obey and speak. As YHWH's speech ends, the recurring literary marker the יד־יהוה 'was among him there' alerts the hearer to an ensuing vision scene. The literary portrait begins with a command from YHWH to the prophet 'arise and go out to the valley and I will speak with you' (3.22). Ezekiel narrates that he is once again obedient to follow the דבר־יהוה. Ezekiel claims to encounter YHWH's glory again and describes it anthropomorphically, והנה כבוד־יהוה עמד שם ('Behold, the glory of YHWH stood there' 3.23). The hearers certainly would perceive that the current encounter with the glory of YHWH is similar to that which he experienced by the river Chebar. Although this time, the כבוד־יהוה is anthropomorphically described as standing, and the prophet's language of ambiguity is replaced with a clear sense of what he is seeing and hearing.[87] In the Ezekiel text, YHWH speaks in the midst of a vision of the כבוד־יהוה and he is depicted as 'standing'. Again, the 'seeing' as

---

[85] Dreytza, יד ('hand'), *NIDOTTE, II*, p. 404, argues that the Hebrew idiom YHWH's יד is not only present in Ezekiel's 'irresistible call ... but also during his lifetime as the Lord seizes him on special occasions'.

[86] Block, *The Book of Ezekiel*, pp. 152-53, refutes Zimmerli's interpretation that this paragraph of the binding of Ezekiel is one of the twelve sign acts performed by Ezekiel. Block observes this initiation process in light of ancient Near Eastern cultural practices for initiation rituals.

[87] The account recalls the story of Moses when he went outside the camp to the tent of meeting to meet with YHWH (Exod. 33.7). In the Moses narrative, the Lord spoke out of the pillar of a cloud.

a way of perceiving and understanding or knowing what he sees initiates the prophet's appropriate response of worship by falling prostrate (v. 23).

In the midst of worship as the יד־יהוה is upon Ezekiel, the distinctive role of the רוח assumes center stage. The prophet announces
ותבא בי רוח כאשר דבר אלי ותעמדני על־רגלי ('The Spirit came into
me as he spoke and caused me to stand to my feet' 2.2; 3.24). For the
second time the רוח actively engages the prophet through 'entering
him' and empowering him to rise to his feet. The recurring and interconnected literary themes of the יד־יהוה to the appearance of the
glory of YHWH, and the Spirit's activities with the prophet link this
scene to the preceding texts by echoing the same motifs.

Summary

Ezekiel 2.1–3.27 is a unique literary unit in Ezekiel's visions as it commences the prophet's call to prophetic service. The vision scenes are
comprised of YHWH's commands, descriptions of the diverse roles
of the רוח with the prophet, and symbolic acts. Ezekiel's visionary
call narrative makes clear that the prophet is called to deliver a warning message to the Israelites, a rebellious nation. The prophet's obedience to follow the דבר־יהוה is paramount as YHWH both warns
Ezekiel not to be rebellious or afraid, as well as commands him to
perform symbolic acts. These images of Ezekiel's obedience to eat
the scroll with the words of lament, mourning, and woe speak to
YHWH's impending judgment upon the Israelites. The themes of
motion and judgment continue to prevail from Ezekiel's inaugural
vision to his call narrative. Yet, the commissioning vision scenes also
uniquely emphasize the numerous descriptions of the activities of
the רוח that are linked to the seer (2.2; 3.12, 14, 24) and his encounters with the כבוד־יהוה (3.12; 23).

YHWH's Spirit enters the prophet and raises him to his feet,
which coincides with the prophet hearing YHWH's first commissioning speech (2.2).[88] YHWH's Spirit is conveyed as a dynamic power in
which the same activities are ascribed to the יד־יהוה.[89] YHWH's Spirit

---

[88] Rea, *The Holy Spirit in the Bible*, pp. 101-105, argues God promises his indwelling Spirit is only for the future time of the new covenant.

[89] Scheepers, *Die Gees van God en die Gees van die mens,* pp. 316-17, argues that the
'hand' and the 'spirit' both represent a power in 1.3; c.f. 8.1 with 11.5 in Ezek. 8.3
and 2.2.

lifts the prophet up to the dwelling place of the כבוד־יהוה and then transports Ezekiel back down among the exiles (3.12-15). YHWH's Spirit enters the prophet again and raises him to his feet as YHWH's commands him to perform symbolic acts. Each visionary encounter Ezekiel has with YHWH's Spirit involves the themes of empowerment, submission, inspiration, and/or transportation. The symbolic action of Ezekiel eating the דבר־יהוה written on the scroll and the רוח described as entering the prophet support the notion that Ezekiel's hearers would understand that the prophet embodied YHWH's word and YHWH's Spirit in this vision narrative. They would also understand that the messenger of YHWH would need inspiration and the empowerment of YHWH's Spirit as communicated by the infusion of YHWH's Spirit.

Ezekiel's call also highlights the visionary encounters with the כבוד־יהוה that are closely related to two recurring literary motifs: (1) the רוח, and (2) the יד־יהוה. The combination and close proximity of the רוח and the יד־יהוה intensifies the literary portrait of YHWH's empowerment that is needed for Ezekiel's call to execute his prophetic service. The symbolic and anthropomorphic descriptions of the כבוד motif support the claim that Ezekiel's vision of the יהוה־כבוד is indeed representative of a revelation of YHWH's attributes of his sovereign power, holiness, and immanent majestic presence.

Ezekiel reports to the hearers that most of his senses are engaged in these visions. He reports to see the כבוד־יהוה and its chariot throne, hear the living beings and the voice of YHWH, eat and taste a scroll, and affectively respond to these dramatic events. YHWH's overwhelming power is also underscored by Ezekiel's emphasis upon the affective language used to describe the emotional disposition of Ezekiel's own 'spirit' in response to the dramatic activities in the visions. First, Ezekiel reports that he falls face down in worship as he finally discerns that what he is seeing is a vision of the כבוד־יהוה. The act of worship is an affective response of reverential fear and awe to the appearance of YHWH's glory who dramatically displays authority in a foreign land. The inaugural vision elaborately describes a vision of the mobile chariot-throne of the glory of YHWH highlighted by the fire and the storm theophany motifs that would elicit fear of judgment in the prophet and the hearers.

Second, Ezekiel's call as God's messenger, is to the disobedient and stubborn Israelites. Ezekiel uses variations of the word מרר ('rebellious') seven times to describe the Israelites. The repetitive use of this affective term likely instigated fear among the hearers, as they were considered the rebellious Israelites exiled in Babylon.

Third, Ezekiel is described with unexpected and noticeable anger or bitterness in his own רוח when he is caught up by the divine רוח, and then taken away from the glory of YHWH. There is a sharp contrast between the prophet's mood and the previous delight that he enjoyed with eating the scroll. The overwhelming control of the prophet's movements by the רוח and YHWH's יד in this vision scene seem to produce overwhelming affections in Ezekiel.

Fourth, YHWH's יד or variations of the term (eg. יהוה־ליע חזקה ויד) is used to convey YHWH's power anthropologically as it executes its divine force upon the prophet and causes him to become overwhelmed for seven days. The hearers, who Ezekiel claims to be present while he sat overwhelmed, may have discerned that the prophet was stunned by all the dramatic events that took place in his visions. The affective literary portrait of the prophet and the exiles serve to accentuate the intense nature of Ezekiel's call to the nation of Israel. YHWH tested the prophet's will and obedience as he was charged as a watchman and symbolically embodied the words of judgment for the rebellious Israelites. Certainly, Ezekiel's stunned disposition would enhance how the hearers would perceive the gravity of their situation.

D. Signs, Visions, and Messages of Death (4–7)

Chapter 4 marks the beginning of Ezekiel's messages for his fellow exiles given through a series of sign-acts or dramatic performances.[90] These literary devices are used in tandem with the visual genre of the book. Ezekiel's visions function as the major structural markers for the book and the sign-acts are additional ways in which Ezekiel's messages are given in visual form. The hearers once again are enticed to use their imagination in the hearing of Ezekiel's visions. The first literary scene is marked by a series of actions (4.1-5.4) and appear to

---

[90] B. Lang, 'Street Theater, Raising the Dead, and the Zoroastrian Connection in Ezekiel's Prophecy', *Ezekiel and His Book*, pp. 302-305, for an extensive bibliography.

be syntactically linked to the previous description of Ezekiel's binding in 3.33-27.

The first set of sign-acts symbolize the inevitable fate of Jerusalem as it reveals YHWH's first ministerial charge. The use of the affective language is underscored as the signs were sensually perceived by Ezekiel.[91] The vision continues with YHWH's commands to Ezekiel to perform symbolic acts (chs. 4–5) as in part, his duty as a watchman to warn Israel of the impending judgment. Although these symbolic acts are often interpreted as public performances, the narratives report only that the prophet was commanded to perform them, not that he acted upon them. It is perhaps difficult for the contemporary hearer to discern the meaning of symbolic acts. However, in the context of prophetic visions, it is not difficult to glean its theological message that is discerned through 'affective aids'. In other words, symbolic language is a tool to elicit affective responses. Effective literary tools not only use words but also combine pictures or symbolism to communicate and capture the attention of its hearers and demand a response. Ezekiel 4–5 declare the themes of judgment falling upon the covenant breakers.

Ezekiel 6–7 builds upon the judgment themes depicted in the symbolic acts of chs. 5 and 6. The דבר־יהוה decrees judgment and destruction to the 'house of Israel' because of their idolatrous abominations that will result in a threefold judgment of (1) sword, (2) famine, and (3) plague (6.11).[92] YHWH is a God who upholds the terms of the covenant. When his people breach the covenant stipulations, as the Israelites did, he takes appropriate disciplinary measures, some of which may be unprecedented, to register his disapproval of the people's sins. What this implies is that his punishments, although they are painful and may cause intense suffering, are deserved and justified because of the Israelites' persistence in the worship of idols and other abominable practices. YHWH's punishments are based on moral and cultic violations.

---

[91] Broome, 'Ezekiel's Abnormal Personality', pp. 277-93, opines that the abnormal mental state of Ezekiel is supported through the sign-acts.

[92] The threefold judgment recalls Leviticus 26, Ezekiel 5, and they are three of the four 'horsemen of the Apocalypse' in Revelation 6.

III. The Temple Vision (Ezekiel 8–36)

A. The Vision of the Glory of YHWH Departing from the Jerusalem Temple (8–11)

The second major vision, Ezekiel 8–11, is rhetorically and affectively connected to Ezekiel's inaugural vision and call narrative (Ezekiel 1–3).[93] As the inaugural vision proclaims and introduces the coming of YHWH's transcendent glory to Ezekiel by the power of YHWH's יד and the call narrative introduces the רוח as one of the main characters, so too Ezekiel's second major vision highlights (1) the כבוד־יהוה, (2) the רוח, and (3) the יד־יהוה. Affectively, the narrative harkens back to the previous vision with its emotive language used to describe (1) Ezekiel's response to the יד־יהוה and the רוח, and (2) YHWH's detestation for Israel's wickedness, idolatry, and abominations.[94] The broader literary structure for Ezekiel's second major vision can be divided as follows: (1) Ezekiel's vision and tour of Jerusalem's sins of idolatry (Ezekiel 8), (2) Ezekiel's vision of YHWH's execution of judgment (Ezekiel 9), (3) Ezekiel's chariot-throne vision of the glory of YHWH leaving the Jerusalem Temple (Ezekiel 10), and (4) Judgment for those who remain in the land and YHWH's promise for renewal (Ezekiel 11).

It is noteworthy in the present narrative that at times the language appears more intense than the inaugural vision. For example, the title of YHWH is extended to the 'Lord YHWH' (אדני יהוה 8.1). It is possible that the added description, the Sovereign Lord, may serve to convey to Ezekiel's hearers something of the intensified tone of the present visionary events. In other words, the hearers may feel the seriousness of YHWH's messages given to the prophet in images and words to a greater degree than in the previous visionary scenes.

The setting of the second major vision of Ezekiel is introduced with the familiar dating formula that continues to alert the hearers to the time, place, and situation of Ezekiel's first temple vision narrative

---

[93] See Block, *The Book of Ezekiel Chapters 1–24*, p. 272, who highlights the chiastic structure of Ezek. 8.1–11.25.

[94] Iain M. Dugaid, *Ezekiel* (NIVAC; Grand Rapids: Zondervan, 1999), argues that the underlying structure of this single vision makes the message clear and cohesive, yet he gives minimal attention to one of the main characters portrayed in the narratives, the Spirit, pp. 146-58.

(8.1).⁹⁵ These chronological indicators provide the hearers with a way in which to move through the narrative. The consistent first-person language reminds the hearers that Ezekiel identifies himself as one of the main characters in the book. As such, the recurrent date notices that introduce the vision and oracular narratives also serve to associate the language with what could be called a 'prophetic diary'.⁹⁶ Yet, this does not mean that the story intends to portray Ezekiel's visions as a private affair because in both the inaugural vision and now in the present temple vision there is the presence of Ezekiel's community who serve as witnesses to his visions.⁹⁷ Although, they are not described as active participants in the vision, they are mentioned in such a way to convey their importance. The occasion identifies Ezekiel as 'sitting in his house' while the 'elders of Judah were sitting before' him, which implies the elders regard Ezekiel as a prophet and accord him a measure of authority (8.1).⁹⁸ While the elders sat before him, Ezekiel is carried off in visions of YHWH to the temple in Jerusalem.

The literary repetitions of the יד־יהוה, the רוח, the כבוד־יהוה, and the mysterious figure are highlighted in varying degrees in Ezekiel 8–11, which function to cue the hearers to the continuity between Ezekiel's first two major prophetic visions (cf. Ezekiel 1–3 and 8–

---

⁹⁵ Many scholars agree that the dating signifies the year of Jehoiachin's exile on September 18, 592 BCE, and occurs approximately fourteen months after the initial opening vision. See Block, *The Book of Ezekiel*, p. 278; Duguid, *Ezekiel*, p. 130; Block, Odell, *Ezekiel*, p. 103.

⁹⁶ Odell, *Ezekiel*, p. 1, appears to be the first to associate the book with the idea of the prophet's personal recordings of his visions.

⁹⁷ William Brownlee, *Ezekiel 1–19* (WBC; Waco: Word Books, 1986), pp. 129-31, interprets the spiritual journey as a literal transportation because he argues that real events cannot take place at the same time as visionary events. He assumes that the vision occurs at night and that it would be improbable that the elders would meet in the middle of the night.

⁹⁸ Second Kings 24.14 records that those who went into exile with Ezekiel were a total of 10,000 people and included King Jehoiachin, members of the royal family, government officials, trained soldiers, smiths, artisans, and the elite of the land. Although the narrative does not give the reason for the elders meeting with Ezekiel in his house, see Block, *The Book of Ezekiel Chapters 1–24*, pp. 28-34, 278-79, who concludes that the exiles were allowed to live together and maintain some aspect of their ethnic and social customs. Therefore, it is possible the elders mentioned in this narrative met with Ezekiel to inquire of YHWH through their pre-Judean religious-social practices of seeking the word of YHWH through a prophet.

11).[99] Ezekiel's narration reiterates the opening vision as he reports the ותפל עלי שם יד אדני יהוה ('hand of the Lord YHWH fell upon me' 8.1). The hearers would recall that Ezekiel's inaugural vision was introduced with a variation of this phrase. However, the verbal nuance between אליו (1.3) and נפל (8.1; cf. 11.5) would not go unnoticed as the intensity demonstrated by the term נפל in the present vision is accentuated because it highlights the sudden and overwhelming nature of YHWH's involvement with Ezekiel. The power of YHWH's hand is not simply upon the prophet, it 'falls' on the prophet.[100] The serious tone of the story is compounded by the description of the weightiness and force of delivery of the power of YHWH *falling* upon the prophet. Likewise, as in Ezekiel's inaugural call narratives (Ezekiel 1–3), the hearers may perceive that once the יד־יהוה is reported to be upon the prophet prior to the beginning of the vision, then the יד־יהוה would remain upon the prophet as representing an empowering presence upon the prophet for the duration of the vision.

Immediately after YHWH's hand falls upon the prophet, Ezekiel reports not only to ראה ('see, have visions, look at') the mysterious figure, but he הנה ('beholds') the luminous mysterious figure. The appearance of the structural markers, ראה combined with הנה alters the narrative setting from Ezekiel's house to a vision (8.2). Again, the language used in this narrative clearly delineates between the cursory narratives and the active vision scenes. The term הנה ('behold'), as a demonstrative participle, serves to stress for the hearers the

---

[99] G.R. Berry, 'The glory of Yahweh and the Temple' *JBL* 56.2 (1937), pp. 115-17, points out that the vision of ch. 1 is referred to several times later, but without any great significance. The vision appeared in 3.12-15, as a 'concomitant of the transportation of Ezekiel by the Spirit'. It is found also in 3.23, as 'an adornment of the scene in which the Spirit gave him another message'. It comes again in 8.2-4, as 'an incident in connection with the miraculous transportation of the prophet to Jerusalem'. It appears in 9.3, when the glory went from the cherubim to the threshold of the temple. It is found several times in ch. 10, the glory of Yahweh, now back again with the cherubim, going from the cherubim to the threshold of the house, v. 4, and back again from the threshold to the cherubim, v. 18, after which the cherubim and the glory removed themselves to the east gate of the temple, v. 19. In 11.22, 23, the cherubim and the glory moved from the city to the mountain on the east, this being their final appearance until ch. 43.

[100] Block, *The Book of Ezekiel Chapters 1–24*, p. 279, describes the function of this preamble in terms of 'a divine seizure'.

significance of that which Ezekiel's gaze is fixed upon.[101] Not only does Ezekiel see, but he is also rendered motionless as he appears to be enamored by what he sees. The anticipation mounts as the hearers would recall that in Ezekiel's inaugural vision the יד־יהוה preceded the grandiose entrance of the glory of YHWH. From this perspective, the hearers may discern it is the יד־יהוה as representative of the power of YHWH and is closely associated with the prophet's ability to receive the supernatural vision of the כבוד־יהוה.

Similar to the description of the transcendent glory of YHWH in Ezekiel 1 is the description of the 'likeness as the appearance of a man' in Ezekiel 8. Ezekiel describes, 'what appeared to be from his waist down he looked like אש ('fire'), and 'from there up his appearance was כעין חשמל' (8.2; cf. 1.26b-27).[102] Through the use of the unique term חשמל and the recurrent term אש, Ezekiel highlights the brilliant and illuminous colors and distinct features of this mysterious being.[103] The hearers probably would not initially perceive his identity as he is still shrouded in mystery. Again, Ezekiel uses metaphorical and anthropomorphic language to describe the figure as a means to describe what might, otherwise, be indescribable.[104] In Ezekiel 8, the mystery figure actively participates in the vision as 'he stretched out what looked like a hand and took me [Ezekiel] by the hair of my head' (8.3). Since the hearers do not actually see what Ezekiel sees, they are required to use their imagination to visualize the mysterious figure through Ezekiel's description. From this perspective, Ezekiel's audience is able to participate to some degree in the vision through the pictorial words used to describe the vision. The images provide the story with a dimensional quality. Meaning, Ezekiel's descriptions

---

[101] Naude, 'ראה' ('see, have visions') *NIDOTTE,* III, pp. 1007-15.

[102] Zimmerli, *Ezekiel 1*, p. 234, compares the heavenly being in 1.27 with the 'man' in 8.2 and concludes that that since YHWH encounters Ezekiel in the form of the כבוד, then the 'man' in 8.2 must refer to a heavenly messenger. Odell, *Ezekiel*, p. 104, argues that although the figure resembles the likeness of the divine glory in 1.26-27, it is identified as 'the Spirit' (8.3) and not the glory.

[103] Zimmerli, *Ezekiel 1*, p. 234, argues that these Ezekiel texts are a precursor to the apocalyptic tradition that underscores a heavenly mediator (Zech. 5.9) lifting the prophet between heaven and earth.

[104] Paul Joyce, *Ezekiel: A Commentary* (New York: T & T Clark, 2007), pp. 73-75, recalls Dan. 7.13, 'I saw one like a human being coming with clouds of heaven. And he came to the Ancient One and as presented before him.' See Kutsko, *Between Heaven and Earth*, p. 81, argues that while Ezekiel never directly uses the phrase 'image of God' to refer to humans, this priestly prophet employs the idea.

of the vision would likely affect most of the senses in the hearers. They could use their imagination to see the message and they would hear Ezekiel's words as he described the images or words of YHWH. The narrative even describes how the hearers would at times be affected in their emotions to what they saw and heard. In essence, their senses would enable the hearers to participate and likely would aid in their understanding of YHWH's messages. Additionally, the authoritative role of the words of the prophet proclaiming YHWH's words seen and heard serve to paint the picture of reality in the unseen (by most) visionary world.[105] The affective language functions to stimulate the emotions in the hearer, which also serves to engage their participation.

However, in this second major vision, a surprising turn of events takes place as the mysterious figure is reported to grab Ezekiel's hair with 'a form of a hand' (8.3). In the first major vision the hearers envision and witness the prophet responding to the vision of the mysterious figure. In this vision, the prophet is forcefully seized by the mysterious figure. It is not clear how the hearers would initially understand whether or not the mysterious figure is indeed the anthropological description of the glory of YHWH as described in the inaugural vision. Yet, in v. 4, the prophet clarifies that it is the glory of YHWH who is like the appearance which he saw in the plain (cf. Ezek. 3.22-23). The present vision narrative is linked once again, to the previous visionary call narrative as they both anthropomorphically describe the glory of YHWH. The distinction here, lies in the interaction of the glory of YHWH with the prophet. YHWH's glory is described and visualized in form, but it also acts upon the prophet. Thus, it is likely that the hearers would perceive that the prophet not only is portrayed as engaging *in* and responsive *to* the mysterious figure as the glory of YHWH, but also, engaged *by* the glory of YHWH in the vision.

As the main characters in this first temple vision are revealed: (1) Ezekiel, (2) the יד־יהוה, (3) the divine Spirit and (4) the mystery figure anthropomorphically described as the glory of YHWH; it appears

---

[105] See Grey's examination of the acts of the רוח in Ezekiel 37, 'Acts of the Spirit' pp. 69-81, as she applies speech-act theory to the narrative of Ezek. 37.1-14 and builds upon the work of John Austin who argues that speech-act theory contributes to biblical studies in that words or speech are more than referential or informative, but are also performative and indicative of a reality.

the divine רוח assumes one of the leading roles. Ezekiel reports it is the רוח who lifts him 'between heaven and earth' and brings him in 'visions of God' to Jerusalem (8.3b). Likewise, as in the call narrative, the transporting activity of the רוח is emphasized in the first temple-vision narrative (8–11). Ezekiel's hearers would likely recall how the רוח lifted Ezekiel and took him away (3.14), and now it is the heavenly figure that 'takes or [grasps] Ezekiel by the hair of his head' as 'the רוח lifts him between heaven and earth' (8.3b).[106] The close association between the main characters of the רוח and the anthropomorphic description of the glory of YHWH suggests a cooperation in their participation with the prophet in 'visions of God' to Jerusalem.[107] The question is, how would Ezekiel's audience perceive the tandem forces acting upon the prophet? Ezekiel is unique among the classical prophets in that the story portrays Ezekiel being transported by the Spirit in a vision hundreds of miles away from Babylon to Jerusalem. While it is not altogether clear who or what transports Ezekiel in this visionary spiritual journey, in the context of both vision narratives, it is more likely the hearers would perceive it is YHWH's Spirit acting upon the prophet.[108]

---

[106] Blenkinsopp, *Ezekiel*, p. 53, argues that the transporting activity of the רוח is a form of 'soul travel', which he proposes is described when the conscious self leaves the body behind and the being is transported to another place. Pilch, *Flights of the Soul,* p. 217, argues that the activity of the Spirit in light of Ezekiel's usages can best be understood in light of the pre-classical ecstatic prophets, Elijah and Elisha, in whom the Spirit was very active. For Ezekiel, the Spirit is an energy originating in the divine sphere which manifests itself as a force that propels and transports (Ezek. 8.1; 11.1, 24; 37.1), and energizes and renews both individuals and community (Ezek. 11.19; 18.31; 36.26-27; 37.14; 39.29).

[107] There are various views that attempt to describe Ezekiel's visionary journey. For the parallels between Ezekiel and Elijah and Elisha, see Zimmerli, *Ezekiel 1*, p. 42, who states that 'the hand of the Lord lifts Ezekiel out of ordinary time and space into the very presence of God'. Blenkinsopp, *Ezekiel*, p. 53, argues that Ezekiel's transportation is indicative of a kind of 'soul travel', in which the 'sensation of the conscious self is leaving the body behind and being transported to another place'.

[108] For example, Zimmerli, *Ezekiel 2*, p. 567, draws upon linguistic distinctions to designate meaning to the term רוח in this context. He argues that the simple use of the term רוח without the article points to an 'independently effective power' that is 'brought about by Yahweh'. In this way, Zimmerli likened the activity of the רוח to pre-classical prophets and their 'prophetic experience of a call'. Similarly, Hildebrandt, *An Old Testament Theology of the Spirit of God*, p. 190, argues that the רוח functions to 'prepare the prophet for his prophetic proclamation'. Greenberg, *Ezekiel 1–20*, pp. 167-68, argues that the רוח is a 'wind' that transports the prophet

The phrase, ורוח נשאתני describes a unique role and characteristic of the Spirit and accentuates the sensory or physical aspects of the literary portrait of the prophet in connection to the רוח (cf. Ezekiel 1–3).[109] It is as if the prophet is described as not having control of his body in these visionary scenes. The hearers may perceive that the רוח is controlling the prophet and events in the vision as Ezekiel is taken to undisclosed places by the רוח (cf. 3.12-14; 8.3). In the inaugural call narrative, the prophet is taken upward to heavenly places, and this vision portrays the prophet transported from his surroundings by the רוח to a place faraway yet known to the prophet and the hearers (Ezek. 8.1; cf. 37.1; 40.1).[110] This activity of the רוח transporting the prophet in a vision is unique and would likely provoke feelings of amazement in the hearers. Since, the main character of the divine רוח is portrayed as actively engaging the prophet in the previous visionary scenes (cf. Ezek. 3.12, 14a, 24) and appears to be engaging the prophet in similar ways in his first temple vision (Ezekiel 8–11), then narratively and contextually the רוח likely represents the divine Spirit here as well.

After the prophet is taken up by the Spirit and describes seeing the glory of YHWH, the narrative proceeds with a series of literary repetitions: (1) 'he said to me' (Ezek. 8.5-6; 8-9; 12-13; 15-17) and (2) 'he brought me' (Ezek. 8.7; 14; 16).[111] Since, the text uses the

---

in a vision as if in a 'night dream'. He chooses to emphasize the nature of the vision without assigning the רוח any supernatural properties. In an opposing view, Block, *Ezekiel 1*, p. 280, proposes that the term רוח is ambiguous and if the רוח transports the prophet, then the term could be rendered 'wind', but since the רוח levitates the prophet between heaven and earth, then the term should represent the divine Spirit. Through a NT lens, Horton, *What the Bible Says*, pp. 68-69, proposes that Ezekiel's visionary transportation can be liked to Paul's experience of his vision of Paradise and the third heaven (2 Cor. 12.3).

[109] Hosch, 'רוח in the Book of Ezekiel', p. 115, points out that the 'motion equated with the activity of the divine ("spirit") was important for Ezekiel, and it may define his understanding of the ("spirit") in a special way as reflected in the prophet's encounter with the רוח'.

[110] The nearest analogies in the biblical texts are found in the Elijah and Elisha accounts. The narratives in 1 Kgs 18.12; 2 Kgs 2.1-12, 16-18 describe Elijah as being 'carried by the Spirit' in a physical transportation. The narratives of 2 Kgs 5.26; 6.17, 32-33 describe Elisha as having some extrasensory powers. Each of these texts are similar to Ezekiel, but these aforementioned texts are not vision reports as in the Ezekiel texts.

[111] Block, *The Book of Ezekiel Chapters 1–24*, p. 283, names the tour guide as YHWH.

masculine pronoun that corresponds grammatically with the masculine noun, glory of YHWH, then the hearers may perceive it is the glory of YHWH who speaks, commands, and brings or leads the prophet through the temple complex. Yet, the hearers may be forgiven if they readily do not perceive who is speaking or leading the prophet in the context of a vision narrative. Since, the divine Spirit 'lifts Ezekiel between heaven and earth' and brought him in 'visions of God to Jerusalem', they may be uncertain due to the contextual ambiguity that is present in the narrative. The 'Son of man' title may prove helpful. The previous vision (Ezekiel 1-3) introduces the title as a transitional marker, which Ezekiel employs frequently throughout his visions to introduce prophetic speech by the glory of YHWH. Therefore, it may provide the hearers with some clarity as to who is speaking. However, since the act of bringing the prophet to various places has previously been designated to the רוח (cf. 3.12; 15), then the reader and the hearers may wonder if the רוח is actually the one leading the prophet through the temple complex as well.

When the setting changes somewhere between 'earth and heaven' the hearers envision, albeit through their imagination, the divine רוח transporting Ezekiel to the Jerusalem Temple (8.3). Ezekiel reports that he is shown atrocities occurring inside the Jerusalem Temple. Ezekiel is first taken to the entrance to the north gate of the inner court.[112] He identifies the doorway as the location or the 'seat' of the image of jealousy.[113] This first atrocity introduces the main theme of idolatry named 'the idol that provokes to jealousy' (v. 3).[114] The hearers would likely understand that the idol provoked YHWH to jealousy because according to the Mosaic covenant, YHWH is the one and true living God above all other gods, and the worship of any

---

[112] For a discussion of the location of the north gate, see Greenberg, *Ezekiel 1–20*, p. 168, who argues that the north gate of the inner court probably represents the 'altar gate' in v. 5, which was opposite of the great altar of sacrifice.

[113] H.C. Lutzky, 'On "the image of jealousy" (Ezekiel viii 3,5)', *VT*, 46.1 (Jan 1996), pp. 121-25, proposes an alternative reading according to a textual reason. He argues the term קנה ('jealousy') had an original meaning ('procreate'), which bears creation, and belongs to the cultic vocabulary. He supports this view by drawing correlations between the Ugaritic equivalent of the term קנה that occurs in the epithet of Asherah ('Creatress of the gods'), (IIAB [CTA 4] I, p. 23, IV, p. 32). Thus, Lutzky concludes that the root קנה applies to Asherah as well as to her divine consort El.

[114] For a treatment of the distinctions between the temple Ezekiel saw in his vision and the actual temple, see Kaufmann, *The Religion of Israel*, pp. 406-407.

other gods is considered idolatry.[115] Ezekiel also conveys to the hearers that not only is the idol present, but the כבוד אלהי ישראל is present as well (v. 4). The vision scene is intense as the image of idolatry is found in the holy Temple where only the כבוד אלהי ישראל is to reside. The drama is exaggerated as the profane occupies the same space as the sacred. This revelation would likely terrify Ezekiel's hearers as they would realize the consequences of YHWH's wrath for the sins of idolatry.

As the first part of the second vision (Ezek. 8.1-11) underscores the diverse roles of the divine רוח, it also draws attention to the prophet's relationship to YHWH, by the recurrent naming of Ezekiel, the 'Son of man'. Again, the narrative emphasizes the divine nature and power of YHWH either described anthropomorphically by the יד־יהוה, or by the descriptions of the activities of the divine רוח, which are both in sharp contrast to Ezekiel as a mere mortal. In other words, the story portrays YHWH as in control of the vision events and conveys to the hearers that Ezekiel is portrayed as submissive to YHWH's power.

Next, the glory of YHWH commands Ezekiel to look upon the altar at the detestable 'idol of jealousy' (vv. 5-6) to reveal to him that Judah's idolatry is reprehensible.[116] YHWH speaks to his prophet, 'But you will see things that are even more detestable' (v. 6). The language recalls a court drama in which a case is built against the defendants. In this case, YHWH is developing his case against Israel. Ezekiel serves as the main witness to Israel's crimes, and the hearers are secondary witnesses. The vision of the hidden idolatry in YHWH's most holy place, the Jerusalem Temple, is the crucial setting, which provokes the glory to depart the Temple. The glory manifesting in the sacred place of the Jerusalem Temple is in keeping with the priestly idea of the divine presence of YHWH. The narrative also emphasizes the divine רוח as the one who transports, possibly leads, and is closely connected to YHWH who speaks to the prophet.[117] These events occur in the context of a vision that acts as the medium

---

[115] See Exod. 20.1; Deut. 4.16; 32.16, 21.
[116] Odell, *Ezekiel*, p. 105, argues that the conventional interpretation of the image of jealousy is that this is the image of another god.
[117] Block, 'Empowered by the Spirit of God', pp. 20-28.

in which hidden revelation is provided to the prophet as the יד־יהוה
is upon the prophet.

The hearers could only participate in this vision by their imagination as they discover step-by-step what awaits them as they make their
way to Jerusalem with Ezekiel and into the sacred space of the Temple and its environs. The scenes create somewhat of a suspense
drama as the hearers would anxiously await to see and hear what
would be in the next room. All of these smaller scenes emphasize
abominations occurring in the most holy place, the Jerusalem Temple, which would leave the hearers wondering how these crimes could
possibly be surpassed.

In the following scene (Ezek. 8.7-13), Ezekiel continues to describe the ways in which he is guided through the temple courts: 'He
brought me to the entrance to the court. I looked, and I saw a hole
in the wall. He said to me, "Son of man, now dig into the wall". So,
I dug into the wall and saw a doorway there' (v. 7).[118] The activity is
strange, and it is not clear how the hearers would perceive the
prophet's digging into a hole in the Temple. However, the metaphorical meaning is reasonable, in the sense that what is hidden is being
revealed. The prophet is brought to the entrance to the temple and
shown a hole, but not the presence of a doorway. The prophet is
commanded to participate by digging into the hole in order to see the
doorway. The language used in the narrative conveys again that the
prophet's participation and obedience in the vision is essential to the
plot of the story. In contemporary terms, the active participation in
the vision narrative is analogous to a 'virtual reality' scene.

YHWH responds as he asks Ezekiel a rhetorical question as if to
emphasize the shock of what is happening (v. 12). Ezekiel is asked if
he sees what the elders are doing in darkness. The juxtaposition between ראה and חשׁך is notable, especially in the context of a vision.
Ezekiel is shown sins occurring in the darkness or in secret. In other
words, the glory of YHWH reveals to the prophet the hidden sins of
idolatry by the seventy men of elders.[119] The theme of seeing continues as the narrative underscores the hidden motives of the elders,

---

[118] It is possible that the enlarging of the hole puts the focus on the wall and
draws the prophet's attention to 'the crawling things and detestable animals'.

[119] The number of elders is reminiscent of the seventy elders who represented
Moses, Aaron, and Abihu in the ratification of the covenant at Mount Sinai (Exod.
24.1).

'The Lord does not see us, the Lord has forsaken the land' (v. 13). There is a tenor of blame and possibly despair associated with the analogy of the Lord's sight and his abandonment of the land. It is possible that the hearers would understand that it is the sight of the Lord upon his land and his people that reflects his favor. Yet, the irony in the story is clear, YHWH is the only God who sees the actions of his people, and also the deepest parts of their hearts.[120] The accusations of the seventy are false because YHWH sees their idolatry, which leads to the abandonment or departure of the glory of YHWH becoming a self-fulfilling prophecy.

Ezekiel proceeds to be led throughout the Temple from the entrance of the north gate to the inner court where the elders and the high priests are practicing abominations against the holy YHWH (vv. 14-16).[121] Although, this scene is brief, the language used underscores the themes of idolatry as the women were weeping or mourning תמוז (v.15).[122] It is not clear if the hearers would perceive תמוז ('Tammuz') as a god or type of lament. It is possible that Tammuz represents a special genre of lament, rather than the deity himself. Contextually, the narrative supports the idea of some type of idolatrous act. Ezekiel is not only lead through the Temple but is also commanded to ראה the escalating abominations occurring in the Temple. As previously discussed, the idea of seeing is closely related to the ideas of perceiving and understanding. From this perspective, the narrative highlights YHWH as disclosing to Ezekiel, his chosen messenger, hidden knowledge through the medium of visions. This scene is short, but the message is emphatic! YHWH has chosen Ezekiel to see the wicked idolatrous acts of the leaders in the Jerusalem Temple.

In the final scene (Ezek. 8.16-18), Ezekiel is brought back to 'the inner court of the Lord' where 'twenty-five men' are 'bowing down to the sun in the east' (v. 16).[123] The rebellious leaders are performing

---

[120] See Deut. 4.28; Ps. 115.4–8; Isa. 44.12–20.

[121] See Odell, *Ezekiel*, pp. 110-11, who presents the various scholarly views for the reference to Tammuz.

[122] Block, *The Book of Ezekiel Chapters 1–24*, pp. 294-95. It is the only reference to Tammuz in the OT.

[123] The scene is reminiscent of the national lament described in the book of Joel (2.17), this was the designated place for the priests to pray to God, but now it is the place of sun worship. See Block, *The Book of Ezekiel Chapters 1–24*, p. 298, cites 2 Kgs 21.5 to point to the possibility that the sun god, Shemesh/Shamash had

the ultimate act of defilement as they are worshipping other gods in the most sacred place of worship designated for YHWH. The act of prostration towards the idol alerts Ezekiel's hearers that the leaders are turning their backs and allegiance away from YHWH. The drama culminates with YHWH's response to these atrocities. He is provoked by their cultic horrors and declares that he will respond in fury, without pity, and will not spare his wrath nor listen to their cries (v. 17). The affective language surely elicits fear in the hearers as they would know that the Sovereign Lord is full of power and capable of pouring out his wrath.

The vision transitions from the language of reasons for judgment described in Ezekiel 8 to decrees of judgment to slaughter all those who do not possess 'the mark' in Ezekiel 9.[124] The first scene (9.1-2) commences with the introduction of a new character, 'a man clothed in linen'.[125] The heavenly scribe is to mark with a sign on the foreheads of all those who appear to be dismayed by the national apostasy occurring in their midst. The significance of this marking would not be altogether clear to the hearers at this point. It is possible they would recollect the Passover accounts in Egypt where the blood was painted above the doorposts and the marking was used as symbol to the Israelites who would be saved from the coming judgment of YHWH. It is conceivable that Ezekiel's hearers might understand the supernatural scribe who was charged with marking the foreheads of those considered righteous might hope that the mark was one of preservation. Although, the identity of the man is not revealed, he

---

'gained royal sponsorship during the reign of Manasseh, who built altars for the entire host of heaven in the courts of the temple'.

[124] For explanations on the interpretations of the 'mark', see Tuell, *Ezekiel*, p. 50, who proposes that there is a connection between Job 31.55, which uses the same word as the one in Ezekiel 9 and may be understood as God's signature or seal, declaring those marked belong to God. For a different view, see Eichrodt, *Ezekiel*, pp. 130-31, who proposes that the mark is 'designated as *tau* the last letter in the Hebrew alphabet, and probably took on the shape of a sloping cross, the most archaic form of that letter'. However, the context is similar to those described in the Exodus texts related to the Passover in Egypt (Exod. 12.7, 13, 22-23, 27). In this way, it could be a mark designated to preserve or protect those who remained faithful to YHWH.

[125] Block, *Ezekiel Chapters 1–24*, p. 305, relates the man clothed in linen to the angels wearing linen in Daniel (Dan. 10.5), which accounts for the rabbinic identification of the seventh figure here as the angel Gabriel.

appears to receive directions to participate in the judgments from the Lord (vv. 3-11).[126]

The scene intensifies as the prophet is left alone in the temple court (v. 8). In an emotional outburst, Ezekiel expresses his own terror of despair at the impending judgment of the Lord. No longer would the prophet be in total submission as he falls on his face before YHWH in a vain attempt of intercession on behalf of the remnant of Israel. However, the Lord's sovereignty would prevail. In other words, the narrative highlights that YHWH's impending judgment cannot be overturned or disputed. The judgment upon the leaders of the house of Israel and Judah will be executed because their sin is too great (vv. 9-11).

The theme of judgment for Israel's idolatry continues in Ezekiel 10.[127] The scene echoes the previous texts (cf. Ezekiel 1) and transitions the hearers to a chariot-throne vision filled with imagery of clouds, brightness, fire, and the thundering sound of the wings of the cherubim.[128] The hearers would recall Ezekiel's descriptions of the 'throne of sapphire', 'the living beings', 'the wheels', and the יהוה־כבוד from Ezekiel 1.[129] Three things are pointedly unique to this vision sequence: (1) the setting takes place in the Jerusalem Temple instead of Babylon (10.3), (2) the כבוד־יהוה departs from over the threshold of the temple (10.18), and (3) Ezekiel realizes that the living beings are cherubim who carry 'coals of fire' that the 'man in linen' is commanded to scatter over the city as a sign of judgment (10.20).[130] Here, Ezekiel 10 is a literary reflection of Ezekiel 1, which

---

[126] Tuell, *Ezekiel*, p. 48, understands the priestly portrayal of Ezekiel and argues that the prophet would understand the linen garment to represent a priestly role (Exod. 39.27-29; Lev. 16.4, 23), and the writing kit would symbolize both a priest and a writer.

[127] Odell, *Ezekiel*, p. 117, discusses the debate over whether the theme is one of judgment or cleansing, as the coals over the city may represent an act of purification.

[128] Odell, *Ezekiel*, p. 117, highlights the biblical tradition in Num. 14.10; 16.19, which associates the manifestation of YHWH with the theme of judgment.

[129] Charles Sherlock, 'Ezekiel 10: A Prophet Surprised', *The Reformed Theological Review* 42.2 (May – Aug; 1983), pp. 42-44, points out that twice now the voice has spoken of 'whirling wheels' (10.3, 6; this phrase is not used in ch. 1). Ezekiel, however, does not seem to understand what they are, or recognize them. They had no parallel in the temple tradition, and represent the new element in his vision thus far. When he does look at them, it is therefore natural that he describes them in some detail (10.9-12).

[130] Block, *The Book of Ezekiel 1–24*, p. 185.

invites the hearers to interpret the present vision in light of the previous one. Ezekiel and the hearers would surely understand the gravity of the glory leaving the sacred Temple, for the promise of YHWH's dwelling among his people was a covenantal sign of his favor and his promise to forsake his people would be a consequence of their continued rebellion.[131]

In the next vision scene, one of the leading actors returns to the stage. Ezekiel 11 not only emphasizes the activities of the divine רוח but also introduces to the hearers a new role of the רוח. The hearers would recall the transporting activity of the רוח depicted in Ezekiel 3 and now portrayed in this scene. By the Spirit and in divine visions Ezekiel is transported to the east gate of 'the house of the Lord' (11.1; cf. ch. 3). This unique transporting activity of the רוח allows Ezekiel, in divine visions, to observe the evil practices of the leaders in the Temple. The transporting activity of the רוח, in essence, becomes the primary means of communicating to Ezekiel what is or has occurred in the Jerusalem Temple. The hearers likely would perceive that the divine visions which Ezekiel sees are clearly caused by the activity of the Spirit in this temple vision narrative. However, in this scene the Lord is identified as the one speaking to Ezekiel about the evil men and commanding him to prophesy against them (11.2-4) followed by the רוח־יהוה falling on the prophet again prior to commanding Ezekiel specifically what to prophesy (11.5). It is not clear if the hearers would be confused by the moves from the רוח speaking to the Lord in ch. 8 and the רוח־יהוה speaking in Ezekiel 11. It appears that in this scene, there is an integration of the communicative acts of seeing and hearing by the divine רוח, the רוח־יהוה, and YHWH (11.1-24).

The overall story takes a dramatic turn from YHWH's judgments to the possibility of hope. The current literary scene peaks with a description of these forthcoming promises by the Sovereign Lord (11.16-20). The first promise is to return YHWH's scattered people to the land of Israel again (11.16-17).[132] The hearers undoubtedly, would perceive this as the first sign of hope to escape YHWH's

---

[131] See Deut. 4.29, 31.17; Hos. 9.2-3.

[132] Block, *Ezekiel 1–24*, pp. 350-52, argues the oracle of future deliverance requires 'undoing their past' in order to establish a new order, which the first step would be to gather the exiles and return them to their homeland.

judgment. Second, YHWH announces that 'I have become their sanctuary' (11.16b) as a replacement to the destruction of the Jerusalem Temple.[133] The hearers likely would be surprised as the sanctuary was considered the cultic site for the sacred presence or the יהוה-כבוד to dwell. Ezekiel's vision displays the departure of the יהוה-כבוד from the sacred Temple and then the כבוד-יהוה appearing to him in a foreign land, a detail that would propose radical ideas about worship. Remarkably, YHWH promises to change the locus of the כבוד-יהוה, which would profoundly change the worship practices of Israel. Additionally, YHWH personalizes the place of worship, as the text uses the first person to describe YHWH as their sanctuary instead of the temple building.

The third promise, and possibly most surprising for the hearers, is YHWH's declaration to his people that he will give them 'an undivided heart and put a new spirit in them' (11.19a).[134] Although, this temple vision is quite clearly painting the spiritual depravity of the leaders of Israel and Judah, it must have been unanticipated for the hearers to discern exactly what was meant by YHWH's promise of putting 'a new spirit in them'.[135] In this context, the hearers could possibly perceive the idea of a new spirit as a new disposition or moral willingness to become obedient to YHWH's covenantal laws. They may not have understood the dynamic of a new spirit, but the message of how this spiritual renewal would be received was clear. The new spirit would only come through the power of YHWH.

Ezekiel's vision at this juncture communicates to the hearers that YHWH will reinstitute his covenant with his people. It proposes that YHWH will cause them to become a people who will be able to worship as he will provide a heart and mind transformation.

---

[133] Block, *Ezekiel 1–24*, pp. 349, argues that YHWH's announcement is revolutionary because it is unparalleled in the OT, and the sanctuary was normally viewed as a sacred place or cult site designated for the divine presence to dwell.

[134] Joyce, *Divine Initiative*, p. 111, posits that the use of רוח is pointing to the 'will' in such a way as to describe the moral sense of the word לב ('heart, mind'). He uses this point to argue that the reference to a new heart and spirit (11.19; 36.26-7; 37.14) is the gift or the result of the outpouring of YHWH that provides the capacity of corporate Israel to obey YHWH's commands.

[135] Rea, *The Holy Spirit in the Bible*, pp. 101-107, through grammatical, contextual, and theological perspectives identifies two 'renewing functions' for the role of the רוח ('Spirit') in the book of Ezekiel: (1) God's promise of his indwelling Spirit (Ezek. 11.19; 36.27; 37.14), and (2) the outpoured Spirit as covenant sign (Ezek. 39.29).

Furthermore, the text states, 'I will remove from them their heart of stone and give them a heart of flesh' (11.19b).[136] The concept may have been totally foreign to the hearers, but Ezekiel's vision introduces an anthropological idea that through the power of YHWH a human *heart* or *will* can be given the capacity to be tender, flexible, and ultimately desire to seek and obey God. The expression, 'stony heart' would cause the hearers to recall the previous description of the Israelite's hearts in Ezekiel's call to become a prophet to a people who were 'obstinate and stubborn' (Ezekiel 2–3). The metaphors likely were clear to the hearers in that the 'stony heart' would represent their hardheartedness and unwillingness to obey YHWH's laws.

The literary unit culminates as Ezekiel is given more detail and revelation to his vision. As it was the Spirit who brought Ezekiel in the vision, the hearers may assume it is the Spirit who gives Ezekiel the revelation needed to see more clearly. He states that 'the cherubim, with the wheels beside them, as the כבוד־יהוה' is above them and is now moving upward from within the city of Jerusalem stopping above the mountain east of it (11.22).[137] The recurrent theme of mobility is underscored once again as the narrative highlights the transporting activity of the רוח as it lifts Ezekiel and brings him back to the exiles in Babylonia (11.24; cf. 1-3).

Summary

Ezekiel 8–11 is a single vision composed of several visionary scenes in which the Spirit reveals to Ezekiel that things are not what they appear to be. The priests and leaders in the sacred Temple were supposed to be offering true worship acceptable to YHWH. Yet, in the secret chambers they were committing idolatry and performing abominable acts of false worship. In the beginning and ending of these chapters, it is the Spirit that is emphasized as one of the main characters in this first temple vision. The Spirit transports the prophet 'between heaven and earth in visions' to the Jerusalem Temple. Although, the question remains as to whether it is the Spirit who brings Ezekiel to the entrance of the east gate and reveals to the

---

[136] Odell, *Ezekiel*, p. 124, proposes that the promise speaks of giving them 'one heart' (11.19-20), and this unifying aspect of one communal heart is the 'gift of unity that heals communal rifts' (cf. 37.15-23).

[137] Block, *The Book of Ezekiel Chapters 1–24*, p. 278, calculates a possible time frame since his first vision and proposes that Ezekiel has had fourteen months to reflect on his first vision and therefore understand more clearly what he saw.

prophet all abominations that are occurring by Judah's leaders and the house of Israel, it is the Spirit's presence who works in concert with YHWH (chs. 8 and 11). The glory of YHWH speaks to Ezekiel and commands him to enlarge a hole through the temple walls so that he can see the mass idolatry occurring in the sacred Temple courts (8.8-18). The Spirit may guide Ezekiel through the temple complex so that he can look upon all the detestable acts occurring in secret (8.8-18). The glory of YHWH declares the impending judgments that will be executed for their mass idolatry (ch. 9). In these ways, it is the glory of YHWH working in tandem with the Spirit and the hand of YHWH assisting the prophet to discern true and false worship.

In Ezek. 10.1-22, the prophet is shown the chariot throne again; however, as it is the Spirit who brought Ezekiel, it is also the Spirit who revealed to him that the living beings are 'cherubim'. The vision scene climaxes with the כבוד־יהוה departing the Jerusalem Temple and rising above the cherubim. Ezekiel 10 is thus an important part of Ezekiel's message as it describes the divine abandonment of the glory of YHWH from the desecrated Temple. YHWH departs from the Holy of Holies to the threshold (10.4), from there to the east gate (10.18-19), and finally away from the city altogether (11.23). The theological implications are paramount as YHWH's glory abandons his chosen city and Temple, which results in leaving his people defenseless to the enemy. Through their offensive acts and false worship towards YHWH, they have provoked YHWH to decree judgment. It is in this setting that the glory of YHWH reveals true and false worship to Ezekiel and is chosen to receive YHWH's message of impending judgment.

It is the Spirit who comes upon the prophet again in Ezekiel 11 and sets the stage for YHWH's promises to restore his covenant. YHWH promises to perform a renewing work in the hearts of his people to enable them to become true worshippers. The Spirit assumes one of the leading roles in Ezekiel's first temple vision as the Spirit transports the prophet to YHWH and works in tandem with the glory of YHWH who speaks to the prophet regarding the fate of the house of Israel. The hearers likely would discern that it is the divine רוח who inspires Ezekiel to see visions, brings the prophet to YHWH, and also inspires him to hear the voice of YHWH.

There are two meaningful variations from the ways in which the רוח, the יד־יהוה, and the כבוד־יהוה are described in the first temple vision report in Ezekiel 8–11. First, the role of the רוח is unique in Ezekiel's first temple vision as it seems to be more closely connected to the יד־יהוה. The hearers would likely understand that the anthropomorphic phrase, יד־יהוה, is utilized to describe YHWH's power as a means to inspire the vision (cf. 1.3; 8.1). This view is narratively supported because Ezekiel describes that he feels the יד־יהוה simultaneously as he reports to ראה a vision. The vision of the luminous mysterious figure, 'like that of a man from what appeared to be his waist down he was like fire and from there up his appearance was as bright as glowing metal' (8.2) immediately precedes the transporting activity of the רוח (8.3) and the vision of the כבוד אלהי ישראל (8.4). The close associations of these literary markers indicate that the יד־יהוה, the רוח, the כבוד־יהוה, and the mysterious figure not only serve as the main characters, but also appear to function cooperatively. Both the יד־יהוה and the רוח represent an empowerment that not only has profound effect upon the prophet, but also precedes the initiation of a vision.[138] As the יד־יהוה 'falls' upon the prophet before seeing the vision of the 'figure like that of a man' so also the רוח 'lifts' the prophet before seeing a vision of the כבוד־יהוה. It is the יד־יהוה that 'falls' upon Ezekiel in 8.3 prior to seeing, and functions in the same manner as the רוח that 'falls' upon Ezekiel in 11.5 prior to the prophet hearing.[139] From this perspective, the narrative hearing further supports that the יד־יהוה and the רוח both function in the act of inspiration.[140]

Second, Ezekiel's narration expands the activities of the anthropomorphic description of the glory of YHWH (cf. 1.27-28; 3.23; 8.2-3). In Ezekiel 1, the 'figure like that of a man' is elaborately described and later stands (3.23), but now is portrayed as grabbing the prophet by his hair (8.3). The direct interaction with Ezekiel in his vision

---

[138] Robson, *Word and Spirit in Ezekiel*, pp. 105-70. Block, 'Empowered by the Spirit of God', pp. 32.

[139] Zimmerli, *Ezekiel 2*, p. 567.

[140] Joyce, *Ezekiel*, p. 67, argues that the two phrases, 'word of the Lord came to Ezekiel' and 'the hand of the Lord was on him there' are two recurrent and important formulas for the divine inspiration of the prophet, the latter being especially distinctive of Ezekiel (cf. Ezek. 1.14, 22; 8.1; 33.22; 37.1; 40.1).

points to the ways in which YHWH stimulates the prophet's senses in the midst of his vision. Ezekiel not only hears and sees, but he also describes that he physically and affectively feels (cf. Ezekiel 1–3).

B. Sign-Acts, Judgment Oracles, Metaphors, and Parables (12.1–24.27)

Chapters 12–24 constitute numerous sign-acts, judgment oracles, metaphors, and parables that occur amidst Ezekiel's vision reports.[141] Chapter 12 begins with reminders that Ezekiel dwells among a 're-bellious house' (12.2-3; 9; 25). The hearers would be reminded of this recurrent phrase from Ezekiel's call (2–3). The first sign-act also recollects Ezekiel's call as YHWH commands the prophet to dig a hole through the wall (12.5). The dominant theme of seeing and hearing is juxtaposed with the theme of 'not seeing' and 'not hearing' as it reflects the spiritual blindness and deafness of YHWH's people (12.1-28). The subsequent oracles and sign-acts in the story anticipate the siege of Jerusalem and declares that Ezekiel's vision of destruction will soon be fulfilled (12.17-20). Ultimately, the oracles and sign-acts reveal the spiritual depravity of the house of Israel.

Ezekiel 12.21–14.11 contains five prophecies reflecting the prophet's disdain for false prophets. A unifying thread throughout these prophecies is provided by the term חזון ('vision') which appears five times in 12.21-28 and once in ch. 13. The term חזון is juxtaposed with the words 'flattering divination' as a means to emphasize that false prophets are a part of the rebellious house and will be held accountable for prophesying from their own inspiration (chs. 13–14.1-11). It is likely the hearers would know that these counterfeits are ones who claim to see visions inspired by YHWH, yet the prophet accuses them that they see and hear nothing from YHWH, and speak from their own spirits.

The succeeding chapters signal a new collection of prophecies followed by the use of metaphors and parables as visual aids to accentuate the messages (1) Jerusalem in 14.12-23; 17.1-10; 21–24, (2) the dynasty in 17.11-24, 19, (3) Israel in 20–22, and (4) the King of

---

[141] The literary devices of sign-acts and unusual metaphors utilized in Ezekiel's visions have long been noted with discussions of Ezekiel's 'madness' and have not escaped an interpretative lens of psychoanalysis. For this view, see Broome, 'Ezekiel's Abnormal Personality', pp. 277-92; and Halperin, *Seeking Ezekiel: Text and Psychology*. For a more nuanced perspective, see Steven Tuell, 'Should Ezekiel Go to Rehab? The Method to Ezekiel's "Madness"', *PRS* 36 (2009), pp. 289-302.

Babylon and the sons of Ammon in 21.18-23.[142] Once again, the book of Ezekiel emphasizes the visual medium of YHWH's message given in visions through the symbolic language used to engage the hearer's imagination. The crux of these messages from YHWH underscores one of the central themes of the book. The sacred city of Jerusalem is central to the life and faith of his people, yet not even the temple is more sacred to YHWH than his people. The hearers likely would see and hear through the images and words used that YHWH despises idolatry and desires for his people to be faithful and holy. The vivacity of the messages comes to life as ultimately Ezekiel was called to become a sign. The message of YHWH was to become incarnate in the body of the messenger.[143] Ezekiel was tested in personal tragedy and required to respond selflessly to the hand of YHWH that was upon his life and calling (24.15-27).

C. Prophecies Against the Nations (25–32)
Ezekiel 25 marks a transition in the collection of his oracles as his prophecies previously dealt with the judgment and fate of Jerusalem, now the story turns to judgment upon the foreign nations (Ezekiel 25–32; 35).[144] However, since these judgment oracles are directed to the enemies of God's people, then they could well be conceived by Ezekiel's hearers as messages of hope for their future.[145] In this change of focus they would likely perceive that YHWH's punishment may be turning away from them and towards other nations, though the language consists of the same themes previously underscored, that of sin and idolatry, which were proclaimed against Israel and Judah.

---

[142] See Block, *Ezekiel 1–24*, for an extensive description of the various forms of oracles depicted in these narratives.

[143] Odell, *Ezekiel*, p. 320, discusses how elsewhere in the OT, the term 'sign' occurs to signify supernatural signs and portents, as the signs and wonders in Egypt, but human beings rather appear as signs (Ps. 71.7; Isa. 8.18; 20.3; Zech. 3.8).

[144] Block, *Ezekiel 25–48*, pp. 117-19, proposes that Ezekiel has Genesis 2–3 in mind with the reference to creation (Ezek. 28.13, 15), and to the first creation account as Ezekiel's cherub is linked with the cherubim stationed by YHWH at the entrance of the garden (Gen. 3.4).

[145] There is a noticeable resemblance to the language used in the books of Isaiah and Zephaniah where oracles of judgment upon the nations were described in ways to combine messages of hope.

D. Ezekiel as a Watchman (33)

The literary motifs and language in Ezekiel 33 harken back to the themes from previous narratives. For example, the metaphor of the watchman in vv. 2-9 echoes Ezekiel's call and commissioning in 3.16-21.[146] The language in vv. 10-18 summarizes the disputations of ch. 18. Ezekiel reports that the prophecies from 24.25-27 are fulfilled (vv. 21-22), and vv. 23-29 reiterate the judgment of the inhabitants of Jerusalem. Chapter 33 also draws attention to the communal response to the prophetic message. The metaphor of the watchman assists the hearers to recall that Ezekiel was called as YHWH's messenger and given authority to speak on his behalf. As the hearers remembered from his commissioning report, the prophet was empowered and inspired by the hand of YHWH and by the Spirit. The hearers would possibly discern that YHWH's hand has never left the prophet and the Spirit was always present to come upon the prophet, dwell in the prophet, and inspire the prophet to see, hear, and deliver YHWH's messages. The theme of responsibility is underscored in this chapter as previously referenced in ch. 3. The prophet as a watchman was responsible and held accountable to sound the alarm and the hearers were responsible to heed to the warnings given by the messenger. The outcome would remain unclear and dependent upon their response.

The story unfolds with a new twist, as for the first time, Ezekiel's warnings are taken to heart with the language of guilt as the community laments, 'our transgressions and our sins weigh upon us, and we waste away because of them; how can we live?' The themes of death and life are juxtaposed with the themes of sin/death and obedience/life. As the community laments, it appears that their hearts perceive that the impending judgment may not be irrevocable. They also discern that their disobedience would result in death.

E. Prophecies Against the Leaders of Israel (34)

The metaphorical language persists in Ezekiel 34 with shepherd and sheep imagery.[147] The hearers probably would conclude that the

---

[146] Odell, *Ezekiel*, pp. 413-15, highlights the characterization of the watchman as a sentinel called to pronounce judgment but also to rescue them from their guilt.

[147] Katheryn Pfisterer-Darr, 'The Book of Ezekiel: Introduction, Commentary and Reflections', in (Leander E. Keek (ed.), *The New Interpreter's Bible: A Commentary* vol. VI (Nashville: Abingdon Press, 1996), pp. 1465-66, notes that the image of a deity as a shepherd may be drawn upon by the ANE texts.

shepherd imagery is alluding to the Israelite leaders, whom Ezekiel has earlier condemned in chs. 13 and 22, and the sheep imagery refers to the people who are entrusted to the leaders to lead. Thus, it is not surprising that these oracles are YHWH's response to those who were left injured and abandoned. YHWH announces: (1) judgments against these shepherds in vv. 1-10, (2) vows to gather the scattered sheep in vv. 11-16, (3) YHWH's rule over the flock in vv. 17-24, and (4) a covenant of peace in vv. 25-31. Ezekiel's use of metaphor no doubt would allude to the hearers that the sheep belong to YHWH as their sovereign shepherd. The imagery would elicit positive feelings as shepherds were a symbol of nurture and care for the flock which they were responsible to protect. Yet, the allusion to cannibalism does not go unnoticed in v. 5. Because the sheep were left unattended by their shepherd, they 'became meat to all the beasts of the field'.[148] The end of this chapter reminds the hearers of YHWH's promise, which declares that after the judgment of Jerusalem, he would remember his everlasting covenant (cf. 16.60).

F. Prophecies against Edom and Israel (35–36)

The oracle in Ezekiel 35 resembles a court case in which, (1) the judge is YHWH, (2) the nation of Edom is the accused, and surprisingly, (3) Israel is the victim. Ezekiel 35 explicitly names the foreign nation, Edom, as YHWH vows to avenge Israelite blood. The text reads, 'Because you harbored an ancient hostility and delivered the Israelites over to the sword at the time of their calamity, the time their punishment reached its climax, therefore as surely as I live, declares the Sovereign LORD, I will give you over to bloodshed and it will pursue you' (35.5-6).[149]

Ezekiel 36 continues with the court drama emphasizing the familiar theme of judgment, however now, nuanced with new perspectives. Unexpectedly, YHWH positions himself in the narrative as Israel's defender, which may leave the hearers somewhat surprised. The

---

[148] See Nathanael Warren, 'A Cannibal Feast in Ezekiel', *JSOT* 38.4 (2014), p. 504, for a literary-rhetorical analysis of the cannibalistic rhetorical allusions in Ezekiel. He argues that the element of necrophagia plays into Ezekiel' s corpse desecration motif to highlight the similar fates of Jerusalem and Gog.

[149] Block, *Ezekiel 24–48*, p. 329, proposes an historical perspective in that Ezekiel describes the experience of the mountains of Israel in the wake of the Babylonian conquest and the enemies pursued them and took advantage of them in their destitution.

affective disposition of YHWH is emphasized in the narrative as Ezekiel describes YHWH as a jealous God who speaks in wrath and pronounces judgments due to his jealousy and anger (36.5-6). The reference of YHWH's באשׁ קנאתי ('in the fire of my jealousy') speaks of YHWH's passion, which evokes intense emotions and ultimately, drives him to action.[150] Yet, while YHWH's intense affections are directed towards 'the remaining nations' in v. 6, the hearers would soon find out that it is for the sake of his honor as the rightful owner of the land.[151] YHWH responds with an answer for the land as Ezekiel begins to describe a new day (36.8-15)![152] A day in which YHWH envisions complete restoration of the relationship between YHWH, his people, and the land he gave as their inheritance.[153] Yet, this particular promise is conditional upon: (1) the covenantal relationship between YHWH and his people restored and (2) the exiled nation of Israel will be restored to their land.[154]

Amidst this explanation for a new day, an unanticipated plot twist occurs in Ezekiel's description of YHWH's pronouncements. The text reads, 'It is not for your sake, O house of Israel, that I am going to do these things, but for the sake of my holy name' (36.22-23). The accusatory tone highlights that YHWH seeks to vindicate the holiness of his name, which leads to a view that Ezekiel's hearers would perceive they were being charged with desecrating YHWH's holy name. The theme of holiness in the context of a court drama points to the single objection at the fore is that what once was holy and now desecrated, must be consecrated. The aim is restitution for the crimes committed. It is likely that the hearers would ask themselves as to how this grievous transgression could be rectified.

In this highly emotional characterization of YHWH, a new theme is introduced through the use of metaphor, that of 'cleansing with

---

[150] Heschel, *The Prophets*, II, p. 263, developed the idea that YHWH is a God who possesses pathos and shares his affections with his prophets, which ultimately influences the affections of his prophets.

[151] Cf. Ezek. 11.5 and 33.24, where similar claims to the same land had been made by the Judeans who had escaped the deportation.

[152] See Zimmerli, 'The Land in the Pre-exilic and Early Post-exilic Prophets', *Understanding the Word* (JSOTSup 37; Sheffield: JSOT Press, 1985), pp. 255-58.

[153] The sign of a new day is marked with fruitfulness of the land as promised in the covenantal blessing (cf. Lev. 26.1-13).

[154] Cf. Ezek. 7.7; 30.3 for earlier predictions of the 'day of YHWH'.

water'.[155] The text reads, 'I will sprinkle clean water on you, and you will be clean; I will sprinkle clean water on you, and you will be clean; I will cleanse you from all your filthiness and from all your idols' (36.25).[156] Such words would likely bring a glimmer of hope to the hearers as they encounter YHWH's remedy for defilement as being executed through the cleansing of water.[157] The metaphorical repetition of this new theme also adds to the significance of the message. Certainly, the hearers would understand water as a cleansing agent in a natural sense, but how would the water cleanse their immorality and disobedience? Ezekiel, who was earlier identified as a priest or son of a priest, now appears to assist the hearers to view the oracle in this light.[158]

For example, the metaphor of water as a symbol of cleansing may be alluding to the priestly cleansing rituals, suggesting that the hearers would perceive that the cleansing of water as the cleansing by blood in the priestly rituals were in some way synonymous. Contextually, Ezekiel points to the cleansing as a means of preparation for what follows. YHWH, again proclaims that he will give his people a 'new heart and put a new spirit' in them (v. 26). In light of Ezekiel's identification with a priestly heritage, the hearers may discern that YHWH's cleansing is necessary before what could be called a 'heart transplant' could occur. From this perspective, the terms 'water' in Ezek. 36.25 and the 'new spirit' of v. 26 could possibly be understood

---

[155] The concept of ceremonial uncleanness is a distinctive feature in the Torah. For example, the categories of what was 'clean' and 'unclean', or 'sacred' and 'profane' were described in the Levitical laws.

[156] Verena Schafroth, 'An Exegetical Exploration of Spirit references in Ezekiel 36 and 37', *JEPTA* (2009), pp. 61-77, argues that though the verb זרק ('sprinkle') in v. 25 is usually connected with the sprinkling of blood, the sprinkling with pure water here should be understood as a ritual cleansing and recalls the Mosaic rites of purification (cf. Num. 19.17-19; Isa. 4.4; Zech. 13.1) as well as Ps. 51.7, which refers to sprinkling and cleansing of the worshipper. See also C.R. Biggs, *The Book of Ezekiel* (London: Epworth Press, 1996), p. 116; Charles Feinberg, *The Prophecy of Ezekiel* (Chicago: Moody Press, 1969), p. 209.

[157] E.F. Davis, *Swallowing the Scroll* (Sheffield: Almond Press, 1989), p. 40; B. Vawter, & L.J. Hoppe, *Ezekiel: A New Heart* (Grand Rapids: Eerdmans, 1991), p. 11.

[158] Schwartz, B., 'A Priest Out of Place: Reconsidering Ezekiel's Role in the History of the Israelite Priesthood', in Stephen Cook and Corrine Patton (eds.), *Ezekiel's Hierarchical World Wrestling with a Tiered Reality* (Boston: Brill, 2004), pp. 61-67.

by the hearers as a means to describe how YHWH would fulfill his covenantal promise to give them a new heart and a new spirit.[159]

Immediately following, YHWH reiterates his previous promise to give the house of Israel 'a new heart' and 'a new spirit', yet this time he elaborates, 'I will remove the heart of stone from your flesh and give you a heart of flesh. I will put My Spirit within you and cause you to walk in my statues, and you will be careful to observe my ordinances' (36.36-37).[160] It is not clear at this point as to how the hearers would perceive the idea of YHWH's Spirit indwelling them. Yet, it is conceivable they would remember the Spirit entering Ezekiel in his calling and possibly discern that YHWH's Spirit would act upon them in like manner once they were cleansed from their sins of idolatry (cf. 2.2). In this light, the hearers may have made the connections between YHWH's Spirit indwelling functioning to empower the prophet to become obedient to his ministry call and YHWH's Spirit empowering them to become obedient.

The parallelism of the terms 'new heart' and 'new spirit' appear to be synonymous (v. 26).[161] It is representative in chiastic arrangement as the word order in v. 26a–b is verb–noun, noun–verb. From this viewpoint, the 'new spirit' does not refer to YHWH's Spirit. It is likely conceivable that the hearers would perceive the 'new heart' or 'new spirit' as a new heart attitude towards YHWH.[162] Ezekiel's language used to describe what can be called a 'heart transplant' may have been perceived by the hearers to use their imagination to envision the hearts as soft and pliable to YHWH's will and through the empowerment of the Spirit in them, then they will finally be able to obey YHWH's decrees.[163]

---

[159] Rea, *The Holy Spirit in the Bible*, pp. 102-10, argues that although, 'Ezekiel did not employ the term "new covenant", these concepts of "inner cleansing and regeneration" with God's promise to impart YHWH's Spirit to indwell believers was a new feature not previously provided in his [YHWH's] covenants with Abraham, Moses, and David', yet the promise to circumcise the hearts of Israel is alluded to in Deut. 30.6.

[160] For references to the infusion of the רוח in the life of the OT believer, see Block, 'The Prophet of the Spirit' *JETS* 32 (1989), p. 40. See also Joyce, *Divine Initiation*, pp. 108-109, who rightly points out that the antecedent texts, 'heart' and 'spirit', represent the person's internal locus of emotion, will, and thought.

[161] See Lys, *Ruach*, pp. 140-41.

[162] Dreytza, *Der theologische Gebrauch von RUAH im Alten Testament*, p. 14, classifies Ezek. 36.26 anthropologically rather than theologically.

[163] Odell, *Ezekiel*, p. 443, notes a distinction between Ezekiel's heart metaphor and Jeremiah's. She points out that Jeremiah's description of the promise of the

IV. Ezekiel's Visions of Hope (Ezekiel 37-39)

A. The Vision of the Valley of Dry Bones (37.1-14)

Third and shortest, but very pivotal, is Ezekiel's vision of the dry bones in 37.1-14.[164] This literary unit is presented in the form of an autobiographical narrative. As such, Ezekiel reports the vision and the conversations between the prophet and YHWH as if to convey a private affair to his listeners. In the vision report, the narrative combines oracles and symbolic acts, which serve to enhance the multi-dimensional quality of the vision. In this passage, it is revealed to the hearers from the outset that it is by the יד־יהוה and the רוח־יהוה that Ezekiel is enabled or inspired to see a vision (v. 1). In addition, while the יד־יהוה is upon Ezekiel, it is the רוח־יהוה who transports and sets him down in a valley full of bones; as well as inspires him to hear the Sovereign Lord (vv. 1-3).[165] The recurrent statement, 'the hand of YHWH was upon me' (v. 1), links the present vision with Ezekiel's other visions (Ezekiel 1–3; 8–11), inviting the hearers to view this scene in this light. The term רוח occurs 10 times in Ezek. 37.1-14 with various semantic meanings, which emphasizes the work of the divine רוח.[166] The transportation and inspiration by the רוח־יהוה is

---

new covenant, the Torah is written on the heart so that the knowledge of YHWH's laws become innate (Jer. 31.31-34).

[164] There exists a variety of proposals for the structure of this literary unit. Zimmerli, *Ezekiel 2*, pp. 256-58, observes the relationship between vv. 1-10 and 11-14 as an image and interpretation (cf. chs. 17 and 21). He cites v. 11 as a turning point in which vv. 1-10 look back at the imagery of the vision and vv. 11-14 introduce the disputation between God and the people. L.C. Allen, 'Structure, Tradition and Redaction in Ezekiel's Death Valley Vision', in P.R. Davies and D.J. Clines (eds.), *Among the Prophets: Language, Image and Structure in the Prophetic Writings* (JSOTSup 144; Sheffield: JSOT Press, 1993), pp. 126-34. Allen structures the vision account: (1) a negative picture of Israel's condition (vv. 1-3), (2) a positive and transforming event (vv. 4-8), and (3) oracular pronouncement of salvation (vv. 9-14).

[165] Christopher R. Seitz, 'Ezekiel 37.1-14', *Int* 46 (1992), pp. 53-56 and Francesca Stavrakopoulou, 'Gog's Grave and the Use and Abuse of Corpses in Ezekiel 39.11-21', *JBL* 129 (2010), pp. 64-85, identify a rhetorical-literary purpose for Ezekiel's corpse motif and draw correlations to Ezekiel 11, 24, and 34.

[166] As previously discussed, since the Hebrew uses the same word for the English concepts of 'wind' as a meteorological phenomenon, and 'spirit' as a supernatural manifestation, it might be ambiguous as to how the ancient Israelites made distinctions. See also Goldingay, 'Was the Holy Spirit Active in Old Testament Times? What Was New About the Christian Experience of God?' *Ex Auditu* 12 (1988), pp. 14-28. Goldingay argues that the OT terms, 'Holy Spirit' and 'the Spirit of God (or the LORD)' and the theology associated with them 'depends on

highlighted from the onset of the passage (v. 1), and the indwelling activity of the Spirit is emphasized at the end of the passage (v. 14). The hearers would recollect that this was not the first vision in which Ezekiel had been led by the divine Spirit to a valley (cf. 3.22). Yet, the backdrop of the valley in ch. 3 was YHWH's glory. The backdrop in the present vision is quite different.

The beginning scene of the vision narrative underscores the theme of the divine Spirit leading the prophet to the valley. As the רוח־יהוה brought Ezekiel in a vision to a valley full of bones, the רוח־יהוה also leads him 'back and forth among them' as if urging the prophet to take a closer look at the bones. The hearers likely would recall the recurrent theme of mobility and leading by the Spirit from Ezekiel's description of his first vision (Ezekiel 1–3). As the divine Spirit leads Ezekiel to view the bones more closely, Ezekiel is able to depict the number and quality of the bones. Ezekiel pronounces that he was הנה ('surprised' or 'astonished') to see how exceedingly numerous they were on the floor of the valley (v. 2).[167] The hearers will soon learn the significance of their number (v. 10). Ezekiel again emphasizes his emotional disposition by reiterating his surprise with the duplication of the term הנה ('surprised' or 'astonished') as he sees how extremely dry the bones were (v. 2).[168] The repetition of the affective language would suggest to the hearers that they pay special attention to what is provoking such an emotional response by the prophet. They would recall how the Spirit's interactions with the prophet evoked such intense affections in his previous visionary

---

grasping the significance of the fact that, in about 40% of its occurrences, the Hebrew word רוח basically means "wind or breath", not "spirit". Furthermore, certain passages draw out the correspondence between the Spirit of God and the human spirit, that vivifies the spirit of the people to God (Ezekiel 37).' He also points out that the metaphor changes from 'wind' to 'water' in which water represents a physical purification and wind corresponds to the purification of the human spirit (Ezekiel 36). With regard to a possible chiastic arrangement, see Michael Fishbane, *Biblical Interpretation in Ancient Israel* (New York, Oxford University Press, 1985), pp. 451-52.

   [167] For the full treatment of how the particle הנה ('behold') relates to the verb ראה ('see') see Jackie A. Naudé, *NIDOTTE*, III, pp. 1007-15. The particle הנה is common in dream or vision reports and implies a visual experience with a quality of surprise and amazement at what is being seen.

   [168] D.J. McCarthy, 'The Uses of הנה in Biblical Hebrew', *Bib* 61 (1980), pp. 332-33, discusses how that in dreams and visions הנה expresses a strong emotional reaction to an awesome sight.

descriptions and now may recognize that the Spirit is directly responsible for producing Ezekiel's feelings of awe and amazement (cf. Ezekiel 1–3; 8–11).

Ezekiel's hearers would no doubt associate the bones or skeletal remains with death.[169] The term עצמות ('bones') occurs several times in this short passage. Ezekiel is: (1) taken to a valley full of bones (vv. 1-2), (2) asked if these bones can live (v. 3), (3) commanded to prophesy to the dry bones (vv. 4, 7), (4) the Sovereign Lord promises to bring the bones to life (v. 5), (5) the Lord reveals that the bones are the house of Israel (v. 11), and (6) Israel states that their bones are dried up and hopeless (v. 11). Ezekiel's use of repetitive language not only emphasizes the Spirit's role in leading, but also the theme of death through its metaphor of the term עצמות ('bones'). As the vision continues, Ezekiel is shown the quantity and quality of the bones, the purpose of the metaphor, and YHWH's promise regarding the message. Once again, as previously noted in Ezekiel's visionary descriptions, it is as if the vision has a progressive revelatory quality by the way in which Ezekiel is increasingly given more understanding of the vision (cf. Ezekiel 1 and 10).

The narrative juxtaposes the theme of death with that of life as the Sovereign Lord questions Ezekiel with what appears to be an absurd question, 'Son of man, can these bones live?' (v. 3).[170] It seems Ezekiel's earlier question, 'Will you completely destroy the remnant of Israel' (11.13), has now been answered. The hearers may well perceive that as the house of Israel is totally destroyed for their sins, this vision portrays corpses that are left unburied. Yet, at this point it is not clear if they would associate the vision of the valley of dry bones with themselves. Ezekiel does not describe how the hearers respond to such a horrendous idea, but it is conceivable they would have been devastated by the idea of unburied corpses.

---

[169] Odell, *Ezekiel*, p. 449, rightly points out that the metaphor of bones is frequently seen in the HB associated with death or disease, yet she argues that Ezekiel's use of the metaphor is unique. Odell proposes that the bones represent a 'treaty violation as with the Assyrian depictions of its slain enemies'.

[170] Jacqueline Lapsley, 'Can Theses Bones Live? The Problem of the Moral Self in the Book of Ezekiel', *Beihefte zur Zeitschrift für die alttestamentliche Wissenschaft* (Berlin/New York: Walter de Gruyter, 2000), p. 32, points to OT references where the power of God brought corpses back to life. Cf. 1 Kgs 17.17-24; 2 Kgs 4.18-37, 13.21.

Since the previous chapter cites the Sovereign Lord as the speaker to Ezekiel, it would be reasonable that the hearers would conclude that the Sovereign Lord is continuing to speak to the prophet. A distinction is made here, as the story reveals that it is the prophet who will prophesy to the dry bones (v. 4). At the Lord's command, Ezekiel prophesies to the bones to hear the word of the Lord (v. 4). Now, Ezekiel, the prophet, not only sees the word of YHWH and receives the 'word of YHWH', but also is commanded to participate in the vision. Once again, the active participation of Ezekiel is required in the vision narrative not only through physical symbolic acts, but now in prophesying as a symbolic act.

Ezekiel is obedient to the Lord's commands, and with his obedience the Lord responds with a promise that he will cause the רוח ('breath') to enter the bones and cause them to come alive (v. 5).[171] It is not clear if Ezekiel's hearers would discern that the participation with YHWH results in the ensuing promise, yet they would understand that YHWH's covenant required obedience in order to receive blessings and may relate the two concepts here. More importantly, how would the hearers discern the promise of the רוח as giving life to the bones? They would understand that YHWH is the only one to give this life-giving breath, yet it appears that the רוח is the participating force in which the word of YHWH becomes a reality. Here, the hearers may perceive the term רוח as representative of a life-giving breath since it is not clear at this point if the divine רוח is at play.

However, the hearers may recall that twice in Ezekiel's ministry he laid prostrate amidst the presence of the glory of YHWH (1.28; 3.23), and each time the divine Spirit entered him, inspired and empowered him to his feet (2.2; 3.24). In a similar way, Ezekiel's vision of the dead bones depicts the divine Spirit as reforming and infusing the bones with a life-giving רוח. In both of these occurrences, the divine Spirit is infusing a life-giving force that causes the recipient to

---

[171] As previously discussed, the semantic range for the term רוח can extend to 'breath', 'wind', 'spirit', and 'Spirit' to name a few. The term רוח can denote 'breath' in the sense of air in motion. In the context of Ezek. 37.5, it is likely referring to YHWH's breath as in Job 26.13, 'By his רוח ('breath') the skies became fair; his יד ('hand') pierced the gliding serpent'. Contextually, both instances are referring to YHWH. The Job passage parallels YHWH's רוח and the power of YHWH's יד similarly to Ezekiel 37.

become animated. The hearers may also recall an earlier visionary parallel in which the hearers may recall Ezekiel was required to eat the words of YHWH before speaking them. On that occasion, Eze-kiel actively participated in the vision through a symbolic act before the word of YHWH could be spoken to the whole house of Israel (Ezekiel 2-3).

The next commands, the Sovereign Lord says, 'I will make the רוח enter you, and you will come to life. I will attach tendons to you and make flesh come upon you and cover you with skin; I will put my רוח in you, and you will come to life. Then you will know that I am YHWH' (vv. 5-6). YHWH answers his own question as to whether these bones can live (v. 3). The regeneration of these dead bones can only be accomplished by the infusion of the רוח in response to the prophetic word and then, it is by this miracle that they will know the lordship of YHWH. Anticipation mounts with the imagery of the dead bones as Ezekiel's hearers are alerted to the impending activity of YHWH's life-giving activity by the רוח invigorating and bringing the dead bones to life.[172]

While Ezekiel prophesies to the dry bones, he hears a noise, a rat-tling sound, and the bones come together, bone by bone (v. 7). It would not be surprising if the hearers were astonished with Ezekiel's description of the demonstration of the power of the רוח. Next, Ezekiel sees that the tendons and flesh have appeared on the bones, but there is no רוח or life-giving quality in them (v. 8). Would Ezekiel's hearers be dismayed to learn that even though the bones came to-gether with flesh covering their bones, there was still no life found in them? It appears that before they could respond, the Lord immedi-ately commands Ezekiel, 'Prophesy to the רוח, prophesy, Son of man' (37.9).[173] The command is somewhat surprising and ambiguous as

---

[172] Cf. Eccl. 12.7. The text reads that only God can revive dead bones because he is the creator and originator of all life. Additionally, the רוח represents the ani-mating force without which no life is possible (Judg. 15.19). See also, Frederick Tatford, *Dead Bones Live* (Heathfield: Errey's Printers, 1977).

[173] Robert Koch, *Der Geist Gottes im Alten Testament* (Frankfurt am Main: Peter Lang, 1991), p. 24, suggests that the concept of the divine breath of life in human-kind originates in Egyptian myths, while the idea of an extraordinary vital power stems from Babylonian religious beliefs. See Neve, *The Spirit of God in the Old Tes-tament*, p. 12 and Ma, *Until the Spirit Comes*, p. 27, whom both recognize the similar-ities, but rightly point out that there is no concept in ancient Near Eastern litera-ture, which could have served as preparation for the Spirit of God as it is described

Ezekiel was commanded previously to prophesy to the bones, but now, he is commanded to prophesy to the רוח.

The Lord specifically tells Ezekiel what to prophesy, 'Come from the ארבע רוחות ("four winds") and נפח ("breathe") into these slain, that they may live' (v. 9). The emphasis is placed not only upon the רוח, but its movement. Contextually, the hearers would recall that the רוח סערה ('windstorm') in Ezekiel's opening vision was not an actual natural wind, but a wind caused by YHWH. So too, they may perceive the ארבע רוחות ('four winds') are not referring to natural winds, but winds given by YHWH. More specifically, the hearers may discern the ארבע רוחות ('four winds') represent the four corners of the earth. Like Ezekiel's opening vision displaying the glory of YHWH moving sovereignly into enemy territory riding upon his chariot throne with a mission, so too the ארבע רוחות ('four winds') appear to be moving at the bidding of YHWH via Ezekiel's obedience to prophesy with a mission to bring life to death.

Ezekiel remains obedient. He prophesies exactly as the Lord commands and the רוח sweeps into the valley and fills the bodies, which stand up, alive, as 'a vast army' (37.10).[174]

In Ezek. 37.11-14, the Lord interprets this symbolic vision for the prophet: 'Son of man, these bones are the whole house of Israel' (37.11). As discussed previously, the reference to the whole house of Israel would cue Ezekiel's hearers that the Lord was referring to Israel and Judah in exile. Although Ezekiel's fellow exiles say, 'Our bones are dried up, and our hope is lost; we are cut off completely' (37.11), the Lord declares, 'I am going to open your graves, and bring you up from your graves, O my people; and I will bring you back to the land of Israel' (37.12). Now, it would seem virtually impossible for the hearers not to understand that Ezekiel's vision of the dry bones is a metaphor for Israel's exile and restoration. The text reads, 'Our bones are dried up and our hope is gone; we are cut off' (37.11). In light of the devastation to their sacred Jerusalem Temple and subsequent exile to Babylon, the hearers would probably perceive this prophecy by

---

in the vast majority of the Biblical texts. Hildebrandt, *An Old Testament Theology of the Spirit of God*, p. 5, further stresses that there is no evidence that the meaning for 'Sprit' exists outside the Hebrew canon. The OT is, thus, the only ancient literature that develops this term to portray a people's experience with their God.

[174] Cf. The creation account in Genesis 2, which describes the life-giving breath breathed into Adam.

the Spirit to be a vision of hope that YHWH had not forgotten them.[175]

Now, YHWH's promise is certain. He states that he will put רוחי ('my Spirit') in them and will cause them to live (37.14). The power of YHWH appears to work through the Spirit to infuse life into dead bodies, causing them to stand and live (cf. 1.28; 3.23). The concept of the Spirit as a life-giving force may well lead the hearers to recall how the divine Spirit entered the prophet twice and empowered him to stand to his feet when he was prostrated before the majestic appearance of the glory of YHWH (cf. 2.2; 3.24). From this perspective, it is conceivable that the hearers would associate the activity of the Spirit's infusion of life with Spirit empowerment as well.

The Spirit's role is not only underscored by its transporting and leading the prophet in a vision, but also through a promise of life and empowerment from the Sovereign Lord to indwell the whole house of Israel (36.26-27). The indwelling of YHWH's Spirit may also be understood by the hearers as pointing to the promise of the glory of YHWH returning to the temple.[176] Yet, it is not inconceivable that the hearers may also distinguish between the Spirit's activities of 'breathing life' into what is considered dead and 'indwelling' in the context of Ezek. 36.26 because the text speaks of a new heart for God's people (cf. 18.31), and the subsequent verse refers to God's indwelling presence.[177] Although, the hearers maybe forgiven as they may be uncertain at this point, however what is clear, is that the promise of the indwelling life and power of the Spirit is executed

---

[175] For historical and cross-cultural perspectives, see Odell, 'Ezekiel Saw What He Said He Saw: Genres, Forms, and the Vision of Ezekiel 1' in *Changing Face of Form Criticism for the Twenty-First Century* (Grand Rapids: Eerdmans, 2003), pp. 162-76, who presents a thorough analysis of the Assyrian and Babylonian influences upon the writer(s) of the book of Ezekiel. See also Lipschits, *The Fall and Rise of Jerusalem*, pp. 36-133.

[176] Hamilton, *God's Indwelling Presence*, pp. 51-55, argues that Ezek. 36.27 is a promise of God's Spirit to dwell in the restored temple and not in the individual. Essentially, there are two primary opposing views as to the notion of the 'indwelling' of YHWH's Spirit. First, some scholars argue that there is no indication of the Spirit's indwelling a person nor any such idea developed afterward in the OT and propose that an eschatological interpretation of the text is warranted.

[177] Hamilton, *God's Indwelling Presence*, p. 52, posits that while both promises are still in the future, the text supports an argument that the 'believing remnant of Ezekiel's audience had experienced a heart change'. See also, W.C. Kaiser, Jr., 'The Indwelling Presence of the Holy Spirit in the Old Testament', *EQ* 82.4 (2010), pp. 308-15.

through the obedience of Ezekiel 'to prophesy to the [YHWH] breath' and 'to breathe into the slain, that they may live' by the activity of the Spirit (vv. 9-10; cf. 39.29).[178] Ezekiel elucidates for the hearers the importance of obedience to the prophetic word while working in tandem with the Spirit to produce life and restoration.

An interesting development in the story is the recurring theme of the indwelling activity of the Spirit (cf. 36.27). In the present scene, YHWH promises that he will put רוחי ('my Spirit') in them and will cause them to live (37.14).[179] This promise of the indwelling of the divine Spirit is coupled with the promise of life and a return to their land. Previously, the hearers would have recalled how the Spirit came during Ezekiel's call in which he narrated (2.2). After which, YHWH promises to put his Spirit in the whole house of Israel to cause them to become obedient (36.27). Lastly, YHWH's promise of the indwelling divine Spirit was linked with a life-giving force to bring what was dead back to life (37.14).[180]

---

[178] See Tuell, 'True Metaphor Insights into Reading Scripture from the Rabbis', *Theology Today* 67 (2011), pp. 467-75, who discusses rabbinic views of metaphor as a hermeneutical lens. He notes that in the Talmud, most rabbis cited in *b. Sanhedrin* 92b talk as though Ezekiel 37 was describing an actual miraculous resurrection. He further adds that the rabbis debate who was raised (Ephraimites, perhaps), where the resurrection took place (the plain of Dura), and when it occurred (at the same time that Nebuchadnezzar cast Shadrach, Meshach, and Abednego into the furnace; cf. Dan. 3.19-30).

[179] The relationship of the phrase 'I will pour out my Spirit' to YHWH's promise that he will 'give' the divine Spirit 'within them' in 36.27 and 37.14 has been disputed. Generally, the debate usually revolves around the significance of the different verbs and prepositions in the respective passages. For example, see D.I. Block, 'Gog and the pouring out of the Spirit: reflections on Ezekiel 39.21-29', *VT* 37.3 (1987), pp. 257-70, argues for a change of meaning from 36.27 and 37.14 to 39.29, stating that in 39.29 the outpouring of the Spirit serves as a guarantee of the future unbroken fellowship between God and his people. He further comments that the pouring out of God's Spirit upon his people represented an assurance of new life, peace, and prosperity, and also served as the definitive act of claiming ownership of Israel. While this is accurate, it still seems more coherent a shift in essential meaning between the texts, as an analysis of God's 'giving' the Spirit and his 'pouring' it, points to them describing essentially similar actions. Furthermore, on a conceptual basis, it seems that the reason for the bestowing of the Spirit was Israel's disobedience, i.e. in all three texts, God's Spirit will ensure the obedience of the restored people.

[180] Rea, *The Holy Spirit in the Bible*, pp. 101-107, through grammatical, contextual, and theological perspectives identifies two 'renewing functions' for the role of the 'Spirit' in the book of Ezekiel: (1) God's promise of his indwelling Spirit and (2) the outpoured Spirit as covenant sign (Ezek. 39.29).

Summary

The significance of Ezekiel 36–37 is that it envisions the necessary preparations for the return of the glory of YHWH. The content of these chapters makes clear that the people of Israel, who have been characterized many times as a rebellious house, now will be totally renewed. The effect of this total renewal will be that a future turning-away from YHWH will be impossible.

The רוח references in Ezekiel 36 and 37 are rich and meaningful for any theology of the Spirit.[181] While there are only two references to the רוח in ch. 36, there are ten references to the רוח in Ezek. 37.1-14. Nowhere else in the book is there such a high number of literary occurrences found in such a short literary unit. So, in Ezek. 37.1-14, YHWH's Spirit is identified or associated with 'breath' and the four 'winds' in the vision. The vision begins with YHWH's Spirit transporting and leading the prophet through the valley of dry bones and ends with the promise of YHWH's Spirit to revive the house of Israel with the divine Spirit dwelling in them.

Interestingly, the spoken word only becomes effective after the prophet obeys the commands of the Lord to prophesy to the dead bones. Ezekiel's obedience leads the hearers to discern that his willingness to obey YHWH will result in the fulfillment of the promise of the Spirit breathing life into the dead bones, thereby underscoring the need for the Spirit's empowerment of the prophet in preaching. The prophet's obedience to speak exactly the message given to him also results in YHWH's involvement in Israel's heart transplant and the indwelling of the Spirit (37.5, 14; cf. Ezek. 36.26-27).[182] YHWH later discloses that the bones represent the nation of Israel. As such, the metaphor of death represents the Israelites' religious unfaithfulness that pervaded the Jerusalem community prior to the Exile, which greatly escalated after the destruction of Jerusalem (Ezekiel 18).[183] Set against Israel's sin and disobedience with her experience in

---

[181] Schafroth, 'An Exegetical Exploration of 'Spirit' references in Ezekiel 36 and 37', p. 66.

[182] Block, 'The View from the Top: The Holy Spirit in the Prophets', p. 197, asserts that Israelite religion was not just adherence to the Torah, but 'it was from the beginning a heart religion' (cf. Deut. 10.16; 30.6; Jer. 4.4). He uses this premise to emphasize that Ezekiel's anticipation of this internal transformation was formed by these earlier ancient foundations.

[183] Block, *The Book of Ezekiel*, pp. 1-12, argues that although the exiles were allowed to maintain some sense of distinct ethnic and social community (Ezra 2;

the Exile, the רוח in this light is linked to a life-giving force to cause them to become obedient. Hopefully, the promise of a new heart and a new spirit given to them through the power of YHWH will enable the people to walk in YHWH's ways again through their obedience and faithfulness to God's laws.[184]

The promise of the indwelling Spirit in this vision was foundational in: (1) bringing life to the dead (37.1-14), (2) hope to the hopeless (vv. 12-14), (3) restoration of the house of Israel to their land (v. 13), and (4) knowledge that YHWH was faithful to keep his covenant to his people (vv. 9-14).[185] In essence, YHWH will reclaim his people and bring them back to the land of Israel. The promise of the indwelling Spirit also subsumes the ideas that 'by the Spirit' hearts will be renewed through the act of 'indwelling' in the lives of the people. From this perspective, the Spirit is described as external to YHWH, yet summoned by him. Ultimately, this vision portrays a promise that YHWH will bring life out of death; a new spirit in exchange for an old spirit; and hope for the hearts of Israel to receive YHWH's indwelling Spirit as a means of empowering them to become obedient to YHWH as their Lord.

B. YHWH's Promise of Restoration, Cleansing, and Holiness (37.15-39)

The narrative in Ezek. 37.15-39 contains another sign-act and oracle concerning the future restoration of God's people: Israel and Judah. This particular passage acts as the transition between the oracles of hope that begin in chs. 34–37 and the future. The sign-acts involve Ezekiel's description of two sticks, on each of which he is to inscribe a name (37.16). It is likely that the hearers would sense that the symbolism speaks of the anticipated restoration between the northern and southern kingdoms, following which, YHWH would save them

---

Nehemiah 7; Isa. 56.2-4; 58; Ezek. 8.1; 14.1; 20.1; 44 –46), their spiritual condition was gravely altered.

[184] Lipschits, *The Fall and Rise of Jerusalem*, pp. 69-76. Although some scholars argue that the destruction of the temple left the land empty, Lipschits argues with the support of archaeological evidence that the land was not empty. For Lipschits the death of Gedaliah did not cause a decline in the population of Judah. He concludes the area occupied by the Judeans grew smaller but was not vacant.

[185] Block, 'The View from the Top: The Holy Spirit in the Prophets', p. 199, admits that the HB does not use the same language of 'new birth' or speak of the NT 'indwelling of the Spirit', but argues that the ideas did exist in the people's minds and they did experience the reality as described in the biblical texts.

and cleanse them of all their sin and defilement. Ezekiel's description emphasizes that after these signs, God's people will (1) be ruled by one king and shepherd, (2) obey God's laws and decrees, (3) live in the land that was promised, (4) have future generations living in their promised land, (5) establish an everlasting covenant of peace, and (6) establish an everlasting sanctuary to dwell among them (Ezek. 37.24-27). The theme of holiness is once again highlighted as YHWH is described as restoring, saving, cleansing, and now able to dwell among his holy people. The Sovereign Lord is given all the credit as he boasts that all the nations would know that he alone is responsible for making Israel holy again (Ezek. 37.27-28).

C. YHWH's Promise to Defeat Israel's Enemies (38–39)

The oracles in chs. 38–39 are usually structured as a single unit with two narratives that describe the execution of the wrath of the Sovereign Lord against Gog (38.1-23) and the cleansing of the land through the death of Gog (39.1-29).[186] Ezekiel's recurrent use of the literary marker, 'the word of the Lord came to me' cues the hearer that YHWH is about to speak (v. 1). The story commences with a directive to the 'Son of man' [Ezekiel] to set his face against Gog and its allies and to prophesy that the Sovereign Lord is against them (38.2-9).[187] YHWH's passions are underscored again as the text reads, 'This is what will happen in that day: When Gog attacks the land of Israel, my hot anger will be aroused, declares the Sovereign Lord. In my zeal and fiery wrath, I declare that at that time there shall be a great earthquake in the land of Israel' (vv. 18-19).[188]

In ch. 39, the attention is shifted from YHWH's emotions to his actions. Once again, YHWH unleashes his holy wrath upon the offenders who came against his land and profaned his holy name (39.1-7; cf. 36–37). The recurrent themes of burial and death, cleansing

---

[186] Block, 'Gog in Prophetic Tradition: A New Look at Ezekiel 38.17', *VT* 42 (1992), p. 157.

[187] See Duguid, *Ezekiel*, pp. 443-51, who proposes that Gog 'transcends historical categories and takes on mythical proportions'. He suggests that Ezekiel foresees the nations bombarding God's holy people and land in the latter days. He juxtaposes the Ezekiel text with that of Isa. 2.2-4.

[188] Duguid, *Ezekiel*, pp. 456-57, points out that the message of Ezekiel 38–39 is 'not a coded message for those who live in the "last days", who by carefully unlocking its secrets will be able to determine the symbolic identity of the key participants in the final struggle. Rather, it is a word of encouragement to all the saints of all times and places that no matter what the forces of evil may do, God's purposes and victory stands secure.'

and holiness are framed in the story, which highlights YHWH's un-yielding sovereign power. YHWH's power is illustrated by the anthro-pomorphic description of his 'hand' that is unleashed upon Gog when his land and his holy name are defiled (39.8-21). Even though, the house of Israel has been an active participant in these atrocities through their unfaithfulness, YHWH decides that he will show com-passion upon them as he keeps his covenant to defend his land and holy name (39.22-27). YHWH chooses to deliver his people once again from all evil forces coming against them. The impetus de-scribed in these narratives culminates with the declaration: 'Then they will know that I am the Lord their God' and YHWH's recurring promise: I will pour out רוחי on the house of Israel (v. 28).[189]

It is possible that the hearers would draw distinctions between the Spirit in Ezekiel 36–37 as an act for Israel's 'reception of new life' and the Spirit in Ezek. 39.29 as 'an ongoing witness to Israel as well as to the nations that he is their God'.[190] From this perspective, it is possible that they may have connected the 'outpoured Spirit' as some kind of seal of the everlasting covenant of peace (Ezek. 37.26) and is 'a divine mark of ownership' that would ratify the covenant rela-tionship'.[191] Yet, on a broader level the act of pouring out YHWH's Spirit and giving the divine Spirit may have been perceived by the hearers as representing the same functions.[192] It is promising that the work of spiritual renewal in God's people, Israel, had begun with his cleansing process of judgment by the Babylonians in Ezekiel's own day and now was perceived as a future promise from God through an 'outpoured Spirit' (Ezek. 39.29).[193] Preceding Ezekiel's final major

---

[189] Cf. Ezekiel 28.24; 33.29; 34.30; 37.13; 39.29.

[190] Rea, *The Holy Spirit in the Bible*, p. 106.

[191] Rea, *The Holy Spirit in the Bible*, pp. 106-107. See also, Block, 'The View from the Top: The Holy Spirit in the Prophets', pp. 202-203, highlights the liquid idiom 'outpouring of the Spirit' that occurs in six contexts in the Prophets, three times in Isaiah (29.10; 32.15; 44.3), once in Joel (3.1-2), once in Ezekiel (39.29), and once in Zechariah (12.10) as a way in which to distinguish the different functions. He ar-gues that all five use it in a way to denote acts of divine favor, signaling a turn in their divine fortune given by the outpouring of the Spirit.

[192] Robson, *Word and Spirit in Ezekiel*, pp. 252-62, argues that the outpouring of YHWH's Spirit on his people and the giving of YHWH's Spirit within them are essentially synonymous.

[193] Rea, *The Holy Spirit in the Bible*, p. 105, posits that 'although the outpouring of God's Spirit prophesied by Ezekiel did not occur in his time, it was nevertheless a completed action in God's mind'. Neve, *The Spirit of God in the Old Testament*, pp. 116-18. Neve highlights that for the first time in the book of Ezekiel the

vision narrative, Ezekiel 38–39 describes the annihilation of the surrounding hostile peoples who invade the land of Israel.[194]

V. Ezekiel's Vision of the New Temple (Ezekiel 40–48)

Chapters 40–48 record the final vision of the glory of YHWH in the book of Ezekiel. Although, the promise of the new sanctuary was described briefly in Ezek. 37.26-27, now it is given in detail.[195] The story develops in the narratives as they are further divided thematically into five sections: (1) the vision of the new Temple with the glory of YHWH returning (40–43.11), (2) YHWH's new directives for the Temple (43.12–44), (3) the divisions of the land and directives regarding Holy Days and Festivals (45–46), (4) the new Temple with water flowing from the throne (47.1-12), and (5) the allotted distribution of the healed land to the Twelve tribes (47.13–48.1-35).[196]

Ezekiel's final vision paints a picture of YHWH's promise to return to the cleansed Jerusalem Temple, the sacred city with its renewed worship, and the spiritually transformed and revived people; thereby, demonstrating that YHWH is their ultimate king.[197] It is generally accepted that Ezekiel's visionary temple underscores the theme of spatial dimensions because the language of holiness is juxtaposed

---

uncommon reference to the 'spirit' as the presence of YHWH ('fullness of his being') is used (Ezek. 39.29; cf. one other text Ps. 139.7).

[194] See Jacob Milgrom and Daniel Block, *Ezekiel's Hope: A Commentary on Ezekiel 38–48* (Eugene, OR: Cascade Books, 2012), who argue that the structure of Ezekiel 38–39 can be arranged in four literary units: (1) YHWH's program for Gog's attack against Israel in the future (38.2-13), (2) YHWH's anger in view of Gog's advance against Israel (38.14-23), (3) The annihilation of Gog's army and its armaments (39.1-16), and (4) The corpses of Gog's army devoured by birds and beasts (39.17-29).

[195] The tabernacle (Exod. 25.1-9) and Solomon's temple (1 Chron. 29.1-9) are depicted in the form of the Israelites gathering materials. Yet, the vision of the sanctuary in Ezekiel's final vision is solely based upon YHWH's sovereignty.

[196] Greenberg, 'The Design and Themes of Ezekiel's Program of Restoration', *Int* 38 (1948), pp. 189-90, focuses on the law codes as providing the major structure and themes in Ezekiel 40–48. See also, Tuell, *The Law of the Temple in Ezekiel 40–48* (HSM; Atlanta: Scholars Press, 1992), pp 35-49, who provides an arrangement for chs. 40–48 giving special emphasis to the legislation or law code at its center. For a chiastic structure of chs. 34–38, see Renz, *The Rhetorical Function of the Book of Ezekiel*, p. 128. However, this structure is somewhat too organized and not entirely convincing.

[197] Pieter de Vries, 'Ezekiel: Prophet of the Name and glory of YHWH – The Character of his Book and Several of its Main Themes', *JBPR* 4 (2012), p. 105.

between what is deemed holy and what is unholy.[198] The theme of cleansing and holiness is also brought to the fore as the symbol of water is again highlighted in Ezekiel 47, prompting the hearers to remember YHWH's promise of 'cleansing by water' as previously discussed in Ezekiel 36.

Like all four visions in the book, Ezekiel's second vision of the temple begins with Ezekiel's recurrent Hebrew idiom, 'the hand of YHWH was upon me', which serves to introduce and remind the hearers that another vision is about to commence (1.3; 8.1; 37.1). Particularly, chs. 40–48 are linked with chs. 1–3 and 8–11, the other two visions of the glory of YHWH. The story explicitly reiterates that this vision is linked to Ezekiel's opening vision, 'And it was according to the appearance of the vision which I saw, even according to the vision that I saw when I came to destroy the city: and the visions were like the vision that I saw by the river Chebar, and I fell upon my face' (43.3).

Ezekiel's final vision is also linked to the other two visions of the glory of YHWH by its literary structural markers. The specific dating is once again given (cf. 1.1; 8.1; 40.1).[199] The phrase, מראות אלהים ('in visions of God') reminds the hearers that from the outset Ezekiel has received visions of God (cf. 1.1; 8.3; 40.2). The book begins and ends with Ezekiel's symbolic and anthropomorphic descriptions of his visions of God. Although, the text does not specifically mention the Spirit in the introductory scene, the hearers likely would understand that it is the Spirit who is again responsible for transporting the prophet. After all, it is the Spirit who transports Ezekiel in all of the other three major visions. Contextually, it appears that the terms the 'hand' and the 'spirit' are pointing to the leading role of the Spirit

---

[198] Jo Bailey Wells, *God's Holy People: A Theme in Biblical Theology* (JSOTSup 305; Sheffield: Sheffield Academic Press, 2000), p. 165.

[199] Duguid, *Ezekiel*, pp. 470-71, posits that the dating is read literally and states that 'like the opening vision of the heavenly king on his throne had been dated from the exile of the earthly king Jehoiachin, this vision of the heavenly city is dated from the destruction of the earthly city, Jerusalem'. Duguid posits that the repetitive date, the tenth day, is used to point to the Jubilee year (cf. Lev. 25.8-13) and is used to draw correlations between the exiles 'present landlessness, enslaved state and the predicament of many in former times who lived in between Jubilees'. However possible, it is not certain that the hearers would draw these connections. See also, Tuell, *The Law of the Temple*, pp. 35-37, who provides additional details regarding the shared literary markers and the unity of the chs. 40–48.

(40.2-3).[200] Additionally, in Ezekiel's previous visions, it is the Spirit who (1) inspires, transports, and leads the prophet to the glory of YHWH (2.2; 3.12-15; 8.2), (2) the gift of the indwelling Spirit cleanses and prepares for the glory to return (36.25-27), (3) the work of the Spirit who transforms the people of Israel (37.1-14), and (4) the outpouring of the Spirit (39.7). Given that Ezekiel has described the importance of the role and activities of the Spirit throughout his major visions, it is likely the hearers would be prepared for the Spirit to be present in the current vision report.[201]

A. The Vision of the New Temple with the glory of YHWH Returning (40.1–43.11)

This section emphasizes that the new Temple is consecrated in preparation for the return of the glory of YHWH. The scenes can further be structured: (1) the new Temple, its gates, courts, and rooms (40.1–49), (2) outer sanctuary and rooms for the priests (41–42), and (3) the glory returns (43.1-12). The theme of holiness is emphasized as the glory of YHWH enters the new Temple, and the nameless man instructs Ezekiel regarding (1) the altar, (2) the offerings, (3) the sacrifices to be offered by the Levitical priesthood who are the sons of Zadok, and (4) the festivals.

Ezekiel's final vision begins with the hand of YHWH that is upon Ezekiel and the implied reference to the Spirit transporting the prophet to a very high mountain in Israel (40.1-2).[202] The new Temple, which is described as having city-like structures (40.2) thematically echoes Ezekiel's vision of the valley of dry bones. The imagery of death in Ezekiel 37, may remind the hearers that just as the dry bones were brought to life, so also here, the valley has been exalted

---

[200] Rea, *The Holy Spirit in the Bible*, p. 107, emphasizes that water is often used in Scripture to symbolize the Spirit, power, birth and life, and/or a cleansing agent. In Ezek. 47.1-12, Rea connects 'an outpoured Spirit' to the idea of God's Spirit as a 'life-giving river to flow from his sanctuary in Jerusalem and water the Dead Sea valley' (cf. Joel 3.18) to the symbolic idea of 'cleansing, sanctification, renewal, and healing' (2 Chron. 4.2-10; Titus 3.5; Eph. 5.26). He utilizes other Scriptural references to water to emphasize the relationship between God's Spirit and water (Ps. 46.4; Zech. 13.1; 14.8; Jn 7.37; Rev. 22.2).

[201] de Vries, 'The Relationship between the glory of YHWH and the Spirit of YHWH', *OTE* 28.2 (2015), pp. 326-50.

[202] Jon D. Levison, *Theology of the Program of Restoration of Ezekiel 40–48* (HSM 10; Missoula, MT: Scholars, 1976), pp. 7-39, argues that the reference to 'the high mountain' in Ezekiel can only represent Mount Zion. He posits that Ezekiel, like Moses, imparts legislation to the people.

to the land of Israel that 'looked like a city' on a high mountain (40.2; cf. 37). The mysterious bronze figure once again makes his appearance, holding a linen cord and a measuring rod in his hand (v. 3; cf. ch. 8). In the final Temple vision, Ezekiel is shown the mysterious man again as his tour guide; only this time the man has a line of flax and a measuring rod to measure the dimensions of the new Temple, which appears to be built already. Ezekiel is commanded repetitively to see and hear attentively (v. 4). YHWH's repetitive command has a sense of urgency as he reminds Ezekiel to fix his senses on what YHWH is about to show him. YHWH repeatedly emphasizes that failure to see and hear is an act of rebellion and results in death and destruction (cf. 12.2). Ezekiel as YHWH's messenger is required to see YHWH's commands and hear YHWH's words in order to know and understand the ways of YHWH and thus convey clearly to YHWH's people that they should be ashamed of their sin and repent (43.10). Ezekiel as YHWH's chosen messenger is held to a higher standard of obedience, and it appears that his devotion to 'see and hear' is vital to obedience. The hearers are given repetitive warnings of the importance to see and hear the words of YHWH as 'seeing' and 'hearing' is connected to their understanding and knowing the word of YHWH.

Next, as Ezekiel is led by his bronze tour guide through the vision, he sees the mysterious figure taking extensive measurements of (1) the east gate and outer court (40.5-16), (2) the north and south gates (40.17-27), and (3) the gates to the inner court (40.28-37) of the Temple.[203] Ezekiel is shown (1) the rooms for preparing sacrifices (40.38-43), (2) rooms for the priests (40.44-47), and (3) the Temple (40.48-49).[204] The mysterious man continues with his measurements of the outer sanctuary (ch. 41), and the rooms for the priests (ch. 42).[205] At

---

[203] See Kalinda Stephenson, *The Vision of Transformation: The Territorial Rhetoric of Ezekiel 40–48* (SBLDS 154; Atlanta: Scholars, 1996), p. 19, who argues the rhetorical function of delineating the space with the use of walls is to signify the importance of separating what is 'holy' from 'unholy'. Zimmerli, *Ezekiel 2*, pp. 352-57, likens the gates to excavated sites at Hazor, Gezer, and elsewhere.

[204] de Vries, 'Prophet of the Name and glory of YHWH', pp. 101-103. Additionally, in Hebrew the words meaning 'room' and 'doorway' are singular, while the words meaning 'portico' and 'gateway' are plural. It is not clear if Ezekiel is describing one room to one gate or one room to six gates.

[205] The measurements that overshadow chs. 40–42 cause some interpreters to view chs. 40–42 as a blueprint (Cooke, *Ezekiel*, p. 425; Zimmerli, *Ezekiel 2*, p. 412; Allen, *Ezekiel 20–48*, p. 228), argues against this view.

this point, there is little attention given to the outer court and significantly more attention given to the inside of the Temple. The combination of the language used to describe the separation between the spaces and the amount of attention given to this matter may serve to alert the hearers that Ezekiel is attempting to emphasize the areas that are holy from what is considered unholy. Similarly, to the previous visionary reports, the multi-dimensional quality of the narrative is consistent with Ezekiel's portrayals of his visions.[206] Although the dimensions in this vision are provided with measurements of the Temple, it is not clear as to how the hearers would discern the reason for Ezekiel's emphasis upon the meticulous measurements of the Temple. The last time the bronze tour guide led Ezekiel through the Jerusalem Temple in a vision, it was to show him all the abominations occurring inside (ch. 8). The story climaxed in the departure of the glory of YHWH from the temple (cf. 10.18). It is not unreasonable to think that the hearers may be anticipating another major event that could be on the horizon.

Contextually, Ezekiel's hearers would be aware that YHWH's attention to detail is associated to the specific ways in which he desires and commands to be worshipped. This point is conveyed as Ezekiel's bronze tour guide draws attention to the specific duties of the Zadokite priests and the Levite priests, the rooms, and their garments to be worn. Ezekiel sees two rooms for the Zadokite priests, who have responsibility for the temple and altar (40.44-46), and they are 'the only Levites who may draw near to the Lord to minister before him' (40.46).[207] The theme of holiness and separation of what is deemed holy continues to be in sharp contrast to the previous temple vision in chs. 8–11 that emphasized the unholy. In v. 47, the bronze tour guide measures the inner court and then proceeds to the temple

[206] Tuell, 'Ezekiel 40–42 as a Verbal Icon', *The CBQ* 58 (1996), p. 649, discusses the proposals that Ezekiel used a pre-exilic blueprint for the temple complex.

[207] J.Z. Smith, *To Take Place: Toward Theory in Ritual* (Chicago: University of Chicago Press, 1987), pp. 56-58, observes that these passages in Ezekiel referring to the Zadokites represents a 'Zadokite stratum'. For an opposing view, see Duguid, *Ezekiel and the Leaders of Israel*, pp. 87-90. Tuell, *Ezekiel*, p. 288, traces the biblical literature from the Jerusalem shrine by David (2 Sam. 20.25; 1 Chron. 15.11; 18.16; 24.6) to Solomon's temple priests in which Zadok became the sole high priest (1 Kgs 1.7) to argue that Ezekiel was a Zadokite priest in exile.

with pillars on each side of the jambs (40.49).[208] The mysterious tour guide comes to the innermost room of the temple (41.3-4), where he states, 'This is the Most Holy Place' (41.4).[209] In addition, the mention of the engraved cherubim would not go unnoticed as their primary duty was to guard the most holy place (cf. Ezek. 28.14), thus emphasizing the distinctions between the themes of holiness and what is unholy (41.18).[210]

Ezekiel's description concludes with his mysterious tour guide measuring all four רוח ('sides') of the outside gates to the Temple complex (42.15-19). Yet, Ezekiel's reference to the four directions as the ארבע רוחות ('the four winds') is somewhat surprising (v. 20, cf. 37.9).[211] The text reads that all ארבע רוחות ('the four winds') had a wall around it to separate the holy from the common. Furthermore, the singular form of רוח is used 4 times in Ezek. 42.16-19. It is not clear if this particular use of the term רוח would be discerned by the hearers to have some sort of spiritual or theological meaning. Narratively, the hearers were given the purpose of the wall, which likely may have caused them to recall that the רוח סערה ('windstorm') from Ezekiel's description of his opening visionary scene was not a natural רוח ('wind') but a supernatural רוח ('wind') given by YHWH (1.4). Whether they would or would not have drawn any correlations is unclear.

The hearers' growing anticipation surely was heightened with the close of Ezekiel's description of the measurements of the Temple. The hearers were previously led through Ezekiel's excruciating

---

[208] Cf. 1 Kgs 6.3, a description of the dimensions of Solomon's temple that has freestanding bronze pillars, Jachin and Boaz, which flanked the temple entrance (1 Kgs 7.17-22; 2 Chron. 3.15-17).

[209] See Tuell, *Ezekiel*, p. 291, for a discussion on the idea of inner rooms are particularly referred to as the most holy place of the temple complex in the ancient Near East.

[210] Cf. 1 Kgs. 6.23-28, which states that the most holy place in Solomon's temple which had an olive wood throne covered in gold leaf and two cherubim with wings that formed a seat and their outer wings were armrests.

[211] For a discussion of Ezekiel's various uses of the term רוח see Block, 'The use of Ruah in the Book of Ezekiel', p. 33. He attributes the basic meaning of רוח as 'wind' with a bifurcation of the term. For Block, one fork leads to the meaning of 'side' or 'direction', while the other fork develops five subcategories in Ezekiel: (1) as agent of conveyance, (2) agent of animation, (3) agent of prophetic inspiration as 'mind', (4) as the seal of covenant relationship, and (5) sign of divine ownership.

descriptions of all the sin and abominations occurring in the Temple (8–11), which incited YHWH's wrath of death and destruction. Yet, they were given a glimpse of hope through the promises of YHWH's cleansing by water and his giving of a new heart and a new spirit (36.25-26). More astonishing was YHWH's promise of the gift of the indwelling Spirit of YHWH who would empower them and cause them to become obedient to the covenant (36.26-27). Ezekiel's visions culminated in the work of the Spirit who would transform the people of Israel (37.1-14), and then be poured out upon the house of Israel (39.7). The hearers conceivably would recall these predictions as their hearts may have grown with excitement for what came next. The next scene peaks as the preparations for the return of the glory of YHWH now appear to be complete.

The measurements of the outside dimensions of the temple complex concludes the description of the sacred space; however, the story climaxes as Ezekiel announces for the hearers that he saw the glory of the God of Israel coming from the east and heard YHWH's voice as a roar of rushing water (43.2; cf. 1.24).[212] The scene highlights the glory of YHWH entering the new Temple (43.1–5):

> Then he led me to the gate, the gate facing toward the east; and behold, the glory of the God of Israel was coming from the way of the east. And his voice was like the sound of many waters; and the earth shone with his glory. And *it was* like the appearance of the vision, which I saw, like the vision, which I saw when He came to destroy the city. And the visions *were* like the vision, which I saw by the river Chebar; and I fell on my face. And the glory of the Lord came into the house by the way of the gate facing toward the east. And the Spirit lifted me up and brought me into the inner court; and behold, the glory of the Lord filled the house.

Ezekiel confirms for the hearers clearly that this vision of YHWH's glory is like the one he saw and heard at the Kebar River (1.1-28) and the vision of the destruction of the Temple (8.3). Ezekiel's direct language provides the hearers with knowledge that he was seeing YHWH's glory again, only this time the glory was returning to

---

[212] The concept of the glory of YHWH entering his sacred buildings follow a pattern described in the construction of the Tabernacle (Exodus 25–40), and Solomon's temple (1 Kings 6–8).

the Temple (43.3).[213] As Ezekiel describes the sights and sounds of the powerful and majestic glory of YHWH, the only thing he could do was fall prostrate in worship. The affective response to the glory of YHWH also links this vision with the earlier visions. Ezekiel's hearers would likely be amazed that everything Ezekiel has been through has not deadened his senses to the point that he does not respond with awe and amazement at the sight and sound of YHWH.

Ezekiel describes how YHWH's glory caused the land to shine with radiance (43.2). The overpowering nature of the vision of YHWH's glory affected Ezekiel's physical and emotional senses. Ezekiel's eyes saw in color, his ears heard majestic sounds, and his emotions were overwhelmed to the point of falling prostrate before the glory in worship. There is a sense that YHWH's previous commands to Ezekiel to see and hear prepared him to know and understand the awesomeness of what he was now shown. The use of anthropomorphic and anthropopathic terms with the language of analogy assisted and invited the hearers to participate through their imaginations. Ezekiel repeatedly described the glory of YHWH as likened to sights and sounds that his hearers would recognize in their environment. For example, the glory was likened to fire, bright colors of gemstones, and a figure that looked like a human being. He also likened the voice of the Almighty like the sound of rushing waters. It is possible that Ezekiel's description of the glory might have served as an invitation for the hearers to fall prostrate as well.

Despite the fact that he lay prostrate in worship, Ezekiel knows somehow that the glory of YHWH entered the Temple gate facing east (43.4). The hearers most likely would recollect Ezekiel's first temple vision regarding the twenty-five elders who were facing east (cf. 8.16). The description of YHWH's departure was gradual as if to convey a sense of hesitancy (cf. 8–11), but his entrance appeared to be astonishingly swift as if to communicate a desire and eagerness to return (43.5). Similarly to Ezekiel's inaugural vision in 2.2, the Spirit lifts Ezekiel up and then brings him to the inner court where the glory of YHWH fills the temple (43.5). However, the Spirit does not appear to inspire the prophet to hear YHWH at this point, but rather,

---

[213] It is not uncommon for scholars to use cross-cultural comparison studies as a lens to discuss the return of YHWH's glory to the temple. See Block, *Ezekiel 25–48*, pp. 576-77, who describes Esarhaddon's and Ashurbanipal's accounts of the return of deities in temple-building projects.

the Spirit leads Ezekiel to the inner court.[214] It would not go unobserved that once again, it is the Spirit who leads Ezekiel to the glory of YHWH. It is as if the Spirit's role is not only to take Ezekiel to the specific place that he needs to be, but also to reveal to Ezekiel what he needs to see and behold. Only this time, the Spirit takes Ezekiel inside to the inner court to show him that YHWH's glory is filling the Temple with his holiness (v. 5).

Now, Ezekiel describes someone speaking to him while the mysterious tour guide stands beside him (v.6). The voice states, 'Son of man, this is the place of my throne and the place for the soles of my feet. This is where I will live among the Israelites forever. The house of Israel will never again defile my holy name …' (v. 7a; cf. 20.39; 36.20, 23; 39.7).[215] Likely, the hearers discerned YHWH as the one speaking, because he repeatedly spoke to Ezekiel as, 'son of man'. Yet, the speaker uses the messenger formula in vv. 18, 19, and 27, which suggests that the speaker may not be YHWH himself. The association between the Spirit and the glory of YHWH is underscored as they appear to be working in tandem to reveal to Ezekiel YHWH's message through sight and sound. The theme of seeing and hearing once again is emphasized in the context of Ezekiel's visionary descriptions. YHWH shows Ezekiel the new Temple and then speaks to him. Ezekiel is not only commanded to see and hear, but he is commanded to speak to the Israelites what he sees and hears (vv. 10-12). From this perspective, the hearers are able to participate not only through their imagination via Ezekiel's description of what he sees and hears, but also through a command placed upon them to respond to what they hear.

Ezekiel's vision of YHWH's return is likened to his previous visions of the glory of YHWH. However, the words 'throne' and 'cherubim' are used in new ways in ch. 43. The term 'throne' is used in 1.26 and 10.1 for the chariot, and it is now used in 43.7 for the sanctuary. Thus, the literary and theme is preserved, but the rhetorical effect is changed to provide a sense of newness. The rhetorical emphasis may communicate to the hearers that Ezekiel's final vision is not of the glory of YHWH riding on his chariot throne, but a vision of YHWH's heavenly throne. The hearers may be forgiven, if they

---

[214] Block, 'The use of Ruah in the Book of Ezekiel', p. 33, views this function of the רוח as 'agency of conveyance'.

[215] Tuell, *Ezekiel*, p. 295.

are somewhat confused as this distinction is not readily clear. However, the glory of YHWH filling the temple was made clear to the hearers. They likely would feel relieved and elated as their previous feelings of abandonment, death, and destruction (chs. 8–11), were now replaced with YHWH's glory returning and with God's presence now providing a sense of life and restoration.

B. YHWH's New Instructions for the Temple (43.12–44)

The narrative shifts focus as Ezekiel's attention is now drawn to the altar in the inner court and its importance (43.12-27). The previous section describes what Ezekiel sees, hears, and is commanded to speak. Now, the narrative turns to how the hearers were provided with the regulations and ordinances for the newly consecrated Temple.[216] Ezekiel describes how the renewed worship of Israel is to become holy in the sacred holy sanctuary and in the land. The hearers would perceive the importance of these regulations concerning the altar and the sacrifices, since YHWH has returned to dwell among them (43.12-27).[217] The altar is essential for their cultic worship in the temple, and the priests must consecrate themselves in order to offer the appropriate sacrifices to the Lord.[218] Without these consecrated acts of worship, the Lord would not be able to accept the sacrifices as part of their covenantal relationship. Ezekiel continues to provide his hearers with instructions for the eight-day purification process that fits the altar for sacred use (43.19-27). After which, the Zadokite priests (v. 19) will carry out their task of offering burnt offerings and fellowship offerings on the altar.

Ezekiel 44 continues with the themes of (1) YHWH's glory filling the Temple, (2) the priests' roles and responsibilities, and (3) the theme of holiness as stated in terms of what is allowed in the new Temple and what is not allowed. As the tour guide brings Ezekiel to

---

[216] Tuell, *Ezekiel*, pp. 301-303, argues for an internal law code that deals with access to the divine presence by right priesthood and right liturgy.

[217] S.M. Paul, 'Studies in the Book of the Covenant in the Light of Cuneiform and Biblical Law' (VTSup 18; Leiden: Brill, 1970), p. 34, discusses the biblical precedent for presenting laws regarding the altar at the beginning of a law code. The Old Covenant describes in Exod. 20.22–23.33 laws concerning the altar and sacrifices. Leviticus 17–26 describes commandments to perform sacrifices only before the tent of meeting.

[218] J. Gordon McConville, 'Priests and Levites in Ezekiel: A Crux in the Interpretation of Israel's history', *TynBul* 34 (1984), p. 28, compares Ezekiel's participation in the purification process as a priest with that of Moses who instituted the cult on Mount Sinai.

the front of the Temple, Ezekiel states, 'I looked and saw the glory of the Lord filling the temple of the Lord, and I fell facedown' (v. 4). Ezekiel is once again instructed to gaze upon the glory of YHWH as it fills the Temple and then he responds in reverence by prostrating himself before the holiness of God. Now, he is commanded to hear the instructions from YHWH regarding who is allowed access to the new Temple and who is not. YHWH belabors the point, declaring 'the priests, who are the Levites and descendants of Zadok, who faithfully carried out the duties of my sanctuary when the Israelites went astray from me, are to come near to minister before me. They are to stand before me to offer sacrifices of fat and blood, declares the Sovereign Lord' (v. 15). The tone is intensified as the affective language is used to juxtapose the description of the 'rebellious house of Israel' and their 'detestable practices' with that of the priests who are 'faithful' and the 'only ones to come near any of my holy things' (vv. 6-7, 13-15). YHWH reminds the Israelites of their past sins and abominations and states that they 'must bear the shame of their detestable practices' (v.13).

The concern for holiness is at the fore throughout this narrative as YHWH commands that the priests are to follow strict regulations to bear the responsibility of ministering to the Lord in the most holy place. The priests belong to the Lord and they are to have the Lord as their inheritance alone (v. 28). In these ways, the idea of holiness is tied to faithfulness and obedience. The intense language used to describe the instructions appears to evoke affective responses of shame and fear.[219] Ezekiel's hearers were reminded of their sin, which elicits feelings of shame, and the strict instructions that were demanded for entrance to the most holy place produces a sense of fear. If these instructions were not carried out, then once again the Israelites would be subject to death and destruction or, even worse, the abandonment of YHWH's presence in the Temple.

---

[219] Joanna Stiebert, 'Shame and Prophecy: Approaches Past and Present', *Biblical Interpretation* 8.3 (2000), pp. 255-57, defines shame as 'a human emotion or affect. It tends to be classified as a self-conscious emotion, founded in social relationships where people interact and evaluate themselves and each other. Although, the presence of the "other" or audience, real or eidetic, is a frequent catalyst of shame, the judgment constitutive of the emotion is judgment in terms of some ideal that is one's own' (p. 256).

C. Divisions of the Land and the Festivals (45–46)

The story continues with the theme of YHWH's holiness as it pertains to (1) the temple, (2) the covenant with the Israelites, (3) their inheritance, and (4) the land. Ezekiel 44 describes the new regulations for the consecrated Temple. Now, Ezekiel 45 would address the land and the issue of its possession. The primary focus of the division of the land for Ezekiel concerns YHWH's commands (1) to assign a sacred portion of the land (vv. 1-7) and (2) to instruct the princes and the people regarding the prescribed offerings in accordance to the festivals (vv. 8-21). As true landowner of the territory of Israel, YHWH asserts his authority and ownership by invoking all of the administrative tasks associated with owning land. He delegates, assigns, and delineates portions of the land. His regulations regarding the land are focused upon maintaining its sanctity. YHWH alone decides what portions of the land are most holy and who will have access to the land. YHWH also restricts the priests from owning land.

D. The River Flowing from the New Temple (47.1-12)

The third section in Ezekiel's extended temple vision report describes water flowing from the throne to bring life to the land and every living creature (Ezek. 47.1-12).[220] As Ezekiel's tour of the temple is now complete, the following scene focuses the hearers' attention to his description of the new Temple.[221] The heavenly tour guide returns in the narrative to ensure that Ezekiel is guided to the most important elements of the visionary sequence. Ezekiel describes for the hearers that what he sees is, 'water flowing under the threshold of the house toward the east. The water was coming from under the south side of the temple and south of the altar. He then brought me [Ezekiel] through the north gate and led me around the outside to the outer

---

[220] For the water imagery, as life-giving see Gen. 2.10-14. See also, Revelation 22, as it features a river similar to Ezekiel 47, which flows from the throne of God and the Lamb out to nourish the tree of life, whose fruit appears every month and whose leaves are 'for the healing of the nations' (Rev. 22.1-2). For theological reflections, see Block, *The Book of Ezekiel, Chapters 25–48,* pp. 691-702. He proposes that the restoration of the relationship of God's people is the prerequisite of the renewal of the environment. Block uses a symbolic approach to the text here to draw some theological conclusions. For example, he observes the fact that the 'stream flows out over the desert and down to the Arabah to rejuvenate land and sea', before it passes by the altar is a way to perceive 'God's desire to receive sinful humans and his delight in their worship'.

[221] See Tuell, *Law of the Temple,* pp. 69-70, who identified extra biblical analogues to Ezekiel's association of temple and stream.

gate facing east, and the water was flowing from the south side' (47.1-2).[222] The hearers may be forgiven at this point as it is unclear from where the source of the water is coming. It appears to be coming from the temple itself, yet would they question as to whether there was a river under the temple? Earlier, the guide led Ezekiel inward towards greater holiness, now he is led outward, away from the sanctuary complex.

Ezekiel describes the nature of how the water pours out of the house. He states that each time the heavenly tour guide wades downstream with the prophet, pausing every 1,000 cubits to measure the depth. The water increasingly becomes more unstable, powerful, and deeper as it eventually overflows. Ezekiel's description of the increase of the water pouring out is described in quantitative increments. He states that after a thousand cubits, it is ankle-deep (v. 3), after another thousand cubits, it is knee-deep (v. 4), and then waist-deep (v. 4), and finally it so deep that the waters become too deep, preventing anyone from crossing it (v. 5).[223] The tour guide questions Ezekiel, 'Son of man, do you see this?' (v. 6). The question seems rhetorical as Ezekiel is likely gazing at the images in the vision with sheer amazement at what he sees. As previously discussed, the verb ראה possesses a wide range of meanings, 'see', 'observe', 'gaze', 'discover', 'become aware of', 'perceive', 'experience'. Contextually, the meaning suggests that the guide is questioning the prophet's perception or understanding. Since the focus has been upon Ezekiel's measurements, now the guide shifts the prophet's attention to the meaning of what he sees. The powerfulness of the depth of the water is somewhat surprising, yet it also appears to be transformative and life-giving. Ezekiel describes that he sees trees on the banks of both sides of the water (v. 7). The hearers may recall that the water was symbolic of cleansing and related to a life-giving force in Ezekiel 36. Hearts were cleansed by water (cf. Ezekiel 36), and now the abundance of water pouring out of the newly consecrated temple could only mean that YHWH

---

[222] Cf. 1 Kgs 7.23, 39, describes that on the south side of Solomon's temple was a 'sea' or a bronze pool used for cleansing.

[223] Similar to and perhaps influenced by Ezekiel, Joel writes, 'In that day, the mountains will drip with wine, and the hills will flow with milk. All the gullies of Judah will flow with water; a spring will issue from the temple of YHWH, and water the Wadi of the Acacias' (Joel 3.18).

kept his promise to pour out YHWH's Spirit upon the whole house of Israel.

Ezekiel is now told what effects the water will have upon everything it flows upon. The salty water will become fresh and everything in it will live (vv.8- 9). Fruit trees will also grow upon the banks of the river because of the flowing water from the temple (v. 12). The symbolism of the life-giving water likely encouraged the hearers to be hopeful that a new environment would bring them renewal and restoration.[224] The idea of water as a metaphor used in this narrative suggests that the water imagery represents an energizing force that is able to bring life from death. As previously mentioned, the water imagery also cues to the hearers that some kind of cleansing is also ensuing, which now appears to link the themes of cleansing and healing together. Ezekiel's portrayal of the revitalized land comes at the end of the vision narrative. Ezekiel likely led his hearers to discern that the land would only be restored after YHWH had returned to his people, and the Temple restored through proper holy worship. The renewal of the land and its environs also points the hearers to begin to discern that a possible spiritual renewal was on the horizon. YHWH's desire for holiness matched his desire for blessing his people.

E. The Allotted Distribution of the Healed Land to the Twelve Tribes (47.13–48.1-35)

The final section of Ezekiel's book describes the delineation and distribution of the renewed land (Ezek. 47.13–48.1-35).[225] YHWH's covenant with the Israelites has always included promises of land and a holy temple for YHWH's presence to dwell. The fact that Ezekiel 37 explicitly foretells the removal of the traditional animosity between Judah (representing the south) and Ephraim (representing the north), with the result that there will be a single people to whom one king will be given, is an indication that the reference to the number twelve is not without significance. Not only in Ezekiel 37 but also in the final vision, the equality of all the twelve tribes of Israel is

---

[224] The image of YHWH as a source of 'living' waters appears also in Isa. 44.3-4; 55.11.

[225] For a different perspective, see Block, *The Book of Ezekiel, Chapters 25–48*, pp. 703-704, who argues that 'ch. 48 is given priority over 45.1-8, and the basic text of 47.13–48.29 is seen as the product of reflection in the priestly "school" of Ezekiel'.

stressed. This is part of the future restoration affected by the Spirit of YHWH and finally accomplished with the return of the glory of YHWH.

The narrative begins with Ezekiel's description of the boundaries of the new Promised Land (47.13-23).[226] The first two scenes describe the boundary list of the land (vv. 13-20) and the framework (vv. 13-14, 21-23). The narrative emphasizes YHWH's covenantal promise that this land would be their progeny's inheritance and divided among them. The renewed land represents that YHWH's covenant is still in effect. The restored temple with the returning glory of YHWH is in part, how the hearers would likely perceive that they were forgiven. Now, the fulfillment of the covenant promise is upon them. Each of the twelve tribes is assigned an equal portion (47.14), running in a strip from east to west, excepting the tribe of Levi, which is not given any portion.[227]

Chapter 48 provides the hearers with the division or sacred allotment of the land among the twelve tribes.[228] Ezekiel gives special attention as he describes the sacred portion as the spiritual center of the land (48.8-22). In doing so, Ezekiel continues with the theme of holiness as he specifically reports that the Zadokite priests are assigned 'a sacred portion within the sacred portion of the land' (48.10-12). The Levites will receive an area bordering on the territory of the priest, 25,000 cubits long and 10,000 cubits wide. The entire length will be 25,000 cubits and the width 20,000 cubits. None of this land will be sold, neither traded nor transferred, because it is sacred to YHWH. In the midst, is the sanctuary, which the priests surround and protect. The closing scene of the narrative brings the hearers back to a place of contemplation. Ezekiel invites the hearers to meditate on the city and some of the major themes of the vision of chs. 40–48.

---

[226] Cf. The allotted lands given to Moses in Num. 34.1-12 described the land as the inheritance, but the boundaries were not revealed to the ancient Israelites and they do not correspond exactly.

[227] Block, *The Book of Ezekiel, Chapters 25–48*, pp. 741-42. He highlights that Ezekiel's vision of Israel's territorial arrangement offers a theology of land due to the fact that the land belongs to God and this constitutes his residence at the center of gravity.

[228] See Milgrom and Block, *Ezekiel's Hope*, p. 247, who observe that ch. 48 fulfills the expectations of 47.13-14, 21.

Ezekiel recalls that the vision started with the temple and the city (40.2) and now they are where the vision ends. Both are transformed visions of the defiled and destroyed earthly institutions. The earthly place is contaminated by the sins of the people and results in the abandonment of YHWH's glory (chs. 8–11). In the present vision, Ezekiel is shown an undefiled temple, restored and refilled by YHWH's glory (chs. 40–48). In place of the adulterous city, Jerusalem, which was destroyed on account of her sins, Ezekiel was shown a holy city named 'THE LORD IS THERE' (48.35).[229] This renewed land would become the new dwelling place for the renewed people of God and the glory of God. In place of a devastated land, Ezekiel was shown a land that flourished because of the pouring out of the river of life. Ezekiel's final temple vision unfolds from his earlier prophecy: 'I will make a covenant of peace with them. It will be an everlasting covenant. I will establish them and increase their numbers, and I will put my sanctuary among them forever. My dwelling place will be with them. I will be their God and they will be my people' (37.26-27).[230]

Summary

In this final part of the book, we see how the Spirit of YHWH, who transforms and revives Israel, paves the way for the return of the glory of YHWH portrayed in the last vision. In the final vision, we read of a stream of water flowing from the temple. The water imagery is closely related to the Spirit of YHWH. The water starts from the place where the glory of YHWH is present. Since the language harkens back to the introduction of water as a symbol of cleansing associated with a promise of new life (cf. Ezek. 36.25-27), then it is more likely that the hearers would discern that the symbol of water in the present vision also represents cleansing and the giving of life. The previous vision narratives highlight the idolatry and abominations that were occurring in the Temple (1–3; 8–11), now in Ezekiel's

---

[229] Block, *The Book of Ezekiel, Chapters 25–48*, p. 746. He argues that the primary issue in this final vision deals with cultic concerns and not political ones. Thus, the issue is not that of the return of David, but of YHWH's presence.

[230] Block, *The Book of Ezekiel, Chapters 25–48*, p. 745. He emphasizes the theme of divine presence as it is announced in 37.26-27 and describes the spiritual reality in concrete terms, employing the familiar cultural idioms of temple, altar, sacrifices, and land.

final temple vision, not only has YHWH's glory returned, but it is pouring out life-giving, cleansing water.

The people and the land are transformed. The message of transformation of a community by the Spirit of YHWH is followed by the final vision where the glory of YHWH is evidently present in the sanctuary and even the land itself is transformed by the Spirit of YHWH; this is the climax of the message of Ezekiel. The presence of YHWH in the hearts and lives of the people of Israel is closely related to the presence of YHWH in the sanctuary. The book ends on a profound note: 'The name of the city from that time on shall be, The LORD is there!' The affirmation that YHWH's presence is in the city, which was previously described as defiled and unholy and now has been made holy, is the highlight of the story. Throughout the book, Ezekiel emphasizes the location of the holy, but more importantly, it emphasizes the holy God who dwells in the midst of his people. The promise is that the Lord will always be there to keep his covenant with his people.

7

OVERTURES TOWARD A PENTECOSTAL THEOLOGY OF SPIRIT-INSPIRED VISIONS

I. Introduction

The final chapter contributes to the Pentecostal tradition by offering some overtures toward a theology of Spirit-inspired visions in light of the conclusions drawn from this examination of Ezekiel's visions.[1]

Current studies about Spirit-inspired visions are largely descriptive or overshadowed as they are part of a larger examination on Spirit baptism, pneumatology, or eschatology. Thus, a thorough proposal for a theology of Spirit-inspired visions has yet to emerge. The purpose of this study is to contribute to the discussion of Spirit-inspired visions and to inspire Pentecostal and Charismatic communities to read Ezekiel in a fresh new way so as to hear what the Spirit has to say about the diverse ways in which the activities of the Spirit are engaged in Ezekiel's visions. Additionally, it is hoped that the Pentecostal and Charismatic academic communities will further the theological discussions so as to benefit the academy and the church at large.

While the biblical witness is replete with dreams, visions, angelic visitations, and prophecies, the Bible does not convey information about visions in a systematic way. Yet, the mere presence of so many meaningful examples in the canon validates their existence and use

---

[1] As mentioned previously, the distinctions between visions and dreams are not the pursuit of this study. Ezekiel uses terminology that is reflective of 'visions', therefore the theological conclusions will limit its discussion to the topic of visions. Perhaps, in a subsequent research endeavor, dreams will be a natural way forward.

by God as a means of communicating to his people. Visions are one of the central tenets of Pentecostal beliefs, in part, attributed to the outpouring of the Spirit. In Pentecostal spirituality, the mode of visions is one of the ways in which God encounters and speaks to his people because they are perceived as part of the apostolic witness, a result of the outpouring of the Spirit on the day of Pentecost (Acts 2). A theological discussion about visions may be of importance throughout the Christian traditions,[2] however it can be argued that for the Pentecostal tradition(s) the expectation of God to encounter, speak, and baptize his people through the Spirit is of prime importance. The expectation of encounter with the living God through the Spirit and Scripture is not only anticipated, but also fundamental to Pentecostal lives and mission. Thus, Spirit inspired visions as prophetic messages are perceived to encourage them for their mission in the last days as they await the second coming of Christ.

This investigation examined the literary and theological relationships between the recurring activities of the divine רוח ('Spirit'), the יד־יהוה ('hand of YHWH'), and the prominence of affective language showcased in Ezekiel's visions (Ezek. 1–3; 8–11; 37.1-14; 40–43). Though space only allowed for a more in-depth analysis of the four major visions that provide the overall structure of the book, the examination revealed that the Spirit's characteristics and diverse activities played a significant part in Ezekiel. Three of these four visions are underscored by the theme, the כבוד־יהוה ('the glory of YHWH'). As previously discussed in Chapter 2, a Pentecostal reading strategy that is informed and shaped by the Scripture, the Spirit, and the community, was also used as a contextual lens to read Ezekiel's visions. In this view, a Pentecostal approach to reading Scripture is synchronic and theological, allowing for the ethos of the tradition to inform the interpretation theologically. A Pentecostal reading strategy includes a communal participation with the Spirit, which informs a theology of encounter or expectation of the reader to experience while hearing

---

[2] For a literature review of some biblical theologies regarding visions see, Abner Chou, *I Saw the Lord: A Biblical Theology of Vision* (Eugene, OR: Wipf & Stock, 2013), pp. 2-19. Chou utilizes an innertextuality and intertextuality of vision to argue for the unity of Isaiah, Ezekiel, Daniel, Paul, and John's visions. He concludes that all saw and wrote about the same vision from different perspectives: the summing up of all things in Christ.

the text.[3] As such, a theology of encounter intersects with the discussion of the roles of experience and the affections in the task of hermeneutics. Daniel C. Maguire remarks, 'It is not for nothing that the rationalist is upset by the inclusion of affectivity ... Affectivity imports mystery and depth. We can feel more than we can see or say.'[4] For this reason, biblical scholarship has given little attention to the affective dimensions in the biblical texts. The affective language in Ezekiel was not only used to describe the emotive disposition of the main characters, which provides depth and dynamic to the plot in the narratives, but also enhances the meaning for the hearers of the visions. The emotional vocabulary utilized helps articulate the affective impact of Ezekiel not only in the narratives, but also instructs the hearer to experience the text.

This study provides not only a review of contemporary Ezekielian literature, but also examined the early Pentecostal literature as it relates to Ezekiel's visions with hopes to glean insights from their voices and compare to contemporary contributions, which ultimately provides a method owing to a narrative-theological hearing of the text. My method for comparing and contrasting the early Pentecostal literature with the conclusions from the analysis of Ezekiel's visions does not assume a direct relationship between them. Rather, I seek to observe convergence and differentiation in the variety of religious phenomenon between what is described in the Ezekiel texts and in the early Pentecostal periodicals. First, I recognize that the literary features in the early Pentecostal narratives are stories, testimonies, sermons, and teachings, all of which belong to various groups of Pentecostals observed in this study from 1906-1923. Individual testimonies or sermons must be read within their contextual limits, notwithstanding that according to Land, they also represent the theological roots and heart for the early Pentecostal movement. Second, in the task for constructing theological overtures, pertinent questions were considered: (1) how were these biblical symbols in Ezekiel's visions retrieved? and (2) how have they continued to function in Pentecostal spirituality and piety?

Chapter 5 provided an overview of the book and proposed a new structure based upon the identification of the book's genre, central

---

[3] Waddell, *The Spirit of the Book of Revelation*, p. 101.

[4] Daniel C. Maguire, 'Ratio Practica and the Intellectualistic Fallacy', *JRE* 10.1 (1982), pp. 22-39 (23).

themes, and its literary markers. Ezekiel's visions provide support that the four major vision narratives mark the overall literary structure (Ezekiel 1–3; 8–11; 37.1-14; 40–48), and the numerous recurrent themes in these visions support literary and theological connections.

The previous chapter offered a literary theological hearing of these four major vision narratives underscoring their pneumatological emphasis, which identifies the main ways the hearers may have perceived the descriptions of the visions. All four of Ezekiel's significant visions examined, feature language that describes the power and sovereignty of God through the use of the Hebrew idiom, the יהוה־יד, and the diverse activities of the divine Spirit. It is proposed here that the conclusions from this theological hearing of Ezekiel's visions offer the basis to discuss how Ezekiel's visions are grounded pneumatologically, which provides a way forward to explore their theological implications.

In order to contribute to the conversation of Spirit-inspired visions on a broader scale, OT pneumatology, these conclusions will be structured thematically to reflect what Ezekiel contributes to the discussion of visions and how the Spirit's characteristics and activities relate to Ezekiel's visions. These conclusions will also be put into conversation with Pentecostal spirituality (past and present). The overtures will also consider an appreciation for the affective dimensions that are showcased in Ezekiel's visions.

II. What does Ezekiel Reveal about Visions?

A. Ezekiel's Visions are 'Visions of God'

First, this study has demonstrated that Ezekiel is at its heart a narrative about visions. The phrase, מראות אלהים ('visions of God'), reminds the hearers that from the outset Ezekiel has received visions of God (cf. 1.1; 8.3; 40.2) as prophetic events. Although it is not perceived that Ezekiel actually saw God in a literal sense, it is proposed that they were visions of a supernatural reality. This reality includes, but is not limited to, a vision of the majestic glory of God, the throne-room of God, and the living creatures that were later identified as cherubim. The book begins and ends with Ezekiel's use of bizarre symbolic imagery, anthropomorphic and anthropopathic words and phrases, and language of ambiguity to describe the visions of these supernatural realities. The vocabulary of visions is observed in the term ראה ('see, have visions, look at, appear, make oneself visible') and its noun form מראה ('sight, appearance, supernatural vision').[5] The phrase, 'the heavens were opened' seems to lead the hearers to perceive that the prophet saw the heavenly throne-room, where he described intimate encounters with YHWH.

B. Ezekiel's Visions, the Hand of YHWH, and Worship are Connected

Second, all four major visions reveal that YHWH's hand, as a metaphor for the power of God, is used to *introduce* the vision narratives (1.3; 8.3; 37.1; 40.1) and is described as also *upon* the prophet during his visions. For example, the beginning of the book reports that the word of YHWH will come to Ezekiel and he will see visions of God while the hand of YHWH is upon him (1.1-3). Additionally, at the end of Ezekiel's inaugural vision and call narrative, the hand of YHWH is observed again to emphasize YHWH's power upon the prophet during the vision (3.12-15). Ezekiel describes that he lay prostrate in awe before the glory of YHWH (1.28), while the hand of YHWH was upon him. In other words, the power of YHWH comes upon the prophet and does not leave him for the duration of the visions. The Hebrew idiom, the יד־יהוה, is more than a structural marker. It is an insightful theological statement about the role of the power of God and visions that are inspired through the hand of YHWH. Ezekiel's visions are a sovereign gift given and dependent upon the power of God. The term gift is used to describe visions of God's glory as the revelation of God and the word of YHWH that is communicated in symbolic form through the medium of visions.

As the prophet saw the heavenlies by the power of God, he was deeply affected as demonstrated by his humble act of worship (1.1-28). Worship was evident by the prophet's bodily prostration as he beheld and perceived the glory of YHWH. The encounter with the power of God and the revelation of his glory caused the prophet to submit in humility, which is a form of worship. Subsequently, the prophet hears the voice of YHWH and receives his prophetic call to the rebellious house of Israel (2.1-7; 3.4-11). Interestingly, the encounter with YHWH in the form of a vision affected the prophet

---

[5] Naude, ראה ('see, have visions') in *NIDOTTE*, III, pp. 1007-15. The term ראה occurs approximately 73 times in the book, see Even-Shoshan, *A New Concordance of the Old Testament*, pp. 1041-45.

prior to his commission to prophetic service. Part of his commissioning includes a warning not to be rebellious like his compatriots. The theological significance is profound as Ezekiel's first major vision not only proclaims the transcendence and holiness of the glory of God, but also engages and calls the prophet to his prophetic ministry.

The affective dimensions of the narrative are undeniable and also provide theological implications about the connections between visions, the power of God, and worship. Worship is an affective response to a revelatory encounter with the power of God. Worship creates the context in which the voice of God is heard. Worship precedes the commissioning of the prophet. Worship fostered intimacy with God, which ultimately led the prophet to perceive and discern God's heart (motives, will, affections) about his people. Heschel's innovative idea of, 'divine pathos', asserts that God's heart is joined to the prophet's heart through 'sympathy' or the affections and enables the prophet to speak for God to humanity.[6] He states that

> the analysis of prophetic utterance shows that the fundamental experience of the Hebrew prophet is a fellowship with the feelings of God, sympathy with the divine pathos, a communion with the divine consciousness, which comes about through the prophet's reflection of, or participation in, the divine pathos.[7]

Following Heschel, the revelation of God's will through divine pathos leads the prophet to discern God's will, inspires worship, and ultimately obedience. The intimate visual encounter with YHWH precedes the commands from YHWH. Therefore, it can be concluded that the visual nature of prophetic activity in Ezekiel is a conduit for God's pathos to affect the prophet in such ways as to prepare him to speak on behalf of YHWH and obey his commands. The story of Ezekiel's call and commissioning is a testimony to the ways in which God was perceived to reveal himself and his supernatural world, encountered the prophet intimately, and transformed the prophet's heart (motives, will, and affections) for the purpose of God's mission.

This initial observation that Ezekiel is first and foremost about visions of God's supernatural realities are instructive for Pentecostals

---

[6] Heschel, *The Prophets*, II, pp. 99-103.
[7] Heschel, *The Prophets*, II, p. 263.

who have often read Ezekiel through a NT lens or eschatology without mention of the impact of the affective language. This type of reading ignores the affective dimensions in the text. Yet, some early Pentecostals, as discussed in Chapter 4, were deeply affected by reading Ezekiel's inaugural vision. Martha Lewis specifically cites Ezekiel 1 as a way to describe her own experience of seeing Jesus upon a throne and concludes that this visionary encounter caused her to confess her sin. She states, her 'stubborn will was broken', which 'prepared her to become a witness'.[8] Her response to the experience was not unlike Ezekiel. However, Miss Lewis also thought of her visionary encounter as part of her Spirit baptism.[9] It was not uncommon for early Pentecostals to perceive that their visionary encounters of God were given as part of their Spirit baptism for the sake of purpose and mission based on the prophetic fulfillment of the outpouring of the Spirit (Joel 2.28-32).[10]

In addition, a testimony from Mattie Ledbetter recounts her visions of Jesus on a throne of glory,

> I had visions of Jesus on a throne of glory, and the Holy Ghost used all my powers to praise and adore Him for some time. I did not talk very much in tongues, but on Thursday the Holy Spirit manifested Himself in a much more wonderful way. I had two visions of Jesus, and I was filled with rapturous love and it seemed that if God did not stay His hand, I would die of pure love and joy, and desire to praise and adore Him, as it was revealed to me that He deserved I beheld Him on the throne of His glory.[11]

First, Ledbetter describes that the throne-room vision took place while the powerful hand of God was upon her. In fact, she states that God's power might cause her to die of pure love and joy if he did

---

[8] *TP* 1.3 (November, 1908), p. 7.

[9] *TP* 1.3 (November, 1908), p. 7.

[10] *TBM* 1.18 (July, 1908), p. 5. Susan A. Duncan's testimony relates Spirit baptism to God's hand,

> While a meeting was going on in the church, a few had gathered in Elim's home for further waiting, and it was there the power fell. During the day about seven were prostrated under the hand of God, speaking in tongues, singing, and prophesying. Truly the 'Latter Rain' had come, and God was doing a new thing in the earth. Later, many others were baptized in the Spirit and prostrated under the power of God.

[11] *TBM* 1.18 (July, 1908), p. 3.

not remove it. Second, Ledbetter's visions of God were so over-whelming that it caused her heart to be filled with 'rapturous love'. Third, as her heart was deeply affected by this revelatory vision of God, it led her to respond with worship. She was completely over-whelmed with awe and wonder of seeing Jesus upon his throne of glory, not unlike Ezekiel. These testimonies bear witness to the importance of Ezekiel's visions of God's supernatural realities.

To hear Ezekiel in this light might cause contemporary Pentecostals to rediscover how prophetic visions inspired by the power of God not only inform, but transform the hearer through affective responses. Worship in this context is perceived as an affective response in Ezekiel and in the early Pentecostal testimonies. In Ezekiel, the prophet's act of worship as he lay prostrate at the sight and revelation of the glory of YHWH preceded his call. The Spirit and the hand of YHWH prepared the prophet's heart to receive his call for ministry. In some of the early Pentecostal testimonies, the visions of God filled their hearts with love, adoration, and worship, which also prepared their lives for ministry. As discussed in Chapter 3, most Pentecostals desire to encounter God through the Spirit, Scripture, and the community. Most Pentecostals would consider that worship is the part of the liturgy where the Spirit speaks through the gift of prophecy. However, visions in contemporary Pentecostal churches are usually regarded with suspicion and devalued as a legitimate sign of an encounter with the Spirit. Perhaps contemporary Pentecostals should reflect on the nature of prophetic visions that produce a heart to worship God in light of the close connections between visions and worship in Ezekiel, as well as observed in the early Pentecostal literature. Perhaps a fresh perspective of Ezekiel's visions could provide a deeper understanding of how God's communication by the Spirit through visions in the context of worship can produce a greater impact for mission.

C. Ezekiel's Visions are Considered 'the Word of YHWH'

Third, this study reveals that Ezekiel's visions are 'the word of YHWH' given through the medium of visions.[12] Ezekiel is a

---

[12] Ezekiel's superscription reveals that the visions in v. 1 is 'the word of YHWH' that comes to Ezekiel in v. 3.

prophetic book given to Ezekiel, a prophetic figure.[13] The primary genre of the book that is revealed in the first few verses of the text: השמים ואראה מראות אלהים נפתחו ('the heavens were opened and I saw visions of God') alerts the hearers that they are invited to hear Ezekiel's visions through words used to describe them. The fact that the primary genre of this prophetic book is vision, also provides the hearers with the expectation that visions are, in part, a mode of communication between God and the prophet. Notwithstanding, direct speech from YHWH is observed in the midst of the vision narratives, which provides the story with a full range of audio-visual effects. The revelation that comes to the prophet in the form of both verbal or visual experiences produce what Brueggemann calls, 'an alternative consciousness'.[14] In other words, the impact of such encounters with God not only provide revelatory information to the prophet, but also transforms how the prophet interprets his reality.

However, the focus of this study is upon 'the word of YHWH' as observed through the medium of visions. Ezekiel's visions as 'the word of YHWH' categorize the four major vision narratives as prophetic visions. According to Burke Long, a prophetic vision, as a mode of revelation, arises by means of a visible or visualized experience, which often is received in the form of symbolic images.[15] Contextually, Ezekiel's prophetic visions are: (1) highly symbolic, (2) provides revelation given by the יד־יהוה, (3) initiates an encounter with the divine Spirit, (4) is considered 'the word of God', and (5) results in a participation with God.

Theologically, the use of ראה in Ezekiel's visions indicates not only 'seeing', but also 'to discern', 'to discover', 'to encounter', 'to know', 'to perceive', and 'to understand',[16] which adds to the

---

[13] See Moore, *The Spirit of the Old Testament*, pp. 58-59, who discusses how the prophetic literature can be presented as something that is seen, as well as heard or spoken.

[14] Brueggemann, *The Prophetic Imagination* (Philadelphia, PA: Fortress Press, 2nd edn, 2001), p. 13. He defines the terms to include that this type of 'alternate consciousness' changes or transforms the prophet and the prophet's perception of reality.

[15] Burke Long, 'Reports of Visions Among the Prophets', *JBL* 95 (1976), pp. 353-65. Long provides various definitions for visions in the prophetic literature.

[16] See Brown, *et al.*, *The New Brown, Driver, Briggs, Gesenius Hebrew and English Lexicon*, p. 919; Koehler & Baumgartner, *The Hebrew and Aramaic Lexicon of the Old Testament*, II, pp. 1156-61.

discussion of epistemology.[17] The prophet was inspired to see and discern the glory of YHWH in the form of visions through highly symbolic imagery, which informed his understanding of the supernatural realities of God.[18] However, the message is often times obscured by the symbolism. As the visionary sees, hears, and experiences the supernatural realities, he/she not only receives God's word, but is also required to discern and discover God's will communicated through the imagery. The act of discovery and discerning is central to understanding the messages imbedded in the visions. Since the imagery used to convey the message is primarily symbolic, it is also in need of interpretation.

It is observed here, through the use of imagination, the hearers are able to participate in the visionary world that Ezekiel describes using metaphors, anthropomorphisms, and anthropopathic language. This act of imagination assists the hearers to 'see' and 'perceive' the images as information, thus the images provide understanding of the prophetic message given by the power of God. The hearers (past and present) are challenged through the use of imagination to perceive and understand the supernatural realities. The revelation of the word of YHWH through visions as a direct encounter with God and the Spirit creates a place for human-divine partnership in the act of interpretation.

Ezekiel's prophetic visions as the 'word of YHWH' are compatible with Pentecostal beliefs and practices because, generally, Pentecostals believe that God can speak to the community through a variety of means. However, contemporary Pentecostals primarily focus

---

[17] Naude, ראה ('see, have visions') in *NIDOTTE* III, pp. 1007-15. The terms used to designate visions in both Testaments include verbs of 'seeing' and 'perceiving'.

[18] There are many debates surrounding prophetic inspiration by YHWH's Spirit in the exilic period. Many scholars observe that the book of Ezekiel recovers the role of inspiration by the Spirit in Ezekiel's ministry after this apparent paucity is observed among the classical prophets. Robson, *Word and Spirit in Ezekiel*, pp. 99-126; 146-70, provides an outline of the concept of רוח inspiration depicted in the classical prophets and a discussion of the רוח as an agent of inspiration in Ezekiel directly related to the word of YHWH. He observes that in the pre-exilic classical prophets there was a decline in the use of רוח related to prophetic inspiration. See also, Ma, *Until the Spirit Comes*, pp. 11-13. Ma and Robson have provided significant contributions to the discussions of prophetic inspiration by the Spirit in the HB. Both scholars observe that after the relative lack of the reference 'the spirit of God or the spirit of YHWH' in relation to prophetic inspiration in the pre-exilic classical prophets, the idea receives a revived emphasis during the Exile as seen in Ezekiel.

upon the prophetic word spoken through preaching, tongues and interpretation, prophetic words, and testimonies. In many contemporary Pentecostal churches, there is seldom, if any space given for the interpretation of prophetic visions. Albeit, the gift of prophecy generates numerous debates, past and present, which typically revolve around how to distinguish between genuine and false prophecy. Pentecostals might look to Ezekiel for evaluating prophetic visions as the text associates the sin of rebellion with false visions.[19] From this perspective, it is not the vision itself, which is judged, but the character of the one claiming to receive a vision from God. Ezekiel, called as a watchman, warned that people who give false prophecies would be held accountable (Ezek. 3.16-21). Ezekiel not only legitimizes prophetic visions and highlights the importance of distinguishing true prophetic visions from false visions, but also instructs on how to discern the two. Pentecostals could benefit from the instructive nature of prophetic visions found in Ezekiel.

The trepidation for false prophecies is voiced in *The Bridegroom's Messenger* as they were concerned with deception occurring in the 'last days'.[20] The editor writes, 'False prophets will continue to prophesy lies, and many will be deceived'.[21] Yet, the evidence of numerous vision reports also suggests that they revered prophetic visions as revelatory encounters with God. Agreeing with Hocken, that visions and dreams were considered part of the experiential aspect of early Pentecostal worship, and despite their concern for false prophecy, visions and dreams were still an expectation for their communities to encounter.[22] Perhaps a fresh interest in reading Ezekiel's visions as a

---

[19] As such with the nature of prophecy, Ezekiel contrasts between true and false prophets. Ezekiel 12.21–14.11 contains five prophecies reflecting the prophet's disdain for false prophets. A unifying thread throughout these prophecies is provided by the root חזה ('vision') which appears five times in 12.21-28 and once in ch. 13. The term חזה is juxtaposed with the terms 'flattering divination' as a means to emphasize that false prophets are a part of the rebellious house and will be held accountable for prophesying from their own inspiration (chs. 13–14.1-11). It is likely the hearers would know that these counterfeits are ones who claim to see visions inspired by YHWH, yet they see and hear nothing from YHWH, and speak from their own spirits.

[20] *TBM*, 1.18 (July, 1908), p. 3.

[21] *TBM*, 1.18 (July, 1908), p. 3.

[22] Hocken, *The Challenges of the Pentecostal, Charismatic, and Messianic Jewish Movements: The Tensions of the Spirit*, p. 9.

means for understanding visions may lead Pentecostal communities to a renewed interest in this spirituality.

D. Ezekiel's Visions include Prophetic Speeches filled with Affective Language

Fourth, Ezekiel's prophetic visions function as audiovisual modes of communications, and at times, include prophetic speeches from YHWH that are embedded in the vision narratives. Narratively, the communication between the main characters provides meaning and understanding to the plot of the vision reports. Similar to a film, the visual effects are enhanced with audio effects.

The dialogue is primarily observed between God and the prophet. Odell suggests that Ezekiel's visions are like a 'prophetic diary', which she states are like 'private conversations with God'.[23] Ezekiel's visions communicate part of God's message to the prophet, but YHWH often engages in dialogue with the prophet as he reveals the vision, talking and asking questions as part of the process. Often times, the vision is being used by God, in part, to provoke a response or question. Ezekiel's visions as God's word, which include speeches, are not merely monological; but they are also dialogical, interrogative, and interactive. God speaks, questions, listens, responds, and engages in dialogue.

For example, after Ezekiel's inaugural vision (Ezek. 2.28), as part of the prophet's commissioning, a series of commands from YHWH begins (Ezek. 3.27). In Ezekiel's first temple vision, YHWH asks rhetorical questions (Ezek. 8.6, 12, 14, 17). The speeches accentuate the affective dimensions in the text as YHWH's language is filled with anger because of his priests performing acts of rebellion and wickedness in his most holy place. In ch. 10, YHWH's speeches are primarily in the form of revelation to the prophet and the hearers. For example, the living creatures that are visualized in the inaugural vision are now identified as cherubim. In ch. 11, the prophet, for the first time, cries out to YHWH in anguish as he feels and discerns the wrath of YHWH. The prophet feebly attempts to plead with YHWH as he asks if the Sovereign Lord will completely destroy the remnant of Israel (Ezek. 11.13). The passionate tone of the text serves to provide a fuller meaning to the story. First, YHWH as a holy God is angry at the unholy acts occurring in his most sacred space in the

---

[23] Odell, *Ezekiel*, p. 28.

earthly realm. Second, the prophet called to speak on behalf of YHWH's anger is feeling the depth of YHWH's impending consequences for the sin of his people.

While Ezekiel's third major vision does not witness to the recurring theme of the glory of YHWH, it does not go unnoticed that the power of God represented by the hand of YHWH and the Spirit are present to introduce the vision. The text records, 'The hand of YHWH is upon me, and carried me out in the Spirit of YHWH, and set me down in the midst of the valley which was full of bones' (Ezek. 37.1). The beginning of prophetic speech is rhetorical as YHWH asks, 'Can these bones live?' (v. 3). Noticeably, YHWH does not prophesy or command the bones to live but commands the prophet to prophesy to them. It is completely within YHWH's power to command the dead bones to live, yet he does not. Instead, YHWH chooses to use the prophet's voice to prophesy. This vision provides another example of the prophet's participation with YHWH in the midst of the vision.

It is also helpful to understand how Grey examines the words of the prophet and the acts of the רוח in Ezekiel 37.[24] She applies speech-act theory to the narrative of Ezek. 37.1-14 and builds upon the work of John Austin who argues that speech-act theory contributes to biblical studies in that words or speech are more than referential or informative, but are also performative and indicative of a reality.[25] Grey's examination of discourse is not concerned with authorial intent, but rather with the meaning of the discourse itself and what the speaker did during the discourse.[26] A relevant conclusion drawn, 'in this vision, the words of the prophet create a new reality'.[27] Matthias Wenk adds to the conversation, as he asserts, 'prophetic

---

[24] Grey, 'Acts of the Spirit: Ezekiel 37 in the Light of Contemporary Speech-Act Theory', pp. 69-81.

[25] John L. Austin, *How to Do Things with Words* (Cambridge, MA: Harvard University Press, 1962). Walter Houston, 'What did the Prophets think they were doing? Speech acts and prophetic discourse in the Old Testament', *BibInt* 1.2 (1993), pp. 167-88. Matthias Wenk, 'The Creative Power of the Prophetic Dialogue', *Pneuma* 26.1 (2004), pp. 118-29.

[26] Grey incorporates the contributions of Nicholas Wolterstorff, Craig G. Bartholomew, Colin J.D. Greene, and Karl Moller (eds.), 'The Promise of Speech-act Theory for Biblical Interpretation', *After Pentecost: Language and Biblical Interpretation* (Grand Rapids: Zondervan, 2001), pp. 73-90.

[27] Grey, 'Acts of the Spirit', p. 69.

speech is intended to transform, rather than simply inform'.[28] The affective language adds to the speeches as it is used to influence the hearer and add depth to the message. Grey's contribution also supports the legitimate authoritative role of the words of the prophet with the speech acts of YHWH that through proclamation change is affected. Regarding the role of the רוח, Grey concludes that Ezekiel's רוח as ('breath') 'produces the reality, which is actuated by the רוח (Spirit) and inhabits the breath of the prophet's declaration, which works to achieve and fulfill the declaration'.[29] Perhaps contemporary Pentecostals should reflect on the role of prophetic speech in their churches in light of the close connection between the role of the Spirit and prophecy as evidenced in Ezekiel. For example, it is possible that Ezekiel could shed light on how prophetic speech not only informs, but also transforms the hearer.

III. What do Ezekiel's Visons Reveal about the Spirit?

Ezekiel's visions, like the biblical witness, does not present a systematized outline of the work of the Spirit. Ezekiel's visions provide examples of the spiritualities of the Spirit described through symbolic imagery and stories. However, the nature of the Spirit of God is in part, a mystery and the descriptions albeit creative, are ambiguous at times.[30] The mystery is compounded through the use of anthropomorphisms, metaphors, and poetic language. Identifying the activity of the Spirit in Ezekiel can also be elusive because the Hebrew term רוח can be even more ambiguous, at times, because of its wide range of semantic domains, some of which are: ('air in motion', 'breath', 'wind, a blowing breeze', 'vain things', 'spirit', or 'mind'). Somewhat distinctly, Heschel expounds on the idea of the 'mind' to argue that the רוח can also reflect the 'pathos', 'passion', or 'emotion as a state of the soul'.[31] The next sections will categorize and discuss the conclusions drawn from this study as it connects the diverse roles of the Spirit with Ezekiel's visions.

---

[28] Wenk, 'The Creative Power of the Prophetic Dialogue', pp. 118-29.
[29] Grey, 'Acts of the Spirit', p. 79.
[30] The difficulty of producing an OT pneumatology has led to a number of approaches to the task, each one categorizing the biblical material in different ways. See Chapter 2 of this study for a literature review of OT pneumatology.
[31] Heschel, *The Prophets*, II, pp. 2-3; 95-97.

A. The Hand of YHWH is closely Connected to the Spirit

First, as previously discussed, the hand of YHWH is an anthropo-morphic phrase used to describe the power of God. In this study, it is also observed that the hand of YHWH is closely connected to the activity of the divine Spirit. From the beginning, Ezekiel's visions direct the attention of the readers to the correlation between the יהוה־יד and the רוח observed in the vision narratives. Structurally, the hand of YHWH and the Spirit are interwoven into the very fabric of the narrative through the diverse ways in which the term רוח and variations of the phrase, the יד־יהוה are positioned and thematically intertwined in Ezekiel's visions (Ezek. 3.12-14, 22-24; 8.1-3; 37.1; 40.1-3).

As the hand of YHWH functions to introduce Ezekiel's inaugural vision narrative, it also serves to introduce the preliminary variable uses of the term רוח (wind, Spirit, spirit, 1.4; 12, 14, 20-21). The term רוח is first used to introduce Ezekiel's inaugural vision as a theophanic windstorm which begins the chariot-throne vision of the glory of YHWH (1.4). In the midst of the bizarre images of the four living creatures, the Spirit is introduced as leading or guiding the living creatures because they possess a spirit (1.12, 14, 20-21; cf. 10.17). The Spirit also inspires the prophet to hear YHWH's voice (2.1), indwells the prophet and (2.2), transports the prophet (3.12, 14; cf. 8.3; 40.1), all the while YHWH's hand is upon him (1.3; 3.14; 8.3; 40.1). The variable meanings for the term רוח and the יד־יהוה contribute to the themes of mobility, power, leadership, guidance, and are closely connected to the prophet as he sees, hears, and experiences the vision.

Theologically, the connections between YHWH's hand and the divine רוח result in underscoring the leitmotifs of (1) inspiration, in the sense that the Spirit inspires the prophet to hear and perceive, (2) empowerment, in the sense that the Spirit enables the prophet to stand in the presence of YHWH; endowment of power for the prophetic ministry to the rebellious Israelites that lay ahead of the prophet, and (3) mobility, in the sense that the Spirit and the hand of YHWH transports the prophet from place to place in the vision. These numerous examples convey to the hearer the significance of the close connections between the power of God and the Spirit.

Early Pentecostals, as documented in Chapter 4 of this study, also describe the hand of God as a power that falls upon them. One example, Susan A. Duncan testifies to the connections between the manifestations of the Spirit by the power of God's hand as it came upon Pentecostal believers. She writes,

> While a meeting was going on in the church, a few had gathered in Elim's home for further waiting, and it was there the power fell. During the day about seven were prostrated under the hand of God, speaking in tongues, singing, and prophesying. Truly the 'Latter Rain' had come, and God was doing a new thing in the earth. Later, many others were baptized in the Spirit and prostrated under the power of God.[32]

B. Ezekiel's Visions are Prophetic Encounters that are Inspired by the Spirit

Second, the biblical witness affirms that the HB prophets or seers were inspired by God and called to be recipients of divine revelation through visionary encounters. In the context of Ezekiel's visions, the theological theme of inspiration points to the ideas that seeing and hearing the words of YHWH as prophecy, is given through the medium of visions and inspired by the Spirit. Contextually, both the יד־יהוה and the רוח represent an empowerment that not only has profound effects upon the prophet, but also precedes the initiation of his visions. The hearers would likely understand that the anthropomorphic phrase, the יד־יהוה, describes YHWH's power as a means to inspire the visions (Ezek. 3.12-14, 22-24; 8.1-3; 37.1; 40.1-3). It is the יד־יהוה that is upon the prophet (1.4) and 'falls' upon Ezekiel in 8.3 prior to seeing, and functions in the same manner as the רוח that 'falls' upon Ezekiel in 11.5 prior to the prophet hearing. From this perspective, the narrative theological hearing further supports that the יד־יהוה and the רוח both function in the act of inspiration. As the יד־יהוה 'falls' upon the prophet before seeing the vision of the fiery 'figure like that of a man' so also the רוח 'lifts' the prophet before seeing a vision of the כבוד־יהוה.

The רוח as an agent of divine inspiration is a recurring theme in Ezekiel that is especially prominent when linked with the verbal utterances of YHWH. Ezekiel reports that the prophet was commanded to stand up on his feet and instructed that YHWH will speak to him (2.1-2). This is the first mention of the Spirit in relation to the prophet and it is closely associated with Ezekiel's hearing YHWH's commissioning speech (2.1-10), which adds to the significance to the role of one of the main characters, the Spirit. Although the Spirit is not mentioned in conjunction with the prophet until after the inaugural vision, the act of inspiration does not go unnoticed as it is pivotal to the plot of the story. Ezekiel is inspired to see and hear the words of YHWH prior to his empowerment for his prophetic ministry. Hildebrandt argues that the רוח in Ezekiel is: (1) 'the motivational guiding force behind the creatures' (Ezek. 1.12, 21, 20-21; 10.17), and (2) transports and raises Ezekiel, which is associated to 'the phenomenon related to inspiration of the prophet' (Ezek. 2.2; 3.12, 14, 24; 8.3; 11.1, 5, 24; 43.5).[33] He also draws connections between the יד־יהוה and the term רוח as an indication of prophetic empowerment, and concludes that the term רוח is related to 'prophetic inspiration, whether visionary or auditory, and is a result of the divine רוח'.[34] Hildebrandt's contribution goes so far to identify the function and identity of the Spirit, however he does not reflect on these theological implications.

This study in Ezekiel's visions has sought to engage in dialogue with Pentecostal scholars regarding Spirit-inspired visions as a way to offer theological overtures. However, the paucity of works relating to the discussion of Spirit-inspired visions spurred an interest to examine Augustine's theological constructions of interpreting prophetic visions. This is not to suggest that there are no other scholars outside the Pentecostal traditions that write about this subject, but Augustine, in particular, offers a way to move the discussion forward that does not betray a Pentecostal ethos.

Borrowing from Augustine's theory of interpreting prophetic visions, it is observed that Augustine contributes to the theological conversation regarding Spirit-inspired visions.[35] He describes various

---

[33] Hildebrandt, *An Old Testament Theology of the Spirit of God*, pp. 26-27.

[34] Hildebrandt, *An Old Testament Theology of the Spirit of God*, pp. 27; 189-90.

[35] Augustine, *On Christian Doctrine* (trans. D.W. Robertson; New York: Macmillan, 2nd edn, 1987), 1.36, p. 41. He asserts that the poetic and symbolic language used in the biblical text was a means to describe prophetic vision reports. In *On Christian Doctrine* 2 and 3, Augustine articulates a way to interpret the meaning of obscure passages of Scripture based on his theory of signs. From this perspective, symbolism is used as a stylistic device to point towards something beyond itself. Augustine incorporates principles of signs and analogy in his writings to explain how the visionary interprets symbolic images. In the end, he views symbolic images as signs to be interpreted metaphorically to express what may be considered as indescribable ideas, emotions or states of mind.

ways in which the Spirit of prophecy 'touches' people. The first way is depicted as the Spirit of prophecy gives instruction through the use of images or symbols. The person is instructed by the Spirit of prophecy through mental images in their imagination; however, they are not given the interpretation or understanding of these images.

The second way in which the Spirit touches or instructs the individual is accomplished by giving the understanding of the images. The Spirit comes upon them and gives them an interpreting effect in which they are given images, and are also given an interpretation or understanding of the images. Augustine explains that this is a higher degree of prophecy.

The third way of instruction is given by inspiration, in which one receives the images and understanding of the images or symbols.[36] Inspiration is given by the Spirit of prophecy in which it touches a person to instruct them by images, and also touches them with the understanding of the images through words. Augustine further explains how the Spirit provides instruction through these mental images in two ways: (1) dreams and (2) visions.[37] The dream happens when one is asleep, and the vision experience happens while one is awake. Particularly, for Augustine, prophetic visions are 'ecstatic states' described in affective language, such as *pavor* ('awe').[38] He generally defines ecstasy or ecstatic states as an overpowering phenomenon that occurs when 'the mind is alienated from the bodily senses so that a person's spirit, having been caught up in a vision by the divine Spirit, might be open to receiving revelation from God'.[39] He asserts that this ecstatic manifestation or awe is 'when the mind is alienated from the body's senses so that a person's spirit, having been caught up by the divine Spirit, might be open to receiving and contemplating images'.[40] This ecstatic experience alters the senses in one aspect, because the mind is somewhat disengaged from the bodily

---

[36] Augustine, *Response to Simplician* 2.1.1, p. 210.

[37] Augustine, *Response to Simplician* 2.1.1, p. 209.

[38] Augustine, *Responses to Miscellaneous Questions: Miscellany of Eighty-Three Questions* (trans. Boniface Ramsey WOA: A Translation for the 21st Century, I/12, Hyde Park, NY: New City Press, 2008), 2.1.1, p. 209. He uses the Greek word ἐκστάσιν and translates it into Latin, *ecstasis* in the sense of *mentis excessus* ('mental transport, movement') in the context of revelation. Lewis and Short, *Latin to English Lexicon,* Online electronic word study tool. Retrieved on 09/8/2019 from http://perseus.uchicago.edu/Reference/lewisandshort.html.

[39] Augustine, *Responses to Miscellaneous* Questions, 2.1.1, p. 209.

[40] Augustine, *Response to Simplician*, 2.1.1, p. 209.

senses. However, as the person ceases to be aware of their bodily senses, they are still aware of their mental senses. This lack of awareness of the bodily senses and the increased awareness of the mental senses provides the context in which the Spirit of prophecy gives these mental images or instructions.

Consequently, Augustine combines his philosophical, psychological, and theological commitments to formulate constructs regarding how the human soul and the body respond to divine-human visionary encounters.[41] According to these commitments, he postulates that numerous affective movements ('loves or desires') are occurring in the rational part of the soul *mens* ('mind, intellect') and induce ecstatic states, as a response to divine-human encounters.[42] It is important to note at this juncture that Augustine does not interpret ecstasy as a type of madness, or state of emotional frenzy, as if drunk with rage or identified with an intensified form of anger. The notion of prophecy as an altered mental state in which one is not in control of one's mental faculties is not the way in which Augustine describes ecstasy.

This idea of how one is 'caught up' provides more insight into how he perceives this type of ecstatic divine encounter. These terms provide the reader with a framework for Augustine's theology of encounter within this context. Also, the term *alienato mentis* further explains the nature of the relationship between the soul or mind and its bodily senses as it is discussed as an ecstatic encounter in relation to prophecy. As Augustine understands the mind's ability to be alienated from the bodily senses, it thus, allows one's mind to be in a passive position for receiving from the divine Spirit, as it is 'caught up' or in 'union with the Spirit' in this divine encounter, as in a state of awe. This state of awe is an affective movement of the soul in its response to the external activity introduced by the Spirit of prophecy.

---

[41] Augustine's early works that address varying perspectives of the *anima* were written approximately during the same period before his baptism in Milan, p. 387: *De Ordine, De Immortalitate Animae* and *De Animae Quantitate*. In his later works, in *De Trinitate*, Augustine's theological perspectives became more sophisticated in relation to his anthropology.

[42] Augustine, *On Genesis: A Refutation of the Manichees Unfinished Literal Commentary on Genesis: The Literal Meaning of Genesis* (trans. John Rotelle, in WOA: A Translation for the 21st Century, 1/13, New York: New City Press, 2002), 12.3, p. 465. See also, Augustine, *The Trinity* (trans. Roland J. Teske; WOA: A Translation for the 21st Century, 1/26, Hyde Park, NY: New City Press, 1999), 15.7.11. 9.3.8.

It appears that Augustine's views of prophetic visions, which are inspired by the Spirit, and his theology of encounter are somewhat aligned with Pentecostal spirituality. Dale Coulter has expounded upon the affective predilections in the writings of Augustine, Catherine of Siena, Bernard of Clairvaux, Richard of St. Victor, Catherine of Genoa, and Martin Luther, concluding that their common theology of 'encounter centers upon affectivity as the point of contact between the divine and human'.[43] For the aforementioned theologians and Christian mystics, a trinitarian perspective is a central belief, which informs their theology of encounter. In other words, prophetic encounters with God include the belief that it is given by God through the Spirit, and centers upon affectivity. For Augustine, not unlike Pentecostals and Ezekiel, the ways in which the Spirit of prophecy touches a person is a gratuitous gift from God that affects the soul deeply. The category of experience is fundamental to understanding Pentecostal spirituality, and one way to approach this attribute is to situate it within the context of the Christian mystical tradition. However, Pentecostals generally are not aware of the rich heritage provided through Christian mysticism.

Most Pentecostals, doctrinally embrace a Trinitarian theology, and through this lens incorporate their views that the gifts of prophecy are primarily interpreted through the biblical promise of the outpouring of the Spirit based on Joel 2.28-32, Acts 2.17-18, and 1 Corinthians 12 and 14. From this perspective, the gift of prophecy is inspired by the Spirit often times in the midst of a worshipping community. At the heart of Pentecostalism is the desire to encounter God through his word, Spirit, and the community of believers in order to experience and nurture a relationship with God, receive his purposes for life and mission, and often times results in a variety of affective responses. The charism of Spirit-inspired visions is one such avenue to encounter God by the Spirit.

C. Ezekiel's Visions Connect the Transporting Spirit with the Hand of YHWH and Worship

Third, one of the most contested features in Ezekiel's visions is reflected in the visionary transportations (Ezek. 3.12-15; 8.3; 11.1; 37.1;

---

[43] Dale M. Coulter, 'The Spirit and the Bride Revisited: Pentecostalism, Renewal, and the Sense of History', *JPT* 21.2 (2012), pp. 123-34.

40.1).[44] The Spirit transports the prophet from one place to another in a vision and lifts Ezekiel up to the throne and then away from the divine presence all the while under the power or the יד־יהוה (3.12-15). The Spirit transports the prophet 'between heaven and earth in visions' to the Jerusalem Temple (Ezekiel 8–11). The Spirit comes upon the prophet again in Ezekiel 11 and assumes one of the leading roles in Ezekiel's first temple vision as the Spirit transports the prophet to YHWH and works in tandem with the glory of YHWH who speaks to the prophet regarding the fate of the house of Israel. Ezekiel's third prominent vision begins with the hand of YHWH and Spirit transporting and setting the prophet in the middle of the valley of dry bones (Ezek. 37.1).

In Ezekiel's final vision, the Spirit is not mentioned in the introductory scene, but since it is observed in the preceding narratives, it is likely that the hearers would understand that it is the Spirit who is again responsible for transporting the prophet, as it is the Spirit who transports Ezekiel in all of the other three major visions. Contextually, the narrative points to both the 'hand' and the 'spirit' as transporting the prophet in visions (Ezek. 40.2-3). Ezekiel's visionary transportations elicit the idea that the Spirit is representing the power of God at work to initiate these visions. The nuance is that the Spirit comes into the prophet in 2.2 and hears the word of YHWH, but in the subsequent visionary transportation, it is observed that the Spirit is somewhat active from the outside to lift, transport, and setting the prophet places in the vision. Yet, the visionary transportations are described to occur for the purpose of providing the prophet with revelation of God's will and his prophetic word for his people. The transporting Spirit is above all else the most active description of the Spirit's activities. The idea of taking the prophet from place to place in a vision in order to see what God wants to show him, rather than, the prophet remaining stationary is interesting. The narrative highlights the Spirit as leading the visionary and taking him to a place in which YHWH will provide revelation.

At the center of Ezekiel's visionary transportations is the theme of worship. Ezekiel describes a magnificent vision of the glory of YHWH; lays prostrate; is transported to the throne room of YHWH

---

[44] For the various views of a literal transportation and a visionary transportation, see Greenberg, *Ezekiel,* pp. 40-42.

where he sees and hears worship (1.28; 3.12); is transported to the sacred Temple where idolatrous worship is occurring (chs. 8-11); is transported to the valley of dry bones where he witnesses the promise of the Spirit to renew the Israelites' disobedient hearts so that they may become true worshippers (ch. 37; cf. 36); and is brought to a high mountain where the promise of the Spirit's outpouring will bring cleansing, life, and healing to the nation and land of Israel for the purpose of renewing worship to YHWH as their rightful King (chs. 40–48).

For some contemporary Pentecostals, 'worship' is synonymous with the 'presence of God'. Pentecostals believe strongly in the manifest presence of God and consider worship as an encounter with the divine mediated through his divine presence and power, which shapes them spiritually. Since, Pentecostal worship is an encounter with God, then re-visiting Ezekiel's visionary transportations, which is closely connected to worship may prove fruitful. Some of the hallmark signs of Pentecostal churches is a belief and desire for: (1) the Spirit to lead the worship, (2) to hear from the Spirit during worship both individually and communally, and (3) for the community to worship God in the Spirit. Contemporary Pentecostals could benefit from Ezekiel's context of the close associations between visions and worship. The worship creates a space not only for prophetic words, but also prophetic words given in visionary form. Therefore, gleaning from Ezekiel in a fresh new way, can provide examples of how the Spirit inspires and makes known the will of God for the worshipping community through visions.

As documented in Chapter 4, early Pentecostals linked the manifestations of visions with the power of God and Spirit baptism. For example, a testimony from a missionary from India exclaims, 'And the Spirit of God came upon me, after which I saw the vision of the Almighty, falling into a trance but having my eyes open. I was left alone, and saw this great vision, and there remained no strength in me; and I became dumb.'[45] Writing in *The Pentecost*, Martha J. Lewis from Canada recounts her experience with the baptism of the Spirit at a church altar call. She tells of her 'stubborn will' and how she became broken and willing to confess her sins. She reports that she continued to pray at home for the next three days for the baptism of

---

[45] *AF* 1.8 (May, 1907), p. 3.

the Spirit and then was awakened out of her sleep by the 'sound of a roar of fire':

> I saw fire all about me and fire above me. I saw nothing of earth. The fire above me was in strips or widths. Cloven tongues of fire were in the background. Truly the heavens were opened onto me and I saw the Spirit of God, like a dove descending and lighting upon me at my throat. The dove was all fire and had a circle of light about Him.[46]

For most of the testimonies in this study from the early Pentecostal literature, it was observed that the reception of visions came primarily during worship. They believed that visions are an encounter with God and essential for their spiritual transformation. Some early Pentecostal testimonies of visions of God specifically describe that it is the 'hand of God' that carried them in visions from earth to heaven. Generally, these early Pentecostals viewed that the 'hand of God' symbolized the power of God that was responsible for 'transporting' them in a vision. For example, Mattie Dennis describes her throne room visionary experience,

> Then I was carried, or led upward through a heavenly atmosphere with the light remaining over my head. Then I saw the walls of the great city of God. Oh, the beautiful colors can never be told! And it dazzled like the sun. I now saw many bands of angels flying over and about the city. Then the 'hand of God' led me through a shining gate, and all the host of heaven was praising God with voices with all the music of heaven, and I saw it was the Lord.[47]

This idea of transportation by the Spirit in a vision while the hand of the Lord is upon someone is echoed elsewhere. Brother Myland emphasizes the close connection between 'the hand of the Lord' and the Spirit that carried him away,

> That was my first Pentecostal message. I tell you it wasn't I that spoke. It was God's 'the hand of the Lord was strong upon me' like Ezekiel. When the Spirit of the Lord gets you, then the hand of the Lord is upon you. Your spirit may shrink, but the hand of

---

[46] *TP* 1.3 (November, 1908), p. 7.
[47] *TBM* 5.105 (March 1, 1912), p. 3.

the Lord is upon you. He carried me away. First, He carried me up, then He carried me out.[48]

These early Pentecostal testimonies make the connections between the Spirit's power that comes upon them and the hand of God. The idea is that they are rendered almost powerless as the power of God comes upon them. They also link these visionary experiences with worship as they see the throne of God in its glory, likened to the narratives in Ezekiel.

D. Ezekiel's Spirituality and the Use of Affective Language

Martin states, 'the passionate tone of Psalm 63 along with its prominent theme of divine encounter, resonate deeply with the Pentecostal ethos, which values both passion and encounter'.[49] So too, Ezekiel's impassioned quality is expressed through the widespread use of affective language; which begs the question, 'How do the affective dimensions in the text influence Ezekiel's spirituality?'

First, Ezekiel connects the encounter with the Spirit and YHWH's יד to the affective dimensions in the vision narratives. Hebrew prophets were portrayed as impassioned messengers of YHWH. They received YHWH's power through the Spirit, and at times communicated metaphorically by the Hebrew phrase, the 'hand of YHWH'. Ezekiel's visions demonstrate that the activities of the Spirit were at times controlling and overwhelming. For example, Ezekiel is described with unexpected and noticeable anger or bitterness in his own רוח when he is caught up by the divine Spirit.[50] The encounter with the Spirit causes him to become overwhelmed for seven days (3.15). Ezekiel's visions describe the prophet's emotions of fear, anger, awe, and delight in the midst of the visions. At various times, the prophet was distressed, confused, angry and imbittered in his own spirit, and overwhelmed by the divine Spirit.

---

[48] *TLRE* 2.3 (December, 1909), p. 6. See Chapter 4, *AF*, *TBM*, *TP*, *PE*, and *TBC* for other testimonies of visions that relate to worship.

[49] Martin, 'Psalm 63 and Pentecostal Spirituality: An Exercise in Affective Hermeneutics', pp. 263-84.

[50] Tuell also observes that the combination of YHWH's יד and YHWH's רוח in Ezek. 3.12-15 suggests the presence of ecstasy. He interprets Ezek. 3.12, 14a as the 'prophet's mystical transportation from God's direct interaction'. Tuell states that the phrase יד־יהוה 'the hand of YHWH' reflects the concept of ecstatic prophecy in Ezekiel and is an important formula for the divine inspiration of the prophet (1.3; 3.14, 22; 8.1; 40.1).

Since the Spirit's presence is prevalent in the prophetic experiences described in Ezekiel, the prophet's odd or 'ecstatic'[51] behaviors are related to the influence of the Spirit. Moore states that YHWH's Spirit can be described as the 'untamable energy and dynamic controlled only by God. It is a force that can come upon persons, seize them, and cause them to get beside themselves in prophetic ecstasy, unnatural, abnormal, and even crazy to civilized society, something to be kept out of bounds.'[52] Some contemporary interpreters conclude that Ezekiel's behavior seemed symptomatic of psychosis, paranoia, and schizophrenia.[53] At times, interpreters use the affective dimensions to psycho-analyze the historical figures to conclude that some prophets must have been mad-men, frenzied and out of control. However, this hermeneutical approach to psycho-analyze a historical figure is untenable and lacks an understanding of the workings of the Spirit and prophecy. Interestingly, Ezekiel's visions as discussed throughout this study, associate the affective dimensions in the text with either the prophet's responses to encounters with YHWH and his Spirit, or YHWH's responses to sin, his people, or his Temple.[54]

Land offers a more fruitful approach, he argues that religious affections (gratitude, compassion, and courage) are the 'integrating core of Pentecostal spirituality'.[55] Agreeing with Land's definition of Pentecostal spirituality, 'Spirituality is the beliefs and practices in the

---

[51] See Augustine, *The Trinity*, 9.1.8, and Augustine, *Expositions of the Psalms*, Psalms 9 and 30, for his theories of visions, prophecy, and ecstasy. Through these treaties, he offers a way to interpret Ezekiel's symbolic visionary language as signs given by God. Augustine integrates his theological and pneumatological commitments with his understanding of the basic psychology of human nature to inform his theories of prophetic visions as ecstatic states. He uses the Greek word ἐκστάσιν and translates it into Latin, *ecstasis* in the sense of *mentis excessus* ('mental transport, movement') in the context of revelation. In congruence with Augustine's pneumatological convictions and his anthropology, he insists 'there is never a time when the mind, in virtue of its nature as a center of self-awareness, does not remember, understand, and will itself', see Augustine, *The Trinity*, 15.7.11, p. 266.

[52] Moore, 'The Prophetic Calling: An Old Testament Profile and Its Relevance Today', pp. 35, 64.

[53] Halperin, *Seeking Ezekiel: Text and Psychology*; and E.C. Broome, 'Ezekiel's Abnormal Personality', pp. 277-92. Broome also believed that Ezekiel displayed symptoms of catatonia, psychosis, and paranoia.

[54] See *AF* 1.3 (November, 1906), p. 1; *AF* 1.6 (February-March, 1907), pp. 1, 2, 8; *AF* 1.7 (April, 1907), pp. 1, 4; *AF* 2.13 (May, 1908), p. 1.

[55] Land, *Pentecostal Spirituality*, pp. 2, 75, 97, 120. See also, Cartledge, 'Affective Theological Praxis', pp. 34-52.

affections which are themselves evoked and expressed by those beliefs and practices'.[56] He describes Pentecostal spirituality as 'a passion for the kingdom',[57] which necessitates that the affections have a
role to play in the act of biblical interpretation.[58] As believers in the
fivefold gospel, contemporary Pentecostals regard the ministry gifts
of Jesus and the Spirit's empowerment for mission as essential. Similar to the ways in which Ezekiel presents the prophet as an impassioned messenger, so too, contemporary Pentecostals perceive themselves as impassioned messengers for Christ.

Pentecostals, owing to their spirituality and mystical proclivity, do
not question the legitimacy of the prophetic scriptures. In fact, Ezekiel's visions resonate with Pentecostal spirituality that emphasizes
and expects the supernatural realm to invade their worship services
and produce a heart that is transformed and responsive to the Spirit's
encounter. Pentecostals tend to claim that their encounters cause
them to be filled with the love of God, which in turns causes them
to become empathetic to other people's needs.

In ways similar to Ezekiel's descriptions, some early Pentecostals
describe their own affections while under the power of God in the
midst of vision experience. Some report to have experienced visions
of Jesus, the throne of heaven, angelic beings, all while having the
ability to communicate how they were feeling during the vision. A
testimony from Mattie Ledbetter recounts her visions of Jesus on a
throne of glory, 'In a vision I saw Him far above my head beneath a
dome of rainbow of light and glory. As I sang and wafted my hand,
He descended, coming down upon me, which was the longing desire

---

[56] Land, *Pentecostal Spirituality*, p. 1.

[57] Land, *Pentecostal Spirituality*, pp. 2, 97, 120. Cartledge, 'Affective Theological
Praxis', pp. 34-52.

[58] For examples of scholarship incorporating the affections and scripture, see,
Land, *Pentecostal Spirituality*; Baker, 'Pentecostal Bible Reading: Toward a Model of
Reading for the Formation of the Affections', pp. 95-108; Martin, 'Psalm 63 and
Pentecostal Spirituality', pp. 263-84, who provides a historical overview of theolo-
gians who regarded the importance of the role of the affections in spirituality; and
Jared Runck, 'A Pentecostal "Hearing" of the Confessions of Jeremiah: The Liter-
ary Figure of the Prophet Jeremiah as Ideal Hearer of the Word' (PhD Thesis,
University of South Africa, 2017). One of the first scholars who examined the role
of the affections in the Hebrew prophets was Heschel, *The Prophets*, vol. 2.
Heschel's groundbreaking work not only examines the affections of the prophetic
consciousness, but also the 'pathos of God'.

in my soul. All day and all night I was thrilled with waves of joy and glory in every fiber of my being.' [59]

Second, Ezekiel's visions connect worship, as an affective response, with YHWH's overwhelming power by his hand and his Spirit. The prophet falls face down in worship as YHWH's hand is upon him, as he finally discerns that what he is seeing is a vision of the glory of YHWH. This particular act of worship is an affective response demonstrating reverential fear and awe to the appearance of YHWH's glory. For Hollenweger, one of the distinct characteristics of early Pentecostalism, is the 'inclusion of dreams and visions into public and personal worship'.[60] A testimony found in *The Pentecost* from Martha Lewis, communicates how she was rendered powerless to move hand or foot, as she saw a vision of 'the fire I saw above me came also on my body and burned through my flesh like ashes going through a sieve. I was speechless. I was filled with the Holy Ghost in all my being, worshipping God, for the first time, in spirit and in truth.'[61] Her testimony and many others described above highlight how their visions represented vivid and bright colors seen in heaven, the hearing of heavenly choirs, and feelings of joy as they were under the power of God by 'the hand of God', all the while in the context of personal or public worship. These stories also reflect how these believers respond to their visions either with verbal praise, repentance, or decisions to answer a call to follow Christ. But also, these testimonies record their physical bodily responses of prostration and shaking in response to 'the hand of God upon them' in these visions that were given by the Spirit. In these ways, similar to the prophet Ezekiel, they saw themselves receiving visions by the Spirit of God and participating in their visions through all of their senses. The connection between prophetic visions of heavenly realities were closely connected to worship, which is a result of their revelation of God that was given by the power of the Spirit through the medium of visions.

Like their spiritual ancestors, contemporary Pentecostal spirituality affirms that divine-human encounters are 'overwhelming' and may

---

[59] *TBM*, 1.18 (July, 1908), p. 3. The mention of 'false prophets' in the context of the 'last days' is also prevalent throughout this periodical, 'False prophets will continue to prophesy lies, and many will be deceived.'

[60] Hollenweger quoted in Land, *Pentecostal Spirituality*, p. 52.

[61] *TP* 1.3 (November, 1908), p. 7.

be identified by various terms (Spirit baptism and baptism in the Holy Spirit being among the most common), yet understood in various ways. However, there seems to be a general belief among Pentecostals and Charismatics that the overwhelming experience of God by the Spirit is something they share in common. The overwhelming experience is usually described in affective language in which they feel connected to or in communion with God. Similar to the way Heschel provides an analysis of prophetic utterance, in which he argues that 'the fundamental experience of the Hebrew prophet is a fellowship with the feelings of God, sympathy with the divine pathos, a communion with the divine consciousness, which comes about through the prophet's reflection of, or participation in, the divine pathos'.[62] In addition, they understand that visions and dreams are manifestations of the prophetic and eschatological gifts of the Spirit.[63] From these perspectives, as the prophet, Ezekiel submitted to and participated with the power of YHWH by the Spirit and through the medium of visions, his experience was not only informative, but as he participated *with* God he was also affected emotionally *by* God. So too, early pentecostal testimonies and contemporary Pentecostals and Charismatics share similar beliefs and practices related to prophetic encounters.

Third, Ezekiel connects the recurring themes of the affections with visions and obedience. The prophet responds affectively as he lays prostrate in awe and wonder, which leads to worship at the sight of the glory of YHWH (Ezek. 1.28). Specifically, in the call narrative, the affective dimensions play a vital role in the prophet's acts of obedience. The prophet demonstrates gratitude as exhibited through worship, feels the empowerment of the Spirit as he is raised to his feet to stand in the presence of YHWH (Ezek. 2.2), and is commanded twice by YHWH not to be afraid (Ezek. 2.6; 3.9). Ezekiel's call as God's messenger, is to the disobedient and stubborn Israelites. The variations of the word מרר ('rebellious') are used to describe the Israelite's attitude. The repetitive use of this affective term likely instigated fear among the hearers, as they were also included among the rebellious Israelites exiled in Babylon. Yet, YHWH also promises the prophet that he will make Ezekiel 'unyielding and hardened' for the

---

[62] Heschel, *The Prophets*, vol. 2, p. 263.
[63] Roger Stronstad, *The Prophethood of All Believers: A Study in Luke's Charismatic Theology* (JPTSup 16; New York: Sheffield Academic Press Ltd, 2003).

sake of his prophetic ministry to a rebellious people, if he chooses to obey (Ezek. 3.8). Thus, the promise of YHWH is associated with his Spirit's empowerment to afford the prophet the opportunity to become obedient.

Fourth, at the heart of Pentecostalism is the art of story-telling. Pentecostal language is typically not only descriptive, but also emotive. A story is not fully experienced unless the affections of the story teller connect with the affections of the hearer. Pentecostals, typically connect with testifying as a way to witness to 'what God has done' in their lives, which leads to thanksgiving and praise. Likewise, Ezekiel's visions provide meaning to the hearers through story-telling, which describes the prophet's visionary experiences through the lens of the affections. Ezekiel invites the hearers to see, hear, and feel through language that evokes the passions. The vision narratives are interconnected through the recurrence of the main characters, themes, language, and plot. The visions introduce and describe the actions of the main characters. The visionary sees, hears, and responds to the characters. YHWH is portrayed at various times as angry and compassionate. The recurring themes provide the hearers with additional revelation and understanding despite the symbolic imagery and metaphorical language used to describe the visions. The artistic language used to describe the images are colorful and dynamic, which can stimulate the hearers affectively. The emotive language used in the story also assists the hearers to envision the story through the art of imagination. In these ways, the plot or drama of the story introduced in the first vision is connected to the subsequent visions. It is as if the visions are scenes in a film. Each scene or vision narrative is connected to the previous scene.

From this perspective, Ezekiel's visions as described above, could be compared to a contemporary understanding of a 3-D film or a virtual reality experience. The characters and images described are not stagnant or one dimensional. They are mobile, interactive, and multi-dimensional, which adds to the perception of an interactive experience. The visionary is not an observer of the vision, but rather is one of the main characters in the vision. As such, the vision texts describe the visionary engaging all of the senses. For example, the prophet (1) sees symbolic imagery (1–3; 8–11;17–22; 37; 40–47), (2) hears angelic singing and voices that resemble the voice of the Almighty, and the voice of the Lord, (3) tastes a scroll (2.8–3.3), (4) touches a scroll (2.8–3.3), and (5) feels physically and emotionally (2–3). He is lifted up and transported from place to place in some of the visions (2.2; 3; 8). The visionary participates in the vision, through symbolic acts (4.1–5.4).

Ezekiel's literary world is intensified through the use of fire language, illustrations of unpredictable movements, vivid electrifying colors, commanding voices, allusions of majestic imagery, and dynamic forces at play, which all work in ways that naturally elicit the affections of the hearers. The fire and storm language used to describe the glory of YHWH elicits volatility and passion with its association with intense colors of red, orange, and silver. The inaugural vision elaborately describes a vision of the mobile chariot-throne of the glory of YHWH highlighted by the fire and the storm theophany motifs that would elicit fear of judgment in the prophet and the hearers. Thus, this 3-D film, if you will, is complete with its appeal to an ancient sight and sound generation, a prophetic generation that responds not only cerebrally but also affectively.

Pentecostal spirituality affirms the passionate pursuit of God in Pentecostal communities and Pentecostals should find encouragement that a fresh reading of Ezekiel's visions can further guide Pentecostals to desire an encounter with God through visions and find freedom to express their passions *in* and *to* these encounters. On this view, the affections play a role in the task of hermeneutics, beliefs and practices, and mission. I would argue that hearing and reading the biblical texts are both an intellectual and affective endeavor, yet the affective aspects have been generally unnoticed in the academy in the task of hermeneutics.[64]

Land argues that 'Christian affections integrate and undergird Pentecostal beliefs and practices', which is characterized by orthodoxy (right belief), orthopraxy (right practice), and orthopathy (right affections).[65] Hopefully, hearing Ezekiel from this theological

---

[64] As cited previously in this study, see Baker, 'Pentecostal Bible Reading: Toward a Model of Reading for the Formation of the Affections', pp. 34-48 (46). Cf. Martin, *The Unheard Voice of God*, pp. 70-71. See also Edgerton, *The Passion of Interpretation*, who agrees that every interpretation involves the passions of the interpreter. See also Cartledge, 'Affective Theological Praxis', pp. 42, 51.
[65] Land, *Pentecostal Spirituality*, p. 1. See also, *TBM*, 1.18 (July, 1908), p. 3. The mention of 'false prophets' in the context of the 'last days' is also prevalent throughout this periodical, 'False prophets will continue to prophesy lies, and many will be deceived'.

perspective contributes to a fresh reading of the affective dimensions embedded in the vision narratives.[66]

E. Ezekiel's Visions Demonstrate that the Spirit Indwells

In this examination, it has been revealed that Ezekiel's visions are primarily pneumatologically grounded. At the heart of Ezekiel's vision narratives are numerous descriptions of the Spirit's activities. One of the most distinct characteristics of the Spirit in Ezekiel's visions is how the Spirit indwells the prophet and later, the same indwelling activity of the Spirit is promised to the whole community (2.2; 36.27-28).[67]

As previously noted, it is the power of God that is realized in the Spirit and anthropologically described by the phrase, the יד־יהוה. In Ezekiel's call narrative, the Spirit enters the prophet and raises him to his feet (2.2; 3.24).[68] In the midst of worship, or as the prophet lay prostrate before the glory of YHWH, it is observed that the יד־יהוה never left Ezekiel and the distinctive role of the רוח assumes center stage as twice in the narrative, the prophet announces, 'The Spirit came into me as he spoke to me and caused me to stand to my feet' (2.2; 3.24). The presence of this distinguishing pneumatological feature of Ezekiel's visionary call narrative, the sentence 'The spirit came into me' (2.2; 3.24), points to divine inspiration, and is observed again as the text reads, 'the spirit of YHWH fell upon me, and he said to me' (11.5). Additionally, in 36.27, the Spirit is linked with the house of Israel's obedience to YHWH's word. In 37.1–14, the Spirit comes at the command of YHWH's word, spoken by the prophet. The Spirit's indwelling activity is linked to inspiration and a dynamic power as it causes the prophet to stand in the presence of YHWH's

---

[66] James K.A. Smith, *Desiring the Kingdom: Worship, Worldview, and Cultural Formation* (Cultural Liturgies,1; Grand Rapids, MI: Baker Academic, 2009), argues that human life is shaped largely by the affections.

[67] For a discussion of the inward work of the Spirit in the OT, see G. Fredricks, 'Rethinking the Role of the Holy Spirit in the Lives of Old Testament Believers', *Trinity Journal* 9.1 (1988), pp. 81-104; and E.J. Hamlin, *At Risk in the Promised Land: A Commentary on the Book of Judges* (Grand Rapids, MI: Eerdmans, 1990), p. 95. See also, Kapelrud, 'The Spirit and the Word in the Prophets', p. 46. He regards that Ezekiel and Micah are two of the later prophets who emphasize the spirit of YHWH as the divine רוח, who seized and filled them, and inspired them to speak the word of YHWH.

[68] Leonard P. Maré, 'Ezekiel, Prophet of the Spirit', *OTE* 31.3 (2018), pp. 553-70.

glory. These theological implications are profound as they link the indwelling power of the Spirit with inspiration and the presence or glory of YHWH. It is the Spirit who indwells the prophet empowering him to stand in YHWH's presence and hear his voice.

Contextually, the vision narrative directs attention to Ezekiel's call as a messenger of YHWH to the rebellious nation of Israel. As such, the language accentuates Ezekiel's dependency upon the indwelling power of God by the Spirit. It is the Spirit in and upon Ezekiel that empowers him to become a prophet for such a difficult task. From this perspective, the indwelling activity of the Spirit empowers the prophet not only to stand before the sacred presence of the glory of YHWH, but also to hear his voice and become an obedient messenger.

The indwelling activity of the Spirit is noted again as YHWH promises to remove their stony hearts and give them a heart of flesh. Yet, he also promises to put 'My Spirit within you and cause you to walk in my statues, and you will be careful to observe my ordinances' (36.27-28).[69] The Spirit again, is directly linked with empowerment and obedience in that it is the promise of the indwelling activity of the Spirit that will empower them to become obedient. In a sense, the indwelling Spirit will cause a transformation from their previous rebellious spirit or will, and they will become a new purified spirit, willing and obedient. So, as the prophet, Ezekiel was empowered to become or be transformed into a messenger of YHWH and be obedient to YHWH's commands, likewise the Israelite community would become empowered to become obedient to YHWH's commands.

The indwelling activity of the Spirit may also be understood by the hearers as pointing to the promise of the glory of YHWH returning to the temple. It might not be going too far to suggest that the hearers might also distinguish between the Spirit's activities of 'breathing life' into the dead and the indwelling activity of the Spirit in Ezek. 36.26, which speaks of a new heart and the subsequent verse that refers to God's indwelling presence.[70] Clarity comes as the

---

[69] For references on the infusion of the רוח in the life of the OT believer, see Block, 'The Prophet of the Spirit', p. 40. See also Joyce, *Divine Initiation*, pp. 108-10, who rightly points out in the antecedent texts, 'heart' and 'spirit' represent the person's internal locus of emotion, will, and thought.

[70] Hamilton, *God's Indwelling Presence*, p. 52, posits that while both promises are still in the future, the text supports an argument that the 'believing remnant of

promise of the indwelling life and power of the Spirit is executed through the obedience of Ezekiel 'to prophesy to the [YHWH] breath' and 'to breathe into the slain, that they may live' and by the Spirit (vv. 9-10; cf. 39.29). Ezekiel elucidates for the hearers the importance of obedience to the prophetic word while working in tandem with the Spirit to produce life and restoration. The ideas of restoration are not only linked with the glory of YHWH returning to the physical temple, but to their communal and individual lives becoming a spiritual place of worship through YHWH's promise of the Spirit.

The indwelling activity of the Spirit is also linked with the concept of life as YHWH promises that he will put his Spirit in them and will cause them to live (37.14). This promise of the indwelling of the divine Spirit is coupled with the promise of life and a return to their land. Previously, the hearers would have recalled how the Spirit came into Ezekiel at the initiation of his call (2.2). After which, YHWH promises to put his Spirit in the whole house of Israel to cause them to become obedient (36.27).

Last, YHWH's promise of the indwelling divine Spirit is linked with a life-giving force to bring what was dead back to life (37.14). The promise of the indwelling Spirit was foundational in: (1) bringing life to the dead (37.1-14), (2) hope to the hopeless (vv. 12-14), (3) restoration of the house of Israel to their land (v. 13), and (4) knowledge that YHWH was faithful to keep his covenant to his people (vv. 9-14). In essence, YHWH will reclaim his people and bring them back to the land of Israel. The promise of the indwelling Spirit also subsumes the ideas that 'by the Spirit' hearts will be renewed through the act of 'indwelling' in the lives of the people. From this perspective, the Spirit is described as external to YHWH, yet summoned by him. Ultimately, this vision portrays a promise that YHWH will bring life out of death; a new spirit in exchange for an old spirit; and hope for the hearts of Israel to receive YHWH's indwelling Spirit as a means of empowering them to become obedient to YHWH as their Lord.

Ezekiel's audience had experienced a heart change'. See also, Kaiser, Jr., 'The Indwelling Presence of the Holy Spirit in the Old Testament', pp. 308-15.

In contemporary scholarship, there are numerous debates surrounding the idea of the indwelling Spirit in the OT.[71] Some Pentecostals scholars maintain that the Spirit in people's lives in the OT was intermittent and transitory, or came upon certain people when they began to prophesy or perform a miraculous act. Yet, this study suggests that in Ezekiel, the Spirit came into the prophet as he was continuously empowered and enlivened by the Spirit. The text seems to indicate a more permanent presence of God's Spirit in his life and ministry. Wood has indeed argued that most of the prophets were filled continuously by the Spirit.[72] As summarized above, the Spirit in Ezekiel offers several evidences for the Spirit's abiding in and upon the prophet. Some Pentecostals might testify to the Spirit abiding in or coming upon individuals in Spirit baptism, yet it is not to say that they mean the Spirit was not already present. The Spirit functions in Ezekiel in a variety of ways that can offer Pentecostal scholarship and the church at large, valuable insights to investigate further the work of the Spirit in the OT.

F. Ezekiel's Visions Validate that the Spirit Leads

The Spirit in Ezekiel's visions connects the indwelling aspect to the activity of the Spirit leading. First, it is mentioned in the inaugural vision narrative as the living creatures followed the lead of the Spirit because they possess a spirit (1.12; 19-21). At first blush, the leading attribute of the Spirit in the context of the living creatures may not seem relevant to the story, however the narratives juxtapose the leading characteristic of the Spirit and the living creatures with that of the Spirit leading the prophet in his call narrative (2.1-3.27).[73] Notably, Ezekiel accepts the direction of YHWH's commands to become

---

[71] For an overview of the various positions, see Hamilton, *God's Indwelling Presence*, pp. 9-24. He argues that the OT texts indicate that the Spirit was with God's people and the individuals, but not in them as under the new covenant, pp. 26. See also, W.C. Kaiser, Jr., 'The Indwelling Presence of the Holy Spirit in the Old Testament' *EQ* 82.4 (2010), pp. 308-15. Block, 'The View from the Top: The Holy Spirit in the Prophets', p. 199, admits that the HB does not use the same language of 'new birth' or speak of the NT 'indwelling of the Spirit', but argues that the ideas did exist in the people's minds and they did experience the reality as described in the biblical texts.

[72] Wood, *The Holy Spirit in the Old Testament*, pp. 44-49, 58.

[73] John Levison, *Filled with the Spirit* (Grand Rapids: Eerdmans, 2009), p. 98, argues that the spirit that gives movement to the living beings is the energizing power of God and represents a turning point in Israelite conceptions of the 'spirit within'.

a prophet only after the indwelling Spirit has endued him with power (2.2). Contextually, the theme of obedience is also directly linked with the leading of the Spirit. Ezekiel can choose to follow the Spirit or be disobedient like his compatriots.

Ezekiel's vision of the dry bones (37.1-14) also stresses the theme of the divine Spirit leading the prophet. As the רוח־יהוה brought Ezekiel in a vision to a valley full of bones, the רוח־יהוה also leads him 'back and forth among them' as if urging the prophet to take a closer look. The hearers likely would recall the recurrent theme of motion and leading by the Spirit from Ezekiel's description of his first vision (Ezekiel 1–3). As the divine Spirit leads the prophet to view the bones more closely, Ezekiel is able to depict the number and quality of the bones. In this sense, the leading aspect of the Spirit's guidance provides revelation to the prophet, which is necessary for discerning the message in the vision.

A central tenet of Pentecostal spirituality regarding the role of the Spirit in the life of the believer, as well as the community, is related to the Spirit's presence leading and guiding. An experience of the Spirit's presence in this way often times is subjective and requires discernment because the Spirit is observed to lead in various ways. A common belief in the Pentecostal traditions is that the biblical witness testifies to the various ways in which the Spirit leads. For example, in the NT, the text 'speaks' of the Spirit giving instruction, warnings, and exhortations (1 Tim. 4.1-2). Pentecostal believers (past and present) hold to a belief that they are led by the Spirit of God as they hear the Spirit's revealed message of truth, and believe, and obey it. Like Ezekiel, the Spirit's leading is linked with revelation and obedience. This is possibly an OT example of how believers perceive to 'walk after the Spirit', 'mind the things of the Spirit', are 'in the Spirit', 'live in the Spirit', and are 'led by the Spirit' (Rom. 8.1, 4, 12, 13, 14). Generally, the NT is preferred over the OT for examples of the Spirit's leading, especially for instructional purposes. Perhaps a fresh reading of Ezekiel could provide a fuller appreciation of the Spirit's leading attributes. Ezekiel underscores the correlation between the activities of the indwelling Spirit and the leading of the Spirit.

G. Ezekiel's Visions Reveal that Participation with YHWH Leads to New Life by the Spirit

Particularly, Ezekiel's vision of the dead bones (Ezek. 37.1-14) exemplifies how participation with YHWH leads to new life by the Spirit. Structurally, this vision serves to transition the entire book. It anticipates new life to the community that has been stricken with death and destruction. The previous visions emphasize the glory of YHWH moving from the desecrated Temple to a foreign land to demonstrate his sovereignty in a foreign land and pronouncing the impending doom to the community as a result of their idolatrous sin. The vision of dead, unburied bones represents death and uncleanness. Yet, the vision ends with a promise of new life. The vision begins with the Spirit transporting and leading the prophet through the valley of dry bones and ends with the promise of YHWH to revive the house of Israel with the Spirit dwelling in them. As such, the activities of the Spirit serve as bookends around the narrative.

Several observations are identified that imply YHWH desires participation with his prophet in order to accomplish his purposes by the Spirit in this pericope. First, the Spirit is upon the prophet as the 'hand of YHWH' is a metaphor used to describe the power of the Spirit. The power of the Spirit is accentuated as the metaphor of a dead, unclean community that is in need of a miracle to restore life and purity. The combination of YHWH's rhetorical question to the prophet, 'Can these bones live?' (v. 3), and the humble response of the prophet, 'you know', reveals to the prophet that he is in need of the Spirit's power as well. The theme of partnership is depicted as the power of the Spirit is available to the prophet, once again, for YHWH's purposes towards his community.

Second, YHWH does not speak to the dead bones. YHWH commands the prophet to prophesy and the spoken word only becomes effective after the prophet obeys the commands of the Lord. As the prophet is empowered by the Spirit, it is obedience to YHWH that will result in the fulfillment of the promise of the Spirit breathing life into the dead bones. From this perspective, it is through the obedience of the prophet and partnership with YHWH that new life is achieved.

Third, YHWH's promise of new life to the dead community is achieved by his Spirit. The Sovereign Lord says, 'I will make the רוח enter you, and you will come to life. I will attach tendons to you and make flesh come upon you and cover you with skin; I will put my רוח in you, and you will come to life. Then you will know that I am YHWH' (vv. 5-6). The pronoun 'you' is the plural form, which points to the collective community. The regeneration of these dead bones can only be accomplished by the infusion of the רוח in response to the prophetic word. Then, they will know the lordship of YHWH. YHWH partners with his Spirit to cause the dead to come alive.

Fourth, visions are a medium for God to speak or partner with humanity by his Spirit. Visions are like a window into the spirit world. By God's sovereignty, he allows the window to be opened according to his purposes, and it is by the Spirit that these divine-human encounters are made possible. Ezekiel's visions illustrate through storytelling and symbolic imagery how the Spirit is the conduit for YHWH's purposes to be accomplished in this divine-human partnership.

H. Ezekiel's Visions use Water Imagery as a Metaphor to Accentuate the Healing and Cleansing work of the Spirit

Symbols for the Spirit are not only illustrated in scripture, but they are also widely accepted by the church at large for the use of teaching and preaching. However, the interpretation and application of the biblical symbols of water associated with the Spirit are broadly debated.[74] For example, some of the theological doctrines include, water baptism, Spirit baptism, regeneration, cleansing, and forgiveness of sins, which are commonly associated with water imagery and the

---

[74] Although not conclusive, the following are some of the various perspectives revolving around baptism. Broadly speaking, in Christian churches, the theology of baptism has been influenced by two foundational texts, Rom. 6.3-4 and Mk 1.9-11. The Western churches primarily stressed baptism as participation in Christ's death and resurrection according to the theology in the epistle to the Romans. The act of baptismal immersion is the sign of Christ's dying and rising signifying new life and Christian identify. The Eastern churches tend to emphasize Mark and parallel texts. They view baptism as the reenactment of Jesus' baptism in the Jordan. The Gospel texts underscore the pneumatological and trinitarian aspects of baptism. These texts incorporate the gift of the Spirit, the presence of the Father, Son, and Spirit associated with the water baptism in the Jordan. The baptized believers become the adopted heirs of the Father and receive the anointing of the Spirit. Pentecostal and Charismatic believers ascribe to various views regarding the meaning of Spirit baptism as a subsequent baptism to water baptism. Infant baptism versus baptism of the believer has long been debated among Catholic and Protestant believers.

Spirit.[75] The Ezekiel texts, which associate water imagery to the Spirit, serve to add to this discussion. The imagery of an 'outpouring' illustrates an immersion or a contemporary view of water or Spirit baptisms. First, as the book introduces a new theme, that of spiritual cleansing with water; it emphasizes the necessity of spiritual cleansing of the entire community that must precede the covenantal promise of a 'new heart' and a 'new spirit'.[76] YHWH declares,

> I will sprinkle clean water on you, and you will be clean; I will cleanse you from all your filthiness and from all your idols. I will give you a new heart and put a new spirit within you; I will take the heart of stone out of your flesh and give you a heart of flesh. I will put my Spirit within you and cause you to walk in my statutes, and you will observe my ordinances and do them ... I will save you from all your uncleanness ... Then you will remember your evil ways and your deeds that were not good; and you will loathe yourselves in your own sight, for your iniquities and your abominations (36.25-31).[77]

Ezekiel's visions emphasize that the spiritual act of cleansing comes from YHWH, as the sovereign God who is able to forgive his people of their sins. The vision continues to draw the hearer's attention to the Spirit's activity, as YHWH's promise to give the house of Israel 'a new heart' and 'a new spirit'.[78] The theological precedent is underscored again as the cleansing agent of water is connected YHWH's Spirit indwelling his people. From this perspective, one

---

[75] Baptism has multiple meanings reflected in various biblical texts. Some NT texts describe corporate baptism (1 Cor. 12.13), Christ's priesthood (1 Pet. 2.5; 9; Rev. 1.6; 5.10), spiritual circumcision as a way in which to describe the participation in the new covenant (Col. 2.11-12).

[76] The concept of ceremonial uncleanness is a distinctive feature in the Torah. For example, the categories of what was 'clean' and 'unclean', or 'sacred' and 'profane' were described in the Levitical laws.

[77] Schafroth, 'An Exegetical Exploration of Spirit references in Ezekiel 36 and 37', pp. 61-77, argues that though the verb זרק ('sprinkle') in v. 25 is usually connected with the sprinkling of blood, the sprinkling with pure water here should be understood as a ritual cleansing and recalls the Mosaic rites of purification (cf. Num. 19.17-19; Isa. 4.4; Zech. 13.1) as well as Ps. 51.7, which refers to sprinkling and cleansing of the worshipper. See also, Biggs, *The Book of Ezekiel*, p. 116; Feinberg, *The Prophecy of Ezekiel*, p. 209.

[78] For references to the infusion of the רוח in the life of the OT believer, see Block, 'The Prophet of the Spirit', p. 40. See also Joyce, *Divine Initiation*, pp. 108-10.

could say that the cleansing or forgiveness of sins is a requirement for receiving YHWH's Spirit.

Certainly, the Spirit's empowerment is observed as the indwelling activity of the Spirit enables the community to obey. Yet, not only will YHWH's Spirit empower the people for obedience, but it will also transform their hearts by giving them a 'new heart' and a 'new spirit'. It is not surprising that the work of the Spirit in the OT is primarily a work of power. Yet, in Ezekiel, the Spirit's work is also linked to spiritual cleansing, or otherwise known in contemporary Pentecostal churches, as sanctification or transformation. Ezekiel's descriptions of transformation are similar to what can be called a 'heart transplant'. In this context, as the heart is the locus of the will and the emotions, thus a 'soft heart' is symbolic for a new spirit that is submissive to YHWH's will and thus obedient to 'keep' his words or statues. The theme of newness creates the hope of what was considered 'dead' will be renewed with 'new life'. Agreeing with Rea, as he utilizes grammatical, contextual, and theological perspectives to identify two 'renewing functions' for the role of the רוח ('Spirit') in the book of Ezekiel: (1) God's promise of his indwelling Spirit (Ezek. 36.27; 37.14), and (2) the outpoured Spirit as covenant sign (Ezek. 39.29).[79]

The theme of transformation has insightful theological implications for spiritual cleansing and 'new life' mediated through the power of the Spirit. The Spirit will enable them to live in obedience and to 'walk' in God's statutes. It is through the empowerment of the Spirit in them, that will ultimately cause them to obey YHWH's decrees and be free from the bondage of idolatry.[80] The theological themes of cleansing, transformation, new life, and empowerment are given by the Spirit and symbolized through the use of water imagery.

Rea also highlights that, 'Although Ezekiel did not employ the term new covenant, these concepts of inner cleansing and regeneration with God's promise to impart YHWH's Spirit to indwell believers was a new feature not previously provided in his [YHWH's]

---

[79] Rea, *The Holy Spirit in the Bible*, pp. 101-107. He argues that Jesus used the term 'water' from Ezek. 36.25 and the 'new spirit' of v. 26 to describe the 'new birth' to Nicodemus in Jn. 3.5.

[80] Odell, *Ezekiel*, p. 443, notes a distinction between Ezekiel's heart metaphor and Jeremiah's. She points out that in Jeremiah's description of the promise of the new covenant, the Torah is written on the heart so that the knowledge of YHWH's laws become innate (Jer. 31.31-34).

covenants with Abraham, Moses, and David'.[81] The imagery of the indwelling and outpouring of the Spirit suggests that the promise of a new transformed life was not only promised by YHWH, but achieved by the Spirit through the acts of cleansing, transformation, renewal, and empowerment for the sake of obedience. In ways unlike any other OT writing, Ezekiel's visions reveal the revolutionary impact of the Spirit will have upon the community.

The life-giving imagery of water is also expanded to include the ideas of healing in Ezekiel's final vision (Ezekiel 40–48). Ezekiel sees a river of living water flowing out of the restored temple in Jerusalem and emphasizes that wherever the water flows, everything will live (Ezek. 47.9). The healing water turns salt water to fresh water; fish will increase; trees will bear fruit and their leaves will be used for healing. There will be a very great multitude of fish, because these waters go there; for they will be healed, and everything will live wherever the river goes' (Ezek. 47.10-12). Although the word 'Spirit' is not found in the text, most interpreters agree that the river represents the life-giving presence of God or the Spirit of God that goes forth into the world.[82] The water starts from the place where the glory of YHWH is present in the Temple. Since the language harkens back to the introduction of water as a symbol of cleansing associated with a promise of new life (cf. Ezek. 36.25-27), then it is likely that the hearers would discern the symbol of water in the present vision as also representing a cleansing and the giving of life. As previously discussed, in Ezekiel, the power of life resides by the Spirit (Ezek. 37.6, 9-10, 14).

The water imagery is once again connected with the activity of the outpouring Spirit as promised by YHWH in the preceding chapter (ch. 39). Ezekiel clearly draws connections with the Spirit and the water imagery to the ideas of healing. The prophet sees a river of living water flowing out of the restored temple in Jerusalem. The healing river grows deeper and wider as it flows farther from the temple. Cooper argues, 'Everything in Ezekiel's description presents a

---

[81] Rea, *The Holy Spirit in the Bible*, pp. 102-103.

[82] J.B. Taylor, *Ezekiel: An Introduction and Commentary* (Tyndale OT Commentaries; Downers Grove, IL: Inter-Varsity Press, 1969), p. 270; Blenkinsopp, *Ezekiel*, pp. 231-32; Zimmerli, Hanson, and Greenspoon, *Ezekiel* 2, p. 511; Tuell, *Ezekiel*, p. 330.

picture of the life-giving, healing, and life-sustaining properties of the water from the sanctuary'.[83]

Two of the three previous vision narratives highlight the idolatry and abominations that were occurring in the Temple (1–3; 8–11). The vision of the valley of dead bones emphasizes the Spirit's role is renewing life to that which is dead. Now, in Ezekiel's final temple vision, not only has YHWH's glory returned, but it is dependent upon the Spirit that will be poured out to cleanse and renew life. Just as the natural life without water is impossible, so too is the spiritual life impossible without YHWH's Spirit. The themes of life and death continue as previously the Spirit breathed new life to the dead bones, and now pours out a life-giving force to renew the people and the land. The message of transformation of the nation of Israel and the land by the Spirit is followed with the glory of YHWH returning to the sanctuary. The presence of the Spirit in the hearts and lives of the people of Israel is closely related to the presence of the of YHWH in the sanctuary. The promise that the work of spiritual renewal in God's people, Israel, had begun with his cleansing process of judgment by the Babylonians in Ezekiel's own day and now was perceived as a future promise from God through an outpoured Spirit.

It should not go unnoticed that early Pentecostals write about Ezekiel's final Temple vision from the themes discussed above. Sexton associates the water imagery with the Spirit's outpouring of the Pentecostal Spirit baptism with love. In keeping with a Wesleyan Holiness view of Spirit baptism, Sexton perceives that the outpouring of the Spirit is given to a heart that is pure allowing it to love God fully.[84] She writes, 'Waters to swim in. The saints now stand on the brink of a grand ocean of love, too broad to pass over, too deep to fathom. You may wade in the borders of it, and plunge into its healing currents; you may view the river of life on either side of it, but the fullness of the glory is not yet.'[85] Hannah A. James also writes

---

[83] L.E. Cooper, *Ezekiel* (New American Commentary; Nashville, TN: Broadman & Holman Publishers, 1994), p. 43.

[84] Archer, *A Pentecostal Hermeneutic for the Twenty-First Century*, pp. 14-15. Archer traces the Holiness movements and their influences upon early Pentecostalism. He distinguishes a Keswickian Spirit baptism, which according to Archer is a second experiential work for empowerment for service, with that of a Wesleyan Holiness Spirit baptism, which views that Spirit baptism totally eradicates Adamic sin and comes to the purified heart to love God fully.

[85] *TBM* 3.48 (October, 1909), p. 1.

that the temple vision with the emphasis upon the water imagery in Ezekiel 47 is like the baptism of the Holy Spirit and love. She states, 'Ezekiel's wondrous vision of the ever-deepening river should be like the baptism. Oh! That we all should plunge into the mighty torrents of God's love and be swept along upon its waters ... to be without measure.'[86]

Contemporary Pentecostal and Charismatic believers identify themselves as people of the Spirit through their central beliefs in the Spirit's outpouring through Spirit baptism. However, at times, the emphasis is more upon the empowering aspects of the Spirit through signs of healing, miracles, and various other charisms. Ezekiel's water metaphor, and the illustrations associated with the water imagery and the outpouring and indwelling Spirit suggest that spiritual cleansing, moral transformation, and infilling of love are at the heart of the Spirit's immersion in and upon the believer.

Early Pentecostals often times associated the Spirit with symbolic imagery, such as a dove, oil, or water. It was not uncommon to connect the Spirit's activities with the healing and life-giving properties of water. For example, Sexton, a writer from the *TBM* interprets the entire chapter of Ezekiel 47 in light of how she perceives the working of the Spirit in the 'sanctified life of Pentecostal baptism'.[87] Sexton writes,

> This [Ezekiel's] vision marvelously applies to the Spirit's working. Where the Holy Spirit goes, it carries life and healing as this stream of living water. Our first going through the waters is with the waters to our ankles. It suggests the walking in newness of life, born of the Spirit and walking by faith. The second bringing through the waters, takes us deeper, but in the same water. The waters are to the knees.[88]

It is apparent that for Sexton the water that overflows the temple in Ezekiel 47 symbolically represents the Spirit whom she associates with 'the rivers of living water that flows from the throne of God' and comes to bring life, healing, cleansing, and holiness.[89] Sexton observes that Ezekiel's temple vision illustrates how the 'water cleanses

---

[86] *TBM* 7.58 (July 1, 1914), p. 3.
[87] *TBM* 3.48 (October, 1909), p. 1.
[88] *TBM* 3.48 (October, 1909), p. 1.
[89] *TBM* 3.48 (October, 1909), p. 1.

from physical filth and the Spirit cleanses from sin and the pollutions of sin'.[90] Early Pentecostals recognized that the Spirit was not only given for empowerment, but also for cleansing and holiness.

IV. Summary

In this chapter, I sketched out the central message of Ezekiel's visions as pertaining to the activities of the Spirit and have made overtures toward the construction of a Pentecostal theology of Spirit-inspired visions.

It was also observed in this study, through reception history of the early Pentecostal literature that there were numerous reports of visions that occurred in the midst of public and personal worship, and perceived as somewhat of a normative event. The testimonies of their visionary experiences typically described how they perceived visions as a gift from the Spirit and led them to praise and worship God. As such, visions are pneumatologically grounded in early Pentecostal spirituality. Generally, these early Pentecostals read the OT texts through the lens of the fivefold gospel. The fivefold gospel is a theological paradigm that expresses the core tenets of Pentecostal soteriology: Jesus is Savior, Sanctifier, Spirit-baptizer, Healer, and Soon-coming King.[91] The early Pentecostals, as well as some contemporary Pentecostals view themselves as living in the last days, awaiting the soon coming King. From this perspective, at times Ezekiel's visions were interpreted eschatologically, and frequently associated directly with the work of the Spirit. More specifically, some of the vision testimonies associated with Ezekiel's visions perceived that the encounters were a direct result of the outpouring activity of the Spirit through Spirit baptism.

More than in any other prophetic book, the prophet's ministry emphasizes the activities of the Spirit. Ezekiel's visions demonstrate a direct correlation between two recurring motifs, the יד־יהוה and the diverse activities of the divine רוח, establishing an immediate emphasis on the involvement of the characteristics of YHWH and the Spirit in the vision narratives. It seems that all the primary vision activities

---

[90] *TBM* 3.48 (October, 1909), p. 1.
[91] Land, *Pentecostal Spirituality*, p. 38. Cf. Wolfgang Vondey, *Pentecostal Theology: Living the Full Gospel* (New York: Bloomsbury T&T Clark, 2017).

are accomplished in, with, and by the Spirit, and closely associated to the power or hand of YHWH. Beyond these explicit literary markers, other indicators in the text suggest that the whole of Ezekiel's visions are comprised of the numerous ways in which the Spirit inspires and reveals YHWH's messages through the medium of visions and oracles to his prophet, Ezekiel, and subsequently to the hearers (past and present). Ezekiel's visions begin and end with powerful workings of the Spirit as one of the leading characters in his narratives. Most of these dynamic activities of the Spirit are associated with the prophet, yet the Spirit is also promised to work in his community (Ezekiel 36 and 37). The promise of the Spirit's power to the community is linked to the themes of cleansing, healing, and the outpouring of the Spirit that ultimately renews life.

The Spirit is closely associated with the power of YHWH and anthropologically described by the יד־יהוה, and yet overshadowed by the revelation of the glory of YHWH. Specifically, the Hebrew idiom, the hand of YHWH is emphasized in all four of Ezekiel's major visionary accounts (Ezekiel 1–3; 8–11; 37.1-14; 40–43). The phrase, 'the hand of the Lord' is used in the narrative reports of Ezekiel to describe how the prophet: (1) hears the word of the Lord and, at times, angelic beings, (2) falls prostrate after seeing a vision of the glory of the Lord, (3) is lifted and transported to a heavenly throne vision, and (4) sees a mysterious man with, at times, angelic beings. Frequently, this phrase is used in tandem with the Spirit of the Lord in the context of Ezekiel's vision reports (Ezek. 3.12-14, 22-24; 8.1-3; 37.1; 40.1-3). Ezekiel's multi-dimensional approach to describe his visions serves to stimulate the hearers through most of the senses, (1) sight, (2) hearing, and (3) the affections. From this multi-dimensional perspective, the seer is inviting the hearers to imagine what he is seeing so as to entice participation in the drama that is unfolding. In these ways, the idea of seeing a prophetic message is distinguishable from hearing a prophetic message, as Ezekiel's presentation of the vision requires a multi-dimensional interpretation instead of a linear understanding. Pentecostals perceive visions as an experiential encounter with God, thus they value experience as part of their spirituality. Pentecostals can find in Ezekiel's visions affirmation that the Spirit affects the whole person, and the workings of the Spirit are dynamically part of the vision experience.

The diverse activities of the Spirit (1) inspire the prophet to see, hear, and experience; transports the prophet; and leads the prophet to the glory of YHWH, (2) the indwelling Spirit enables or empowers the prophet to accept his prophetic ministry and become obedient, and (3) breathes or restores new life. Although, God's sovereignty and glory are overarching themes in the book of Ezekiel, it is also significant that imbedded in the four major visions of Ezekiel are stories of the Spirit's activities as they relate to YHWH, the prophet, and the people of Israel. The visions are packed with biblical theological themes, which are primarily associated with the Spirit's activities: (1) inspiration, (2) revelation, (3) empowerment, (4) restoration and regeneration, (5) healing and cleansing, and (6) covenant. While Ezekiel's visions affirm the work of the Spirit is primarily with the prophet, as an individual, it is apparent that the Spirit's goal is to benefit the covenant community.

A Pentecostal spirituality also includes the dimensions of the affections in the task of biblical hermeneutics. The idea of the literature portraying God's personality[92] or disposition is compatible with the anthropomorphisms and anthropopathisms that were used in the narratives. This type of metaphorical language describes God's attributes not only in the more common idea of power, but also the idea of the affections or emotions. The anguished passions of YHWH and his chosen messenger serve to accentuate the character's roles, and engage the passions of the hearers. My own view is in agreement with the insights of Land, Baker, and Martin, who argue generally that an affective approach to Scripture is three-fold: (1) Pentecostal spirituality is informed theologically through the affective biblical language, (2) the hearer(s) must attune to the affective dimension of Scripture, and (3) the hearer(s) seeks to engage the affective language as a dynamic and living word that transforms the hearer(s) by the Spirit.

---

[92] Johnson, *The One and the Many in the Israelite Conception of God*, pp. 6-8, 20, 36-38.

8

CONTRIBUTIONS, REFLECTIONS, AND TASKS FOR FURTHER STUDY

I. Contributions

This study makes several contributions to the scholarship on Spirit-inspired visions in the book of Ezekiel.

First, this is the first study specifically examining Ezekiel's four major visions from an explicitly Pentecostal reading methodology. The Pentecostal reading strategy attempts to hear the narrative of Ezekiel's visions as a method owing to the Pentecostal ethos and its spirituality. In addition, this reading strategy combines the most up to date developments in hermeneutics, namely *Wirkungsgeschichte*, and a literary theological approach to discern meaning in the texts.

Second, this study provides the most comprehensive overview to date of the most recent scholarship on the themes of visions and the Spirit in Ezekiel. This survey reveals that there is a paucity in Pentecostal scholarship regarding these aforementioned theological themes, and attempts to responds to this concern.

Third, this study provides the first reception history of how Ezekiel's visions impacted early Pentecostals as recorded in the early Pentecostal periodical literature (1906–1923). This is significant because despite the theological differences noted between the two streams, *Wesleyan Holiness* and the *Finished Work*, the spiritualities found in this study were found to be similar. Both traditions read Ezekiel's visions in light of their beliefs about the Spirit and the outpouring of the Spirit upon their generation, Spirit baptism, and Jesus as the soon coming king.

Fourth, this study proposes a structure generated by the narrative based upon its primary genre of prophetic visions. The structural framework derived by its visions feature the theological themes of the Spirit, the glory of YHWH, the hand of YHWH, and the leitmotif of the affections, which affords the basis for constructing overtures towards a holistic theology of Spirit inspired visions. Uniquely, in all four of Ezekiel's visions, the term רוח and variations of the phrase, the יד־יהוה are emphasized in the narratives and are linked to the affective descriptions of Ezekiel's prophetic encounters with YHWH. As such, it presents the most extensive theological approach to the four major visions in Ezekiel from a Pentecostal perspective. It also emphasizes the role of the Spirit as the Spirit's activities are intricately connected to the visions in dynamic ways, which adds to the conversation concerning OT pneumatology.

Fifth, this study is the first to give specific attention to the affective dimensions prevalent in these narratives, which enhances the complexity of the characters and accentuates the spiritualities discovered in the stories.

Finally, drawing from early Pentecostal literature and my hearing of Ezekiel's visions, this study is the first to offer overtures toward the construction of a Pentecostal theology of Spirit-inspired visions based on Ezekiel. While there are works proposing theological reflections regarding the Spirit in the OT, none to this point have come from a Pentecostal reading of Ezekiel.

The predominant themes related to visions were put into conversation with Pentecostal spirituality as a way to offer a fresh perspective for reading Ezekiel's visions and hopefully, inspire contemporary Pentecostal and Charismatic believers to re-discover Ezekiel as a dynamic book, which speaks the language of heaven in visionary form.

II. Reflections and Tasks for Further Study

The findings from the literature review suggest that while reflecting on a theology for Spirit-inspired visions may not be a primary task for the academy at large, it is especially so for Pentecostal-Charismatics. First, a pneumatological orientation towards scripture is a natural lens through which our communities approach reading, hearing, and interacting with the scriptures. Given that the book of Ezekiel is by and large a book about visions in which the role and activities of the

Spirit are central to the narratives, an examination of these themes through various other methodologies may prove fruitful. For example, since this study was limited to the book of Ezekiel, the findings could be put into conversation with other OT vision and pneumatological texts. An intertextual approach could extend the scope of discussions and analyses in such a way as to contribute to overtures towards an overall OT pneumatology.

Second, as the doctrine of the Spirit is central to all Christians, therefore it can be said that the Spirit is the essential conduit for all life between God and the world or the expressed personality of God in this time-space continuum. Ezekiel is but one voice in the canon. As such, an in-depth biblical theological task to study the continuities and discontinuities of the vision narratives and Spirit references from a Pentecostal-Charismatic context could also contribute to the wider theological discussions of pneumatology.

Third, while the primary genre observed in Ezekiel is visions, it was also identified that symbolic acts were integrated in the vision narratives and also played a significant role. Given that the primary focus of this study was limited to the theme of visions and their relationship to the activities of the Spirit, a subsequent study of the relationship between the symbolic acts and visions could add to the theological conversation regarding Ezekiel.

Fourth, as previously discussed, Pentecostal and Charismatic communities especially value the role of affections, which are integral for the formation of believers. As the present study identified the affective language in the vision narratives, a further study could appreciate Ezekiel not only as a witness to right theology and practice, but also as an aide in the formation of the affections in the contemporary hearers. Martin specifically outlines four cooperative moves to an affective approach.[1] Recognizing the affective language in the biblical texts is a starting point to discerning the role of the affective dimensions in the narratives, and following Land and Martin, a future study could discuss how the hearer of the text could allow the affective language to transform their own affections.

---

[1] Martin, 'Psalm 63 and Pentecostal Spirituality', pp. 59-60.

BIBLIOGRAPHY

Early Pentecostal Periodicals

The *Apostolic Faith* (Azusa Street Mission, Los Angeles, CA)
The Bridal Call (Echo Park Evangelistic Assoc., Los Angeles, CA)
The Bridegroom's Messenger (The Pentecostal Mission, Atlanta, GA)
The Christian Evangel (Assemblies of God, Plainfield, IN; Findley, OH)
The Church of God Evangel (Church of God, Cleveland, TN)
The Pentecost (J. Roswell Flower, Indianapolis, IN)
The Pentecostal Evangel (Assemblies of God, Springfield, MO)
Weekly Evangel (Assemblies of God, St. Louis, MO; Springfield, MO)

Other Works Cited

Alden, R., 'Ecstasy and the Prophets', *BTES* 9.3 (Sum. 1966), pp. 149-56.
Alexander, K., *Pentecostal Healing: Models in Theology and Practice* (JPTSup 29; Blandford Forum: Deo Publishing, 2006).
Allen, L.C., *Ezekiel 20-48* (Word Biblical Commentary 29; Dallas: Word, 1990).
—*Ezekiel 1-19* (Word Biblical Commentary 28; Dallas: Word, 1994).
—'The Structure and Intention of Ezekiel I', *VT* 43.2 (1993), pp. 145-61.
—'Structure, Tradition and Redaction in Ezekiel's Death Valley Vision' in P.R. Davies and D.J. Clines (eds.), *Among the Prophets: Language, Image and Structure in the Prophetic Writings* (JSOTSup 144; Sheffield: JSOT Press, 1993), pp. 126-34.
Alter, R., *The Art of Biblical Narrative* (New York: Basic Books, 1981).
Althouse, P., 'Toward a Theological Understanding of the Pentecostal Appeal to Experience', *JES* 38.4 (2001), pp 399-411.
Anderson, A., *An Introduction to Pentecostalism: Global Charismatic Christianity* (Cambridge: Cambridge University Press, 2004).
Archer, K., *A Pentecostal Hermeneutic: Spirit, Scripture and Community* (Cleveland: CPT Press, 2009).
Archer, M., 'The Worship Scenes in the Apocalypse, Effective History, and Early Pentecostal Periodical Literature', *JPT* 21.1 (2012), pp. 87-112.
Augustine, *On Christian Doctrine* (trans. D.W. Robertson; New York: Macmillan, 2nd edn, 1987).
—*On Genesis: A Refutation of the Manichees Unfinished Literal Commentary on Genesis: The Literal Meaning of Genesis* (trans. John Rotelle; WOA: A Translation for the 21st Century, 1.13, New York: New City Press, 2002).
—*Responses to Miscellaneous Questions: Miscellany of Eighty-Three Questions* (trans. Boniface Ramsey, WOA: A Translation for the 21st Century, I.12, Hyde Park, NY: New City Press, 2008).
Baker, R., 'Pentecostal Bible Reading: Toward a Model of Reading for the Formation of the Affections', *JPT* 7 (1995), pp. 34-48.
Bal, M., *Narratology: Introduction to the Theory of Narrative* (Toronto; Buffalo: University of Toronto Press, 1985).
Baltzer, K., 'Considerations Regarding the Office and Calling of the Prophet', *HTR* 61 (1968), pp. 563-70.

Baumgartel, F., 'Spirit in the Old Testament', G. Kittel (ed.), *Theological Dictionary of the New Testament*, VI (1968), pp. 359-367.

Berry, G.R., 'The Title of Ezekiel (1.1-3)', *JBL* 52 (1932), pp. 54-67.

—'The glory of Yahweh and the Temple', *JBL* 56.2 (1937), pp. 115-117.

Biggs, C.R., *The Book of Ezekiel* (London: Epworth Press, 1996).

Blenkinsopp, J., *A History of Prophecy in Israel* (Louisville: Westminster Press,1983).

—*Ezekiel* (Interpretation, a Commentary for Teaching and Preaching; Louisville: John Knox, 1990).

Block, D.I., 'Gog and the pouring out of the Spirit: Reflections on Ezekiel 39.21-29,' *VT* 3 (1987), pp. 257-270.

—'Text and Emotion: A Study in the Corruptions in Ezekiel's Inaugural Vision Ezekiel 1.4-28', *CBQ* 50.3 (1988), pp. 418-42.

—'The Prophet of the Spirit: The Use of RWH in the Book of Ezekiel', *JETS* 32 (Mar. 1989), pp. 27-49.

—*Ezekiel* (Louisville: Westminster/John Knox Press, 1990).

—'Gog in Prophetic Tradition: A New Look at Ezekiel 38.17', *VT* 42 (1992), pp. 154-67.

—'Empowered by the Spirit of God: The Holy Spirit in the Historiographic Writings of the Old Testament' *SBJT* 1.1 (Spr. 1997), pp. 42-61.

—*Ezekiel 1-24* (NICOT 2; Grand Rapids: Eerdmans, 1997 and 1998).

—*Ezekiel 25-48* (NICOT 2; Grand Rapids: Eerdmans, 1998).

—'The View from the Top: The Holy Spirit in the Prophets', in David Firth and Paul Wegner (eds.), *Presence, Power and Promise* (Downers Grove: IVP, 2011), pp. 175-207.

Block, D.I. and R.G. Bratcher, 'Biblical Words describing Man: Breath, Life, Spirit', *BT* 34.4 (1983), pp. 201-209.

Bloesch, D.G., *The Holy Spirit: Works and Gifts* (Downers Grove, IL: IVP Academic, 2000).

Blumhofer, E. *Aimee Semple McPherson: Everybody's Sister* (Grand Rapids: Eerdmans, 1993).

Bowen, N., *Ezekiel* (Nashville: Abingdon Press, 2010).

Broome, E., 'Ezekiel's Abnormal Personality', *JBL* 65 (1946), pp. 277-93.

Brownlee, W., *Ezekiel 1 – 19* (WBC; Waco; Word Books, 1986).

Brueggemann, W., *Hopeful Imagination: Prophetic Voices in Exile* (Philadelphia, PA: Fortress Press, 1986).

—*A Commentary on Jeremiah: Exile and Homecoming* (Grand Rapids: Eerdmans, 1998).

—*Theology of the Old Testament: Testimony, Dispute, Advocacy* (Minneapolis: Fortress Press, 1997).

—*The Prophetic Imagination* (Philadelphia, PA: Fortress Press, 2nd edn, 2001).

Bryant, H.O., *Spirit Christology in the Christian Tradition: From the Patristic Period to the Rise of Pentecostalism in the Twentieth Century* (Cleveland, TN: CPT Press, 2014).

Carley, K., 'Ezekiel Among the Prophets: A Study of Ezekiel's Place in Prophetic Tradition' (*SBT* 2nd Series 31; Naperville: SCM Press, 1974).

—*The Book of the Prophet Ezekiel: A Commentary* (Cambridge: Cambridge University Press, 1974).

Collins, J., 'Introduction: Towards the Morphology of a Genre', in John J. Collins (ed.), *Apocalypse: The Morphology of a Genre* (Semeia 14; Missoula: Scholars, 1979), pp. 359-70.

Cook, S., and C.L. Patton (eds.), *Ezekiel's Hierarchical World Wrestling with a Tiered Reality* (SBL Symposium 31; Leiden: Brill, 2004).

Cooper, L.E., *Ezekiel* (New American Commentary; Nashville, TN: Broadman & Holman Publishers, 1994).

Coulter, D.M., 'The Spirit and the Bride Revisited: Pentecostalism, Renewal, and the Sense of History', *JPT* 21.2 (2012), pp. 123-134.

Cox, H., *Fire from Heaven: The Rise of Pentecostal Spirituality and the Reshaping of Religion in the Twenty-First Century* (Reading: Addison-Wesley, 1995).

Craigie, P., *Ezekiel* (Philadelphia: The Westminster Press, 1983).

Cross, T., 'The Divine-Human Encounter: Towards a Pentecostal Theology of Experience', *Pneuma* 31.1 (2009), pp. 3-34.

Davis, E., *Swallowing the Scroll: Textuality and the Dynamics of Discourse in Ezekiel's Prophecy* (Sheffield: Almond, 1989).

Dayton, D., *Theological Roots of Pentecostalism* (Peabody: Hendrickson Publishers, 1987).

Dreytza, M., *Der theolgische Gebrauch von RUAH im Alten Testament: Eine wort-und satzsemantische Studie* (Basal: Brunnen, 1992).

Duguid, I., *Ezekiel: The NIV Application Commentary* (Grand Rapids: Zondervan, 1999).

Edgerton, W.D., *The Passion of Interpretation* (Literary Currents in Biblical Interpretation; Louisville, KY: John Knox Press, 1992).

Eichrodt, W., *Ezekiel* (London: SCM Press, 1970).

Eisemann, M., *Yechezkel, A New Translation With A Commentary Anthologized From Talmudic, Midrashic and Rabbinic Sources* (Artscroll Series; Hebrew Edition. Brooklyn, NY: Mesorah Publications, 2005).

Elliott, M., 'Effective-History and the Hermeneutics of Ulrich Luz', *JSNT* 33.2 (2010), pp. 161-173.

Ervin, H., 'A Pentecostal Hermeneutical Option', in Paul Elbert, (ed.), *Essays on Apostolic Themes: Studies in honor of Howard M. Ervin* (Peabody, MA: Hendrickson Publishers, 1985), pp. 23-35.

Everts, J.M., 'Filled with the Spirit from the Old Testament to the Apostle Paul: A Conversation with John Levison', *Pneuma* 33 (2011), pp. 63-68.

Faupel, W.D., *The Everlasting Gospel* (JPTSup 10; Sheffield: Sheffield Academic Press, 1996).

Feinberg, C.L., *The Prophecy of Ezekiel* (Chicago: Moody Press, 1969).

Firth, D.G. and P.D. Wegner., *Presence, Power, and Promise: The Role of the Spirit of God in the Old Testament* (Downers Grove, IL: IVP Academic, 2011).

Fishbane, M., *Biblical Interpretation in Ancient Israel* (New York, Oxford University Press, 1985).

Fisher, W., *Human Communication as Narration: Toward a Philosophy of Reason, Value, and Action* (Columbia: University of South Carolina Press, 1987).

Flattery, G.M., *A Biblical Theology of the Holy Spirit: Old Testament* (Springfield: Global University, 2009).

Flattery, G.M., *et al.*, *A Biblical Theology of the Holy Spirit, Old Testament* (Springfield, MO: Global University, 2009).

Fredricks, G., 'Rethinking the Role of the Holy Spirit in the Lives of Old Testament Believers', *TJ* 9 (1988), pp. 81-104.

Goff, J.R., *Fields White unto Harvest: Charles F. Parham and the Missionary Origins of Pentecostalism* (Fayetteville: University of Arkansas Press, 1988).

Goldingay, J., 'Was the Holy Spirit Active in Old Testament Times? What Was New About the Christian Experience of God?' *EA* 12 (1988), pp. 14-28.

Green, C.E., *Foretasting the Kingdom: Toward a Pentecostal Theology of the Lord's Supper* (Cleveland TN: CPT Press, 2012).

Greenberg, M., *Ezekiel I-20: A New Translation with Introduction and Commentary* (AB 22, Garden City, NY: Doubleday, 1983).

—'The Design and Themes of Ezekiel's Program of Restoration', *Int* 38 (1948), pp. 180-93.

Grey, J., 'Acts of the Spirit: Ezekiel 37 in the Light of Contemporary Speech-Act Theory', *JBPR* 1 (2009), pp. 69-81.

Gunn, D.M., 'Narrative Criticism', in Steven L. McKenzie and Stephen R. Haynes (eds.), *To Each Its Own Meaning: An Introduction to Biblical Criticisms and Their Approaches* (Louisville, KY: Westminster, John Knox Press, 1993).

Habel, N., 'The Form and Significance of the Call Narratives', *Zeitschrift für die alttestamentliche Wissenschaft* 77.3 (1965), pp. 297-323.

Halperin, D. *Seeking Ezekiel Text and Psychology* (State College, PA: Pennsylvania State University Press, 1993).

Hals, R., *Ezekiel* (FOTL XIX; Grand Rapids: Eerdmans, 1989).

Hamilton, J.M., and R. Clendenen, *God's Indwelling Presence: The Holy Spirit in the Old & New Testaments* (Nashville, TN: B & H Pub. Group, 2006).

Hanson, P., *The Dawn of Apocalyptic: The Historical and Sociological Roots of Jewish Apocalyptic Eschatology* (Philadelphia: Fortress, 1975).

Hays, J., *An Introduction to Old Testament Study* (Nashville: Abingdon, 1979).

Hayes, E.R., and Lena-Sofia Tiemeyer, *'I Lifted My Eyes and Saw': Reading Dream and Vision Reports in the Hebrew Bible* (Library of Hebrew Bible/Old Testament Studies; London: Bloomsbury/T&T Clark, 2014).

Heschel, A.J. 'Prophetic Inspiration: An Analysis of Prophetic Consciousness', *Judaism* 11.1 (1962), pp. 3-13.

—*The Prophets* (2 vols.; New York: Harper & Row, 1962).

Hildebrandt, W., *An Old Testament Theology of the Spirit of God* (Peabody, MA.: Hendrickson, 1995).

Hocken, P., *The Challenges of the Pentecostal, Charismatic, and Messianic Jewish Movements: The Tensions of the Spirit* (Farnham: Ashgate Pub. Ltd, 2009).

Hollenweger, W.J., 'Pentecostals and the Charismatic Movement', in Cheslyn Jones, Geoffrey Wainwright, and SJ Edward Yarnold (eds.), *The Study of Spirituality* (New York, NY: Oxford University Press, 1986), pp. 549-53.

—*The Pentecostals* (Peabody, MA: Hendrickson, 1988).

Horton, S.M., *What the Bible Says about the Holy Spirit* (Springfield, MO: Gospel Pub. House, 1976).

Hosch, H., '*Ruah* in the Book of Ezekiel: A Textlinguistic Analysis', *JOTT* 14 (2002), pp. 77-125.

Jauss, R.H., *Toward an Aesthetic of Reception* (trans. T. Bahti; Minneapolis, MN: University of Minnesota Press, 1982).

Johnson, A., *The One and the Many in the Israelite Conception of God* (Cardiff: University of Wales, 1961).

—*The Vitality of the Individual in the Thought of Ancient Israel* (Cardiff: University of Wales Press, 1964).

Johnson, D., *Pneumatic Discernment in the Apocalypse: An Intertextual and Pentecostal Exploration* (Cleveland, TN: CPT Press, 2018).

Joyce, P., *Divine Initiation and Human Response in Ezekiel* (JSOTSup 51; Sheffield: JSOT Press, 1989).

—*Ezekiel: A Commentary* (LHBOTS 482. New York: T & T Clark International, 2009).

Kaiser, W.C. Jr., 'The Indwelling Presence of the Holy Spirit in the Old Testament', *EQ* 82.4 (2010), pp. 308-315.

Kapelrud, A., 'The Spirit and the Word in the Prophets', *ASTI* 11 (1977–78), pp. 40-47.

Karkainnen, V.M., *Pneumatology: The Holy Spirit in Ecumenical, International, and Contextual Perspective* (Grand Rapid, MI: Baker Academic, 2002).

Kaufmann, Y., *The Religion of Israel: From Its Beginnings to the Babylonian Exile* (trans. Moshe Greenberg; London: Allen & Unwin, 1961).

Kinlaw, P., 'From Death to Life: The Expanding רוח in Ezekiel', *Perspectives on Religious Studies* 30 (2003), pp. 161-72.

Klein, R., *Ezekiel, The Prophet and His Message* (Columbia, SC.: University of South Carolina Press, 1988).

Koch, R., *Der Geist Gottes im Alten Testament* (Frankfurt am Main; New York: P. Lang, 1991).

—*Geist und Messias: Beitrag zur Biblischen Theologie des Alten Testaments* (Wien: Herder, 1950).

Kutsko, J.F., *Between Heaven and Earth: Divine Presence and Absence in the Book of Ezekiel* (Winona Lake, IN: Eisenbrauns, 2000).

Land, S.J., *Pentecostal Spirituality: A Passion for the Kingdom* (JPTSup 1; Sheffield: Sheffield Academic Press, 1993).

Lapsley, J.E., 'Can Theses Bones Live? The Problem of the Moral Self in the Book of Ezekiel', *Beihefte zur Zeitschrift für die alttestamentliche Wissenschaft* (Berlin/New York: Walter de Gruyter, 2000), p. 32

Launderville, D.F., *Spirit and Reason: The Embodied Character of Ezekiel's Symbolic Thinking* (Waco: Baylor University Press, 2007).

Levison, J.R., 'Two Types of Ecstatic Prophecy According to Philo', *SPA* 6 (1994), pp. 83-89.

—*Of Two Minds: Ecstasy and Inspiration in the New Testament World* (North Richland Hills, TX: BIBAL Press, 1999).

—'Prophecy in Ancient Israel: The Case of the Ecstatic Elders', *CBQ* 65.4 (2003), pp. 503-21.

—*Filled with the Spirit* (Grand Rapids: Eerdmans, 2009).

Levison, J.D., *Theology of the Program of Restoration of Ezekiel 40–48* (HSM 10; Missoula, Mont: Scholars 1976).

Levy, S., *The Targum of Ezekiel, The Aramaic Bible* 13 (Wilmington DE: Glazier, 1987).

Lindblom, J., *Prophecy in Ancient Israel* (Oxford: Blackwell Publishers, 1962).

Lipschits, O., *The Fall and Rise of Jerusalem: Judah under Babylonian Rule* (Winona Lake, IN: Eisenbrauns, 2005).

Lipschits, O, and J. Blenkinsopp, (eds.), *Judah and the Judeans in the Neo-Babylonian Period* (Winona Lake, IN.: Eisenbrauns, 2005).

Long, B., 'Reports of Visions Among the Prophets', *JBL* 95 (1976), pp. 353-65.

Lutzky, H. C., 'On "the image of jealousy" (Ezekiel viii 3,5)', *VT* 46.1 (Jan 1996), pp. 121-25.

Luz, U., *Matthew in History: Interpretation, Influence, and Effect* (Minneapolis: Fortress Press, 1994).

Lys, D., *Rûach: Le Souffle dans l'Ancien Testament: Enquête Anthropologique à Travers l'Histoire Théologique d'Israël* (Etudes d'Histoire et de Philosophie Religieuses 56; Paris: Presses Universitaires de France, 1962).

Ma, W., *Until the Spirit Comes: The Spirit of God in the Book of Isaiah* (JSOTSup 271: Sheffield: Academic Press: 1999).

Maguire, D., 'Ratio Practica and the Intellectualistic Fallacy', *JRE* 10.1 (1982), pp. 22-39.

Maré, L. 'Ezekiel, Prophet of the Spirit', *JSOT* 31.3 (2018), pp. 553-570.

Markus, R., *Signs and Meanings: World and Text in Ancient Christianity* (London: Liverpool University Press, 1996).

Martin, L.R., 'Power to Save!?: The Role of the Spirit of the Lord in the Book of Judges', *JPT* 16 (2008), pp. 21-50.

—*The Unheard Voice of God: A Pentecostal Hearing of the Book of Judges* (JPTSup 32; Blandford Forum: Deo Publishing, 2008).

—'Longing for God: Psalm 63 and Pentecostal Spirituality', *JPT* 22 (2013), pp. 54-76.

Martin, L.R. (ed.), *Toward a Pentecostal Theology of Worship* (Cleveland, TN: CPT Press, 2016).

Mays, J.L. & P.J. Achtemeier (eds.), *Interpreting the Prophet* (Philadelphia: Fortress Press, 1987).

McCarthy, D.J., 'The Uses of הנה in Biblical Hebrew', *Bib* 61 (1980), pp. 332-33,

McPherson, A., *This is That: Personal Experiences of Aimee Semple McPherson, Evangelist,* (Douglas Harrolf [ed.]; HJ Publishing, 1919).

McQueen, L., *Joel and the Spirit: The Cry of a Prophetic Hermeneutic* (JPTSup 8; Cleveland, TN: CPT Press, 2009).

Montague, G.T., *The Holy Spirit: Growth of a Biblical Tradition* (New York: Paulist Press, 1976).

Moore, R.D., 'A Pentecostal Approach to Scripture', *Seminary Viewpoint* 8 (Nov. 1987), pp. 4-5.

—'Canon and Charisma in the Book of Deuteronomy', *JPT* 1 (1992), pp. 75-92.

—'Deuteronomy and the Fire of God: A Critical Charismatic Interpretation', *JPT* 7 (1995), pp. 11-33.

—'And Also Much Cattle': Prophetic Passions and the End of Jonah', *JPT* 11 (1997), pp. 35-48,

—*The Spirit of the Old Testament* (JPTSup 35; Blandford Forum: Deo Publishing, 2011).

Moore, R., and B. Peterson, *Voice, Word, and Spirit: A Pentecostal Old Testament Survey* (Nashville, TN: Abingdon, 2017), pp. 206-215.

Mowinckel, S., 'The Spirit and the Word in the Pre-exilic Reforming Prophets', *JBL* 59.3 (1940), pp. 199-227.

—*The Spirit and the Word: Prophecy and Tradition in Ancient Israel* (K.C. Hanson [ed.]; Minneapolis: Fortress Press, 2002).

Neve, L.R., *The Spirit of God in the Old Testament* (CPT Classics Series; Cleveland, TN: CPT Press, 2011).

Niditch, S., *The Symbolic Visions in Biblical Traditions* (HSM; Chico, CA: Scholars Press, 1983).

Nielson, K., 'Ezekiel's Visionary Call as Prologue: From Complexity and Changeability to Order and Stability', *JSOT* 33.1 (2008), pp. 96-108.

Odell, M.S., 'Ezekiel Saw What He Said He Saw: Genres, Forms, and the Vision of Ezekiel 1' in M.A. Sweeney and E. Ben Zvi (eds.), *The Changing Face of Form Criticism for the Twenty-First Century*, pp. 162-176 (Grand Rapids: Eerdmans, 2003).

—*Ezekiel: Smyth & Helwys Bible Commentary* (Macon, GA: Smyth & Helwys, 2005).

Odell, M.S., and John Strong, (eds.), *The Book of Ezekiel: Theological and Anthropological Perspectives* (Atlanta, GA: SBL, Symposium Series. No. 9, 2000).

Oliverio, L.W. Jr., *Theological Interpretation in the Classical Pentecostal Tradition: A Typological Account* (Leiden: Brill, 2012).

Overholt, T., 'The Ghost Dance of 1890 and the Nature of the Prophetic Process' *Ethnohistory* 21 (1974), pp. 37-63.

Perdue, L., *The Collapse of History: Reconstructing Old Testament Theology* (Minneapolis: Fortress Press, 1994).

Petersen, D., *Late Israelite Prophecy, Studies in Deutero-Prophetic Literature and in Chronicles* (SBLMS 23; Missoula: Scholars Press, 1971).

—*The Roles of Israel's Prophets* (Sheffield: Sheffield Academic Press, 1981).

Pfisterer-Darr, K., 'The Book of Ezekiel: Introduction, Commentary and Reflections', in *The New Interpreter's Bible: A Commentary in Twelve Volumes*, vol. VI in Leander E. Keek (ed.), (Nashville: Abingdon Press, 1996), pp. 1465-66.

Pilch, J., *The Flights of the Soul: Visions, Heavenly Journeys and Peak Experiences in the Biblical World* (Grand Rapids, MI: Eerdmans, 2011).

Pinnock, P., *Scripture Principle, Reclaiming the Full Authority of the Bible* (Grand Rapids: Baker, 2006).

Rea, J., *The Holy Spirit in the Bible: All the Major Passages about the Spirit* (Lake Mary: Creation House, 1990).

Renz, T., *The Rhetorical Function of the Book of Ezekiel* (Leiden: Brill, 1999).

Roberts, J.J., 'The Hand of Yahweh', *VT* 21 (1971), pp. 244-51.

Robson, J., *Word and Spirit in Ezekiel* (LHBOT 447; New York: T & T Clark, 2006).

Routledge, R., 'The Spirit and the Future in the Old Testament: Restoration and Renewal', in D. Firth and P. Wegner (eds), *Power, Presence and Promise* (Downers Grove: IVP, 2011), pp. 353-60.

Rowland, C., *The Open Heaven: A Study of Apocalyptic in Judaism and Early Christianity* (New York: Crossroads, 1982).

Sakenfeld, K.D., 'Ezekiel 18:25-32', *Int* 32. (1978), pp. 295-300.

Schafroth, V., 'An Exegetical Exploration of Spirit references in Ezekiel 36 and 37', *JEPTA* (2009), pp. 61-77.

Scheepers, J.H., *Die Gees van God en die Gees van die mens in die Oud Testamentische Studien* (Kampen: J.H. Kok, 1960).

Schoemaker, W.R., 'The Use of rûah in the Old Testament and of Pneuma in the New Testament', *JBL* 23 (1904), pp. 13-67.

Schüngel-Straumann, H. *Rûah Bewegt die Welt: Gottes Schöpferische Lebenskraft in der Krisenzeit des Exils* (Stuttgart: Verlag Katholisches Bibelwerk, 1992).

Schwartz, B., 'A Priest Out of Place: Reconsidering Ezekiel's Role in the History of the Israelite Priesthood' in Stephen Cook and Corrine Patton (eds.), *Ezekiel's Hierarchical World Wrestling with a Tiered Reality* (Boston: Brill, 2004), pp. 61-67.

Seitz, C.R., 'Ezekiel 37.1-14', *Int* 46 (1992), pp. 53-56.

Shantz, C., *Paul in Ecstasy: The Neurobiology of the Apostle's life and Thought* (Cambridge, New York: Cambridge University Press, 2009).

Sheppard, G., 'Word and Spirit: Scripture in the Pentecostal Tradition – Part Two', *Agora* 2.1 (1978), pp. 14-19.

Sherlock, C., 'Ezekiel 10: A Prophet Surprised', *RTR* 42.2 (May-Aug,1983), pp. 42-44.

Sklba, R., 'Until the Spirit from on High is Poured out on Us' (Isa. 32:15); Reflections on the Role of the Spirit in the Exile', *CBQ* 46 (1984), pp.1-17.

Smith-Christopher, D., 'Ezekiel in Abu Ghraib: Reading Ezekiel 16.37-39 in the Context of Imperial Conquest', in *Ezekiel's Hierarchical World: Wrestling with a Tiered Reality* (SBL Symposium Series 31; Atlanta: Society of Biblical Literature, 2004), pp. 141-58.

Snaith, N., *The Distinctives Ideas of the Old Testament* (New York: Schocken, 1964).

Spittler, R., 'Scripture and the Theological Enterprise: View from a Big Canoe', R.K. Johnston (ed.), *The Use of the Bible in Theology* (Atlanta: John Knox, 1985), pp. 56-77.

Stanley, W.M., 'An Investigation of the Divine Spirit in the Old Testament' (PhD, Butler University, 1960).

Stavrakopoulou, F., 'Gog's Grave and the Use and Abuse of Corpses in Ezekiel 39.11-21', *JBL* 129 (2010), pp. 64-85,

Stead, M.R., 'Prophetic Visions' *Dictionary of Old Testament Prophets* (Downers Grove, IL: IVP Press, 2012), pp. 818-24.

Stephenson, K., *The Vision of Transformation: The Territorial Rhetoric of Ezekiel 40–48* (SBLDS 154; Atlanta: Scholars, 1996).

Stibbe, M., 'This is That: Some Thoughts Concerning Charismatic Hermeneutics', *Anvil* 14.3 (1998), pp. 181-93.

Stiebert, J., 'Shame and Prophecy: Approaches Past and Present', *Bib Int* 8.3 (2000), pp. 255-77.

Stronstad, R., Spirit, Scripture and Theology: A Pentecostal Perspective (Baguio City, Philippines: Asia Pacific Theological Seminary Press, 1995).

—'Pentecostal Experience and Hermeneutics', *Paraclete* 26.1 (1992), pp. 14-30.

Sweeney, M., 'Ezekiel, Zadokite Priest and Visionary Prophet of the Exile', *Form and Intertextuality in the Prophetic and Apocalyptic Literature* (FAT 45; Tübingen: Mohr Siebeck, 2005) pp. 125-43.

Synan, V., *The Century of the Holy Spirit: 100 Years of Pentecostal and Charismatic Renewal* (Nashville, TN: Thomas Nelson, 2001).

Tatford, F.A., *Dead Bones Live* (Heathfield: Errey's Printers, 1977).

Taylor, B., *Ezekiel: An Introduction and Commentary* (Tyndale OT Commentaries; Downers Grove, IL: Inter-Varsity Press, 1969).

Thomas, J.C., 'Women, Pentecostals, and the Bible: An Experiment in Pentecostal Hermeneutics', *JPT* 5 (1994), pp. 41-56.

—'Reading the Bible from within Our Traditions', in *The Spirit of the New Testament* (Leiden: Deo, 2005).

—'Pentecostal Interpretation', in Steven McKenzie (ed.), *The Oxford Encyclopedia of Biblical Interpretation* (Oxford: Oxford University Press, 2013), II, pp. 89-97.

—'What the Spirit is Saying to the Church – The Testimony of a Pentecostal in New Testament Studies', in Kevin Spawn and Archie Wright (eds.), *Spirit and Scripture* (London: T & T Clark, 2012), pp. 115-29.

Thomas, J.C. and K.E. Alexander, '"And the Signs Are Following": Mark 16.9-20 – A Journey into Pentecostal Hermeneutics', *JPT* 11.2 (2003), pp. 147-70.

Thomas J.C., and Frank Macchia, *Revelation: Two Horizons New Testament Commentary Series* (Grand Rapids: Eerdmans, 2016).

Tribe, R., 'Spirit in the Old Testament Writings', *Theology* 59.5 (1936), pp. 256-69.

Tuell, S., *The Law of the Temple in Ezekiel 40–48* (HSM 49; Atlanta: Scholars Press, 1992).

—'Ezekiel 40–42 as Verbal Icon', *CBQ* 58 (1996), pp. 649-61.

—*Ezekiel* (New International Bible Commentary; Peabody, MA: Hendrickson, 2009).

—'Should Ezekiel Go to Rehab? The Method to Ezekiel's 'Madness', *PRS* 36 (2009), pp. 289-302.

—'True Metaphor Insights into Reading Scripture from the Rabbis', *TT* 67 (2011), pp. 467-75.

Uffenheimer, B., 'Prophecy and Sympathy', *Immanuel* 16 (Sum. 1983), pp. 7-24.

—'Prophecy, Ecstasy, and Sympathy', *CV* 257-269 (Leiden: Brill, 1988), pp. 257-69.

—*Prophecy in Ancient Israel* (trans. David Louvish; Jerusalem: Magnes Press, 1999).

Vanhoozer, K., *Is there a Meaning in this Text? The Bible, the Reader, and the Morality of Literary Knowledge* (Grand Rapids: Zondervan, 1996).

VanGemeren, W., *Interpreting the Prophetic Word: An Introduction to the Prophetic Literature of the Old Testament* (Grand Rapids: Academic Books, 1990).

—*New International Dictionary of Old Testament Theology and Exegesis* (Grand Rapids: Zondervan, 1997).

—W., 'The Spirit of Restoration', *WTJ* 50 (1988), pp. 81-102.

Vawter, B. & L.J. Hoppe, *Ezekiel: A New Heart* (Grand Rapids, Mich.: Eerdmans, 1991).

Vondey, W., *Pentecostal Theology: Living the Full Gospel* (New York: Bloomsbury T&T Clark, 2017).

Vries, P., 'Ezekiel: Prophet of the Name and Glory of YHWH – The Character of his Book and Several of its Main Themes', *JBBR* 4 (2012), pp. 105-108.

—'The Relationship between the Glory of YHWH and the Spirit of YHWH', *JSOT* 28.2 (2015), pp. 326-350.

Wacker, G., *Heaven Below: Early Pentecostals and American Culture* (Cambridge, MA: Harvard University Press, 2001).

Waddell, R.C., *The Spirit of the Book of Revelation* (JPTSup 30; Blandford Forum: Deo Publishing, 2006).

—'Hearing What the Spirit Says to the Churches: Profile of a Pentecostal Reader of the Apocalypse', in Lee Roy Martin (ed.), *Pentecostal Hermeneutics: A Reader* (Leiden: Brill, 2013), pp. 171-204.

Waldholm, R. Jr., *A Theology of the Spirit in the Former Prophets: A Pentecostal Perspective* (Cleveland, TN: CPT Press, 2018).

Warren, N., 'A Cannibal Feast in Ezekiel', *JSOT* 38.4 (2014), pp. 501-12.

Welker, M., *God the Spirit* (trans. John F. Hoffmeyer; Minneapolis, MN: Fortress Press, 1994).

Wilson, R., 'Prophecy and Ecstasy: A Reexamination', *JBL* 98 (1979), pp. 321-37. Reprinted in *Anthropological Perspectives on Old Testament Prophecy*, Robert C. Culley and Thomas W. Overholt (eds.), *Sem* 21 (1982), pp. 404-22.

—*Prophecy and Society in Ancient Israel* (Philadelphia: Fortress Press. 1980).

—'Prophecy: The Problem of Cross-Cultural Comparison', *Sem* 21 (1981), pp. 55-78.

—'Seeing is Believing: The Social Setting of Prophetic Acts of Power', *JSOT* 23 (1982), pp. 3-31.

Wink, W., *The Bible in Human Transformation: Toward a New Paradigm for Biblical Study* (Philadelphia: Fortress Press, 1973).

Winkle, R., 'Iridescence in Ezekiel', *Andrews Seminary Studies* 44.1 (2006), pp. 51-77.

Wood, L., 'Ecstasy and Israel's Early Prophets', *BETS* 9.3 (1966), pp. 25-137.

—*The Holy Spirit in the Old Testament* (Grand Rapids: Zondervan, 1976).

Woodhouse, J., 'The Spirit in the Book of Ezekiel', in B.G. Webb (ed.) *Spirit of the Living God* (Sydney: Lancer, 1991).

Wright, C.J.H., *Knowing the Holy Spirit Through the Old Testament* (Downers Grove, IL: IVP Academic, 2006).

Wyckoff, J.W., *Pneuma and Logos: The Role of the Spirit in Biblical Hermeneutics* (Eugene, OR: Wipf & Stock Publishers, 2010).

Yong, A., 'Pentecostalism and the Theological Academy', *TT* 64.2 (2007), pp. 244-50.

Zimmerli, W., *Ezekiel 1: A Commentary on the Book of the Prophet Ezekiel Chapters 1–24* (trans. Ronald. E. Clements; Hermeneia; Philadelphia: Fortress, 1979).

—*Ezekiel 2: A Commentary on the Book of the Prophet Ezekiel Chapters 25–40* (trans. James D. Martin; Hermeneia; Philadelphia: Fortress, 1979).

—*I am Yahweh* (ed. W. Brueggemann; trans. Douglas W. Stott; Atlanta: John Knox, 1982).

—'The Special Form and Traditio-Historical Character of Ezekiel's Prophecy', *VT* 15.4 (1965), pp. 515-27.

INDEX OF AUTHORS

www.ingramcontent.com/pod-product-compliance
Lightning Source LLC
Chambersburg PA
CBHW060042100426
42742CB00014B/2662